Relucta

Reluctant Saint?

A Theological Biography
of
Fletcher of Madeley

Patrick Streiff

Translated from the German by
G. W. S. Knowles

EPWORTH PRESS

All rights reserved. No part of this publication may be
reproduced, stored in a retrieval system, or transmitted, in
any form or by any means, electronic, mechanical,
photocopying, recording or otherwise, without the prior
written permission of the publishers, Epworth Press.

Copyright © Patrick Streiff 2001

Translation © G. W. S. Knowles 2001

0 7162 0546 7

First published 2001
by Epworth Press
20 Ivatt Way
Peterborough, PE3 7PG

Typeset by Regent Typesetting, London
Printed and bound in Great Britain by
Biddles Ltd, Guildford and King's Lynn

Contents

Contents

Author's Foreword

John William Fletcher, Methodist theologian and saint, has been largely forgotten. Though he was known and read by nineteenth-century Methodists, no new edition of his works appeared in the twentieth-century, and not much was published about him. This book seeks to redress the balance, and throw new light on the life and work of this leading figure in the Methodist movement in England in the eighteenth-century.

The present book is an abbreviated and revised version of my Dissertation on John William Fletcher, which was published in German in 1984, and went quickly out of print. As the appendix shows, I have drawn on a wide range of archival material, much of it previously unpublished. Ever since I began my work in the 1970s, Peter Forsaith, of Wootton, near Abingdon in Oxfordshire, has been giving me valuable advice on archives in England. I thank him for his help, and extend my best wishes for his own work on an annotated edition of Fletcher's letters.

I have normally drawn attention in the footnotes to additions and alterations to my Dissertation. In order to make the biographical presentation as concise as possible, I have frequently referred the reader to the analyses of the source material in the Dissertation. Use has been made of the most recent literature. New discoveries about Fletcher's life and work are pointed out in just a few places. Those who are familiar with the older literature will find many other examples.

I am glad that at last, after almost twenty years, it has become possible to produce an English version of my work, and I thank the Epworth Press for its readiness to translate and publish the manuscript.

Patrick Streiff

Chronology

1770   'Theological controversy' sparked off by anti-Calvinistic tendency of minutes of Wesley's Conference.

1771   Fletcher resigned presidency of Trevecca college, and published a 'vindication' of the 1770 Conference minutes. Relations with Lady Huntingdon and her circle became strained.

1771–   Various polemical writings published by Fletcher and his
1776   opponents.

1777   A more conciliatory approach adopted. Reconciliation with Lady Huntingdon.

1778–   Fletcher, by now in poor health, visited Continent again,
1781   and stayed for three years in Nyon.

1781   Married to Mary Bosanquet on 12 November.

1785   Died in Madeley on 14 August.

PART I
BEGINNINGS (1729–1750)

Childhood and Background

Even in his lifetime Fletcher became, for many Methodists, a model of sanctification. Was he already a little saint as a child? One might assume so, in the light of statements in an early biography:

> From his childhood he was impressed with a deep sense of the majesty of God, and a constant fear of offending him . . . His filial obedience and brotherly affection were exemplary; nor is it remembered that he ever uttered one unbecoming expression . . .[1]

Such praise is simply hagiography, and has more to do with speculation than with solid facts. The few details biographers give of Fletcher's childhood and youth need to be treated with caution. They are often idealized conceptions, projected back into his youth from later stages in his life.

Very little is known about Fletcher's childhood. No family documents are extant. As his original name, 'Jean Guillaume de la Fléchère', reveals, he grew up in the French-speaking part of Switzerland. The youngest of a family of five girls and three boys, he was born in the Swiss town of Nyon, on Lake Geneva, probably on 11 September 1729.[2] His parents belonged to the lower ranks of the nobility. His father held local political offices, and owned vineyards.[3]

John William referred to his childhood in Switzerland in only two letters, written shortly after his conversion.[4] In both of them he was describing his inner development, rather than external events in his life. He spoke of his past because he wanted to demonstrate from it how, over and over again, God had been at work in his life, and yet for a long time he had not known true faith or its fruits. In both letters he recounted an experience he had had as a boy of seven – an experience which must have made a deep impression upon him. He had evidently been extremely angry with one of his brothers, and had been sent to bed early as a punishment. He had been afraid that he would be cast into hell, but God had freed him from his fear. His proud heart had been softened, and he must have wept a great deal, because a great deal had been forgiven him. He had decided at that time, he wrote, to devote himself to God and to the service of his church. In both letters, again, John William described this event as his first conscious experience of the love of God.[5] His outstanding impression, however, was that he had been a particularly proud, short-tempered child: 'I have often heard from my friends, that there never was a Child prouder more passionate and stubborn than me from the cradle.'[6] In those letters, written soon after his conversion, Fletcher could not get away from the pride and self-will which he saw as evidence of the power of sin. An event in John William's childhood recorded by his brother confirms that he was a proud and often quarrelsome child.[7]

Some biographers were personally acquainted with Fletcher in his later years, but they can add very little to the fragmentary picture we have of his youth. Even Fletcher's wife was unable to tell us much more about the young John William.[8] She had the impression, probably not too wide of the mark, that from his childhood onwards he had a very tender conscience. She too described, among other things, the quarrel mentioned above. John Wesley included in his biography of Fletcher some stories about daring exploits in swimming,[9] directing the reader's attention to God's wonderful guidance and deliverance. Alongside the interpretation Wesley put upon them, the stories reveal that a thirst for adventure and a spirit of daring were no strangers to the young John William. The picture changed in Joshua Gilpin's biographical sketch.[10] Gilpin described the character of the young Fletcher in astonishing detail, and in doing so presented the whole of his childhood and youth in a very positive light, from which almost all negative features were excluded. The last of the biographers who knew Fletcher personally was Joseph Benson, who built upon the works mentioned above, and so produced a picture of an outstandingly pious young man, who was often delivered from life-threatening danger by the intervention of God, and who went astray only as a result of the bad influence of others. This strongly idealized portrait was reproduced, to a greater or lesser degree, by all subsequent biographers. It was the result of a backward projection from Fletcher's later life to his youth.

The statements we have from Fletcher himself can only be supplemented in a very limited way from these biographies. The picture of his early years remains fragmentary, but it is certainly not that of a particularly virtuous boy, of firm religious convictions, who was already making an outstanding impression upon those around him – the picture, so to speak, of a saint in the making. On the contrary, we know from Fletcher's own statements that he was proud, vehement and headstrong. When he looked back, he saw his wilfulness as an expression of his sinfulness. But he also remembered early experiences of the forgiving grace of God, which awoke in him the determination to serve God and to live righteously before him.

The environment in which Fletcher grew up

It is helpful to consider also the environment in which Fletcher grew up. Of particular interest is the development in church life and theological thought which was taking place in French-speaking Switzerland, and the influence of individual personalities. Nyon, the town in which Fletcher was born, lay in the Waadt district, which was governed from Bern. Fletcher's parents, however, chose to send him for his education to neighbouring Geneva. There were important theological differences between the Bernese Pays de Vand and Geneva.

In the seventeenth century, the Reformed regions in Switzerland had been at pains to establish orthodox doctrine. Church representatives from the various districts had drawn up a Consensus Formula (*Formula Consensus Helvetica* 1671–74), as a bulwark against new forms of thought.[11] But this Consensus Formula did not go undisputed. Around the turn of the eighteenth century, three prominent professors of theology from the cities of Basle (S. Werenfels), Neuchâtel (J.-F. Ostervald) and Geneva (J.-A. Turrettini) advocated a departure from the strict orthodoxy of the Consensus Formula, and thus prepared the way for so-called 'reasonable orthodoxy'. They sought to demonstrate the reasonableness of the Christian religion. In terms of effectiveness, the most significant document in French-speaking Switzerland was probably Ostervald's catechism, which first appeared in 1702. It was issued as an introduction to the Heidelberg Catechism, but within a short time superseded it. We can take it for granted that Fletcher came into contact with this catechism, perhaps early on in Nyon, but in any case certainly during his student days in Geneva. What did this new environment in which the young Fletcher found himself look like, and what effect did it have upon him?

Ostervald's catechism

From the outset, Ostervald's catechism differed clearly from the Heidelberg Catechism in both plan and structure. Preliminary notes made
plain its apologetic purpose. In the introduction, the history of God's
dealings with humanity was presented. The catechism proper then
began with a further prolegomenon, dealing with religion in general.
First, Ostervald discussed the necessity for religion, and its essential
elements. He then proceeded to establish the truth of the Christian
religion, and dealt finally with the truth, the godliness and the use of the
Holy Scriptures. Only after laying these introductory foundations
did Ostervald present the first section of his catechism: 'Of faith and
the truths of the Christian religion'. Here the Apostles' Creed was
expounded. A second section then dealt with 'the Duties of Religion'. It
included an exposition of the Ten Commandments and the Lord's
Prayer. This second section turned out to be more than three times
longer than the first. Ostervald's purpose in writing the catechism was
thus revealed. He did not wish to pursue speculative doctrines, but
rather to develop specific guidelines for behaviour. Finally a shorter
third section dealt with the sacraments, and the duties to be undertaken
by candidates for confirmation.

Overall the catechism followed the traditional question and answer
pattern. However, this normal pattern conceals two unusual features:
first, the constantly repeated questions as to how a statement can be
verified and confirmed as certain and irrefutable, and secondly, the
regular question as to the usefulness and the moral consequences of a
doctrine. By this means Ostervald was trying to prove that the Christian
religion was both true and necessary, and, in the process, was bringing
history and morality before the bar of reason. It was reasonable to
believe that the Christian religion was true, and virtuous living would
bring a rich reward. Therefore the person under instruction should and
must assent to the truths of the Christian religion and live accordingly.
The teaching was reinforced by the promise of reward and punishment
which accompanied God's law. The moral-pedagogical emphasis of
reasonable orthodoxy found particularly clear expression in Ostervald's
catechism. Behind his reconstruction and development of the classical
Reformed catechism stood an understanding of theology, apologetics,
pedagogics and hermeneutics which built upon the Dutch-English early
Enlightenment. Ostervald – and the whole of reasonable orthodoxy
along with him – was seeking to enable the thinking of the early

Enlightenment to bear fruit within the church. In doing so they were aiming at the reformation of the church. This new current within the church, inspired by the early Enlightenment, established itself more quickly in Geneva than in the Bernese Pays de Vand where Fletcher's birthplace was located.

Theological awakening in Geneva

In Geneva, it was only after long debates that the Consensus Formula was approved in 1678 and imposed upon all ministers. Once again the old orthodoxy had gained the victory. However, the new currents of thought were being closely followed by the professors at the University of Geneva, the '*Académie de Calvin*', and at the beginning of the eighteenth century close relations were established especially with England and with the Anglican Church.

In 1705, Jean-Alphonse Turrettini, son of the Turrettini who had had a large influence on the orthodox Consensus Formula, became Professor of Theology in Geneva. The son did not follow in his father's footsteps. He completely departed from the orthodoxy represented by the Consensus Formula. By 1706 candidates for the church's ministry were already being examined along much less strict lines, and in 1725 the Consensus Formula was finally abolished. From then on it was required only that candidates should adhere to the scriptural teaching of the Old and New Testaments, as summarized in the catechism. Reasonable orthodoxy had won its way into Geneva. A pupil of J.-A. Turrettini, Jacob Vernet, took theology further along this road, and became a leading figure in the '*Académie de Calvin*'. His influence on Fletcher will be discussed in the next chapter.

Continuing orthodoxy in Bern

In the Pays de Vand, which was under the control of Bern, things developed differently. The Bernese government immediately brought the Consensus Formula into force throughout all its territories. All ministers in the Waadt were obliged to subscribe to the confessional formula. In addition, when Huguenot ministers began to seek refuge in the Waadt after the revocation of the Edict of Nantes in 1685, the Bernese authorities feared for the unity of the faith and ruled that under no circumstances should anyone be admitted to public office without first subscribing to the Consensus Formula. Bern required simply a signature. Paraphrases and explanations could no longer be accepted. Even protests from abroad could not shake the rigid stance of the authorities in Bern. Bern scented danger.

In 1699 the authorities called together not only all ministers but also parts of the political administration and required them, in addition, to take the so-called 'Oath of Association'. This oath was sharpened up in a French version prepared for the Waadt. To counter the influence of Saumur upon some of the ministers, the teachings of Arminianism were added to the condemned doctrines of pietism[12] and Socinianism, and some imprecise expressions in the German form of the oath were more clearly defined. From that time on, the Oath of Association and subscription to the Consensus Formula were to be a condition for admission to any church office. The people of the Waadt did not, however, apply this oath-taking very strictly. A visitation in 1719 revealed that since 1700 the Oath of Association had not been required of anyone taking office for the first time. When the report of the visitation was discussed three years later, it was decided that all the ministers of the Waadt should be required to subscribe to the Consensus Formula and take the Oath of Association immediately, in order to bring them back into line with the German-speaking parts of Bern. Protests followed, from the Kings of Prussia and England, among others. Bern now let it be known officially that the Consensus Formula was not a confession of faith but rather a formulation of doctrine which should be understood in terms of its content rather than its wording. It did not need to be taught, but in the interest of good order and peace in church and state it should neither be spoken, nor written, against. A similarly mild interpretation was put on the Oath of Association. Under these new conditions, both signing and oath-taking were seen by most people as acts of obedience towards the authorities. For a few people, however, difficult questions of conscience were involved. At the end of the long controversy over the issue, there remained four ministers who persisted in their opposition. Three of them went abroad. The only one who remained in the Pays de Vand was Théodore Crinsoz de Bionens, though from that time on he was not allowed to work as a minister. We shall need to come back to this man and his relationship to Fletcher.

Although, with a few exceptions, the people of the Pays de Vand had submitted to the order from Bern, the debate over the theological issues went on. Foreigners also became involved in the discussions. In 1723 the Bernese authorities issued a letter in which they declared that they now wanted peace, and that further controversies were prohibited, but they were not able to stop people thinking. Even the Bern government itself could not remain uninfluenced by new currents of thought. In 1735 they had the *Berner Synodus*, the Reformation document from 1532, officially reprinted, and sent to all ministers in active service. This pointed in the direction of a return to original statements from the time of the Reformation. Eleven years later, in 1746, the Oath of Association was replaced by a more moderate Oath of Religion. Meanwhile in Geneva the move to reasonable orthodoxy had been completed. The differences between the situation in the Pays de Vand and that in Geneva affected the choice of Fletcher's place of study, and also his decision regarding a profession. Crinsoz de Bionens had his own part to play in this.

Théodore Crinsoz de Bionens: an outsider in the Waadt

Even from an external point of view it was significant that from 1732 Théodore Crinsoz de Bionens resided in Nyon. From the simple fact of his being so near, Fletcher must have known him and heard of his writings. But the links between them are closer still. Crinsoz de Bionens was one of Fletcher's uncles![13] When, as a result of his refusal to take the oath, the possibility of working as a minister was no longer open to de Bionens, he lived off the family estate. He devoted himself to the development of charitable works, among them the improvement of schooling for the lower social strata, and to exegetical and theological writing, for which he became well known. Since Geneva was afraid to publish de Bionens's writings, the first of them appeared in Rotterdam. A polemical correspondence developed between J.-A. Turrettini in Geneva and Th. Crinsoz de Bionens. After an exposition of the book of Job and the Psalms, de Bionens turned to exegetical work on the apocalyptic writings, and in 1729 published a study on the book of Daniel, in which he sought to verify historically and to date the biblical visions. He did not regard the events described and the numbers quoted as mysterious, obscure data. His aim was to establish the divine authority of the Apocalypse (the Book of Revelation) and to demonstrate the agreement between apocalyptic texts of the Old and New Testaments. His attempts at dating resulted in the following conclusions: (a) the time of papal power, represented by the little horn in Daniel 7, would come to an end after 1715; (b) in 1745 the sanctuary would be dedicated, i.e., the church would be purified, and the weakening of the power of God's holy people, i.e., Protestant Christendom, would be brought to an end; (c) the time of the Lamb, i.e., the time of the first resurrection, would come, probably in 1790, and the joy of the church would be complete.

De Bionens compiled further works on prophecies relating to the end time. These were never published, but only circulated among friends. When nothing special happened in 1745, de Bionens acknowledged, in another of his writings, that he had been mistaken in trying to fix the date, but insisted nevertheless that his exegetical method was basically correct. The works of de Bionens, and of his friend J.-Ph. Loys de Cheseaux, had great significance for the oppressed and persecuted French Protestants, who derived much comfort from them. The fact that the eschatological events did not occur on the predicted dates did not destroy their expectation that the end was near. They were not the only ones to live with the firm conviction that the apocalyptic promises would soon be fulfilled. Many people in the Pays de Vand also held this view. Thus unpublished works by Crinsoz de Bionens circulated among his many followers. The fact that John William Fletcher knew these writings will help to throw light on certain phases of his later development.[14]

2

A Career in the Church or in the Army?

Although we possess very little reliable information about Fletcher's early years in Switzerland, the year of his matriculation in the University of Geneva is known. He chose Geneva instead of Lausanne, which would have been more natural for someone from that part of Switzerland, and in 1746, a year after his brother Henri Louis, this youngest son in the Fletcher family inscribed his name in the Rector's book.[1] What he studied in Geneva, however, was very different from what is commonly supposed.

At about the age of seventeen Fletcher began his studies in 'Belles-Lettres' (the Faculty of Arts). The normal course of studies for students coming from the Collège (Fletcher's previous school) involved, first of all, two years in the 'Belles-Lettres' department, then two further years in the study of philosophy, followed by a four-year course in either theology or law. Two years' study in 'Belles-Lettres' was required because most of the students were very young, but in exceptional cases the course could be completed in one year. We do not know whether this option was open to Fletcher, seeing that he was older than most students when he entered. The curriculum in 'Belles-Lettres' covered classical Greek and Latin authors, history – including an introduction to the principles of chronology – and geography. At the Academy (the university) a knowledge of Latin, which was the medium of instruction, was taken for granted. Students would have started to learn Greek in their last year at the Collège. Other subjects were left until later: Church history – as opposed to history in general, which was part of the basic humanist course – came under theology. Although the chair in Hebrew belonged to the philological and philosophical side of the course, the subject was dealt with mainly as part of theological studies. Physics and mathematics, together with logic and ethics, made up the area of philosophy.

Jacob Vernet, a representative of 'reasonable orthodoxy'

When Fletcher began his humanist studies in the 'Belles-Lettres' department in 1746, the professorial chair was held by Jacob Vernet. Not only was Vernet a disciple of J.-A. Turrettini (as was pointed out above), but as a leading figure in the university he also consolidated the reorientation of theology in the direction of reasonable orthodoxy. Before beginning his work in Geneva he had been a private tutor in Paris, and had undertaken an extensive journey in Italy. He maintained close relations with high-ranking figures in the Anglican Church, having been very favourably impressed by the freedom and clarity of thought he had found in England on the occasion of an earlier visit there. J. Vernet held the chair in 'Belles-Lettres' at Geneva from 1739 to 1756, after which he became professor of theology.

Between 1730 and 1788 Vernet produced a ten-volume work on the truth of the Christian religion, based on Turrettini's Latin dissertations.[2] Vernet's aim, in his writings, was to appeal to the deists and convince them of the necessity of revelation. His basic thinking may be summed up as follows. Revelation, he maintained, in no way excludes natural reason, but rather enhances it. He described the inadequacy of philosophy, and spoke of the ancient philosophers' longing for revelation. He insisted that there were limits to what could be known by reason alone. Reason had nothing positive to say about the origin of the world. Only God could give the assurance of grace and open up the way of reconciliation. Sinful human beings need more light, encouragement, grace and help, in accordance with their weakness. Revelation gives people the knowledge of immortality and of true life. It has more authority than reason. In addition, not all people are capable of thinking clearly and deeply, and they are in special need of revelation.

In describing the true character of revelation, Vernet made five points. (a) Revelation ought not to be set up in opposition to reason. Divine revelation and clear reason are two infallible rules of truth, since they both spring from the same source. (b) Revelation should never contradict itself. (c) Revelation must confirm and perfect the natural light of reason in respect of divine truths. (d) Revelation must supplement the natural light of reason with such aids as sinners need. (e) Revelation must be accompanied by visible signs, such as prophecy and miracles, to demonstrate its divine authority. In these five points Vernet unfolded the meaning of revelation in opposition to the views of the deists. But at the same time his own understanding of revelation was influenced by those opposing views. In essence, revelation is knowledge. For Vernet it is a God-given, reasonable knowledge of divine truth which complements the knowledge acquired by natural reason.

Fletcher's recollections of his student days

We have no information from Fletcher about the content of what he was taught. We do, however, have a few observations about the way in which he organized his time as a student. In addition there are repeated references to a prize which he is said to have won.

In a letter to Charles Wesley, Fletcher wrote of experiences which had coincided with the beginning of his university studies, or which had happened to him earlier. In describing these experiences he compared them with the development of the Wesley brothers. It all seemed to have happened to him along parallel lines to the experiences of their group in Oxford, though with less success:

> When I was sixteen the Lord shewd me that it was not possible to serve two masters and that if I would Sin on I should soon have the wages of sin: I began to look about me, to strive in earnest to grow in holiness and for 8 month I think I walk'd as became a Follower of Christ. About that time I was also convinc'd of the necessity of having a Christian friend and after many useless trials to find one I at last met with 3 students who formd with me a religious society: we met as often as we could to confess one an other our sins to exhort read & pray, and we could perhaps have been what the Methodists were at Oxford; Had not one of us been led away by a Deist and drank so deep of the poison of his arguments that all endeavours to recall him were useless. as he was remarkable for his great parts and made much of, on account of his wit and learning he had such an ascendancy over our companions that I was soon left alone, and happy would I have been still, had not I provok'd the Lord, grievd and quenchd his spirit by a relapse into sin.[3]

How Fletcher tried to live a religious life is clear from this reminiscence. His piety showed itself in virtuous living, prayer and the confession of sin. Fletcher wrote along similar lines in a letter to his brother in which he recalled his life as an eighteen-year-old student. At that time he was probably still engaged in his humanist studies. He described how very careful he was to observe and to fulfil all the laws and forms of religious life. Prayer and attendance at divine worship had an important place in all this. Such devoutness is thoroughly understandable against the background of the influence of reasonable orthodoxy. What did not fit in with that background, however, was Fletcher's reference to the prophetic literature.[4] We can only assume that Fletcher, stimulated by his study of the relatively new science of chronology, was attempting to apply the principles of chronology to the biblical records. We may further suppose, with a fair degree of probability, that he was also seeking, with the help of chronology, to incorporate the numerical data in the apocalyptic writings into a wider overview of history. Prophetic and apocalyptic ideas exerted an influence on the young student. The expectation of the final tribulation and the return of Christ fired his imagination. It drove him, beyond the virtues which he already esteemed more than most, to lead a religiously and morally blameless life.

Fletcher never had anything to say about the progress of his studies. Yet his early biographers, among them his wife, were able to report that once or twice he had won a first prize. His wife's account speaks of a 'Premium of Piety' which he had received at the university.[5] The reference must be to the *prix de piété* or *thème de piété* which, from the beginning of the eighteenth century, was awarded each year by the Collège. Unfortunately there are no records from Fletcher's time as a student to indicate what work he had undertaken. Once, or possibly twice, Fletcher did receive such a distinction. This confirms that he pursued his studies conscientiously, and not without some success. But the fact that the *prix de piété* was awarded in the Collège, and not in the Faculty of Arts or the Faculty of Theology, raises the basic question of the real scope of Fletcher's studies in Geneva.

The length of Fletcher's studies in Geneva

Generally speaking, we read in the biographies that Fletcher's original intention was to follow a career in the church, that he completed the usual studies in Geneva, but that he then decided not to enter the ministry. Such is the gist of the biographies by John Wesley and Joseph Benson. Benson also quotes Gilpin as saying that before the age of twenty Fletcher had turned away from theology and taken up military studies. But these two statements, though they are presented side by side, conflict with each other. More recent accounts state that it is not known for how long Fletcher studied in Geneva, but they still give the

impression that for a certain time he studied theology. Fletcher himself
wrote in a letter of 1781:

> Having some desires to be a clergyman, I was, for seven years, sent to
> Geneva to persue my studies. But after I had stayed there seven years,
> a fear of being unfit for the Christian ministry, and . . . , made me for
> a time prefer the sword to the gown. I left the academy . . .[6]

Allowing just one year for study in 'Belles-Lettres', the whole course of
study, including philosophy and theology, would have taken exactly
seven years. But such a hypothesis is untenable for several reasons. First
there are several time factors to be considered. A seven-year period of
study would have lasted from 1746 to 1753. But in 1751 we find
Fletcher already in his private tutor's post in England. Before that, he
had made various journeys in connection with his military studies and
plans. The observation of the biographer Gilpin that Fletcher had gone
over to the military side before he was twenty years old is too often
overlooked. It is therefore clear, on the strength of time factors alone,
that Fletcher could not have completed a full course of studies in
Geneva.

Archival material from the University of Geneva enables us to define
the period of study more precisely. The students paid a deposit when
they enrolled as readers in the public library. There are separate entries
for students in philology ('Belles-Lettres'), philosophy and theology.
Fletcher's name appears only once among the philology students and
not at all, later, among those in philosophy or theology. Any period of
study beyond that in 'Belles-Lettres' can therefore be excluded. The
draft of a letter which must date from Fletcher's later years supports this
conclusion. In it Fletcher alluded to his studies in the Collège and in
'Belles-Lettres', but made no reference at all to any further studies.[7]

Thus for at least one year and possibly even for two, Fletcher was a
student under Jacob Vernet in the 'Auditoire de Belles-Lettres' in the
University of Geneva. We do not know whether or not he took an
examination at the end of this part of the course. Before his matriculation in the university in 1746, he had been for six, or possibly only five,
years a pupil at the Collège in Geneva, where once or twice he had
gained distinction for *thèmes de piété*. The total length of his stay in
Geneva was seven years. John William Fletcher, then, came to Geneva
as a boy of eleven or twelve, and received the first part of his education
in the Collège.[8] He acquired his classical education during this total

period of seven years, which included both his time in the Collège and his humanist studies in the university. But he never studied philosophy or theology in Geneva. He gained his knowledge in these fields mainly from personal study.

Plans for a military career

Fletcher broke off his studies in Geneva in 1747 or 1748. There were three reasons for this change of direction.[9] While he wanted to keep his vow to serve God, he still felt unworthy of ministerial office. He was thinking not of the ordinary requirements of candidates for ordination, but was wanting, rather, to meet those high demands which, in his view, were essential for carrying out the work of the ordained ministry. A second reason was of a theological nature. If he ever wished to become a minister in the Waadt, he would be obliged to assent to the Consensus Formula and the Oath of Religion before taking up office. But he was reluctant to subscribe to the strict predestinarian doctrine of the Consensus Formula. Fletcher gave as the third reason for his change of direction pressure from his friends. Many of his relatives had already chosen a military career. A brother of his father was a lieutenant colonel in the service of the United Provinces of the Netherlands. His eldest brother was a lieutenant, also in the Netherlands. The lower nobility of the Waadt was well known for serving in foreign armies, and in some cases attaining high rank within them. It was only after some hesitation that John William took the decision to turn towards a military career. The change did not entail the abandonment of his religious and moral convictions, though it did mean giving up the idea of the ordained ministry.

The time following this change of direction can be described only in broadest outline. Fletcher stayed for a year in Germany, to learn German and the construction of military defence installations. This was probably in 1748. A peace treaty, probably the Peace of Aachen of 18 October 1748, deprived Fletcher of the opportunity to enter the branch of the army he had been thinking of. Once the great powers of the day had made peace, there was little chance of joining an army on the Continent. Fletcher had to return home disappointed. At home, the inner religious unrest continued. Fletcher found no pleasure in the company of his friends. He threw himself into his studies, probably of Hebrew and mathematics,[10] but found no peace there either. He therefore decided to seize the first opportunity of leaving the country. When he was offered the sum of £500 to go as overseer and maintenance man on a voyage to Brazil in the service of the King of Portugal, he agreed. This was probably in 1749.[11] When he was ready to sail, someone dropped a pot of boiling water on his legs, and they were badly scalded. Fletcher was therefore obliged to stay in Europe, to get over the effects of the accident.

When he had finally recovered, he heard that his uncle, the officer serving in the Dutch army, had a post in mind for him. John William travelled to Holland, and for several months waited in vain for an appointment. He writes that he had seen so much of military life during this time that he no longer considered it worth the effort. In addition, his uncle resigned from military service.[12] This happened in the middle of June 1750.[13] Plans for a military career for young John William thus fell apart in the summer of 1750. He did not wish to return home, but he had cherished for six years a secret desire to see England. During that time, while studying in Geneva, he had begun to learn English. The close links between Geneva (especially, in those days, through Jacob Vernet) and England had certainly strengthened this interest, possibly even had given birth to it. Fletcher now abandoned all thought of embarking on a military career. At first he had been held back from it by external events; later he had become disillusioned by his own experiences. He therefore gave up the idea and went to England instead.

PART II
EARLY YEARS IN ENGLAND
(1750–1760)

3

A Private Tutor Interested in the Methodists

In the summer of 1750, then, John William Fletcher made his way to England. His parents consented to the journey, and covered the cost of it. Fletcher had begun to learn English while he was still at school. Moreover, his mother tongue, French, was the language of the higher and educated classes in England. He did not, therefore, come to this foreign land without resources. To improve his knowledge of English language and literature, he went to a boarding school in Hatfield, Hertfordshire. Just over a year later, in October or November 1751, he began work as a private tutor with the Hill family.[1]

Private tutor with the Hill family

Unpublished letters to his family give us an insight into the life of twenty-three-year-old Fletcher. He described his surroundings and the things that were happening to him with precision and irony. He told of a relationship he had formed in Hatfield which could easily have led to a love affair, had he not quickly drawn back. It seems that from then on he trod more warily – all the more so because the Hill family circle included a twenty-year-old daughter from a previous marriage. There was nothing remarkable about this daughter, wrote Fletcher, apart from her ugliness, her good character, and an inheritance of £15,000 from her mother. He knew now, as a result of the experience he had had, that he must maintain a certain distance from her, since 'the perception people here have of Frenchmen, and of all other foreigners along with them, compels me to keep well away from her . . . , in the conviction that women are a reef on which it is difficult for private tutors to avoid shipwreck.'[2] Fletcher was happy to find himself in a family which did not make fun of his serious way of life. It was important to him that people should have a good opinion of him. He wanted never to offend

against the rules of polite behaviour. If he was in disagreement with
the Hill parents on any matter, he sought to explain his position with
politely expressed arguments and diplomatic tact.

Thomas Hill, the father, was about sixty years old when Fletcher
took up his post. He was lord of the manor and Member of Parliament
for Shrewsbury. He seemed to have little time for the social life and,
when at home, was usually to be found with a grammar book in his
hand. Fletcher found this passion for grammar as hard to understand
as his employer's wish that he, Fletcher, should teach the children
grammar above everything else. Yet he did his best to please Mr Hill.
Mr Hill loved the French language, whereas his wife understood
scarcely a word of it. So as not to provoke disagreements, Fletcher
remained silent at the dining table. What he found more difficult to
bear, however, was the bad influence previous tutors had had upon the
children. Fletcher trusted that the good nature and tender age of the
children would enable him to bring them back to the path of virtue. One
of the two sons, probably the elder, was at that time eight or nine years
old. The young Fletcher took an optimistic view of human nature. He
tackled his new task with such enthusiasm that he was reproached by
other private tutors for taking his duties too seriously.

> Mrs Hill is a large handsome woman, who was once very beautiful
> and is so still. Though she has no outstanding qualities, she does not
> lack the good taste and disposition which are characteristic of those
> who attend the court and theatrical performances. She takes as much
> delight in spending money as her husband does in saving it. Like
> other women she knows the secret of leading her husband on and
> extracting from him what she needs for her pleasure and her pomp. I
> often see her with jewellery worth 20,000 gold pieces (*louis d'or*),
> while her husband is wearing a wig worth less than 30 pence.[3]

She had a passion for mussels. After Fletcher had bought her some, she
felt very kindly disposed towards him.

In his first letter to his father, Fletcher said how much he was looking
forward to leaving London and spending the summer on the family's
property at Tern Hall, which was situated on the Welsh border, three
miles from Shrewsbury in Shropshire. He was planning further to
improve his knowledge of the language and the country, and to bathe in
the River Severn. In a later letter, written in December 1752, he gave a
description of Shropshire:

Shropshire is a beautiful, very fertile region. It is watered by the River Severn, a rival to the Thames, and would appear somewhat similar to our own country, if some of our vineyards could be transplanted here. The air is clean, provisions are cheap, and the inhabitants, though a little too fond of drink, are friendly and pleasant.[4]

Fletcher received the offer of another private tutor's post, with a titled family, in which he would have earned £100 a year instead of £30, but since he did not receive Mr Hill's consent he felt obliged to stay where he was. Mr Hill, however, then increased his salary to £50. With this Fletcher hoped to settle his debts with his father, and at the same time to set aside half of what he owed to support Christian welfare work in Nyon.[5]

The piety of the young Fletcher

Along with descriptions of the Hill family and life in England, the twenty-three-year-old Fletcher's two letters also contain passages on religious questions. These statements give us an insight into the piety which characterized the life of the young man. He thanked God for his good health and his simple lifestyle. He wished his father, for the new year, everything that might contribute to his sanctification and true happiness.[6] When the first letter was written, in March 1752, Fletcher was spending his free time in social activities, such as dancing lessons and the cultivation of friendships (female ones, naturally), as well as in quieter leisure pursuits, such as contemplating spiritual truths and studying biblical questions. By the time the second letter was written in December, the balance between these areas of interest had shifted. Fletcher now liked to immerse himself more deeply in spiritual things. He wanted to take time to reflect upon himself and God. Instead of going out hunting, he would pay attention to his own soul. He told of extraordinary examples of God's protection, while he was out riding, and described how he found solitude and isolation more congenial than the receptions which Mr Hill gave before parliamentary elections. Life at Tern Hall suited him better than life in bustling London. Near the estate he got to know a seventy-year-old minister distinguished by his gentle character and his piety – qualities which, according to Fletcher, were rare in this country. At that time, clearly, Fletcher had no contact at all with people who were close to the Methodist movement or who belonged to it. That may have been due in part to the fact that he was

moving at a different level of society. When at a later stage he heard of
the Methodists for the first time, it was only to be expected that he
should immediately want to get to know them.

Fletcher also expressed his thanks, in these letters to his father, for an
anonymous work by his uncle Crinsoz de Bionens which had been sent
to him. Like other works by his uncle, this one too dealt with questions
concerning the dating of eschatological texts. Fletcher was convinced of
his uncle's ability to interpret the prophetic view of the future. Speaking
for himself, Fletcher stressed two things. The first concerned the *nearness* of the eschatological prophecies. Fletcher did not deny the fundamental possibility of deducing the time of Christ's coming from the
prophetic writings, but he urged caution on those who wanted to determine the exact date. Human capacity for knowledge was limited. It was
also possible that his own generation would die before the Second
Coming. The second issue was the *significance* of this expectation for
believers. For the early church it was a powerful incentive. When the
immediate expectation was not fulfilled, the community's hope and
faith were nevertheless strengthened. That was better than slumbering
in dangerous security. So Fletcher concluded that we should hope for
the return of our Lord humbly and patiently, not wavering in our
reverence for God and his prophecies. We should do this with a pure
conscience, and with a heart which has turned away from the world.
Expectation of the end should kindle faith and piety in us also, Fletcher
wrote.[7]

Expectation of the return of Christ brought a strengthening of
Fletcher's own faith and hope. It did not cause him any anxiety. But
believers must turn away from the world, and must have a pure conscience, so that all they long for is to be separated from the flesh in order
to be with Christ. This faith, this humility, this turning away from the
world, this maintaining of reverence for God – all this was described by
Fletcher as the attitude God requires of human beings. Nothing could
separate from God the person with such an attitude. The prophetic predictions of both Old and New Testaments, which might be fulfilled in
this generation, should strengthen people in this attitude that is required
of them. How seriously Fletcher intended this is made clear in one of his
little notebooks. Before the celebration of the Lord's Supper, he engaged
in self-examination and noted down his sins. He mentioned his pride,
his irritability and angry outbursts, his too strict and at times unjust
disciplining of the children entrusted to him, and his neglect of prayer
and of the Word of God.[8] These notes clearly reveal his striving for rest

and peace of soul. Fletcher was seeking to acknowledge his sins, and as far as possible to avoid committing them again. He had heard the religious and ethical imperatives of the biblical message, and applied them most conscientiously as the yardstick for his own life. Fletcher called Christ his redeemer. But the gospel promises of faith, justification and forgiveness were not mentioned, except perhaps as dependent on the fulfilment of the imperative.

The picture we are presented with, then, is neither that of a religiously indifferent person, nor that of someone shaken in his faith. Quite the contrary: the young Fletcher tried very earnestly and single-mindedly to bring religion and morality together in his life, and to live in an exemplary fashion. Examining his conscience and turning to God thus took precedence over engaging in social intercourse.

First acquaintance with Methodism

'The children of God are minish'd from the earth, said I, one I had met in 22 years (and that was a woman I had seen abroad) and it would be folly to seek for an other.'[9] Such was the sharp, sweeping conclusion Fletcher had come to in the period before his conversion. At that time he had as yet no knowledge of the Methodists, but he seized every opportunity to admonish other people. It is not surprising, then, that he was asked whether he did not wish to become a minister. The seriousness which he displayed in religious matters seemed to qualify him well for this office.

It was through such an encounter, in which Fletcher had spoken to another person about spiritual things, that he heard the name 'Methodists' for the first time:

> The [Hill] family had baited and while they drank tea I went to take a walk and get out of the way of the world: I soon met a poor woman who seem'd to be in distress, and asking her what was the matter I soon saw by her answers that she was a Christian: the pleasure and profit I found in her conversation made me forget that I was upon a journey, and when I return'd to the inn I found I had been left behind. However taking a horse, I overtook the family (before it was dark [crossed out]) and told the reason why I had stay'd behind. Don't go says a Lady talking so to Old women. People will say that we have got a Methodist preacher with us: I asked what she meant by a

Methodist and when she had told me I sayd that I would be one of them if there was really such a people in England.[10]

The idea that this private tutor, Fletcher, was well-suited for ministerial office was not disputed, and caused no offence. But the thought of his adopting Methodist practices was abominable. The incident described above took place in the spring of 1753, when Fletcher was travelling with the Hill family from London to their estate in Tern.[11]

It is not surprising that, when Fletcher returned to London with the Hill family towards the end of the year, he immediately sought out the Methodists. He attended Methodist services, listened to their preaching, and joined one of their 'societies'.[12] We do not know exactly when he became a member, but we may suppose that, in accordance with Methodist practice, it had already happened before his conversion. The Methodist movement was about fifteen years old when Fletcher became acquainted with it. It had developed in an amazing way. Anglican ministers who shared the basic beliefs of the Methodists often called themselves 'gospel ministers'. To their contemporaries, John and Charles Wesley were important exponents of Methodism, but the Methodist movement at that time embraced more than the 'United Societies' under the brothers' leadership. In the 1750s the growing movement for revival and renewal had many facets, though it still considered itself to be part of the Church of England.

The beginnings of the Methodist Revival

The Methodist Revival was actually started neither by John Wesley nor by his brother Charles, but by George Whitefield. At the end of 1738 Whitefield came back to England from Georgia. In January 1739 he was ordained priest. Following the example of the layman Howel Harris in Wales, Whitefield began to preach in the open air in England too. So, in February and March 1739, he proclaimed the good news to the miners around Bristol. Bad harvests and their economic consequences, together with some extremely cold winters, had made life harder for the miners. This led to unrest, but scarcely any of the clergy cared about these people. The effect produced by the preaching of Whitefield, who was just twenty-four years old, was extraordinary. His preaching centred on human sin and the grace of God through faith in Jesus Christ. Each time he preached, thousands of people gathered to hear him. Many were so affected that they were ready to turn to God in repentance and seek this liberating faith for themselves. Existing and newly created 'societies' welcomed these seekers and became the place where they experienced their conversion. Whitefield himself, who was a minister in Georgia, was only able to stay in England for a short time. During his stay he was trying to collect money for an orphanage he was planning to build in Georgia. His activity in Bristol went on for a total of eight weeks. He could think of only one man who could continue the work, so that the seekers were not left uncared for: John Wesley, who was eleven years his senior. They had been friends since their student days.

Whitefield wrote to Wesley on 23 March, with an urgent request for Wesley to come to his aid and continue the work he had begun. After much toing and froing, and many discussions in the Fetter Lane Society in London, which was in a sense the mother-society of the new movement, a positive decision was reached by drawing lots. On 31 March Wesley arrived in Bristol. When he was present for the first time at one of Whitefield's sermons, outside a consecrated church building, as a true minister of the Church of England he reacted strongly against such conduct. Yet he could see the need for it and the success it was having. The next day he preached at a meeting of a 'society', and finally, on 2 April, for the first time in the open air, to a large crowd. Having thus successfully introduced his successor, Whitefield left Bristol and went to London, where he also started open-air meetings, before returning to the American colonies. Some members of religious societies had, indeed, already attempted to do this, but they had been chased away by the people. Whitefield, by contrast, succeeded in gathering around him thousands of people who wanted to hear this gifted young preacher. He also introduced Charles Wesley to this new practice of preaching in the open air.

The differences between Whitefield and the Wesley brothers soon became apparent in their work. Whitefield was the great evangelist. He could mobilize tens of thousands, while John or Charles Wesley's hearers amounted to 'only' thousands. The strength of the Wesley brothers, by contrast, lay in their nurture of those who were seeking and coming to faith, gathering them into groups, and leading them to a sanctified life. Important theological differences also arose between Whitefield and the Wesley brothers on the doctrine of predestination. This was already threatening to lead to a break between the former friends in the first months and years of the movement. Several times Whitefield and the Wesley brothers had to come to a kind of standstill agreement on the issue. Their personal friendship and mutual respect helped them to push their doctrinal differences into the background.

In 1770, however, the year of Whitefield's death, various factors led to the old conflict breaking out afresh in a particularly sharp form. It then fell to Fletcher in large measure to determine the course of the controversy. By contrast with the Calvinistic stream, to which Whitefield and most of the 'gospel ministers' belonged, the Wesley brothers were high church Arminians. Thus the Wesleyan stream in Methodism[13] was more strongly influenced by the English-Dutch early Enlightenment than was the Calvinistic branch.[14]

Another member of the group of leading figures within the Methodist movement was the Countess of Huntingdon. She was of noble birth, and sought to exercise her influence at this higher level of society. From the beginning of the movement she was associated with the London Methodists, but she leaned increasingly towards the Calvinistic stream in Methodism, to which most of the Methodist sympathizers among the Anglican clergy also felt drawn. At first all those whose preaching resembled, in content, that of Whitefield or John and Charles Wesley, were, without exception, decried as Methodists. But they all wanted to remain within the Church of England and work for its renewal.

4

From Hell to Heaven

Quite contrary to his expectations, Fletcher's encounter with the Methodists not only brought him friends with whom he shared a common outlook; it also plunged him into a deep crisis, from which he emerged as a changed man. Every change in a person's life arises out of the past and has its effect on the future. This will become clear from what follows. After looking again at the time before Fletcher's meeting with the Methodists, we shall explore what is meant by the term 'conversion', and then examine a little-known document entitled 'Covenant with God'. Finally we shall consider the consequences of the new life of faith.

Prehistory

Two letters written in 1752, together with personal notes, have already given us an insight into Fletcher's life and piety. These were the only letters to have been preserved from the time before his conversion. They showed the extent to which abstention from pleasures, the quest for solitude, meditation on biblical texts, and the study of apocalyptic promises were meant to serve a single purpose: that of strengthening his own faith and hope, through a life well pleasing to God.

All other documents known to us come from the time after Fletcher's conversion. Although they give useful insights into the time leading up to the conversion, it needs to be borne in mind that they were written after this change in his life, and were therefore affected by it. This applies also to an undated letter to his brother, in which he describes the development of his faith.[1] He acknowledges that religion had always had some importance in his life. He recounts how, as an eighteen-year-old, he had devoted himself enthusiastically to the study of prophecy. His deep reflections had led to the conclusion that, in the biblical image, his religion was built on sand. In confirmation of this, Fletcher speaks of a meeting with deists which was to have important consequences. The incident is difficult to date precisely, but Fletcher's statement that he wished to convert the deists makes it likely that the encounter took place near the time when he first heard the name 'Methodists', that is to say, in 1752/1753. At all events, the conversation with the deists resulted in Fletcher's conversion to their Enlightenment conception of Christianity. He thus lost, he says, the religion which until then had been for him no more than outward show. It was not that he had become a worse person. It was simply that his true inward state was now openly apparent.[2] Fletcher also describes the change in himself as a religious one: through deism, he says, he had been led to an open rejection of redemption through Christ. In retrospect this seems to him to have been an unmasking of the enmity towards Christ which was already latent within him.

Unfortunately we have no other evidence to help us grasp more fully the significance of this lapse into deism. Since Fletcher's piety was in large measure conditioned by reasonable orthodoxy, itself influenced by the early Enlightenment, the lapse may be at least partly understood – though it is not thereby explained.[3] This deistic phase lasted for only a few weeks. Fletcher wrote later that he was soon seeking again to draw near to his redeemer. The possible fresh start was hindered however, he said, because he paid too much attention to those around him. Righteousness by works began again to intrude upon the scene – though with the difference that the demands of God now seemed to be less severe: 'Jesus Christ has broadened the way. And if I were damned, then half of all Christians would have to be damned with me.'[4] This he could not believe, since God was merciful.

In another document, a letter to Charles Wesley, Fletcher describes his prehistory from a different point of view. His main theme here is the Methodist one of 'power over sin'. Looking back, Fletcher characterizes his conduct as strictly legalistic. His experience as private tutor has forced him to acknowledge how much anger lurked in his heart. He tells how hard he had striven to overcome sin:

> How many prayers groans fastings tears sighs watchnights Did I go throu' and all [in] vain. Christ alone was to overcome for me, all that while as almost all my life I was lookt upon as a very Odd sort of man and the reason of it was that I kept to myself all my thoughts and shund company as much as possible.[5]

His exaggerated self-condemnation is fundamentally completely consistent with statements made in the letters of 1752. Fletcher describes
himself as a self-centred introvert. This characteristic became stronger
precisely when he was attempting in a legalistic way to justify himself
before God. His individual struggle to overcome sin separated him from
his fellow human beings.

In one of his letters to his brother Henri Louis, Fletcher sums up the
nature of his earlier piety in a theologically interesting way. He had
tried, he says, to sanctify himself by fulfilling the commandments of
God. What was still lacking at his death would be made good by Christ.
Fletcher believed that Jesus Christ had died for sinners, but, as he understood it, the merit of Christ's death was limited to making up what was
still lacking in sanctification at the end of a person's life.[6] This understanding of the redemptive activity of God agrees with that of reasonable orthodoxy, which also understood the atoning death of Christ as
compensation for people's sins, in so far as they had not completely
fulfilled God's law. The saving event was interpreted in moral categories. Here too, then, the strong influence of Fletcher's Swiss past on
his early piety is apparent.

The prehistory of Fletcher's conversion reveals both his attempt to
prove to himself the seriousness of his desire to be a Christian by fulfilling the commandments and turning in upon himself, and also the
shattering of his own piety through his encounter with deistic ideas. The
latter should not, it is true, be overestimated. But it reveals that
Fletcher's development before his conversion did not run in a straight
line. Through the preaching of the Methodists his piety was to be put to
its last and sternest test.

Rejected or accepted by God?

When Fletcher returned to London in the late autumn of 1753 his
immediate concern was to seek out the Methodists. Their preaching tore
his piety to shreds. Among the Methodists, the idea of God's graciousness towards 'better' people did not cancel out his punitive righteousness; righteousness by works, even in its noblest form, was condemned;
the sinfulness of every human being before God was stressed; Christ was
proclaimed as the redeemer and the renewer of life; the Holy Spirit was
promised, bringing assurance of salvation and power for holiness; all
the emphasis was laid on the renewal of a person's whole life, and the

believer was promised deliverance from servitude to sin. Fletcher's crisis of faith was kindled by one particular aspect of this Methodist preaching: the linking of the forgiveness of sins with power over sin. The question of 'power over sin' made the fundamental problem of renewal and sanctification once more the centre of attention. Fletcher's struggle for assurance of salvation and victory over sin took place in London in the winter of 1753/1754, and not as late as 1755, as is most often stated.[7]

Fletcher was beset by a dread of death, that is to say, a dread of not being able to stand before God's judgment:

> The Thoughts which engrossed my Mind, were generally these – I am undone. I have wandered from God more than ever – I have trampled under Foot the frequent Convictions God hath been pleased to work upon my Heart – instead of going strait to Christ, I have lost my Time in fighting against Sin with the dim Light of Reason, and the Use of the Means of Grace; as if the Means could do without the Blessing and Power of God. I fear my Notions of Christ are only speculative, and do not reach my Heart. *I never had Faith*: and without Faith it is impossible to please God. Then every Thought, Word, and Work of mine have only been Sin and Wickedness before God; though ever so specious before Men. All my Righteousness is as filthy Rags – I am a very Devil, though of an inferior Sort; and if I am not renewed, washed, and changed before I go hence, Hell will be my Portion to all Eternity.[8]

Now, as at an earlier stage, Fletcher believed that in order to be received into communion with God one required renewal, that is to say, victory over servitude to sin. The decisive difference, which triggered off the crisis, was the question as to how this renewal could be achieved. Earlier, Fletcher had tried to fight against sin with his own resources. Now, however, the realization that the power must come from God, and that he needed to turn to Christ, seemed to force itself upon him.

One night Fletcher dreamt that at the Last Judgment he was condemned, as a worthless servant, to praise the righteousness of God in hell.[9] In the days that followed he seemed benumbed. When he tried to copy some notes of music, a servant came in and expressed surprise that Fletcher should be doing such work on a Sunday. The servant's words struck home and made Fletcher realize his true condition. The consciousness that he was a sinner before God, that he was capable of nothing good, and that he had failed to appreciate the saving significance of Christ's death, propelled him into a long crisis. The last phase of this crisis was marked by various changing moods: doubt of his salvation – calmness even at the prospect of being cast into hell – mortification – new hope. The order in which these moods came to him was paradoxical: when he thought of his salvation, he was terrified by his sinfulness; when he thought of being cast into hell, the terror receded and gave way to a final sense of security. The God who measured human beings by his righteous standard was feared, while the God who condemned them on the basis of his righteous standard was loved. In the face of God's righteous demands, Fletcher could see only his own failure. The way to salvation was closed to him. On the other hand, as a rejected sinner he was an example of God's righteous judgment, and in this light his fate was a meaningful destiny. Condemnation by God had the effect of lifting his burden. The burden of needing to please God but being unable to do so receded, once Fletcher accepted his inability as God's judgment on him. This fearful state lasted for about ten weeks.

During this time Fletcher was becoming better acquainted with the Methodists and their writings. For example, he read Wesley's Journal, which helped him to take an important step: 'But I found Relief in Mr. Wesley's Journal, where I learned that we should not build on what we feel; but that the surest Way is, to go to Christ with all our Sins and all our Hardness of Heart.'[10] The next day (21 January 1754), Fletcher wrote out a confession of sin and recorded his decision to seek Christ until death. Thus his agonizing self-examination and self-reproach gave way to open confession of sin and the will to turn to Christ. Fletcher described this firm, sincere decision as the beginning of his life as a Christian. Although he was not as yet filled with living, renewing faith, he saw his decision as the indispensable step to consciously receiving God's gracious offer. There followed further periods of disillusionment and hopelessness, because he had sinned. Three days later, on 24 January 1754, he experienced the renewing power of God, for which he had not dared to hope, at work in his own life:

> I thought I committed that Night in my Sleep, grievous and abominable Sins; I awaked amazed and confounded, and rising with a Detestation of the Corruption of my Senses and Imagination, I fell upon my Knees and prayed with more Faith and less Wanderings than usual; and afterwards set about my Business with an uncommon Chearfulness. It was not long before I was tempted to fall into my

besetting Sin, but found myself a new Creature. My Soul was not even ruffled. I took not much Notice of it at first; but having withstood two or three Temptations, and feeling Peace in my Soul through the whole of them I began to think it was the Lord's doing.[11]

After initial doubts, he knew for certain that he was under no illusion. In the assurance that God had had mercy on him, and was giving him power to withstand sin, he lay down to sleep in peace.[12]

Fletcher's Covenant with God

Seven months after he had found peace with God, Fletcher composed a Covenant with God, which was to give direction to his life. His uncompromising approach to this Covenant, and the knowledge of himself and of God reflected in it, clearly show the transformation which had taken place in his life, and point to his future development. The Covenant is mentioned in only one biography, which has been largely ignored.[13] An English translation of the Covenant, reproduced below, was published in an obscure journal.[14] The original document began with a short preamble in Greek, the rest being written in Latin.[15] The surrender of his life, as it is expressed and accomplished in the Covenant, was not a totally new or surprising motif in Fletcher's life. As we gather from one of the little notebooks, Fletcher continued after his conversion to struggle for power over sin. An entry for 21 August contains a long enumeration of failures and omissions, under the heading: 'Faith was weak'.[16] Three days later, on 24 August 1754, Fletcher made his Covenant with God. He did it probably because of his experience of the weakness of his new faith, and because of his need to rely completely on God's promise and renewing power. It is not certain how far Fletcher was influenced by the Methodists in making his Covenant.[17]

   Fletcher's Covenant has a clear structure. Its main body consists of two formally parallel parts. In the first part Fletcher sets out what he is surrendering to God (lines 16–56), and in the second, what he is asking of God (lines 57–89). Each part is subdivided into an introduction (lines 16–21; 57–60) and a six-point statement of his concern (lines 21–56; 60–77). To the second part is added an explanation as to how he presumes to ask for anything at all from God (lines 78–87). These two parts together form the heart of the Covenant. They are bracketed by introductory and concluding arguments – a prologue and an epilogue (lines 2–15; 88–97). The Covenant begins with a preamble (line 1), and ends with date and signature (line 98). The Covenant reads as follows:

In the name of God, Creator of Heaven and earth. Amen.

O most high Jehova, only God, Father, Son, Holy Ghost, I, the worst of the wicked, the vilest of the sons of Adam, a renegade spirit, a man perishing altogether.

5 Having spent the greater part of my life in the service of Satan, by the gracious impulse of Thy mercy torn from the world, the devil and myself, I resolve to consecrate myself wholly and for ever to Thee, my Creator, Redeemer, Sanctifier. I determine to enter upon a treaty with Thee (forgive so great a boldness in so great a sinner). This Jacob did, and it was well with him: striving

10 therefore by his example, and moreover relying on the name of Christ, fasting and praying unto Thee, I creep forth, and most humbly through Jesus crucified, I ask, demand, importune that Thou wilt not refuse to ratify this treaty with Thy vilest slave, and that Thou wilt daily grant to me the help of Thy grace through pity, in Thy Son, that I may be able to play my parts aright to the glory of thy

15 name and the safety of my soul.

I am Thine, O Jehova; Thou didst create me that I might serve Thee: when fallen with my fathers Thou didst redeem me with Thy Son's blood: when rushing into hell Thou madest me stand; thou didst free me from divers dangers; when assailed by manifold want thou didst raise me up: crushed by innumerable

20 sins Thou dost free me. To Thee therefore, urged by my duty, by justice, by gratitude, I give, restore, consecrate, dispose: 1. All my property that now is or that is to be, whether for the relief of the poor or the honour and propagation of Thy gospel, or that with Thy permission it may be carried off by misfortunes or be destroyed: to me grant of them only what is necessary for the sustentation of

25 a humble life: 2. I give, I restore, I consecrate, I dispose to Thee the feelings of my body, the affection of my mind, my talents, my knowledge, my health, my reputation, my good name, all my plans, labours and pleasures: these take away from me, ruin or increase, for Thy pleasure and the increase of Thy glory: I will hold my peace, for Thou wilt do this, O Thou Rock of safety: 3. I give, restore,

30 consecrate and dispose to Thee my every limb and my whole body, that it may be afflicted by diseases as Thou in pity shalt will, or that, with Thy permission, it may be cast into prison by the wicked, that it may be assailed with infamy, or hurt with heathen stripes or swords, and at length when Thou shalt command, for Thy glory and the name of Christ, whether it be hung in a halter or burnt

35 with flames, or whatsoever other manner Thou mayest please, and at whatever time, it may be taken from my spirit. 4. I give, restore, consecrate and dispose the universal faculties of my mind, and my soul itself, that freed from natural and acquired corruption, and inflamed by love of Thee, it may serve Thee all the days of life here, and moreover in another world may adore Thee, and rejoice in

40 Thee. 5. To Thee I give, restore, consecrate, dispose my present office or future, so that if Thou shalt will Thou mayst take it from me, and as long as I perform it I may perform it to Thee alone and last by the grace of Christ: the progress of my pupils of whatsoever kind; all the points of my life, that to Thee

through Jesus my Advocate I may proclaim thy praises, and next may do good,
45 and perform my office, teach or study religion, satisfy my body sparingly,
prepare myself for the last judgment, and lastly may commend to Thee the life
of parents, relations and friends whether they be retained or taken away, for
Thou doest all things kindly and wisely. 6. To Thee I desire to sacrifice my
pride, my appetite for vain-glory, my impatience, also the phantasms of vain
50 plans, the fear of contempt, of poverty and of pain, doubtful expectations of the
future, severity against my neighbour's mistakes, an immoderate use of food,
drink and sleep, all justification by works, all trust in wealth and patronage, and
all mistrust in Christ, whether acquired or inborn: and, protected by the shield of
faith, and armed with the sword of grace, daily to resist these monsters, with
55 Thee, O Christ, for commander and leader, I promise Thee, yet not I, but Jesus
in me by the Holy Ghost.
If a thing created may stipulate with the Creator, if ashes and dust, if a noisome
dunghill may covenant with a Being most holy, the omnipotent Governor of all
nature, I seek, ask, demand, importune from Thee, pitying Father, with most
60 humble and agitated heart, and with all zeal and ardour of spirit. – 1. That all sins
that I have up to this time committed may be so expiated by the sacrifice of Thy
Son that neither their punishments nor their reckoning after death be demanded.
2. That those (sins) which unhappily I shall be able to commit may be, by grace
of the same, either averted, or on speedy repentance blotted out. 3. That I may
65 never be in want of Thy grace in order that I may embrace the gospel with lively
Faith, that I may show myself a living member of Thy Church, that I may be able
at every time to pay every part of my vow. 4. That through Thy Spirit Christ
may dwell in me and, Adam driven out, may reign alone. 5. That in all
temptations, in all calamities, in time of death and in the day of judgemente, Thy
70 help through Christ and Thy divine consolations may sustain and renew me.
6. That I may never neglect to read my Bible frequently, to meditate, to give
alms, to pray diligently day and night, and to receive the Eucharist at each
opportunity: in all these duties be Thou present with me, and breathe upon me
abundantly Thy Holy Spirit, so that, nourished in all the requisites of piety,
75 confirmed in faith, I may triumph, exult in hope, be inflamed with pure zeal,
burn with true love, strive in self-control worthy of Christ, until grace be
changed into glory.
These things, Heavenly Parent, I ask Thee most humbly, not on account of the
confidence recently reposed in Thee, nor the vows just poured forth (and I am
80 persuaded and am certain that Thou wilt not grant to my supplications things
that will be vain and useless), but by Thy pity towards the fallen sons of Adam,
by Thy Word, Jesus Christ, leaving Thy bosom, incarnated and born amongst
beasts, passing life amongst corrupt men, suffering so many insults, submitting
to so many toils, performing so many miracles, applying Thyself to so many
85 prayers on behalf of sinners, drinking so patiently, Himself instead of me, from
the bitter cup of righteous wrath, having shed all His blood after ineffable
anguish giving up the ghost, and now interceding for me at Thy right hand.
So much therefore I ask through Thy Word, that Thou wilt deign to hear me
and grant my prayers with unmerited and free grace, which, if in Thy pity
90 through Jesus Christ Thou wilt in goodness do, Thou wilt present to me in

> Thyself truly a heavenly Father, truly a Divine Redeemer, truly a sanctifying Spirit. Truly, indeed, I, ashes and dust corrupt, shall then be able to perform (yet not I but Christ through me) those things which my mind (O that no deceit may hide in the secret places of my heart) promises, pledges, vows that it will try to perform every day of my life – I, the vilest sinner, an apostate most unworthy of Thy pity, the direct rebel but yet the work of Thy hand, redeemed by the blood of Christ and to be renewed into Thine image by the Holy Spirit. I deliver this, the 24th of August, A.D. 1754.

The introductory preamble (line 1) is a call to God the Creator. In the name of his Creator, Fletcher wishes to make a Covenant with God. This preamble makes it clear right away that we do not have two equal partners to this Covenant. Fletcher owes his very self to the God upon whom he is now calling. This inequality between the two 'parties to the contract' will be explicitly brought out later. Both the introductory and concluding arguments for the Covenant (lines 2–15; 88–97) derive from this fundamental truth.

The introductory argument (lines 2–15), like the preamble, is in Greek. In this first part Fletcher acknowledges what the triune God in his mercy has done for him. Fletcher can only enter into a relationship with God because, through an impulse of divine grace, he has first been torn away from false attachments. He declares quite radically that divine grace has torn him away from the world, the devil and himself. He locates the rule of powers hostile to God not only outside but inside himself. He has been torn away from himself. He can do no other than dedicate himself to God wholly and for ever. Once again (as in the preamble) he refers to God as the three-in-one, but now thinks of him in relationship to the world, as the creating, redeeming and sanctifying God. This way of thinking of the persons of the Trinity in terms of the activity of the triune God in the world is repeated in the concluding argument (lines 90–92). As he determines now to enter into a contract with God, Fletcher himself is appalled by the presumption of such a thought. He appeals to the example of Jacob, as he had done shortly before his conversion. A stronger argument for Fletcher, however, is the mediation of Jesus Christ. Fletcher has found in Christ the intercessor who pleads for humanity before God. In the name of Christ, therefore, he most earnestly begs God not to refuse to confirm this contract with the least of all his slaves. He asks God for the gift of divine grace to be renewed daily, so that he may live his life aright, to the glory of God and for the salvation of his soul.

The concluding argument (lines 88–97) looks to the future, and sets out the promises which have been opened up through God's mercy. At the end of this passage, the necessity for the renewal of the writer's own life is expressed more plainly than ever. Redemption only reaches its goal when a person is made new. Fletcher now sees a new possibility opening up – that of accomplishing, by the grace of God, the good he wills to do (lines 92–95). Redeemed by the blood of Christ, he looks for renewal in the image of God through the Holy Spirit (lines 96–97). His expectation is based on the firm hope that God will ratify the contract, and in doing so grant him the measure of grace he has prayed for in the six points of the second main part of the Covenant. Fletcher repeatedly insists that he will only be able to do this through God's undeserved grace.

Between the introductory and concluding paragraphs we find the actual Covenant, which is divided into two parallel main parts, representing the reciprocal sides of a contract. In terms of substance, however, the two sides are not of equal weight. While in the first part Fletcher commits himself to the surrender of his whole life (lines 16–56), in the second part he can of necessity only express in the form of a *request* what he hopes God may grant him (lines 57–77). And because even this might seem presumptuous, he adds a further paragraph of supporting argument (lines 78–87). It is only in a limited sense, therefore, that we can speak of a reciprocal contract. In the end it is God who must decide whether this Covenant is to have validity.

The first main part (lines 16–56) begins with a sentence which encapsulates the gist of the whole Covenant: 'I am Thine, O Jehova'. The six points which constitute Fletcher's side of the contract are explications of this complete surrender to God. He gives three reasons for the surrender: duty, justice and gratitude. The concept of gratitude brings out most clearly the character of the argument as response. Fletcher's total surrender is rooted in the redemption he has experienced. Because redemption is an undeserved gift, it evokes gratitude. Because God has given himself wholly in the cross of Christ, it is only right that human beings should surrender their whole life to God. Because the object of God's dealings is human renewal, renewal involves the acceptance of the duty of serving God. The character of self-surrender as response is also brought out by the opening words: 'I give, restore, consecrate, dispose'. Fletcher introduces five of his six points with this formula. Self-surrender embraces property (lines 21–24), his own destiny (lines 25–29), and his own body (lines 29–36) – with an increasingly strong indication of his readiness for sacrifice and surrender. Whereas the surrender of his property was accompanied by the request that the basic necessities of life might be allowed him, no similar request that he might retain at least his bare existence is attached to the third point. Fletcher gives himself entirely to God. In sections four to six, concern for the renewal of life is dominant. Fletcher surrenders his talents (lines 36–40), his professional future (lines 40–48), and finally all the things that particularly trouble him (lines 48–56). Once he has incorporated into the surrender of his life to God all the things in himself that he finds displeasing, he can bring this first main part of his Covenant to a close.

In the second main part (lines 57–87), Fletcher formulates his requests to God. Before listing his six points, however, he introduces, in all humility, his particular concern (lines 57–60). His hesitancy comes out even more strongly here than in all the preceding arguments. The six points include, to begin with: the forgiveness of all past sins (lines 60–62); the prevention or forgiveness, upon repentance, of any sins he may commit in the future (lines 63–64); and the constancy of God's gracious dealings with him (lines 64–67). The saving significance of the death of Jesus Christ embraces both Fletcher's redemption *and* his renewal. Everything, in the end, depends upon God's grace. Here again the interplay of the two parts of the contract is in evidence. Even the things that Fletcher has promised in the first main part of the Covenant are subject to the grace of God. But God's grace can only be asked for in humility. Therefore those very promises, though apparently formulated with assurance, are all dependent upon the requests of the second part, which rely for their fulfilment on God's power alone. This is also evident in Fletcher's further requests for the renewal of his life: that Christ may live and reign in him (lines 67–68); that he may experience God's help in all difficult situations (lines 68–70); and that he may receive God's support in the practical living out of his faith (lines 71–77). Fletcher cannot bring this second main part to a close without some further explanation (lines 78–87), in order to exclude any presumption, any thought of reciprocity, any notion of his own merit. His requests, and therefore the whole Covenant, are founded neither on his promises nor on his faith. Their sole foundation is Jesus Christ.

Fletcher signed the Covenant on 24 August 1754. What he had written down and promised in it set a course for his life from which he would never deviate. The all-embracing nature of the six promises and the six requests became apparent in the operation of the Covenant. The surrender of his own life to the will of God and the prayer for renewal by the power of the Holy Spirit stood henceforth at the centre of the

life of John William Fletcher. As with his conversion, so also in this
Covenant, Fletcher laid much more stress on the new birth and sanctification than on justification. Being filled by the Holy Spirit, no longer
seen simply as enlightenment of the mind, but as a force actively at work
in men and women, and as the power by which Christ was revealed and
his image impressed upon believers, was one of the characteristic new
elements in Fletcher's theological understanding of the biblical message.
It opened up for Fletcher new experience and new knowledge, particularly with regard to Christ's atoning death and the triunity of God –
doctrines with which he had long been familiar. Now everything,
including his own actions, was subject to God's grace. In all circumstances Fletcher wanted to maintain the *sola gratia*, 'by grace alone'. But
grace was a power which changed people.

Beginning the life of faith

Fletcher wanted immediately to share his new experience of God and his
fresh understanding of faith with his brother Henri Louis. He therefore
sent him a detailed account of his conversion. He wrote other letters
too, in the hope that his brother, like himself, might be led to true
happiness and real faith. In his letters to his brother, John Fletcher rang
the changes on three main themes: God's goal for human beings is true
love for God and for their neighbour, in fulfilment of the law of Christ;
this goal is only attainable if we relate to Christ as our redeemer in
gospel faith; this faith is not possible without the recognition of our own
sinfulness and dependence upon the operation of God's grace. John
Fletcher was very direct in his criticism of the piety of his brother Henri
Louis:

> Your way of thinking is more refined that that of most people, even
> important people. You do not seek happiness in the enjoyment of
> sensual pleasure, but in moderate satisfaction of the senses; not in
> wealth, but in a disdain for wealth or in gentle moderation . . . You
> imagine that an important aspect of happiness consists in being
> dependent on no one, in never being hindered or controlled by any-
> one; in a word: in having neither great hopes nor great fears . . .[18]

Had not that also been John William's own conviction, prior to the
change in his life? 'We are saved by faith, and this not of ourselves, but
by grace, since faith is the gracious gift of God.'[19] Faith, which is a gift

of God, purifies the heart. The promise of God becomes a living reality when one renounces one's own righteousness, when the pride of one's heart is broken. So wrote John Fletcher. He did not conceal from his brother that he had found it hard to humble himself before God in this way. In his letter he again insisted on the renewal of the self: without redemption and renewal in God's image, no one can enter God's glory. Human beings can only find true happiness when they see themselves before God as sinners in need of redemption through Christ. The human heart is evil. Though our deeds may bring us praise from other people, that does not mean that they are therefore good in the sight of God. Human sin does not consist only in ethical offences.

Although we have found the concept of sin expressed mostly in moral terms, Fletcher could also, after his change of life, emphasize the fundamentally theological aspect of the Fall and its consequences. He asked: 'Do I know that this Fall is fundamentally unbelief, or the frightful arrogance whereby we shut ourselves up within ourselves, separate ourselves from God, and refuse to believe his great promises . . . ?'[20]

All is decided by living gospel faith, which is a working of the Holy Spirit. A consequence of this faith is the gift of the Holy Spirit. The operation of the Holy Spirit is not confined to the days of the first Christians, though special gifts of the Spirit are.[21] Those who do not have this faith do not have the sanctifying Spirit either, and so can love neither God nor their neighbour with their whole heart, for the sake of God's love. Sanctification must be based on justification. Many Christians who recognize their sinfulness make the mistake of striving to keep the commandments without coming to Christ. They would like to sanctify themselves without being justified, to please God without having faith in his Son. By contrast, John Fletcher experienced the presence of God in Christ: 'I never feel stronger signs of God's presence in my heart than when I come closest to his Son.'[22]

John refuted the argument that the kind of gospel faith that has been described was a phenomenon confined to the early days of Christianity, by pointing to the Methodists. They are not mentioned by name, but the description leaves us in no doubt that they are the ones he has in view: 'I know from a trustworthy source and from my own experience that there are at least twenty thousand persons in this kingdom who subscribe, with joy and singleness of heart, to the things I am writing to you.'[23]

Half of these twenty thousand, he says, are still only at the beginning of the road. Most of the rest are like children and young people in

Christ, who are convinced that Christ will complete the work he has begun in them. A third group, of perhaps one thousand people, represent those faithful servants of God who have received five talents and have gained five more. John Fletcher would like to resemble them. He is in no doubt that he will be saved by the blood of Christ, and will therefore also be cleansed, since only those who are perfect in love, and purified from all their sins, will enter God's Kingdom. This criterion, which stood firm both before and after his change of life, was the reason for his strong insistence on human renewal. But after the change in his life Fletcher stressed the radical nature of sin, and the fact that this perfection could be attained only by grace.

5

Private Tutor and Anglican Clergyman

I please her much less by being a Christian than by being her sons'
tutor. She would like me to belong to the world and to the religion of
the day. She suspects that the devil frightened me in my childhood
and that this left deep marks in my brain.[1]

Such, wrote Fletcher, was Mrs Hill's opinion of him. A tutor with the
reasonable beliefs of the Enlightenment would have suited the family
better.

Fletcher's whole life was affected by his new experience of faith. His
life was no longer divided between necessary but burdensome duties,
and special times of devotion. He told how, as a favour, he helped Mr
Hill clean mussels. Such a waste of his time, he said, would previously
have put him in a bad humour, but now he was beginning to discover
that good thoughts could sanctify even a trivial occupation. When his
brother asked him about his plans for the future, he wrote:

They are noble, and very ambitious: a God as my Father; a Saviour as
my brother; an eternity as my lifespan; a kingdom as my inheritance;
a stream of bliss as my drink; the devil and his angels, the flesh and its
lusts, and the world and its pomp as my concern – those are my
prospects, and by God's grace I shall strive after them until I draw my
last breath. That is the fortune I should like to make, and earnestly
beg you . . . to share with me.[2]

Very little is known about Fletcher's daily life in the mid-1750s. The
earliest biographies told how he preferred to return home on foot after
Sunday service, rather than in the waiting carriage, so as to have time
for meditation and prayer. Together with a house servant named
Vaughan, he would devote two or three evenings a week to religious
contemplation and prayer. It was also reported that at times he spent

whole nights in Bible reading, contemplation and prayer, that he was a vegetarian most of the time, and that occasionally he even lived on nothing more than bread, milk and water. Later statements by Fletcher himself confirm this. Once or twice, in 1754 or 1756,[3] he became dangerously ill with tuberculosis. For that reason, one of his biographers claims, a doctor advised him to be a vegetarian.[4]

In 1756, Fletcher's father, Jacques de la Fléchère, died. John wrote of his father:

> But last spring, God visited him with a severe illness, which brought him to a sense of himself. And after a deep repentance, he died about a month ago, in the full assurance of faith. This has put several of my friends on thinking seriously, which affords me great cause of thankfulness.[5]

The predictions of Scripture

On 1 November 1755 the great Lisbon earthquake occurred. A large part of the city was destroyed. More than thirty thousand people lost their lives. News of this dreadful event quickly reached England. That same year the inhabitants of London experienced two strong earth tremors. Inevitably many believers were reminded of what the Bible had to say about the signs of the Last Days. Uncertainty about the future became widespread after the first military clashes between England and France took place in the colonial territories. On the Continent, too, tension between the great powers increased. In 1756 the Seven Years' War broke out.

At the end of November, John Wesley composed a short treatise on the Lisbon earthquake. He argued that God's intervention in this world could have a negative, as well as a positive, dimension, and called his readers to conversion and a true love of God. Fletcher was also staying in London at that time, and attending a Methodist society. Something that was read out there caused him to write a letter, addressed, in all probability, to John Wesley.[6] Fletcher was surprised at the treatise Wesley had just published, on the grounds that very few texts relating to the Last Days were expounded in it, and that it did not go into the dating of millenarian expectations. None of Wesley's teaching sermons dealt with these questions. But, perhaps as a result of the shock produced by the Lisbon earthquake, he began to promote discussion in his meetings on the nearness of the Last Days. Moreover, it was barely two years since Wesley had composed his *Notes on the New Testament*. In writing them he had become acquainted with the eschatological calculations of the German pietist Bengel, and had incorporated some of them into his *Notes*.[7] Fletcher now wanted to reinforce what he had heard, by drawing Wesley's attention to a theologian in continental Europe whom he himself knew well, and who subscribed to the doctrine expressed by Wesley in the letter that had been read out. Fletcher did not mention the theologian's name, but the description he gave undoubtedly points to his uncle, Théodore Crinsoz de Bionens.[8]

Fletcher used two arguments to support the validity of de Bionens' interpretation: that the interpretation agreed with the content of the Bible as a whole, and that it was in harmony with the course of history. Fletcher also addressed the problem that de Bionens' first predictions had not been fulfilled. He therefore admitted the difficulty of arriving at a precise dating, but did not question the fundamental correctness of the interpretation. Its agreement with the historical situation was obvious to him. Fletcher set out in detail calculations based on the data given in the book of Daniel and in the Revelation to John. The dedication of the Holy Place referred to in Daniel 8.14 must, he maintained, take place around the year 1750, or perhaps 1770. What God was doing at present – and here Fletcher had in mind both the Methodist movement and also the hopes of the scattered Protestants in France, who knew de Bionens' writings – had never happened since the days of the apostles. There would be a final battle with papal Rome, which had recovered from the wound inflicted upon it by the Reformation. Protestants, because of their unbelief and their indifference, would be handed over to the wrath of God, since God's judgment always begins in his own house. Only a few would remain faithful witnesses. These, wrote Fletcher, would be filled in extraordinary measure with the Holy Spirit, and would proclaim forgiveness in the name of Jesus. Rome would be destroyed, and with it the Adversary of Christendom. Christ would join in this battle. Fletcher thus drew a distinction between the second coming of Christ to gather together the faithful, and his final return in judgment at the end of the world. Fletcher held that this elucidation of the course of history should be seen as *comforting* news. His aim was no longer to encourage and strengthen faith by exhortation, as it had been in 1752, but rather to promise the salvation in Christ which was going to be revealed. The present affliction, or that which was due to fall upon the human race in the near future, now stood in the shadow of the victory of Jesus Christ, which would shed its light over all, and satisfy every need.

A little while later, in February 1756, Fletcher wrote a poem in French, describing and interpreting contemporary events.[9] In an accompanying letter, however, he wrote to his brother Henri Louis that he should not direct his attention to the interpretation of current events in the light of biblical prophecies, but rather to the experiences described as leading up to faith and flowing from it, since even an honest person could be mistaken about the prophecies. A year later Fletcher spoke yet again about Christ's return. He wrote to John Wesley:

> He [Christ] must, and certainly will come, at the time appointed; for he is not slack, as some men count slackness; and although, he would have all come to repentance, yet, he has not forgot to be true and just. Only he will come with more mercy, and will increase the light, that shall be at evening-tide, according to his promise in Zech. XIV, 7. I should rather think, that the visions are not yet plainly disclosed; and that *the day* and *year*, in which the Lord will begin to make bare his arm openly, are still concealed from us.[10]

The final sentence confirmed and strengthened what Fletcher had earlier written to his brother. Not only was it possible, as he had then pointed out, for a person to be mistaken in trying to determine times: it was also a fact that the day and the year were concealed. Whereas in his letter about the prophecies Fletcher had specified the deliverance of the afflicted believer as the motive for God's intervention, now the emphasis was rather on the revelation of God's grace. God's truth and righteousness, that is, his sovereignty as judge, were not abandoned, but they stood, as it were, in the shadow of the promise of salvation in Christ. The return of Christ led not only to the gathering together of true believers, but also to a final great operation of his grace. The weak light would be strengthened, and weak faith enlightened.

From Fletcher's later years, only very isolated statements about the beginning of the thousand-year reign are to be found, and no calculations about eschatological events.[11] In the 1760s Fletcher was still expecting Christ's return in the near future, but by now the dominant theme was the hope of being filled with the Holy Spirit.[12] Throughout his life, Fletcher's view of the future was marked by the expectation of a new, more comprehensive operation of God's grace, but for the later Fletcher, with his pneumatological preoccupations, apocalyptic gave way more and more to the expectation of a new Pentecost and a church of the Spirit.

Ordination in the Anglican Church

> As I look upon you as my spiritual guide, and cannot doubt of your patience to hear, and your experience to answer a question, proposed by one of your people, I freely lay my case before you.[13]

Fletcher was not ashamed to regard himself as belonging to the Methodists. That was apparent not only from his attendance at Methodist events in London, but also in situations which called for a fundamental decision. He therefore sought John Wesley's advice, in the words quoted above, when the question of ordination was being ever more urgently pressed upon him. Fletcher begins his letter by telling Wesley how the question of the ordained ministry had already been on his mind in his youth. He goes on to describe the course of outward events in the Hill family, and his own inner uncertainty. He could see reasons both for and against ordination. Because he was experiencing this inner conflict, and because the arguments seemed evenly balanced, he was unable to reach a decision. On one side, he says, he was encouraged by small 'successes' within his circle of acquaintances (we might here think of his letters to his family, and of the conversion of two people close to him). On the other side, he was conscious of his lack of gifts, especially that of constant love, and the danger that his wishes might be motivated by his own pride. The discrepancy between the demanding nature of the office and his own self-assessment held him back from seeking ordination. At only one point in his letter to John Wesley does Fletcher introduce a thought which rises above this contradiction: he speaks of his longing to cast himself and his unfitness on the Lord, so that the power of the Lord may be made strong in his weakness.

This inner conflict of Fletcher's was provoked by various questions raised by other people. Three times friends urged him to seek ordination. But there was always something to prevent the plans from coming to fruition. The question of ordination did not, therefore, first arise as a result of his new experience of faith and his contact with the Methodists. Indeed when that happened the idea of ordination was at first pushed into the background, because he was dominated by the feeling that he was a sinful person, lacking in true love. It was only when he received a fresh impetus from outside that he was forced to come to grips with the problem again. Here we must take account of the decisive influence of Mr Hill, whose sons were being taught by Fletcher. Fletcher wrote that Mr Hill had often pressed him to enter the ministry. Whether or not he had already done this before Fletcher's contact with the Methodists is not clear. It is certainly possible that the motive for Mr Hill's suggestion was quite independent of this development.

In the eighteenth century it often happened that prosperous and influential families, who were able to employ a private tutor for the education of their children, would help the tutor to take holy orders and to find a benefice. This was in recognition of the services the tutors had rendered and to compensate them for their rather modest remuneration. The educational background of which they had given evidence seemed to fit them for the ministry. The arrangement was also in the families' own interest, since it freed them from the burden of having to provide a pension. Tutors' posts, then, were greatly sought after, since they offered an excellent opportunity for further advancement, especially when they were with families belonging to the nobility. Towards the end of the eighteenth century Archbishop Moore expressed strong disapproval of this practice. His criticisms were particularly directed against Swiss people, who enjoyed great popularity as tutors, but whose English was so poor that when they became clergymen they were ridiculed by the people.[14]

It is against this background that Fletcher's statement that Mr Hill would find him a benefice may be understood. As Member of Parliament for Shrewsbury Mr Hill had the opportunity, when benefices and livings fell vacant, to exert some influence over the new appointments. Though Fletcher each time declined the suggestion of ordination, on the grounds that he did not know how he could obtain nomination, Mr Hill knew well enough how he could use his influence.[15] Fletcher was surprised when a gentleman whom he scarcely knew actually promised him a benefice, and a clergyman offered him a curacy. Fletcher did not at first think of accepting the benefice and the living. He was hoping for better employment in his own country and in his mother tongue. But he asked himself whether he ought to take advantage of the nomination, seeing that anyone wishing to be ordained had to show that he had been nominated. The obstacles in the way of Fletcher's ordination had been removed by his nomination as curate and by the offer of a benefice, but the question of his personal position remained. John Wesley's advice would help him to come to a decision: 'Persist or forbear will satisfy and influence, Sir, your unworthy servant, J. F.'[16] Wesley's reply has not survived, but it must have been a positive one.

The canons of the Church of England laid down the conditions for ordination. The candidate had to show that he had a nomination, and had to be at least twenty-three years old for the diaconate, and twenty-four years old for the priesthood. Fletcher, who by now was twenty-seven years old, fulfilled these conditions. On the educational level of candidates, the rule said:

> . . . and hath taken some degree of school in either of the said Universities; or at the least . . . be able to yield an account of his faith in Latin, according to the Articles of Religion approved in the Synod of the Bishops and Clergy of this realm, . . . and to confirm the same by sufficient testimonies out of the holy Scriptures . . .[17]

In addition, three or four clergymen were required to provide testimonials of his good conduct. A careful examination by the bishop should precede admission to ordination. This examination was often carried out by the bishop's chaplain, and so it was in Fletcher's case. He was examined, in accordance with the above regulations, by Sir Peter Rivers, chaplain to the Bishop of Hereford.[18]

Fletcher was ordained deacon on 6 March 1757 by James Beauclerk, Bishop of Hereford. On the ordination certificate, the University of Geneva was given as his place of education. It was possible for ordination to the priesthood to follow within a few days – the normal procedure for candidates from the nobility or with influential connections. This happened also in Fletcher's case: just a week later, on 13 March, he was ordained priest by the Bishop of Bangor. On the eve of his ordination, as was the custom, Fletcher signed the Articles of the Church of England. On Monday 14 March John Fletcher was installed as curate in Madeley, about ten miles from the Hill family's estate. A nephew of Mr Hill was patron of the benefice of Madeley. It is not surprising, therefore, that Mr Hill was able to secure Fletcher's nomination as curate, and thus enable him to be ordained. This nomination to the parish of Madeley was of decisive significance for Fletcher's induction as vicar of the same parish in 1760.[19]

The first to benefit from Fletcher's ecclesiastical status were John Wesley and his Methodists. Wesley was at that time in poor health. A minister previously unknown to him came to help him with the service on 13 March, and Fletcher, who had only just been ordained to the priesthood, thinking that Wesley was alone, also hurried to his side. A week later, on 20 March, Wesley received further help from Fletcher. The entry in Wesley's *Journal* contains some words which have become famous:

Mr. Fletcher helped me again. How wonderful are the ways of God! When my bodily strength failed, and none in England were able and willing to assist me, he sent me help from the mountains of Switzerland! And an help meet for me in every respect; where could I have found such another?[20]

Tutor and Anglican clergyman

For more than three years after his ordination, Fletcher retained his position as tutor to the Hill family. He thus spent the winter half of each year in London, and the summer half on the family estate in Shropshire. His work as tutor caused him much concern. Several times in previous chapters it has been noted that he had to fight his anger. He also had difficulty in deciding the right degree of punishment for his pupils. He recorded his struggles in personal entries in a notebook. His thoughts about his work as tutor were at one and the same time prayers and rules for behaviour. Fletcher was trying to approach his work in a new way, in the light of his faith. The grace of Christ which he had experienced, and which also applied to his pupils, should determine his relations with them. The love of Christ should be the standard by which his actions were measured. Fletcher did not want to judge his pupils as strictly as if they were already adults.

After his ordination, in addition to his activities as tutor, he had also to perform other tasks in his capacity as clergyman. This happened in Methodist societies as well as in the wider setting of the Church of England. At first he had difficulties with the English language, so that for a time he wrote out all his sermons in full. In the summer of 1757 he preached in a few churches near the Hill family's estate.[21] Usually, however, he was not invited to do so more than once. The following summer he was disappointed to discover that most of the clergymen round about did not wish to call on his services. At least half of the assembled congregations would gladly have heard him again, but he was never invited a second time. It could even happen that a parish was not served on a Sunday, because Fletcher was not wanted as a preacher. Fletcher nowhere records that he had been able to establish a friendly relationship with any of the neighbouring clergy. Madeley, where Fletcher was curate, was no exception. He was presumably able to preach there in the first summer following his ordination, but after that he was left aside by the vicar. Some people are said to have run after him, because they were afraid they would hear no more about true salvation.[22]

The situation was different among the Methodists, with whom he was in close contact during the winter months in London. Towards the end of the 1750s, the leading figures in Methodism developed personal, sometimes very friendly, relations with Fletcher. Worthy of special note was Fletcher's contact with Charles Wesley. Five letters to Charles Wesley from 1758 have survived, together with eleven from 1759 and nine from 1760. Taking into account the fact that some letters will have been lost, we have a picture of an astonishingly close correspondence. The letters are very personal, and give an insight into Fletcher's condition and his struggles over his faith.

Fletcher among the Methodists

Fletcher was quickly accepted by the Methodists, and was soon highly esteemed among them. He preached mostly in those parts of London in which Huguenots lived, in West Street Chapel, and probably also in Spitalfields.[23] In 1758 he lost two important friends, whom he held in high regard: Thomas Walsh, one of Wesley's leading lay travelling preachers, and Bernon. The name of Thomas Maxfield also began to appear regularly in the correspondence. A few years later Fletcher would find himself grappling with John Wesley's and Thomas Maxfield's differing views on the subject of Christian perfection. After a visit to Bristol in September 1758, Fletcher established contact with Sarah Ryan, who was responsible for domestic arrangements at the 'New Room' in Bristol. In the spring of 1758, through the good offices of John Wesley, Fletcher also became personally acquainted with the Countess of Huntingdon. A letter from the Countess shows how highly regarded Fletcher already was by the leaders of the Methodist movement. Reporting on her first meeting with Fletcher, she wrote:

> I have seen Mr. Fletcher, and was both pleased and refreshed by the interview. He was accompanied by Mr. Wesley, who had frequently mentioned him in terms of high commendation, as had Mr. Whitefield, Mr. Charles Wesley, and others, so that I was anxious to become acquainted with one so devoted, and who appears to glory in nothing save in the cross of our divine Lord and Master.[24]

We do not know at what point Fletcher made the acquaintance of George Whitefield.

Fletcher did not, however, receive only recognition and esteem.

During 1758 controversy arose over the person of a widow, and as a result Fletcher experienced rejection in Methodist circles. Since neither his friend Bernon nor John Wesley rejected his help, Fletcher went on preaching. What remained from the incident was a healthy disillusionment: 'Blessed be his holy name this shows me that there are also dangerous rocks among the children of God.'[25] Fletcher met with opposition of a quite different kind on account of the conversion of Richard, later Sir Richard, Hill. In his search for faith, Hill turned to Fletcher. Fletcher's pastoral guidance, and conversations with other people, helped Richard Hill to find peace with God. Richard Hill's father was a cousin of Thomas Hill, in whose family Fletcher was tutor. Thomas Hill and his wife began to fear that the Methodist plague would ruin their two cousins and the whole family. Fletcher wrote that Mrs Hill, who had wept so much when he was ill, had now said that it would not bother her in the least if he were to starve to death. We shall meet the names of Richard Hill and his younger brother Rowland, who became a dissenting minister, again in the context of the theological controversies of the 1770s.

Only a few references to Fletcher's relationship with John Wesley have survived from the years 1758–1759, but they are significant because they raise theologically interesting topics. In September 1758, Wesley wrote in his *Journal*: 'In the following week I met Mr. Fletcher and the other preachers that were in the house and spent a considerable time in close conversation on the head of Christian perfection.'[26] A month earlier, the annual Conference had met, and had discussed among other things the subject of Christian perfection. The findings were recorded in the conference minutes. The emphasis was placed on the attitude of humility before God to be expected of those who had attained Christian perfection, and on the evaluation of its genuineness through the commandment to love God and one's neighbour. The experience of Christian perfection was attested in the Methodist societies, and in later years it was to become an explosive subject. The correct understanding of Christian perfection was thus a central concern of the Conference, and of a later meeting of a number of ministers and lay preachers.

The findings of this second discussion, in which Fletcher was one of the participants, have remained unknown until now. They are to be found, however, in Fletcher's literary remains, and they appear, in a slightly modified form, in his collected writings, under the heading: 'The Test of a New Creature: or, Heads of Examination for Adult

Christians'.[27] In their original form, the questions listed are expressed in the third person, which shows that they were not primarily intended as self-examination. The booklet is intended to help in testing the genuineness of the testimony of anyone who claims to be living in perfect love. Several questions relate to humility, and are meant to guard against false spiritual pride. Others are concerned with experiences of suffering, which should not detract from love of God and one's neighbour. The introduction and conclusion of the document emphasize growth in grace:

> That which is instantaneous in its descent, is progressive in its increase. This is certain, – too much grace cannot be desired, or looked for & to believe & obey with all the power we have is the high way to receive all we have not.

Sermon on the new birth

John Wesley asked Fletcher to translate two sermons into French, one by him and one by his brother Charles. Fletcher recommended the reading of both sermons, together with an extract from William Law's *Christian Perfection*. The recommendation was contained in a French sermon by Fletcher from the year 1759, published under the title *Discours sur la Régénération*. This is the earliest of Fletcher's published writings to have survived.[28] The new birth was a central theme in Fletcher's own biography. When it was said of him that he was teaching a dangerous doctrine, he felt obliged to publish a sermon on the subject. One person's 'enthusiasm' (fanaticism) had rendered Fletcher's French work in London unfruitful.[29] His own need to respond to the charge of 'enthusiasm' is clearly discernible in the sermon.

The purpose of Fletcher's sermon was to convince readers of their own need to be born again. His text was John 3.3. The sermon began with the story of Nicodemus, retold in order to bring out its meaning. The new birth is the work of the Spirit. The Holy Spirit is effective, new-creating power. The new birth embraces justification, understood as the forgiveness of sins, and sanctification, understood as the renewal of a person's whole being. The goal is the recovery of the image of God, without which eternal salvation cannot be attained. Fletcher's arguments turn on the opposition between the Fall and sanctification. God wills our sanctification, but this only becomes possible through the operation of his Holy Spirit. In this connection Fletcher also spoke of the 'baptism of the Holy Spirit', an expression which will give rise to much discussion later.[30] Several times Fletcher described the new birth as the two great works of the Holy Spirit in the repentant soul: justification and sanctification. In every case justification precedes sanctification. Fletcher's distinctive contribution was to treat the new birth as the inclusive term embracing both justification and sanctification. Sanctification begins as a work of the Spirit in the forgiveness of sins. The body of sin is not thereby destroyed, but its power is curtailed. Sanctification is a long-term, progressive work. When Fletcher included sanctification within the concept of the new birth, he did it with the thought that the renewal of human beings in the image of God – in perfect love for God and their neighbour – could only be attained as the goal of sanctification. In other words, new birth in its fullness corresponded essentially to Wesley's understanding of Christian perfection.

The idea that, taking the new birth as the starting point, human redemption might be understood as a renewal which could be experienced, brought problems. It made God's saving act dependent upon human experience, albeit an experience initiated by that very act. Fletcher became aware of the problems within himself, as he went through the severest doubts and challenges to his faith. It was only in the words of promise at the end of his sermon that the independence of the divine promises over against all human experience found expression, and that the way to liberating experiences of faith was thus opened up.

Throughout Fletcher's life, the new birth continued to be his central concern. Because the new birth is a work of the Holy Spirit, and because its goal is perfection, being filled with the Holy Spirit, or baptized with the Holy Spirit (which for Fletcher amounted to the same thing), became the main content of his hope.

6

What Am I Good for?

Fletcher wrote to Charles Wesley:

> I sense that I do not deserve your advice, much less the title of *friend* which you give me: you are an *indulgent father* to me, and the title of son would fit me much better than that of brother. You ask me if I can confidently commend you to the mercy of God. O yes, I can, and I feel in relation to you what I do not sense for myself.[1]

Charles Wesley called Fletcher a friend, and valued his judgment. Fletcher's self-assessment, however, was fundamentally different from other people's view of him.

In the letters he wrote to Charles Wesley towards the end of the 1750s, there were increasing numbers of statements in which Fletcher spoke of himself as an out-and-out sinner, and counted himself among those who needed to call upon God's grace, having not as yet been filled with it. This outlook affected his relations with other people, so that often he would have preferred to withdraw completely from the world. His lack of an experience of life-changing divine grace led him to seek solitude even among the Methodists in London.[2] For this reason he declined the invitation to go as a missionary to the West Indies with Nathaniel Gilbert. This phase in Fletcher's life was characterized by uncertainty about his own standing before God. He was so uncertain that he even wrote a poem in which he spoke of never having loved Christ, and of not knowing whether Christ loved him.[3] Another sign of the difference between how he himself saw his faith and how Charles Wesley saw it, was the fact that, while Wesley thought that Fletcher was concerned about striving for Christian perfection, Fletcher himself was no longer sure he even had faith.

Respected by others, but despairing of himself

When he examined himself, what Fletcher found in his heart was not the working of God's grace, but only his own pride and unbelief. Over and over again, expressions like 'hardness of heart', 'the wickedness of the heart', and 'pride of heart' appear in his letters. His human self-will, his own self, he said, was driving him away from God. Only God's chastisement could bring him, against his will, to depend constantly on Christ. Fletcher remembered the effects of his earlier fits of temper. Now he saw his self-will and his lack of faith as his points of need. What Fletcher described in these letters was a battle with himself. He was profoundly convinced that he could not expect God's gracious activity if he was not willing to acknowledge his need. With extreme scrupulousness he explored his inmost being. He found the evil in his heart repeatedly confirmed. The use of the word 'doubt' was characteristic of Fletcher's struggle. His doubt was not directed against what the Bible said. God's redemptive activity in Christ was not in question. The doubt had much more to do with his own person. Fletcher doubted himself and his own sincerity.

Occasionally he even expresses deep mistrust of himself. Fletcher saw the secret pride of his heart lurking even in his struggle for inner and outer humility.[4] The evil in his heart was so deeply rooted that no aspect of his life was unaffected by it. The strongest expression of Fletcher's crisis of faith is found in his letter of July 1759:

> Neither doubt nor despair disturbed me for a moment. My temptation followed a different course. It seemed to me that God would be more glorified by my damnation than by my salvation. It seemed to me to be totally against the holiness, the righteousness, and the truth of the Supreme Being for so stubborn a sinner to be admitted to his presence. I could only marvel at God's patience . . .[5]

There are striking parallels between this account and Fletcher's diary entries shortly before his conversion. Here again, in view of his sinfulness, Fletcher could see only the possibility of being rejected by God. He understood the righteousness of God as that of a judge, condemning sinners. God's rejection was then reflected in Fletcher's own attitude, in such a way that he intensely hated himself and other sinners. If God were to lend him an iron sceptre, then he, Fletcher, would be able to make an end of himself, the vessel of dishonour. In contrast to the time shortly before his conversion, his statements about himself and about God now interact. His sense of God's righteous judgment is so overwhelming that he can only break down and acknowledge his failure. His sense of the evil in his own heart is so overwhelming that he can only acknowledge God's righteous judgment. The end prospect is not, as in the diary entry before his conversion, a consignment to hell which paradoxically frees him to praise God, but the wish to destroy himself.

The events just described show very clearly what was on Fletcher's mind both before and after his conversion, and make even more pressing the question as to the motivating forces behind his struggle. Why was he so critical, indeed so mistrustful of himself, that the sinfulness which he discovered in all his actions caused him to lose sight of God's grace towards him in Christ? At all events, the reason had nothing to do with the success or failure of his preaching and pastoral care. In his letters he drew no conclusions about the state of his faith from those areas. His struggle was deeper and more fundamental. His letters to Charles Wesley reveal various factors which influenced his understanding of repentance and faith, and which focus our attention on a central theological problem.

The first of these fundamental attitudes to be mentioned is Fletcher's striving for sincerity. Sincerity was a central theme in his letters:

> Oh dear Sir, I find more and more that it is not an easy thing to be upright before God, many boast of their sincerity and perhaps they may, but as for me I am forced to smite my breast and to say, from all hypocrisy Good Lord deliver me: Oh when I shall be sincere I shall walk on with an even pace, I shall neither stop, nor turn aside.[6]

It was no easy thing to be sincere before the Lord. Fletcher saw his independent will as a threat to sincerity. Accordingly he believed that in order to be sincere it was not enough to recognize the existence of pride and self-love; one was sincere only when this resistance to God had been overcome, and when one trusted him sincerely and without hypocrisy. Fletcher could not speak of sincerity until every egoistic impulse had been overcome.

The second fundamental attitude for which Fletcher was striving was humility:

> Recently I saw so much weakness in my heart, as a Christian and as a minister of the Gospel, that I do not know who should be most

lamented – the man, the believer, or the preacher. But if in the end I
could be truly humble and remain so for ever, I would be happy to
have made these discoveries.[7]

The striving for humility also had as its aim the overcoming of all self-
will. Only in the attainment of full humility could Fletcher hope to find
the assurance of expecting nothing more from himself, and everything
from God.

In the third place mention should be made of some basic presuppositions on which Fletcher himself did not reflect. Both the above
quotations, concerning sincerity and humility, presuppose two things.
First, both these fundamental attitudes are seen as goals to be striven
for. They are imperatives, not indicatives. For Fletcher, true repentance
and true faith could only come with the attainment of these goals.
Secondly, he understood the two attitudes in an absolute, uncompromising way. They must both be complete, otherwise they would be useless. Only in complete sincerity and complete humility could Fletcher's
striving come to an end. Charles Wesley was therefore right in thinking
that Fletcher was engaged in the quest for Christian perfection. All this,
however, does no more than hint at the theological problem.

Fletcher's struggle led him to a deep self-knowledge. He did not
lightly dismiss the forces in his own life which were fighting against
God. He recognized how deep-rooted was his own self-will, and he also
recognized the sovereignty of God, a God whom human beings can
never put under an obligation to be gracious. That was the strength of
those experiences of Fletcher which we have been describing – a
strength which should not be overlooked in any criticism of him. But
Fletcher's anxious struggle arose (and this is where theological criticism
must begin) out of the presuppositions mentioned above – from the
imperative and uncompromising ways in which he conceived of his
goal. As we have already noticed in his sermon on the new birth,
Fletcher was essentially concerned with striving for perfection. Here, in
his personal experience, there came to light, as it were, the negative
reverse side of the concept of the new birth discussed in the sermon.
Fletcher felt himself to be a self-willed, proud person, not one who had
been born again. He was unable to overcome his own self in his own
strength. He felt, therefore, that he must be under the threat of God's
judgment, rather than under his grace.

Fletcher went astray because he failed to realize that one cannot oneself will to overcome self-will. Deliverance from his anxious struggle,

and along with it liberating faith, could only come to him when he allowed God's gracious activity to take place within, and in spite of, the evil in his heart – in other words, when he ceased to make the divine promise dependent on some prerequisite human achievement. In Fletcher's own experience, deliverance from the severe crisis described above only came about, paradoxically, when old ways of thinking, which he thought he had left behind, reasserted themselves, and he saw no other way out than to hope in and trust himself to the help of God's grace. The experience of God's grace was repeated as Fletcher, in fulfilment of his various responsibilities, preached the gospel to others, and in doing so was himself overcome by the grace of God. In the years that followed, Fletcher laid ever increasing stress on the expectation that the Holy Spirit would fill his heart.

Not only has our insight into Fletcher's troubled soul enabled us to discern the reasons for his humble self-criticism and the theological problems concealed behind his struggle; it has also shed light on the trusting relationship between Fletcher and Charles Wesley. The relationship was reciprocal. In his letters, Fletcher sometimes discussed questions put to him by Charles Wesley. He was admitted to the Wesleys' family circle, and became godfather to one of the daughters. The friendship grew, and Fletcher indicated on several occasions how painful it would be for him if he were to be parted from Charles Wesley. The closeness of the bond between them, and Fletcher's high regard for Charles Wesley, are clear from Fletcher's effusive answer to a question concerning Wesley's salvation:

> I am so assured of your salvation that I ask for no other place in heaven than the one I might have at your feet. I even question whether Paradise would still be Paradise if you were not there to share it with me. The very idea, aroused in me by your question, that we might one day be parted, grieves my heart and fills my eyes with tears.[8]

A biographer of the Countess of Huntingdon recounted an anecdote which, precisely by its stereotyped form, is a pertinent illustration of the difference between Fletcher's opinion of himself and others' opinion of him. The story was about Fletcher's first visit, in the spring of 1760, to Berridge, the Vicar of Everton, who was close to the Countess of Huntingdon's circle. Berridge had gathered from his visitor's accent that he was a foreigner, and had discovered that he came from the Bernese area of Switzerland. If he came from Berne, Berridge said, he could perhaps tell him (Berridge) something about a young fellow-country-man by the name of John Fletcher, who was highly praised by the Wesley brothers and had already preached for them. The foreigner had then replied: 'Yes, sir, I know him intimately; and did those gentlemen know him as well, they would not speak of him in such terms, for which he is more obliged to their partial friendship than to his own merits.' When Berridge expressed astonishment, the foreigner answered: 'I have the best reason for speaking of him as I do – I am John Fletcher.'[9]

Offers of future work

Towards the end of the 1750s, the Hills' two sons reached the age for beginning their university education. The time was coming when Fletcher would have completed his work as tutor. What would he do next?

Mr Hill had helped Fletcher to become ordained, and was wanting to obtain a parish and a benefice for him. Fletcher mentioned this for the first time towards the end of 1758, and asked Charles Wesley for his advice. Mr Hill had offered him the living of Shenston, worth £80, which was in his gift, or alternatively, after Fletcher had declined this, the living of Madeley, which was in his nephew's gift, but which would involve more work and would only bring in £60 or perhaps £70. Whereas Fletcher had immediately rejected the first offer, in the case of Madeley he could see reasons in favour of acceptance:

> The extent of [the] Parish, containing near 2000 Souls which are as sheep scatter'd without a Shepherd, & mostly those who enter first into the kingdom, poor labourers, & colliers; the nearness of the Parish of Browsley whence some began to come to listen to the Gospel, & where there are thousands of souls ready for destruction & consequently ready for a Saviour: The apparent success which attended my preaching there while the door was open: The pity I con-ceiv'd for those poor souls which put me then upon praying often I might be suffered to be curate there for nothing, for I would almost as soon have thought of being Pope as of being presented to the living my self . . . If I know any thing of my own heart I have no will in this matter wholly desiring that the will of God may be done & expecting to see plainer intimations of it in your advices and the turn provi-

dence will give to the affair: Your brother is out of Town . . . else I would lay the case before him also.[10]

Fletcher did not yet give Mr Hill a final answer. If these plans were not in accordance with God's will, there would be sufficient hindrances to prevent him from taking the post, including the fact that he was known to the bishop as a Methodist.

By the spring of 1759 Fletcher was certain that his pupils would soon be leaving him. But the Hill family, following Richard Hill's conversion, had become afraid of the 'plague of Methodists', and Mrs Hill gave Fletcher to understand that he would in no circumstances ever be installed by the bishop as Vicar in Madeley. The two sons left Fletcher and their family at the end of April and went off to Cambridge, but they came back as early as the beginning of June, and the whole family moved to its country estate. Fletcher, however, was no longer able to work with the two sons. The sons knew how to exploit the differences between their parents, and they threatened to slander Fletcher to their mother, so that he would lose his post. The way their sons were developing no longer seemed right to the parents, and they regretted having sent their offspring away. After Fletcher made a complaint, Mrs Hill apparently became very obliging again, and several times offered him the appointment at Madeley. He neither accepted nor declined the offer. He would let things run their course. There would still be time to refuse if the offer became more concrete.[11]

A request of quite another kind came to Fletcher from his homeland. His family saw a glimmer of hope that he might return home, and pressed him to do so. Fletcher could see many reasons against returning – so much so, that Charles Wesley, writing on the subject, showed more understanding for Fletcher's mother's situation than did her own son. Finally Fletcher tried to express his refusal to return home as mildly and sensitively as possible. He had decided to stay in England. He neither went as a missionary to Antigua, as he had been invited to, nor returned to Switzerland.

Alongside the offer of the Madeley parish, however, the possibility of service in the Methodist movement also remained open. This offer had been made to him in the spring of 1759 by Charles Wesley. Now, in September 1759, Fletcher expressed his views on an appointment with the Methodists:

What a monstrous idea you have almost led me to consider! What? I

would be paid a *wage* for my service amongst you (*si ulli sint*)! Quite
apart from the fact that up to now I have brought only dishonour to
God, and that in the future I shall not be in a position to do better: if
I were permitted to stand upright in the congregations of the Lord,
would it not be incumbent upon me to make payment, rather than to
receive it? If I receive anything at all from the Methodist Church it
will be like alms which an undeserving beggar receives, and without
which he would perish.[12]

The offer of service in the Methodist societies, which he here calls the
'Methodist Church' (that is to say, that part of the Church of England
which had become Methodist),[13] was not absolutely rejected. It was just
that he did not wish to be paid for such service.

In the late autumn of 1759, Fletcher resolved to leave the Hill family
in London. Mrs Hill was astonished at this plan, and said that she
would regard it as a sign of disdain, if he did not at least continue to live
with them. Charles Wesley advised him not to rush matters, but to stay
with the family until divine providence gave the seal of approval to his
departure. Fletcher therefore waited until the end of December, when
the two sons went back to Cambridge and Mr and Mrs Hill agreed to
his plan.[14] Against John Wesley's advice, Fletcher declined to take a
room in the Foundery (John Wesley's London headquarters). He preferred to have his own room elsewhere, at a distance. In the background, probably, was that offer to take over the parish of Madeley,
about which he had not yet made up his mind. This minor question of
where to live also shows that Fletcher did not feel obliged to follow
Wesley's advice. Considering the high regard which Fletcher had for
John Wesley, and the leading position Wesley held in his societies, this
decision testifies to a noteworthy independence on Fletcher's part – an
independence which was soon to be confirmed on other similar
questions. As for the room, John Wesley was indeed annoyed when, at a
meeting with Jones and Lady Huntingdon, Fletcher told him that he had
rented a room elsewhere.

Another matter also may have caused annoyance to John Wesley.
In November 1759, Lady Huntingdon suggested to Fletcher that he
might celebrate Holy Communion daily in her house fellowship, and
occasionally exhort (expound a Bible text) there. The Countess wanted
her offer to be understood as an interim arrangement, leaving Fletcher
completely free to accept any other call in which he saw God's leading.
The complete freedom which the Countess guaranteed Fletcher, and her

reasonable arguments, were almost sufficient to persuade him. Yet his work with Charles Wesley, his decision to avoid the houses of the upper classes, and his sense that he lacked grace and authority, caused him to delay his response. He asked Charles Wesley for his advice. We do not know what answer he received, though he later confirmed that he had accepted the offer to become the Countess's domestic chaplain. He also spoke often of his activity in the Countess's home, and of his conversations with her. It was important for Fletcher's future relations with the Countess that her meetings in Paddington often helped him to experience the love of God in his own life. John Wesley remained silent, probably because he was afraid of losing Fletcher to Lady Huntingdon's circle.

At the end of February 1760, while Fletcher was still in London, he asked Charles Wesley to return soon so that, together with the Countess of Huntingdon, they could form themselves into a 'threefold cord'. Since there was a good understanding between Charles Wesley and the Countess, such a group of three could come together in London, and its members could maintain close contact with each other. Fletcher was by now serving Wesley's societies in London, as well as the Countess's house congregation in Paddington. For over half a year Fletcher was active among the Methodists. Charles Wesley valued his help: 'He is a great comfort and help to me,' he wrote.[15]

It was not until the end of August 1760 that Fletcher travelled back to Tern Hall, the summer residence of the Hills. Mrs Hill had died quite unexpectedly, following a brief illness, in February. Now Mr Hill had requested him to come. Fletcher doubted whether he would have opportunities of preaching in the area, since Mr Hill would certainly be afraid of harming his chances in the forthcoming election. The course of later events shows, however, that Mr Hill had no such fear. He wanted Fletcher to come, since, as far as lay in his power, he had removed all obstacles standing in the way of Fletcher's installation at Madeley.[16] At this point, however, a fresh offer intervened.

In the late summer of 1760, Lady Huntingdon had to go to Yorkshire to resolve some problems of a theological and disciplinary nature in the societies of Benjamin Ingham, Vicar of Aberford. She was accompanied and supported by Henry Venn, William Romaine and Whitefield. During her stay in Aberford, she recommended Fletcher as tutor for Ingham's nephew, Ignatius Ingham. Once again Fletcher asked Charles Wesley for advice. He set out the reasons for and against his acceptance, but had to conclude: 'If you ask me what I myself think – it seems to me that I have no will in the matter. It is all the same to me where I am, or with whom, since Jesus is not in my heart.'[17] Fletcher was so concerned with overcoming his self-will that he lacked any conviction regarding the various offers he received. Certainly he could make a list of advantages and disadvantages, but he was unable to weigh them up and come to a decision.

Fletcher did not receive an answer within reasonable time. He nevertheless came to a negative decision. The reason lay in a development he could not have foreseen in Shropshire. The nearby ministers, and especially the Vicar of Madeley, appeared to have become reconciled to him, and were offering him any help he might need. From that side too, therefore, there were no longer any obstacles in the way of Fletcher's installation in Madeley. Fletcher did not wish to delay, for selfish motives, a course of events in which he recognized the leading of divine providence. But three main obstacles still remained: Fletcher was not yet naturalized; the chaplain of the Bishop of Hereford had threatened him with trouble, after hearing him preach in London; and the Bishop of Lichfield, who had to countersign the testimonials provided by neighbouring ministers, was hostile to him. These difficulties too, however, were quickly resolved. Fletcher wrote to the Countess that it was very difficult for him to give up his service with her family in London, but that he was obliged to follow providence. The very day after writing this letter, on 4 October 1760, Fletcher was officially nominated as Vicar of Madeley. The Bishop of Hereford sent for him immediately, and on 7 October Fletcher signed all the documents in the Bishop's presence and was appointed Vicar of Madeley. His induction took place ten days later.

It was Fletcher's firm conviction that God had made the way plain for him, and that he must therefore at the very least make the attempt to be Vicar of Madeley. Charles Wesley probably shared this view of things, since he repeatedly urged Fletcher not to resist the ways of God. His brother John Wesley, however, was of a different opinion. He asked Fletcher to give up the parish, even before he had tried to work there. Fletcher mentioned this in a letter to Lady Huntingdon:

He [John Wesley] will have me 'see the Devil's snare, and fly from it at the peril of my soul'. I answer I cannot see it in that light. He adds – 'Others may do well in a Living, you *can* not, it is not your calling.' I tell him I readily own that I am not fit to plant or water any part of the Lord's vineyard, but that *if* I am called at all I am called to preach at Madeley, where I was first sent into the ministry, and where a chain of providences I could not break has again fastened me . . . and that, notwithstanding my universal inability, I am not quite without hope that He who reproved a prophet's madness by the mouth of an ass, may reprove a collier's profaneness even by my mouth.[18]

This reference to John Wesley's opposition in a letter to Lady Huntingdon was probably intended to anticipate and invalidate any similar arguments from her side.

John Wesley's opposition to Fletcher's appointment as vicar was unmistakable. Wesley's own experience led him to see the tendency towards solitude as a temptation of the devil. He was afraid that solitude at Madeley could become just such a temptation for Fletcher. Wesley was also thinking of the situation of the Methodist societies. At that time he urgently needed ordained ministers to celebrate the Lord's Supper and to lead the societies in the larger towns. Fletcher had performed this service in London for over half a year, and by doing so had strengthened John Wesley's hope that he had found a worthy colleague. It was a constant irritation to John Wesley, riding restlessly throughout the kingdom, that his brother Charles had settled down for part of the year with his family in Bristol. It seemed to John Wesley that John Fletcher, the helper whom he, Wesley, valued highly but who undervalued himself, would be lost for ever if he settled in a remote Anglican parish. Although in later years John Wesley learned to appreciate Fletcher's great merits, and could sometimes even see a certain justification for his parish appointment, he was never fully convinced that it was God's leading. Hence his comment in his biography of Fletcher: 'He settled at Madeley, according to his desire, in the year 1760.'[19]

Fletcher longed for rest and seclusion, in which – in contrast to John Wesley – he hoped to be able to resolve his inner struggles and his lack of faith. He was therefore not unhappy to be obliged to leave his work in the Methodist societies in London, although he had specially appreciated his service in the Countess's circle and his fellowship with her. Moreover, Fletcher was so full of the feeling of his own unworthiness and incapacity for service, that, while he was glad of the fellowship of the Methodists, he could not see himself in the position of a leading minister, much less as another Charles or John Wesley. It seemed to him that his place was at their feet. If he, unworthy as he was, was called to any service at all, then it was at Madeley.

Part III
The First Ten Years as Vicar of Madeley (1760–1770)

7

Vicar of Madeley, Shropshire

At the age of thirty-one Fletcher became Vicar of Madeley. He preached his first sermon there on 26 October 1760. A month after his induction Fletcher noted with surprise that on the previous Sunday his church had been full, although the weather was so bad that the streets and lanes were barely passable. Already some people had come in from outlying settlements, and others were 'threatening to come'. Fletcher had made a promising beginning, and had caught a vision: 'Should the Lord vouchsafe to plant the Gospel in this country, my parish seems to be the best spot for the centre of a work, as it lies just among the most populous, profane, and ignorant parishes.'[1]

Industrial and social development in Shropshire in the eighteenth century

Fletcher's parish was situated in the middle of an area which was of crucial importance for the Industrial Revolution in England.[2] East Shropshire was rich in mineral resources. The most important of these was coal, which was mined over a wide area. Iron ore, pyrites, pottery clay, fire-clay, sand, bitumen, limestone and salt were also to be found there. The coalfield lay about fifteen miles from the county town of Shrewsbury to the west, and from the south Staffordshire coalfields around Wolverhampton to the east. The parish of Madeley was at the heart of this coal-mining area, on the northern side of the River Severn. The part of the parish that bordered on the river was called Madeley Wood. The ironworking settlement of Coalbrookdale also belonged to Madeley, and, like most new settlements, was some distance away from the centre of the community which had grown up around the old parish church.

The River Severn provided a link with the port of Bristol, some eighty miles to the south, as well as with Shrewsbury, the main town in the region, and mid-Wales, further up-river. The Severn had been used by shipping from the sixteenth century, and towards the end of that century there had been a notable increase in coal traffic. The earliest mines were on the western side of the coalfield, where, because of geological faults, the seams lay near the surface. Coal had been dug from these shallow seams since the Middle Ages. The deepest seams, in the east, would not be mined until the middle of the nineteenth century. Until the coming of the railways, trade developed mainly along the waterways, and, from the sixteenth century on, the mining and distribution of coal grew into a well-organized, highly profitable undertaking in the Severn Gorge and the communities on its southern side. Since the output from these coalfields was so good, it was possible to undercut the prices of other mining areas in England. New mining methods were developed, and these gradually spread from Shropshire to other coalfields. Coal mining made possible the development of other branches of industry which depended on coal: potteries, the production of tobacco pipes, the extraction of tar, pitch and oil, glass production, salt mining, and lead smelting.

The production of iron was a further important industry in Shropshire. The earliest references to it go back before the time of the Reformation. For hundreds of years iron could only be produced by the burning of charcoal, not coke. For the most part this iron was sold on in the form of wrought-iron bars. It was one of the peculiarities of the trade in charcoal-iron that the iron was transported over long distances, from one production stage to another, as a half-finished product. The greatest concentration of forges was to be found on the banks of the Tern. One of the most important lay at its confluence with the Severn near Atcham.[3] Its annual output of manufactured iron in 1717 totalled 300 tons.

In Coalbrookdale, within the parish boundaries of Madeley, in the year 1707, Abraham Darby I leased an old furnace. From the start he ran it on coke. However, the productivity, and the quality of the iron produced, left much to be desired. It could only be used for cast iron. In 1756 Abraham Darby II renewed the lease of the Coalbrookdale works, which had greatly expanded in the meantime, and now incorporated foundries. The settlement had grown to 450 inhabitants, and the works offered employment for 500 people. So large an operation would not have been feasible without the change to coke, which made possible the installation of more than one furnace on the same site. Where charcoal was still used, capacity was severely limited. The significance of the

Coalbrookdale foundry in the first half of the eighteenth century had to do, not so much with the pots and kettles which were made there, as with the production of cast-iron parts for the Newcomen atmospheric engine. These engines were first employed to drain mines, but were later used to control the water supply in the iron foundries. In Coalbrookdale, one of these machines was set up for the first time in the 1740s, to pump used water back into the storage tanks. This meant that the foundry was completely independent of rainfall patterns, and work did not have to stop during the summer months. Most of the new ironworks set up in Shropshire adopted this innovation.

Somewhere around 1750 Abraham Darby II made the decisive breakthrough and succeeded in producing top-quality forgeable iron using coke as his fuel. His wife, Abiah Darby, reported later that a distinguished gentleman had urged her husband to take out a patent on his discovery, so as to make some profit out of it, but her husband had declined because he did not want to deny the public free access to such an achievement. A new era in the production of iron had begun.

During the first half of the eighteenth century the greatest obstacles to progress in improving the productivity of the iron industry were overcome: for fuel, unlimited quantities of coke were available; the Newcomen atmospheric engine maintained the circulation of water to drive the bellows; railways (with horse-drawn trucks) had been established for decades as extremely useful for handling the raw material from the mines; the choice of particular kinds of iron ore made possible the production of forgeable iron by means of coke, etc. In the middle of the eighteenth century a far-reaching change took place in the running of the industry. Owners of furnaces and foundries, such as Abraham Darby II, began themselves to take over coal- and ore-workings. In Horsehay, Dawley, a neighbouring community to the north of Madeley, Darby and a partner set up a completely new ironworks. The whole landscape had to be changed, a system of water storage tanks dug out, machines constructed, buildings erected.

An influential and experienced contemporary saw the whole enterprise as extravagant and foolish. Nevertheless the new works quickly achieved an output of over twenty tons a week. For the first time a coke blast furnace had proved itself more efficient in the production of forgeable iron than the traditional charcoal furnace. The person who had been so critical became a partner himself in three newly established enterprises.

Over many years 40% of the total output of pig iron in England came

from Shropshire. It was only at the end of the eighteenth century
that Shropshire was overtaken by other regions which, at that time,
expanded very significantly. Those last fifty years of the century were a
time of great social and industrial change in east Shropshire. The
region's economy was dominated by nine large enterprises. Two of
them, Darby's Coalbrookdale and the Madeley Wood Company, from
1776 under the control of Abraham Darby III, were situated in the
parish of Madeley. From the 1780s onwards the Darby family was the
chief property owner in Madeley. The partners in the iron industry
extended their activities, and diversified into porcelain works, tar production, mills, glassworks, etc. In 1776 a Boulton and Watt steam
engine was installed for the first time in Shropshire, to blow air directly
into the blast furnace. Other uses for the new generation of steam
engines quickly followed. Around 1800 the number of steam engines in
Shropshire, relative to the size of the coalfield, was higher than in any
other part of Great Britain – a statistic which can serve as a reliable indi-
cator of the industrial development of a region. The first attempt to
build a steam locomotive was also made in Shropshire, at Coalbrookdale.

When the iron had been produced it had to be transported. The
companies turned their attention to the development of transport
systems, and innovations in this field were no less spectacular than in
that of iron production. The vessels used on the Severn had a capacity of
between twenty and eighty tons each, and a crew of three or four.
Travelling downstream they would drift with the current, using a sail
when possible. Going upstream they were pulled along by gangs of six
to eight men. Even at the time there were those who described this work
as degrading and brutalizing, but manpower was cheaper than horse-
power. However, in 1800 work was completed on the long-awaited
towpath, which speeded up the transfer of the work from men to horses.
In the last quarter of the eighteenth century a series of canals was also
constructed, to improve the links with other parts of England, as well as
a network of local canals to connect the ironworks with the rivers.
Differences in the level of the land were overcome by an ingenious
system of inclined planes. Transport by water was much cheaper than
road transport.

The ironwork partnerships constructed toll roads. However, there
was still no crossing over the Severn in the Madeley area. The famous
Ironbridge, which was cast by Abraham Darby III, caused a sensation
when it was opened in 1781. With a span of over ninety metres, it

crossed the Severn and joined Benthall to Madeley Wood. Anyone wishing to gain an insight into the progress of industrialization in the 1780s or 1790s, or simply to see something out of the ordinary, should visit the Severn Gorge and its Ironbridge.

A permanent problem during the decades of expansion was how to find enough workers. The employers tried to recruit workers from other areas. In 1711 there were around 11,500 people living in the coalfield area. The number had doubled by 1760, and trebled by the turn of the century. Contributory factors, along with the migration of people into the area, were the high birth rate, and the relatively good health of the children in the large families of the miners and ironworkers. Uneducated workers came into the coalfield mainly from the surrounding rural areas. They would work on one of the many farmsteads, while their sons would seek and find work in mining or in one of the new branches of industry. Wages were notably higher in mining or the iron industry than in agriculture: the more dangerous the work, the higher the wages. There were frequent deaths in the pits as a result of roof-falls or explosions. Only a few mineworkers reached the age of fifty. Most were asthmatic by thirty, and no longer fit to work by forty to forty-five at the latest. In order to attract workers, or to discourage them from leaving, the employers gave increasing attention to the provision of living accommodation for their workforce. Settlements grew up in the vicinity of the ironworks, far away from the old village centre. Employers who, like the Darby family, were Quakers, combined industrial development with philanthropy. They were among the first to build workers' settlements, and to provide them with mills, laundries, schools, grocery shops, and houses for widows.

When Fletcher was Vicar of Madeley he visited his flock not only in their homes but in their places of work. In one of his writings he gave an impressive description of the unimaginable working conditions in the mines and at the blast-furnaces:

> To go no farther than this populous parish, with what hardships and dangers do our indigent neighbours earn their bread? See those who ransack the bowels of the earth to get the black mineral we burn: how little is their lot preferable to that of the Spanish felons, who work the silver mines? . . . the murderer's cell is a palace, in comparison of the black spot, to which they repair: the vagrant's posture in the stocks, is preferable to the posture in which they labour . . . Form, if you can, an idea of the misery of men kneeling, stooping, or

Reluctant Saint?

lying on one side, to toil all day in a confined place, where a child could hardly stand: whilst a younger company, with their hands and feet on the black dusty ground, and a chain about their body, creep and drag along, like fourfooted beasts, heavy loads of the dirty mineral, through ways almost impassable to the curious observer.[4]

The nearness of death and the harshness of working conditions in the mines affected the community in many ways. For most workers life consisted either of feasts or fasts. This was reflected in the brutality of their leisure activities. The high point of the annual fair at Madeley every September, in a different spot on each of the three days, was the baiting of a bull by bloodhounds until it collapsed and died. Cockfighting, a form of sport originally indulged in by the higher strata of society but increasingly practised among the labourers, was equally popular. Visits to the public house, and the consumption of alcohol, took place especially on the free days following the payment of wages. On working days there was strict discipline in the ironworks. Punctuality and constant alertness were required of the workers. The employers therefore found it in their interest to discourage the excesses of their workers on their free days. In the course of the years they succeeded in this so far as the blood sports were concerned, but not in the case of alcohol. Employers were accustomed to reinvest their profits, so that their business might grow. Miners, on the other hand, who could lose their lives the next time a pit shaft fell in, squandered their wages as soon as they received them.

Fletcher the vicar

It is estimated that when Fletcher began his ministry there were 1,000 to 1,500 people in the parish of Madeley.[5] Fletcher was soon criticized for his Methodist preaching style: 'There are three meetings in my parish – a Papist [Roman Catholic], a Quaker, and a Baptist, and they begin to call the fourth the *Methodist* one. I mean the Church.'[6]

The opposition to him grew, so that he had to come down to earth and recognize that his vision was too ambitious.

I had a secret expectation to be the instrument of a work in this part of our Church, and I did not despair of being soon a little *Berridge*; and thus warmed with sparks of my own kindling, I looked out to see the rocks broke in pieces, and the waters flowing out. But to the great disappointment of my hopes, I am now forced to look within . . . A crying out – 'He is a Methodist, a down-right Methodist!' While some of the poorer sort say – 'Nay, but he is speaking the truth'. Some of the best farmers and most reputable tradesmen talk often among themselves (as I am told) about turning me out of my living as a Methodist or a Baptist; and spread about such stories as your Ladyship may guess at without my writing them.[7]

Fletcher saw his task specifically in relation to the lowest strata in society. If they did not come to him, he was ready to follow them even into their pits and forges. Fletcher spared no pains to preach the gospel to the whole population. It is reported that when some people made the excuse that they had got up too late to attend Sunday morning service, Fletcher went round his parish at five o'clock in the morning, ringing a handbell.[8] We are not told whether he kept up this practice for any length of time, or whether it was a success or failure.

By small steps Fletcher sought to widen the range of his activities. He introduced Friday evening readings. He held communion services once a month. For the training of children, Fletcher got Charles Wesley to send him some books. He began occasionally to deliver a second sermon on Sunday evenings, after giving instruction in the catechism. On these occasions he read from the homilies of the Church of England. He tried in this way to reinforce what he had said in the morning and to convince his opponents of his ecclesiastical conformity. The church was often full on Sunday mornings. Many people came from neighbouring parishes. In the two settlements of Coalbrookdale and Madeley Wood, groups of people formed themselves into small societies, which he saw as doors of opportunity for an effective ministry. He bought a horse, to enable him to get around the various settlements.

Nevertheless there were setbacks. Symptoms of religious eccentricity appeared in some individuals, and there were conflicts, all of which gave encouragement to Fletcher's opponents. The church leaders wanted to exclude from the church worshippers coming from outside the parish, but Fletcher resisted this. He did, though, decline to hold a service outside the regular hours of worship for a group of eighty workers from a neighbouring parish. Fletcher aroused opposition of a quite different kind in the autumn of 1761, when he attended the annual fair in Madeley for the first time. The elder of the sons of Mr Hill, whose teacher Fletcher had been, overstepped the mark. In a 23-day celebra-

tion he got through over three hundred bottles of wine![9] Fletcher
preached against drunkenness, bull-baiting and other excesses, and
appealed to the conscience of the members of his congregation. The
effect was the opposite to what he intended. Fletcher's church was less
full from now on. There could be different reasons for that, thought
Fletcher: the curiosity of many of his hearers might have been satisfied;
others might have been annoyed by his preaching; the roads might have
become worse because of the bad weather; he might have acquired a
bad name as a Methodist, and the time for God to pour out his Spirit
might not yet have come.[10]

In his second year Fletcher had some encounters with the law.
The first instance was when he wished to take proceedings against a
drunkard who was rousing the rabble in Madeley Wood against him.
The ecclesiastical court, however, delayed its hearing of the case, and
the witnesses refused to testify. The charge was therefore dismissed.
Fletcher had to realize that he did not have the support of the courts in
promoting stricter religious and moral standards. In another instance,
the dilatoriness of the legal processes worked to his advantage: he was
several times accused of contravening the current Conventicle Act. On
this issue the leader of the opposition was a clergyman in Madeley
Wood. The Conventicle Act was a piece of legislation which forbade
gatherings of more than five people in addition to the members of the
household in which the meeting was held. It was explicitly directed
against Dissenters. The Toleration Act allowed Dissenters to hold their
own meetings, provided that the meeting house was properly registered.
An advocate whom Fletcher consulted advised him to check whether
canon law in the Church of England allowed meetings in private houses.
If it did, then it would be contrary to the intention of the legislators to
condemn a clergyman of the Church of England, or the meetings he
arranged, on the grounds that they contravened the Conventicle Act.
But the advocate warned Fletcher to tread carefully, since most of the
magistrates in the area were so ill-informed legally that their decisions
often ran counter to the law. In Fletcher's case the magistrates were of
the opinion that the issue could only be decided by an ecclesiastical
court. And two church leaders threatened to appeal to the ecclesiastical
court:

> The debates about the illegality of exhorting in houses (although only
> in my own parish) grew some time ago to such a height, that I was
> obliged to lay my reasons before the Bishop; but his Lordship

very prudently sends me no answer. I think he knows not how to disapprove & dares not to approve this Methodist way of proceeding.[11]

At first, Fletcher's activity did not extend much beyond the boundaries of his parish. A society had been formed in Broseley, a parish to the south of the Severn. Fletcher visited it, when he was invited, but was uncertain whether he ought to do so on a regular basis, and asked Charles Wesley for advice. Neighbouring clergymen broke off relations with Fletcher. In autumn 1762, for the first time, a clergyman with a similar outlook to Fletcher was inducted into one of the neighbouring parishes.[12]

Fletcher's ministry cannot be divided up into peaceful and turbulent years.[13] That is made particularly clear by his letters from 1763. In April he expressed the wish that God would always give him patience to do his duty, and not abandon his expectation that one day God would bestow the full power of his Word and he would cast the net on the right side of the boat. In May he reported on a fifty-year-old woman who had died in the full certainty of faith. However, grace was specially at work among young people. In June peace seemed to have returned, but by July Fletcher was announcing that the trials he was having to undergo were so severe that they were practically compelling him to leave Madeley. In September he wrote of the 'wolves in sheep's clothing' who were harassing him. Nevertheless, after barely three years in office, Fletcher's verdict was:

> The Gospel of Christ maintains, and I hope gets a little ground in my parish, notwithstanding the general opposition made against it by all the gentry, and by the rabble, who have thirty ale-houses to drown their convictions in. To the great offence of bigotted people, I preach every morning to the colliers of Madeley Wood, a place that can vie with Kingswood for wildness, and I hope in some measure for reformation.[14]

In summer 1764 John Wesley paid his first visit to Shropshire, and to Madeley in particular.[15] He noted in his *Journal*:

> Thence we went on to Madeley, an exceeding pleasant village encompassed with trees and hills. It was a great comfort to me to converse once more with a Methodist of the old stamp, denying himself, taking

up his cross, and resolved to be 'altogether a Christian'. Sun. 22 – At ten, Mr. Fletcher read prayers, and I preached on those words in the Gospel, 'I am the good Shepherd: the good Shepherd layeth down his life for the sheep.' The church would nothing near contain the congregation. But a window near the pulpit being taken down, those who could not come in stood in the churchyard, and I believe all could hear . . . Mr. Grimshaw, at his first coming to Haworth, had not such a prospect as this. There are many adversaries indeed, but yet they cannot 'shut the open and effectual door'.[16]

Fletcher was astonished at how little resistance this visit provoked. The opposition had by no means been silenced, but he did not feel so threatened by it as in his first two years. His activities began slowly to extend beyond the boundaries of his parish. He sought to establish contact with neighbouring clergy, in whose parishes religious societies were meeting. He would preach his first sermon at five in the morning, and would not return home until after midnight. Many of the journeys he undertook were spoken about long afterwards. In 1765 Fletcher felt obliged to take a further momentous step: in one of the neighbouring settlements he preached in the open air, after the local clergyman had denied him the use of his pulpit. Fletcher was now openly threatened with expulsion from Madeley. But this was not the reason why he regarded 1765 as his worst year: the lack of success in what he was doing was a greater burden to him than personal hostility.

By this time Fletcher was receiving frequent visits from different representatives of the Methodist movement, or circles closely related to it. We will come back to this in a later chapter. In 1765 James Ireland, a wealthy merchant and landowner, paid him a visit. From this man Fletcher received regular gifts, which he then shared out among the poor. Ireland wanted Fletcher to accompany him on a journey to Switzerland, but Fletcher declined. In 1768, through the influence of Sir Richard Hill, James Stillingfleet, another clergyman with leanings towards Methodism, was appointed to a benefice in the region. Sir Richard was one of three important landowners in the area who bore personal testimony to the gospel of redemption in Christ, and lent their support to the work. At the beginning of 1769 Fletcher announced that he was now planning a journey to Switzerland, and explained the reasons for his decision:

It hath pleased the Lord to awaken one of my brothers & (I hope) a brother-in-law. The first by the most pressing letters urges me to go to him & shew him the way of God more perfectly, And threatens (if I will not go) to leave his wife & children to come to me here. I have of late begun to consider myself as a debtor to my family, and design next year (if it pleases God to make my way plain) to go and offer them Jesus by words of mouth for a few weeks. But in this and every other matter I desire to have no will of my own.[17]

The brother in question must have been Henri Louis, to whom, both before and after this time, John Fletcher was closely attached.

Marriage and tutorial work

'What between the dead and the living, a parish ties one down more than a wife,'[18] said Fletcher after seven years of ministry. He was disappointed, because he had hoped, thanks to having a single parish and to being unmarried, to remain freer in his work, and undistracted in his love for Christ. At the beginning of his ministry he had written:

The devil, my friends, and my heart, have pushed at me to make me fall into worldly cares and creature snares – first, by the thoughts of marrying, then by the offers of several boarders, one of whom offered me £60 a year, and he is a christian youth, but I have been enabled to cry, *Nothing but Jesus*, and the service of his people.[19]

In fact Fletcher had considered the question of marriage when he first took up his appointment in Madeley. For a while he saw it as a distinct possibility, but he rejected the idea. For the first two and a half years he had a housekeeper in Madeley. When she left him in 1763 his thoughts turned again to marriage. The person who came to mind was the one he had thought of in 1760: Miss Mary Bosanquet. In his typical way, Fletcher decided against marriage on the same grounds as three years earlier:

It is true that Scripture says that a pious woman is a gift from God. It is also true that such a person is one in a thousand. But who would enter a lottery in which there were 999 chances of losing, and only one of winning? And even if I could find this Phoenix, this thousandth one, what would I get then? A disturbing refusal. Who would want a husband like me? If, in spite of all my self-love, I heartily detest myself, could I be so loveless as to expect that another person should do for me what I cannot do for myself, that another person should resolve to treasure me! to love me! to honour me![20]

Another reason put forward by Fletcher for declining marriage was that Mary Bosanquet was a person of substance, and he mistrusted his motives for marrying her: he might be thinking more of her wealth than of her person. The question of marriage worried Fletcher for several years more. But he constantly rejected the idea, even when Charles Wesley tried to encourage him in it. He was prepared to recognize that the married state might be good for others. His rejection of it was an entirely personal matter. He might well need someone whom he could love, but he could not saddle someone he loved with his own burden. So for years Fletcher remained a bachelor.

While Fletcher was continuing to turn his back on marriage, changes were taking place in his attitude towards becoming involved in tutorial work and teaching. When he came to Madeley he told Charles Wesley that he would take on this responsibility only for Charles's son, Charles junior. However, by 1762, William Ley, one of John Wesley's preachers, was living in Madeley. Fletcher gave him some instruction, but reported that his friend was not progressing as well as he might have been. In assessing the validity of this judgment, we need to take into account Fletcher's insistence that his pupil should spend at least twelve hours a day poring over his books. The fact that, some years later, Charles Wesley tried to have Ley nominated for a curate's appointment, suggests that it was probably he, Charles Wesley, who had persuaded Fletcher to take on Ley, in order to give him the necessary classical and theological training in preparation for ordination. All other requests for instruction were declined by Fletcher.

In the middle of the 1760s a Methodist teacher came from London to Madeley, and took over the headship of the local boarding school. The existence of this boarding school is presupposed in an anecdote reported by one of Fletcher's biographers. One morning Fletcher had visited the boarding school while the girls were still at breakfast, which had gone on for a full hour. Finally he had spoken to them, and invited them to breakfast at the parsonage the following day. When they came, he drank his milk and ate the bread which had been soaked in it, all of which took less than two minutes. He spent the remaining fifty-eight minutes in explaining to them the value of time, and in singing and praying with them.

Charles Wesley, who was concerned about the physical well-being of his friend, made enquiries about his diet. Fletcher replied that he himself cooked no meat, but lived mostly on bread and dairy produce. During the early part of his time in Madeley, Fletcher had no health problems, but when, towards the end of the 1760s, he was travelling a great deal and staying in all kinds of different places, his state of health deteriorated. He often suffered from persistent colds. But the really serious, life-threatening illness only broke out in the mid-1770s.

8

The Quest for Empowerment and Effectiveness

Doubts about his own calling

'I am good for nothing, but to go and bury myself in my parish. I have those touches of misanthropy which make solitude my element,'[1] wrote Fletcher to James Ireland in 1770, after Ireland had invited him to go on a journey to Switzerland, and Fletcher had at first agreed. Everything seemed to be against the trip: he had forgotten too much of his French to be able to preach, and it seemed that Ireland was only making the journey on his account. So he asked his friend and patron to cancel the trip, unless he was obliged to go to France for business reasons. However, the journey took place. Ireland and Fletcher visited the persecuted Protestants in southern France, made a detour into Italy, and, in Switzerland, stayed in Fletcher's home town of Nyon.

After his return from the Continent in the summer of 1770, Fletcher gave expression to some fundamental thoughts about his ministry. A clear line of development can be traced in them. During his severe crisis of faith at the end of the 1750s he had spoken of hating himself as a sinner, because his thoughts were dominated by an almighty God, whose judgments were just. Then, in the 1760s, almost imperceptibly, the wonderful grace of God revealed in the incarnation moved back into the centre of his consciousness – a change which had consequences for his relations with other people. And what he tentatively expressed in the form of a question in 1770 slowly unfolded in the course of the theological controversies of the 1770s. He wrote to Charles Wesley:

> I have the impression that we can never have too much compassion for sinners, nor overemphasize for them the love of Jesus, when he himself became incarnate and declared redemption and salvation to tax-gatherers and evildoers. I have also the impression that faith *shows itself gradually* in many hearts, and that it is *our task to nourish* the weakest spark, the faintest signs. *What is your opinion?*[2]

There had been no trace, in Fletcher's utterances in the 1760s, of what he began thus cautiously to recognize early in the 1770s. The 1760s were dominated by questions and doubts about his effectiveness. He was convinced that God had guided him along the way that led to Madeley, but he saw himself as a weak, helpless, inexperienced preacher of the gospel. In a letter to the Countess of Huntingdon he wrote that the opportunities for preaching the gospel in his parish were good, but added:

> But it is well, if after all, there is any work in my parish. I despair even of this, when I look at myself, and fall in quite with Mr. John Wesley's opinion of me, though sometimes, too, I hope the Lord hath not sent me here for nothing . . . Nevertheless I am still fully determined to resign my living after a while, if the Lord does not think me worthy to be His instrument.[3]

Fletcher was hoping for fruit from his preaching. But he felt he could not count on it, since, when he looked at himself, his unsuitability for the ministry was so clearly obvious. However, he had not properly understood John Wesley's opinion of him. What Wesley thought was that it would be a pity if Fletcher were to remain simply vicar of a single parish, and not have a wider field of activity. Fletcher's view, on the contrary, was that, if he could do anything at all in God's vineyard, then at most it would be as a parish priest, and certainly nothing above and beyond that. Over and over again Fletcher had doubts about his own abilities. In difficult situations he never took his congregation to task without taking himself to task much more. He thought that his heart was hard, that he lacked the contrition which, for him, was the essential sign of Christian faith. Pride and self-satisfaction, he thought, were still deeply rooted in him, and were signs of his faithlessness and his lack of contrition and godly fear.

True faith, for Fletcher, included being filled with divine power, which he felt he still lacked. He did not often say, as he did in one letter to Lady Huntingdon, that pride can still cling to a believer, and that it can only be broken when Christ comes in the power of his Spirit. This last great promise, he believed, was still awaited. Fletcher kept his eyes upon it as his goal. In relation both to his own personal life and to the unfruitfulness of the preaching of the gospel in Shropshire, he often spoke of the expectation of a filling with the Holy Spirit, an inbreaking of the kingship of Christ in believers, a Spirit-baptism, a new Pentecost.

With these different designations Fletcher was indicating the one central expectation which became more and more determinative for his life: that the Spirit of God would work in such powerful ways that all human opposition to God would be banished and overcome.

Fletcher's low view of himself was not the result of lack of success. But even the praises of other people were burdensome to him. He wrote to George Whitefield:

> Rev. and dear Sir, I am confounded when I receive a letter from you; present and eternal contempt from Christ and all his members is what I deserve. A sentence of death is my due; but, instead of it, I am favoured with lines of love. God write a thousand, for them, upon your own heart! . . . Your mentioning my poor ministrations among your congregation opens again a wound of shame that was but half healed. I feel the need of asking God, you and your hearers pardon, for weakening the glorious matter of the Gospel, by my wretched broken manner; and spoiling the heavenly power of it, by the uncleanness of my heart and lips.[4]

The few observations we have from the late 1760s on Fletcher's own condition make it clear that he was undergoing the same temptations and doubts about the genuineness of his repentance and faith that had appeared in his correspondence with Charles Wesley at the end of the 1750s. Thus it was that in 1770 an acquaintance of Lady Huntingdon wrote to Fletcher:

> My Dear Christian Friend
> I Take Pleasure in Repeating I Bear you in continual Remembrance before the Throne – I greatly Felt a Hint in your Letter to Lady H– [Huntingdon] To viz. that you was No Christian – gracious Heaven what then are you – Away Away with Unbelieving Tears. Dishonour not God Through Unbelief . . .[5]

Fletcher preferred to remain hidden away in his parish, even when he was invited by Lady Huntingdon, George Whitefield, or Charles Wesley to fresh fields of service. He would rather work among his people in the obscurity of his remote hideout than in the public eye in a city. The 'misanthropy' to which he referred in his letter to Ireland was by no means dislike of people. It was the fear of stepping out into the open, because all his energies were directed towards coming to terms with himself. However, both the work of his own parish and the invitations of his friends forced Fletcher, for his own well-being, to emerge from his hideout.

Preacher

Fletcher wrote out his earliest sermons in full. However, when it came to preaching them from the pulpit, he would be led to depart widely from his notes. Quite soon, particularly at Friday evening prayers, he began to dispense with full manuscripts, and to speak with only brief sermon outlines in his hand. A little while later he ceased, as a general rule, even to write out his Sunday sermons. This observation is supported by the archives, which contain barely two dozen fully written-out sermons, but over two hundred and fifty sermon outlines.[6] The outlines are to be found in little notebooks, which Fletcher could use on his travels, as well as in his parish of Madeley. His sermons would normally have lasted for between thirty and fifty minutes.

In so far as they are datable, the fully written-out sermons belong to the earlier years of Fletcher's ministry in Madeley. They are all variations on a theme, calling sinners to repentance and to faith in Jesus Christ. A common characteristic is that they reveal the sinfulness of human beings in their natural state. Political and social questions receive no treatment in the extant sermons.

Fletcher was prepared for his hearers to be annoyed by his sermons. He did not want to be an 'acceptable', well-thought-of preacher, at the expense of the gospel. This basic attitude is well illustrated by two sermons on Ezekiel. One of the texts comes from the story of the prophet's call, the other deals with Ezekiel's role as watchman. As Fletcher saw it, clergymen had been given this watchman's brief. Therefore they were obliged to deliver a disagreeable message, not because they took delight in annoying people, but because it was their duty to convict them of their sin. Fletcher often enumerated the different manifestations of sin, showing that they were not only to be found in openly sinful deeds, but also in the so-called good works of the self-righteous. His hearers should not be able to say, at the end of the sermon, that they were not sinners. Fletcher also knew all the objections his hearers might raise, took them up in his preaching, and answered them in advance. To the objection 'That is a hard saying; who can hear it?' (John 6.60), Fletcher retorted that he was preaching nothing other than what Jesus, the apostles, and the teaching of the Church all said. To the objection that there was still plenty of time to repent, Fletcher replied that no one knew the hour of his death. Fletcher also warned people against a false sense of security arising from biblical quotations taken out of their context. According to him, the worst kind of sin was not some foul deed, but lack of faith, which violated not only God's law, and his holiness and righteousness, but also God's Son, and his grace. The sin of unbelief was one to which the faithful, outwardly irreproachable churchgoer, who was proud of his own virtue, was particularly prone.

Fletcher distinguished three conditions in which people may find themselves. The first condition is that of the natural, unawakened person (cf. Eph. 5.14). Such persons imagine they are safe, either because they think that there is no God, or that God is not bothered about us, or that God is graciously indulgent towards us; or because they take comfort from the fact that they are good, upright people, who go regularly to church. Such persons also find talk of hell and damnation unacceptable. Therefore, Fletcher stressed, the urgency of the hour and the need for decision must be insisted upon, since God's judgment brings irrevocable separation. This has to be said, in Fletcher's view, precisely because now is still the time of grace. The possibility of repentance still exists. His hearers must remember the importance of the present hour. They should not count on things continuing to go well with them, since it may be that God will punish sinners very soon. Listeners might well be surprised at hearing their own state aptly and clearly described, but, 'if a minister has studied his own heart, he can tell all men theirs too, because we are all alike by nature, all cast into the mould of Adam's corruption.'[7] Fletcher's warnings, and his call to confession and repentance, were not the result of an intellectual process, but sprang from the solidarity he felt with his hearers, as one who was conscious of his own sinful nature.

The second condition is that of those persons who are ready to repent, who have been awakened, and are now bewailing their sins, fearing God, and striving after redemption. It is God alone who thus wakes people up, and brings them to acknowledge their sins and repent. God has countless ways of doing this. Fletcher groups them into 'extraordinary' and 'ordinary' categories. Examples of the 'extraordinary', he says, are St Paul and the Philippian jailer. Mostly, however, God leads sinners to repentance by the 'ordinary' paths, that is, through suffering, or through the witness of another Christian, or, most commonly of all, through the preaching of the Word. Speaking of those who came to church only to be seen, who normally fell asleep, or who said their prayers without any inner involvement in them, Fletcher said that in spite of such negligence, God was able to grant that their hardened conscience should be stirred into life.

The third condition is that of true believers, who have obtained the forgiveness of their sins, who have been born again, and who love God above all things. The Word of God, Fletcher said, needed to be addressed to the three kinds of hearers in different ways. The unawakened sinner should be constantly subjected to the threats of the law. To the awakened sinner, God's grace and the promises of the gospel should be declared. The converted sinner should be exhorted to strive after entire sanctification.

The theme of the new birth, coming straight from the biblical text, was at the very heart of some of the sermons, and was touched on in all of them. It was particularly important for Fletcher because true faith involved the actual renewal of a person. In his preaching the weight lay not so much on a person's being *declared* righteous in a forensic sense through the power of Christ's atoning death, as on his being *made* righteous through the Spirit of God. Sin was so deeply rooted in natural human beings that nothing less than a new creation was necessary for their redemption. Over and over again Fletcher emphasized that our redemption is due to God alone, and that it is to be ascribed to God's grace alone. God works through his Spirit. The new birth is the work of his Spirit.

For Fletcher, the usual means whereby the Spirit worked was the Word, impressed by the Spirit upon the soul. The preacher can lead people to hear outwardly, but only the Spirit can enable the heart to hear truly: 'Men are mere instruments – it is the Lord alone who can make our ministry effectual, and we should therefore have but one end in view, to glorify Christ and save immortal souls.'[8] Fletcher's sermons always included a prayer for God's Spirit to take the preacher's human words and transform them into the Word of God which can touch hearts. But Fletcher also stressed the responsibility of hearers of the Word not to close their hearts to God's activity. In this connection, Fletcher could also say that God lays before a person the choice whether to remain in a fallen condition or to rise to true life through the new birth. The sinner finds life in Christ alone.

Among Fletcher's sermon outlines[9] there are many in which there is a direct or indirect call to repentance and conversion. Many of these and other texts deal with the person of Jesus Christ, his significance and his work. The theme of the new birth is less common in the outlines than in the fully written-out sermons. Biblical texts in which the forgiveness of sins or justification are the central theme are comparatively rare. But many of the sermon outlines take up the theme of sanctification and Christian living.

In form and structure, the sermon outlines have several recurring characteristics. The development of the body of the sermon is usually preceded by an introduction, which describes the context of the passage, or its significance for the hearers. Almost without exception, the ending consists of an application which relates the content of the sermon to the different categories of people in the audience. As a general rule, those are the three categories described above. Often, however, Fletcher sub-divided them further, into sinners, penitents, backsliders, people of little faith, and those firm in their faith. In contrast to this basic pattern for the beginnings and endings of the sermons, there was much variation in the way the contents were developed. Fletcher had no regular three-point structure, or standard questions, which would be applied in every sermon. Most of the sermons have three to five main points, which are then subdivided. Subdivisions vary greatly in length and depth of treatment. Many of the sermon outlines do not fill even one page of his little notebooks, while others cover several pages and in some cases are very similar to the fully written-out sermons.

Though Fletcher himself thought little of his sermons, they were especially appreciated among the Methodists. Thus he wrote to Miss Hatton, with a hint of reproof: 'You talk of hearing me soon – I dare never invite *any one* to hear *me*, though I am glad to see my friends.'[10] The rapturous appreciation expressed by Fletcher's contemporaries must be attributed in part to the prestige and honour which he enjoyed in his later years.[11] John Wesley, who, as a rule, was an impartial observer, made a comparison which undoubtedly drew attention to Fletcher's capabilities. That comparison was influenced by his experiences with the later Fletcher. Even so, it is astonishing that he put Fletcher on a par with George Whitefield, who was known as the great evangelist of the Methodist movement. Wesley concluded:

He [Fletcher, in comparison with Whitefield] had a more striking person, equal good-breeding, an equally winning address: together with a richer flow of fancy, a stronger understanding: a far greater treasure of learning, both in Languages, Philosophy, Philology, and

Divinity: and above all, (which I can speak with fuller assurance, because I had a thorough knowledge both of one and the other) a more deep and constant communion with the Father, and with the Son, Jesus Christ.[12]

Such praise was certainly excessive for the early years of Fletcher's ministry. English was not Fletcher's mother tongue. One of Wesley's travelling preachers heard Fletcher in Bristol in 1772, and gave the following assessment of his preaching style:

We have also had the great Mr. Fletcher here . . . He seems to be an eminent saint indeed. I had the satisfaction to hear him twice, he is a lively, zealous preacher. The power of God seems to attend his word, yet I admire him much more as a writer than as a preacher. He being a foreigner, there is a kind of roughness [which] attends his language that is not grateful to an English hearer; and the English not being his mother tongue, he sometimes seems to be at a loss for words, yet he certainly is a great and blessed man. We have very large congregations to hear both Mr. W. [John Wesley] and Mr. F. [John Fletcher], especially the latter, and I hope that we shall see the fruit of it in a little time.[13]

The cure of souls

Fletcher was very strict with himself. The signs of his lack of faith were more obvious to him than the signs of his faith. He had more to say to Charles Wesley about his hardened heart than about what God had done in him and through him. He took himself severely to task. Was he as unmerciful towards others as he was towards himself?

There are no reports from inhabitants of Madeley on Fletcher's visits and conversations, although it is well known that he visited his parishioners from house to house. He himself wrote to another clergyman:

It is exceeding well to visit from House to house even the *Infidels*, to feel their pulse and to see whether they do not begin to entertain more favourable thoughts of the pearl of great price than grunting swine or snarling dogs generally do[.] Such visits, half upon the footing of *christian love*, and half upon the footing of *human civility*, may tend to remove prejudices. In some cases writing a letter with tender-ness, or giving a little tract suited to the Circumstances of the person, may clear our own conscience, tho' it should do him no good.[14]

Fletcher's pastoral practice can best be gleaned from letters. With some individuals he corresponded over a long period. It is clear from these letters that his aim was to strengthen the faith of anyone who sought his advice. He entered into the situation of his correspondent, offered straightforward help and support, encouraged and consoled. The things he would never say in his dealings with unbelievers, whom he was trying to convince of their sin, nor in relation to himself, he was ready to write to people who were being tempted: 'I am afraid of being too hard in my dealings with those who are tempted.'[15]

A four-year-long correspondence with Miss Hatton, who lived at Wem, north of Madeley, reveals to us a form of pastoral writing which contains many echoes of mystical works such as the *Imitation of Christ*.[16] In his first letter, Fletcher began by thanking Miss Hatton for the confidence she was placing in the advice of a poor fellow-sinner, and linked this with the prayer that God would offer his own counsel through him, worthless instrument though he might be. Fletcher directed attention away from himself and towards Jesus Christ. Christ alone, he said, in all his offices, was the true foundation on which to build. It was Fletcher's conviction that all human thoughts need to be enlightened by God. In the strict sense, the cure of souls can only be effected by God through his Spirit. He, Fletcher, saw himself therefore as an unworthy instrument. This was the presupposition underlying his letters.

Anyone who reads Fletcher's correspondence, ignoring the beginning and ending of the letters, will by no means have the impression that the writer is a 'poor fellow-sinner', or an 'unworthy instrument'. Fletcher's judgments were clear. Thus he wrote in his first letter to Miss Hatton, that although she had received faith as she took communion, she still lacked the seal of forgiveness. The next step was therefore clearly pointed out to her:

Hold fast your confidence, but do not trust, nor rest in it; trust Christ, and remember he says, I am the way . . . May the Lord teach you the middle path, between resting short of the happiness of making your calling and election sure, and supposing you are neither called nor chosen, and that God hath not yet truly begun the good work . . . The

Lord despises not the day of small things; only beware of resting in small things, and look for the seal and abiding witness of God's Spirit . . .[17]

It was a basic presupposition for Fletcher that faith could be experienced, but in several letters he warned against relying too much upon one's own experience. The seal of forgiveness is not the root of faith, nor an essential prerequisite for its existence, but its fruit. Trust should be based on the promises of Jesus. Temptations are not excluded from the way of faith. Indeed they can be signs of one's acceptance by God. Fletcher stressed the necessity of receiving Christ into one's heart. To attain this goal, one should pay attention to where one's own heart stands, and to where God's grace is quietly at work, faintly and almost imperceptibly. For this, recollection is necessary: 'To be able to go on in the way of the cross and that of faith, you stand in need, Madam, of much recollection, and steady watchfulness over the workings of your heart, and diligent attention to the whispers of divine grace.'[18]

What Fletcher meant by 'recollection' – an important word for him – is brought out in another letter. Recollection must take place deep within a person. It is a turning away from the created world, and a turning towards God. Outwardly it may be seen in the avoidance of superfluous words and unprofitable relationships; inwardly in a turning away from the influence of the senses and an attentiveness to the presence of God. Such recollection ought to be possible even amid the bustle of everyday life. Otherwise there would be a danger that one might not focus one's recollection on God even in times of prayer. In such recollection, God's grace would lead either to contemplation of Jesus the crucified, making intercession for us, or to the suppression of one's senses, so as to rest in stillness of heart before God:

But take care here, to be more taken up with the thoughts of God than of yourself . . . Use no forced labour to raise a particular frame; nor tire, fret, and grow impatient, if you have no comfort; but meekly acquiesce and confess yourself unworthy of it; lie prostrate in humble submission before God, and patiently wait for the smiles of Jesus . . . As dissipation always meets its punishment, so recollection never fails of its reward. After patient waiting comes communion with God, and the sweet sense of his peace and love.[19]

Fletcher's view of the human condition stressed the importance of the will. Every deviation from the right path, he believed, began in the will. The will and the understanding are of greater value than the feelings:

> But I apprehend that God's design in withholding from them those gracious influences, which work upon and melt the sensitive, affectionate part in the soul, is to put us more upon using the nobler powers, the understanding and the will. These are always more in the reach of a child of God, while the other greatly depend upon the texture of the animal frame.[20]

In his pastoral letters Fletcher also rated the understanding highly, as a good gift of God. He therefore produced sentences in which mystical-sounding statements were combined with others which seemed to come, rather, from the early Enlightenment:

> That this faith may be the firmer on our part, let it be *rational* as well as affectionate; *affectionate* as well as rational . . . O my friend, we may believe *rationally* . . . And shall we not believe *affectionately* also? Let us stir up ourselves to love this Jesus, who hath given himself to us with all his blood, all his grace, and all his glory.[21]

Even in his last two letters to the ailing Miss Hatton, Fletcher was encouraging her to remain steadfast in faith, since Christ would not break the bruised reed. He took his stand in solidarity with the addressee on the borderline between life and death. He called himself her companion in affliction, and wrote:

> We stand on the shore of a boundless ocean; death, like a lion, comes to break our bones; let us quietly strip ourselves of our mortal robes, that he may do with us, as the Lord shall permit. In the mean while, let us step into the ark . . . Regard neither unbelief nor doubt; fear neither sin nor hell; chuse neither life nor death; all these are swallowed up in the immensity of Christ, and triumphed over in his cross . . . Reason not with the law, but only with Him . . . Hold fast your confidence in the atoning, sanctifying blood of the Lamb of God.[22]

Now, at the gate of death, the only thing that matters is living faith, sincere trust in Christ and his sacrificial death. The statement that the blood of Christ atones for our sin and sanctifies us shows, on the one hand, the close connection between being declared righteous and being made righteous, and, on the other hand, that both our justification and our sanctification depend on Christ.

It is clear from his correspondence with his friend, the solicitous businessman James Ireland, that Fletcher saw everything, even the most 'worldly' matters, in religious terms. If he received from Ireland wine or cloth which he had neither ordered nor could afford, it was for him a reminder of the undeserved, free grace of God. He compared the wine, which did his stomach good, with the wine of the Kingdom, which was good for the soul. If he could clothe himself two or three times with the material, how much more might the soul be arrayed with the cloak of God's love. Though moths might destroy the cloth, the gift that Jesus gives us is beyond the reach of any destroyer. The statement of faith would usually go farther than the comparison justified. Fletcher's intention was to show the difference between earthly and heavenly assets. The heavenly ones are free of the disadvantages attached to the earthly ones. Many of the comparisons are not without humour:

> Every promise of the gospel is a bottle, a cask that has a spring within, and can never be drawn out. But draw the cork of unbelief, and drink abundantly, . . . nor be afraid of intoxication; and if an inflammation follows, it will only be that of divine love . . . I beg you will be more free with the heavenly wine, than I have been with the earthly, which you sent me. I have not tasted it yet, but whose fault is it? Not yours certainly, but mine. If you do not drink daily spiritual health and vigour out of the cup of salvation, whose fault is it? Not Jesus's, but yours.[23]

If in all things Fletcher was able to establish a connection with faith, so it was also with his great aim of calling people to faith and strengthening them in the faith. From the experience of faith people had already had, Fletcher sought, by means of such connections, to make possible further experiences with faith. For him the connections were self-evident. He used the world of everyday experience to bring out the meaning of religious statements, and in this way enhanced the simplicity and comprehensibility of his preaching. John Wesley gave good advice when, in his biography, he urged his readers not to try to imitate Fletcher's style. Many of Fletcher's comparisons may strike the modern reader as strange, because they are not seen as part of the total picture of his personality. But longing, as he did, to permeate every area of life with the gospel, he could do no other than use all the events and circumstances of life, whether everyday or extraordinary, to illustrate statements of religious truth.

In 1776 James Ireland was obliged to leave his very sick daughter in France. Fletcher wrote to her and tried to convince her how important it was to be ready for death, and not to hope for a long life. He put forward a string of reasons why it may please God to call a person away early. His reasons were based, either on the wisdom of God, which nurtures us and knows what is best for us, or on the love of God, which, in the person of the redeemer, is incomparably greater than all that parents and friends can do for us. Fletcher's comments are strongly reminiscent of the *Imitatio Christi*. His thinking and feeling were so greatly influenced by his relationship with God that in his letters to both father and daughter, when faced with the daughter's impending death, he emphasized only the bond of love between God and humanity, which far surpasses all human family ties.

The letters of condolence which Fletcher wrote to James Ireland after the death of Ireland's daughter, like the one he wrote to Miss Hatton's mother, give expression to his conviction that all the ways of God are good. All Fletcher could do, on the death of a family member, was all the more strongly to urge the living to let go all earthly attachments and respond to the love of Christ. The letters of this childless bachelor left little space for human grief and pain. The only response he could make to the greatest manifestations of the love of parents for their children was to observe how much more and greater was God's love in Christ. In only one letter to James Ireland was there any indication of sympathy for a father's sorrow and grief: 'To be cut in the fruit of our body is, sometimes, more painful than to be cut in our own body.'[24] Apart from this, human grief found no place with him. It was taken up into God's all-embracing love for us.

This basic attitude was reflected in Fletcher's own attitude to death:

I had lately some view of death, and it appeared to me in the most brilliant colours. What is it to die, but to open our eyes after the disagreeable dream of this life, after the black sleep in which we are buried on this earth? It is to break the prison of corruptible flesh and blood, into which sin hath cast us . . . O my dear friend, how lovely is death, when we look at it in Jesus Christ! To die, is one of the greatest privileges of the Christian.[25]

Here the certainty of Christ's victory over death led directly to a longing for death. Fletcher's longing for eternal life was stronger because of the temptations and agonies he had suffered in his earthly life. The love of God in Christ shone upon and relativized everything earthly. Fletcher understood this love as requiring him to flee from earthly things and the fallen world. He had not yet grasped the truth that in its incarnational form the divine love makes the earthly the place of God's presence.

Preaching and the cure of souls were central aspects of Fletcher's ministry. Both these activities were for him most intimately bound up with prayer. He summed it up in a short sentence: 'If prayer be the life of any work it must be the work of our whole life.'[26]

9

Theological Convictions

In the 1760s Fletcher published no theological work. But he wrote four theologically relevant, though little known, documents. Three of them are in the form of letters, which were published posthumously. The fourth is a sermon, which Fletcher first published twelve years after it was written, as an appendix to one of his other writings. His extensive correspondence also includes observations on theological themes. Thus we can form a picture of the basic questions and concerns which pre-occupied Fletcher in the 1760s, and on which he took a theological stance.

Calvinist influence on Fletcher

All the secondary literature includes Fletcher in the Wesleyan-Arminian stream in Methodism. The justification for this judgment is to be found in the controversies of the 1770s. Our present enquiry into the Calvinistic influence on Fletcher is undertaken on the basis of one of his own statements. In a document written in 1771, Fletcher related how he first made the acquaintance of John and Charles Wesley, and later of the Countess of Huntingdon and Whitefield, and how the unity of the Methodist movement was of great concern to him. He continued: 'After taking a dangerous turn into the doctrines of election and reprobation, my sentiments settled at last into the anti-Calvinist way, in which Mr. Wesley was rooted.'[1] He then went on to describe events which occurred between 1762 and 1764. The above quotation is astonishing. There are no other statements or comments, either in letters or in other documents written by Fletcher, to indicate that he was influenced by predestinarian doctrine. The only place where we find the terminology of election is as an aside in a letter from the end of 1762, where it is not necessarily to be interpreted in a Calvinistic sense.[2] There are clear indications in statements from 1761 and the beginning of 1762 that Fletcher did not subscribe to the Calvinistic doctrine of predestination.[3] However, it is clear from a letter written in 1764 that he did waver in his judgment on it. The fact that Fletcher asked Charles Wesley for his opinion on 'imputed righteousness' (with reference to Whitefield and James Hervey) and 'evangelical antinomianism' suggests that he was trying to understand what was so bad about them. He was uncertain whether he had rightly assessed their consequences for doctrine and life. Charles Wesley's reply is not extant. From 1765 come fresh clear indications of Fletcher's rejection of predestinarian beliefs.[4]

The questions as to when the tendency towards Calvinism occurred, how deep it went, how long it lasted, by whom it was brought about, and why Fletcher came to abandon it, cannot be conclusively answered.[5] If we attribute it to the influence of Whitefield and the Countess of Huntingdon, which is certainly possible, but not necessarily implied by Fletcher's statement, then the change can have taken place, at the earliest, towards the end of the 1750s. Or did it not happen until 1762, when Hatton came on the scene? Or was it due to the influence of Hervey?[6] Some indications point to this last possibility, but our sources are silent on the subject. Fletcher must have abandoned the tendency by the mid-1760s at the latest. His moves in both directions caused no stir, and are not clearly recorded in the sources. Fletcher's rejection of Calvinist teaching on predestination – indicated chiefly in the 1760s by his silence on the subject, and in the 1770s by his theological arguments against it – should not be allowed to conceal the fact that in other areas, such as pneumatology, Christology and Trinitarian doctrine, he stood firmly in the Calvinian-Reformed tradition.[7]

Criteria for theological debate

It is instructive to take note of Fletcher's basic assumptions, and to understand them in the context of the age in which he lived. Without question, Scripture had supreme authority in theological debate. In his arguments with opponents within the Church, however, Fletcher referred also to tradition, to show that his interpretation of Scripture was in harmony with the reformed tradition of the Church of England. However, this tradition provided no common ground with Baptists and Quakers, and in their case, therefore, Fletcher based his arguments on Scripture and reason. Against the Quakers, experience became an important criterion, embracing facts of life common to humanity as a whole, as well as specifically Christian experiences. The next chapter will have more to say about these various disputations. In a piece he planned to write about the Fall,[8] Fletcher aimed to establish each of his main points on the basis of all four categories: Scripture, tradition, reason and experience. His approach in this was in harmony with John Wesley's own methods of argument.

From the early years of the Reformation, Scripture, tradition and reason were recognized in Anglicanism as the three normal criteria for establishing doctrinal statements. There was the 'threefold test of conformity to Scripture, to tradition and to reason'.[9] Later, in the seventeenth and eighteenth centuries, there was much debate on the place of reason, and its relation to revelation – hence the following brief excursus into the early Enlightenment in Holland and England, with particular reference to John Locke, into deism, and into the scepticism of David Hume.

John Locke sought to determine the separate spheres of reason and faith, and where the boundary between them lay. To the sphere of reason belongs the formation of propositions out of the ideas which a person has acquired by the exercise of his natural faculties, that is, through sensation and reflection. To the sphere of faith belongs the acceptance of propositions which cannot come from reason in this way, but which are given in an out-of-the-ordinary way by God, that is to say, revealed. Within reason's field of knowledge, according to Locke, no proposition can claim to be 'revealed' if it contradicts reason. Whatever falls outside of reason's field of knowledge constitutes, in so far as it is revealed, the proper subject matter of faith. In the area in which the reason cannot get beyond judgments of probability, preference should be given to a revealed proposition, so long as it does not contradict the clear knowledge of reason:

> *Reason* is natural *revelation*, whereby the eternal Father of light, and Fountain of all knowledge, communicates to mankind that portion of truth which he has laid within the reach of their natural faculties. *Revelation* is natural *reason* enlarged by a new set of discoveries communicated by God immediately, which reason vouches the truth of, by the testimony and proofs it gives that they come from God. So that he that takes away reason to make way for revelation, puts out the light of both; and does much-what the same as if he would persuade a man to put out his eyes, the better to receive the remote light of an invisible star by a telescope.[10]

According to Locke, true revelation may be distinguished from the delusions of enthusiasm by the signs of divine authority which accompany it, and which are subject to the scrutiny of reason. The reference here is to outward, visible signs, such as miracles or prophecies. Personal revelations can only claim divine authority when they are in harmony with either reason or Holy Scripture. Reason and revelation are both God-given, and, when rightly understood, cannot contradict each other.

In deism, which flourished from the end of the seventeenth century to around the middle of the eighteenth, the sole authority of reason replaced Locke's synthesis of revelation and reason. Christianity should contain nothing against or beyond reason, and should thereby establish itself as valid from the beginning of creation.[11] The doctrine of the Person of Christ, and its significance for salvation, together with the doctrines of the Fall and original sin, were abandoned. Ethics was at the centre of things. Christianity was absorbed into natural religion.

In the debate over deism in the 1730s, various arguments against it were put forward. Its opponents sought to demonstrate either that the proposed natural religion was neither true nor genuine, or that it was dependent upon revealed religion. The most important opponents of deism based their case on Locke. They recognized natural religion as a phenomenon, but disputed its claim to be the final answer. Their arguments were drawn from what experience had to teach on human depravity, on the historical development of the world, and on the individuality of each human being. In the light of these things, revealed religion had a much better claim.

From the 1740s a more sceptical attitude towards reason developed. It was no longer seen as capable of mediating positive religious knowledge. To demand that faith must be based on rational grounds was to promote doubt, and to invalidate the call to simple, direct faith. Rational faith, in so far as it was at all possible, would be exposed to constant change and every new doubt. By contrast, the Bible demanded faith without proofs, and spoke of the witness of the Spirit.[12] The result was an irreconcilable conflict between faith and reason.

David Hume took scepticism even further, and thereby brought about the dissolution of deism. According to Hume, miracles – and the associated prophecies – are the only basis on which faith in Christianity is possible. However, he went on to argue that no evidence can make miracle-stories probable, or credible. He came to the conclusion that the original religion was polytheism. (Mono)theism had grown out of polytheism, but, among simple people, quickly slipped back into it. Thus the deistic concept of an original, rational, natural religion was refuted and defeated.

Returning to Fletcher, we nowhere find in his writings a lengthy, detailed treatment of these questions, but there are various brief observations on the relationship between experience and reason, between Scripture and experience, and between Scripture and reason. In his publications, Fletcher strung together a multitude of arguments, whether by going through the Bible and quoting texts, or by deducing general conclusions from his observations of human beings and the world, or by referring to tradition or simply using reason in an argumentative way. He liked to answer attacks by enumerating several, often unconnected, arguments. His writings as a whole offer plenty of evidence of this practice.

At many points Fletcher connected with Locke's basic principles. This is clear in his use of the criterion of experience. When Fletcher introduced experience as an argument, he was normally speaking of human experiences in general. In a work from the 1770s, for example, he referred to facts and to sound human understanding, the equivalent of a rational statement in the Lockian sense. However, when Fletcher spoke of the witness of the Spirit in the believer he was breaking out of this thought-world, and was making what, for his time, was a specifically Methodist reference to genuine Christian experience. So far as the relationship between Scripture and reason was concerned, reason, for Fletcher, was not – as for his contemporary Hume – the doubt-inducing critical faculty, but rather – as, again, with Locke – a form of reason capable of a synthesis with revelation, leading to positive statements on religious questions. Unlike Locke, Fletcher attached the greatest importance to revealed religion.[13] But, for him as for Locke, the Christian religion, i.e. revealed religion, was rational religion. Fletcher's use of the fourfold basis for theological statements, also to be found in Wesley, shows, in a limited way, that he was both influenced by and critical of the thinking of his time.

Faith and experience: 'A Letter to the Rev. Mr. Prothero, in Defence of Experimental Religion'[14]

Already in the first year of his appointment in Madeley, Fletcher was challenged to make his theological position clear. During the archdeacon's visitation in the summer of 1761, Prothero, a neighbouring clergyman, delivered a sermon, in the second part of which he attacked Fletcher's Methodist preaching. Another cleric gloatingly called on Fletcher to answer the accusation. Because not only church leaders, but also some members of the congregation, were present, Fletcher felt that it was his duty to let them know where he stood. He prepared a detailed letter, dated 25 July 1761, and sent it to Prothero. In it he invited Prothero to confirm the accuracy of the account, before the letter was made public to the parishioners. Prothero, however, did not reply. On 3 February 1972 Fletcher wrote again, politely but firmly, and requested a reply to his first letter. We have no knowledge of any answer from Prothero. What follows is an account of Fletcher's first letter to Prothero.[15]

Fletcher began his letter with some words of praise for the first part of the sermon, in which Prothero had defended revealed religion against deists and unbelievers, and their blind trust in reason. The second part of the sermon, which was directed against fanaticism ('enthusiasm'), was also necessary, said Fletcher. Prothero's intention could only be applauded. However, so far as the details were concerned, he, Fletcher, was obliged to ask whether the wheat had not been pulled up along with the tares. The charge of 'enthusiasm' was one of the stock arguments used against Methodist preaching.

Fletcher directed his first argument against the belief that virtue and morality constituted the way to salvation. He stressed justification by faith. In the second place, Fletcher questioned the capacity for good of the reason and the will, and expressed the judgment, based on Scripture and tradition, that the will of natural human beings is free only for evil. If a person came to acknowledge his sin and found new life, that was to be ascribed to the prevenient grace of God. If he remained in his fallen state, it was to be attributed to his own obduracy and impenitence. Thirdly, Fletcher took up the charge that the doctrines attacked by Prothero would unleash disorder and strife. Did that necessarily mean that they were false? If so, we would have to give up the Bible altogether, since it brings strife and unrest. Next, with some quotations from Scripture, Fletcher demonstrated the need for the new birth.

A fifth point, which occupied the rest of the letter, dealt with the central question of faith and experience. Fletcher drew a distinction between enthusiasm, which he rejected, and the experience of faith:

To set impulses as the standard of our faith, or rule of our conduct; ... to pretend to miraculous gifts, and those fruits of the Spirit which are not offered and promised to believers in all ages, or to boast of the graces which that Spirit produces in the heart of every child of God, when the fruits of the flesh appear in our life; this is downright enthusiasm: I detest it as well as you, sir . . . But is it consistent with the doctrine of our church to condemn and set aside all feelings in religion, and rank them with unaccountable impulses?[16]

Fletcher began his counter-attack, in which he aimed to demonstrate that faith also has an effect on the feelings, with a string of quotations from homilies and articles of faith. The Latin *sentire* and the French *sentir* could not, he said, be better rendered in English than by the verb 'to feel'. He made a comparison between natural and religious emotions, and then, by means of a whole series of quotations from Scripture, showed that persons in the Bible had religious feelings. The questions he asked were mainly rhetorical ones. With some irony, he put Prothero's words into the mouth of biblical characters:

> Certainly, sir, we must say that Jeremiah was a melancholy enthusiast almost falling into despair through the weakness of his nerves, and lowness of his spirits; or allow that there is such a thing as feeling godly sorrow in religion . . .[17]

Fletcher conceded that certain 'wondrous gifts' of God's Spirit were confined to the time of the apostles. But those were to be distinguished from the work of the Spirit in every believer's heart. This work was a characteristic of saving, justifying faith, which involves an opening up of the spiritual faculties by God, as a consequence of the new birth, and which stands in opposition to a mere speculative, human, historical faith. Fletcher supported his statements with quotations from Pascal, Chrysostom and Bradford (the last of these representing the Church of England), and followed them with extracts from the Augsburg Confession and a French confession:

> Thus, sir, I have endeavoured to prove, from the doctrine of our church, from reason and scripture, from the testimony of the best men, and of all the reformed churches, not only that feeling and rational Christianity are not incompatible, . . . but also that such feelings, so far from deserving to be called madness and enthusiasm, are nothing short of the actings of spiritual life, or, to speak scripturally, 'the power of God to every one that believeth' Rom. I.[18]

Faith is necessarily accompanied by the experience of faith, though of course Fletcher did not want this to be taken to mean that sincerity of devotion should be judged by the feelings a person might have. He frequently stressed, in biblical terms, the work of the Spirit of God in the human heart. This was the core of the biblical message, and if one laid it aside, all that remained would be pagan morality and good-naturedness in Christian dress: 'All that is spiritual and experimental in our bible and liturgy must be, of course, enthusiastic stuff, or, at best, words without meaning.'[19] Fletcher was unwilling to allow the biblical message to be understood in such a way.

The appropriation of salvation: Six Letters on the Spiritual Manifestation of the Son of God

Fletcher concerned himself a great deal with the proper understanding of faith and the efficacy of divine grace. In the summer of 1762 he asked Charles Wesley for advice. The reading of James Hervey's *Theron and Aspasio*, a convinced Calvinist work, had unsettled him. Is faith an imparting of divine power, a participation in the new life, an opening up of the soul's spiritual faculties, or does it consist simply in laying hold of the promises of the gospel, in hoping against hope? The latter seemed to Fletcher to be too little, and he wondered whether, if he were to be content with it, he would not be submitting to the wiles of Satan. This raised again Fletcher's basic question about conquering the power of sin. Presumably he soon received a satisfactory answer from Charles Wesley, since less than two months later he was describing the essence of faith as constant, heartfelt trust in the promises, and drawing a proper distinction between faith and its fruits.

Hervey's book, *Theron and Aspasio*, published in 1755, sparked off several controversies. In 1757 Robert Sandeman (b. 1718) published his letters on Hervey's work, which seemed to him to be too legalistic. He put forward the radical view that justifying faith was to be understood as a purely objective occurrence, a passive assent to the divine testimony to Jesus Christ, based on the supreme authority of Scripture and on election by God. This faith was in no way bound up with any subjective occurrence, any personal experience of salvation. He brought down the accusation of antinomianism on himself and on the so-called 'Glassites', who, under the leadership of John Glas (1695–1773), Sandeman's father-in-law, had broken away from the Church of Scotland. Sandeman's letters, together with a book by Glas, published around

1760, led to great confusion, and to the splitting off of Ingham's
societies in Yorkshire. Fletcher was following these developments
through his contacts with the Countess of Huntingdon, and he too
argued against Sandeman's letters. He wrote to the Countess in 1767:

> Some of our conversations upon the manifestation of the Son of Man
> to the heart, have led me into many an hours consideration. The Holy
> Ghost alone can clear up the points to pursue. Nevertheless I have
> found both comfort and profit in setting upon paper the reflections I
> have been enabled to make upon the mysterious subject; they have
> through mercy, set my soul more than ever against the rampant
> errors of Sandemanianism.[20]

Such were the origins of a work, first published after Fletcher's death,
which took the form of fictional letters: *Six Letters on the Spiritual
Manifestation of the Son of God*.[21] Fletcher's letters are not explicitly
aimed at Sandeman. They begin simply with 'Sir', but they refer to an
earlier personal conversation with an adherent of that school of
thought. Earlier biographers have been unaware of the connection
between these letters and Sandeman and the Glassites. Fletcher raised
again in these letters the question of the experiential nature of faith.[22]
Particular agreements with and differences from Calvinism thus emerge
more clearly.

> That the Son of God, for purposes worthy of his wisdom, manifests
> himself, sooner or later, to all his sincere followers, in a spiritual
> manner, which the world knows not of. The assertion appeared to
> you unscriptural, enthusiastical, and dangerous. What I then
> advanced to prove that it was *scriptural, rational* and of the *greatest
> importance*, made you desire I would write to you on the mysterious
> subject.[23]

In the six letters of his document Fletcher aimed to show that Christ
reveals himself in the heart of every believer.

In the first letter he spoke of the 'spiritual faculties' which are opened
up in every born-again soul and exercised by it. Fletcher pointed to the
collective testimony of Scripture, church and reason. From Scripture he
inferred that Adam had lost the experiential knowledge of God. All
descendants of Adam had lost the faculty for knowing godly things.
Only the person who was born from God would have his spiritual

faculties awakened and would be able to use them. Just as there were
bodily faculties or senses, so Scripture spoke of spiritual seeing, hearing,
smelling, tasting and feeling. To show that he was not misinterpreting
Scripture, Fletcher added the testimony of 'our own excellent church'. A
few thoughtful reflections in support of Fletcher's point of view rounded
off the argument.

In the second letter, Fletcher explained the nature of the revelation of
the Son of Man in the believer's heart. First of all he sought to protect
himself against the suspicion of enthusiasm or self-delusion. An initial
trust in God and his Word was a 'drawing by the Father', rather than
the 'revelation of the Son', because it was more in the nature of a help
towards coming to Christ, than of a divine union with him. But it was
much harder to explain what this manifestation actually was, than to
delimit it negatively. Where descriptive language failed, Fletcher turned
to pictures and comparisons. He compared the spiritual revelation of
the Son of Man with the situation of a person normally living on bread
and water who, hearing about honey and wine, but not being satisfied
with a description of these things, decided to taste them for himself:
doing so gave him a totally new experience and understanding. This
revelation was available to anyone who would honestly seek it. Its
intensity, however, could vary.

In the third letter, Fletcher went into the question as to 'why the Lord
should reveal himself to his children'. Fletcher drew a distinction, as he
did in his sermons, between extraordinary and ordinary forms of revelation, and warned against a hybrid version of the two. A consequence of
revelation was that human beings were humbled to the dust, and were
not able to delude themselves with false pride. Once again Fletcher
identified the conflict which he experienced most strongly in himself.
With a clear allusion to Sandeman's teaching, he issued a warning to
those who proudly claim that they can build on the bare Word of God,
without applying it to their heart:

He [the misguided confessor] thanks God he can now rest upon the
bare word, without an application of it to his heart; that is to say, he
can be fully satisfied with the letter without the Spirit, he can feed
upon the empty husks of notions and opinions, as if they were power
and life . . . We must have fresh food daily, and though we need not a
new Christ, we need, perpetually, new displays of his eternal love and
power. The Lord taught us this important lesson, by making the
manna he gave Israel in the wilderness to disappear every day, and

causing that which was not gathered fresh, to breed worms and stink.[24]

Fletcher's fourth letter began with a question which he himself found unanswerable: why do people experience divine revelation with such widely differing intensity, and at such different points in time? It was one of those questions which, for Fletcher, remained unanswered after his discussion with the Countess of Huntingdon. His arguments, which he described as provisional, displayed a way of thinking characteristic of Fletcher: they were marked by the notion of divine nurture and training. It was God who determined the time and degree of the revelation, in accordance with people's capacity and willingness to receive it. If a person lived and died without receiving any revelation whatever of the love and glory of the Redeemer, the reason for it was probably to be sought in the depths of God's righteousness and grace. In saying this, Fletcher was latching on to the thought of God's foreknowledge: because God knew that such persons would only abuse his condescension, for them there could be no revelation. The core of his argument is to be found in the fundamental statement:

> The Lord considers us as rational creatures, in a state of probation. Were he to indulge us with powerful, incessant, overwhelming discoveries of himself, he would rather violently force, than gently lead us to repentance and obedience.[25]

There is always the possibility of human resistance to God's revelation, as indeed of a falling away from faith. At this point it is evident that Fletcher shared the views of the Wesleyan Methodists. Over against the Calvinist tradition, he adopted leading ideas of the early Enlightenment.[26] He went on to describe the means by which God has promised to reveal himself to genuine seekers. In doing so he opposed any quietist waiting for enlightenment and redemption. God is not restricted to the means he has appointed, but they will normally mark the route by which people are led to salvation. Finally Fletcher warned against counting in any way upon one's own works:

> The sun shines not because we deserve it by undrawing our curtains, but because it is its nature. Jesus visits us, not because of any merit in our prayers &c. but for his own sake, because his truth and compassion fail not. Free grace opens the door of mercy, not to works and merit, but to want and misery.[27]

Whereas in his description of the revelation of Christ in the heart of the believer Fletcher came strikingly close to thoughts in the *Imitatio Christi*, when it came to describing revelations in the Old Testament (the subject of the fifth letter) he tended rather towards the thought of the incarnate mediator, so familiar in Calvinism.[28] After a string of quotations from the Old Testament, interpreted as a revelation of 'Jehovah Jesus', Fletcher gave his answer to the objection that God had only revealed himself directly in the Old Testament because at that time neither the gospel nor the Scriptures were known. In contradiction to Sandeman's position, Fletcher could say:

> If, because we have the letter of Scripture, we must be deprived of all immediate manifestations of Christ and his Spirit, we are great losers by that blessed book . . . O Lord, if because we have this blessed picture of thee [in the Scriptures], we must have no discovery of the glorious original, have compassion on us, take back thy precious book, and impart thy more precious self to us [as] thou didst to thy ancient people.[29]

The last sentence is not to be understood as a fanatical devaluation of Scripture, or as giving the final authority to experience instead of Scripture.[30] For Fletcher, experience had always to be measured against Scripture. However, over against Sandemanianism, he wished to stress that God's revelation comes about not through our intellectual grasp of biblical statements, but through the way they work upon us and in us.

The sixth letter, which was devoted to the New Testament evidence for the revelation of the Son of God, gave Fletcher the opportunity to strengthen his argument: although the Jews knew Jesus in the flesh, it was only through the revelation in their hearts that they came to a knowledge of his divine Sonship. After the ascension there was no diminution in the spiritual revelations of Christ in human hearts, but, rather, they increased, since it was the task of the Holy Spirit to reveal the Son. Thus, in conclusion, Fletcher gave expression to the promise which preoccupied him to the end of his life: the promise of the Holy Spirit.

Faith and works: a sermon on Romans 11.5, 6

On 18 April 1762 Fletcher preached a sermon on Romans 11.5, 6:
'Even so then at this present time also there is a remnant according to
the election of grace. And if by grace, then is it no more of works: otherwise grace is no more grace.'[31] Fletcher wrote his sermon in one of his
little notebooks, so as to make it accessible to the congregation. In the
course of the theological controversies of the 1770s, one of Fletcher's
opponents quoted some short extracts from this sermon, in order to
show that Fletcher had not at that earlier stage succumbed to the
erroneous views of John Wesley. Fletcher thereupon published the
whole sermon, together with a long list of notes, in his 'Checks'.[32] He
retorted that the former sermon contained in essence the same doctrine
that he was teaching now, in 1774. In 1762 Fletcher wished to convince
the pharisees and papists in his parish that salvation was not through
works of the law performed without faith, but only through faith in
Jesus Christ worked out in life. In support of his contention, Fletcher
quoted, in his original introduction to the sermon, from the Homilies of
the Church of England, and from sermons of Bishop Latimer, in order
to counter the impression

> that the Doctrine it contains was never preached in the Church of
> England, before the appearance of the *Methodists*; and to show that
> it is not only the Apostolic *Method* of preaching Christ, but also the
> *Method* which all our Reformers invariably followed.[33]

The actual sermon began with an introduction in which Fletcher
explained the context of the biblical passage from which the text of his
sermon was taken. The subject of the text is election by grace. The
exposition shows that in the early years of his ministry in Madeley
Fletcher was not dogged by the Calvinist doctrine of predestination. It
was never so much as mentioned:

> And even at this present time, says the Apostle, there is a remnant
> according to the election of grace; That is, There are some of them,
> who casting away their dependance on their own righteousness are
> numbered among the *elect*, according to that gracious *decree* of God
> in the covenant of grace, He that believeth shall be saved, &c. Mark
> XVI.16.[34]

What believing means in such contexts is the opposite of the false ideas about human achievement, which Fletcher will go on to criticize.

He divided his sermon into four parts. In the first part he described the nature of the covenant of works and the covenant of grace. The first covenant into which God entered with the human race was made with Adam in a state of innocence in paradise. This was the covenant of works, which required constant and total obedience. In Adam all human beings have broken this covenant:

> this root of original sin, produces in every man many actual iniquities, whereby, as we imitate Adam's rebellion, so we make the guilt of it our own, and fasten the curse attending that guilt upon our own souls.[35]

In this natural condition human beings stand under the curse of the covenant of works, which they have broken. They remain in this pitiable state until they are awakened by divine grace, either through the preaching of the gospel or by some other means. They then recognize their fallen state. After many unfruitful attempts to avert the curse by fulfilling the law, they come to despair of their wretched good works, and begin to seek the way which God, of his free grace, has opened up for lost sinners in Jesus Christ. This is the new covenant of grace, the gospel.[36]

The covenant of the gospel is open to everyone, thanks to the sacrificial death of Jesus Christ, by which he has taken upon himself the punishment due to us, and thanks to the perfect obedience of Jesus, by which he has fulfilled the first covenant. The righteousness of Jesus Christ is recognized by God in place of our own, when we are united to Christ by God-given faith, that is to say, when, by the Spirit of God, we have attained conviction of our sins, and awareness of the righteousness of Christ. The believer receives the power to produce fruits of faith, truly to perform good works. This will be dealt with in the third part of the sermon.

In the second part, Fletcher showed that only faith, the covenant of grace, can lead us along the way to salvation. He quoted passages from Scripture, and from the articles of faith and the liturgy of the Church of England. Yet again he stressed the incompatibility of the two covenants. It would not do, he argued, to perform good works with the idea that God would then overlook persistent sins. Here Fletcher's own conversion experience was reflected:

According to the imaginary, mixed covenant of salvation by our own good works mended, with Christ's merits: man has the FIRST share of the glory; Christ has only man's leavings . . . But by the gospel all is set in a most beautiful order, and exquisite harmony. The merits and sufferings of Christ, the Redeemer of the world, are the only *meritorious cause* of salvation. The glory is entirely ascribed to him . . . Thus, Christ alone *merits*, faith alone *apprehends*, and good works alone *evidence* salvation.[37]

In the third part Fletcher sought to point out the foolishness and injustice of those who complained that he preached against good works. Again he referred to Bible passages and the formularies of the Church of England. He listed three kinds of good works performed by the believer: works of piety towards God; works of love towards one's neighbour; works of self-denial towards oneself. He insisted that he had always preached on these things. In answer to the objection that good works were not necessary, since we could not gain heaven with them, Fletcher used a comparison:

If I say, that eating will never make me immortal, that drinking will never turn me into an angel, and that doing my work will never take me to the third heaven; do I so much as hint that eating is useless, drinking of no service, and doing my business unprofitable? O how does prejudice blind even men of reason and religion![38]

In the fourth part of the sermon Fletcher argued yet again that good works cannot earn salvation, and showed why, nevertheless, they are not a matter of indifference. Both these points had already been dealt with, but in his conclusion Fletcher wanted to explain them once more. He wanted to safeguard the doctrine of justification over against pharisaic false doctrine (a mixture of faith and works) and antinomian false doctrine (faith without works). Good works are necessary as a sign of our obedience, gratitude and love towards God, as a sign of the fruit of our faith towards our neighbour, as well as for the strengthening and growth of our faith itself.[39] Good works will be rewarded in heaven:

To understand this we must remember, that, according to the gospel and our liturgy, God *opens the kingdom of heaven to all believers. Faith alone* when it *works* by *love* takes us to heaven: But as there are stars of different magnitude in the material heaven, so also in the spiritual.[40]

Fletcher formulated his doctrine of justification plainly and clearly. In 1774 he extended his sermon with parentheses and footnotes, in order to guard against any possible misunderstandings. However, its basic assertions remained unaltered. Fletcher held resolutely to his belief that salvation was a gift of God's grace, but his arguments were in no way predestinarian. He was already concerned, in 1762, to exclude any antinomian misunderstanding of the doctrine of grace. Good works are necessary as the fruits of faith – but only that.[41]

The Fall and its consequences: 'A Dialogue between a Minister and one of his Parishioners on Man's Depravity and Danger in his Natural State'

> Six dialogues upon these subjects – The Doctrine of the fall – Salv. by faith alone – The new birth – The Inspiration of the Spirit. The necessity of feeling his operations – The assurance of salvation. Each point proved by scripture, reason, experience, & the authority of the Church, with the most common objections answer'd. The second part would contain an other set of Dialogues between the minister and other Parishioners of different Characters. An infidel 2 a formalist 3 a moralist 4 a worldling 5 a railer at godly ministers & people. with proper answers to their respective objections,[42]

wrote Fletcher to John Wesley in 1766, describing the plan of his work. He wanted to write one of these Dialogues as a sample, and submit it to Wesley. A partial treatment of the first subject was produced, containing three out of seven subsections. The sample had the title 'A Dialogue between a Minister and one of his Parishioners, on Man's Depravity and Danger in his Natural State'.[43] It was to be circulated, and each reader was asked to write his corrections in the margin of the manuscript. Fletcher was concerned about the length of the document, since (as he put it in the foreword) 'a large book is a large evil'. The sample remained a fragment.

The first part of Fletcher's document described the first meeting between the parishioner and the minister. The parishioner told the minister that the doctrine of the fallen state of natural man, as he heard it in church, seemed to him false and dangerous. He would be ready to be convinced of the truth of it, if the minister could demonstrate it on the fourfold authority of Scripture, reason, experience and the tradition of the Church:

Reason and experience will convince a candid deist; and the declarations of our church, supported by revelation, will silence the objections of an honest churchman: you may therefore assure yourself,
that if your doctrine is confirmed by this four-fold authority, I shall
oppose it no more.[44]

In the second part of his document Fletcher sought to produce evidence from Scripture. In doing so he needed not only to quote biblical
passages, but also to establish that his interpretation was correct. He
stressed the enormity and the significance of Adam's sin. By his rebellion
against God, his lack of faith and his disobedience,[45] Adam destroyed
the original, moral divine likeness in the human race. He was punished
with spiritual death, which brought the double death – temporal and
eternal – in its train. After the Fall there still remained some traces of the
natural likeness, in understanding, will and the immortality of the soul.
The whole creation was affected by the Fall, but especially the descendants of Adam. Fletcher understood the transmission of sin to Adam's
descendants in a Traducianist way:[46]

Having infected their whole nature [the nature of the first parents], it
was impossible that they should not infect their remotest posterity,
which they not only represented, as kings do their subjects, but also
seminally contained, as an acorn contains all the future oaks that may
grow from it.[47]

Even after the Flood it held true: the imagination of man's heart is evil
from his youth. The unmistakable words of the prophets about the
fallen state of humanity are to be applied not only to the heathen but to
the whole human race. Jesus Christ is the only exception. Even newborn
children are sinful by their very nature. To the question, how it could be
that natural human beings were always sinning, the minister replied:
'He is not always doing what is evil, but the uninterrupted depravity of
his heart corrupts those actions which otherwise are good or indifferent
in themselves; therefore all that he does is sin.'[48] The conversation
ended, in the second part, with the confirmation that God in Christ
would be judge of the world, and every transgression of his law would
be punished, not just gross and obvious evil deeds such as murder and
manslaughter. There would then be no place to which one could flee
from the terrible judgment, save only the shelter of the Redeemer's
wings.

In the third part of the dialogue the parishioner admitted that he could not contradict the evidence from Scripture, but he asked whether understanding and revelation were in agreement at this point, since many people said that the doctrine of original sin was original nonsense. The minister replied: '. . . If the oracles of God maintain this doctrine, reason is not against it. Sound reason is for it, as I hope to prove by a variety of rational arguments.'[49] By beginning in this way, the discussion is already pointing to a clearer definition of the relationship between Scripture and reason. The final authority is the Word of God, which is not contrary to reason. However, the fact that the adjective 'sound' may be applied to the intellect, indicates that a person can direct his intellect against God and his Word. On the other hand, when the intellect is sound, and not led by any evil intention, it will confirm the truth of revelation. In the strict sense, Fletcher cannot, and does not wish to, derive any direct evidence of human sinfulness from reason. But he maintained that reason led to the point where the statements of Scripture would give a reasonable explanation of what otherwise would remain inexplicable. The minister gives as an example the painful birth of children, their wasting away, and their early death. A gracious God could not allow such things to happen, if our nature were not already sinful.

This part of the dialogue too concludes with extensive quotations from Scripture. First it is established, on the basis of rational observation as well as from Scripture, that the whole of creation, and not just the human race, is affected by Adam's Fall. From people's depraved tendencies and evil deeds we can go back to their root, which is sinful human nature. In this connection a recurring question is tackled. In several places it is pointed out that, since human beings do not understand everything on earth, we cannot be expected to know the answers to all the objections that may be raised. The minister therefore can only try to answer when he is in a position to do so. So, for example, to the objection that since God must have foreseen the sin of Adam, he could have prevented it, the answer is given:

> That God permitted sin to enter into the world, we know by sad experience; and that he does all things in wisdom, we are no less certain: therefore we are sure that wisdom subscribed the awful permission; and till he unfold[s] to us the mysteries of his providence, a modest inquirer will, I apprehend, be satisfied with the following reflections . . .[50]

In conclusion, in this third part too the discussion turns to the subject of hell and eternal punishment. The parishioner raises the objection: 'I do not wonder if some of our neighbours believe, on that account, that hell is an engine contrived by crafty priests and rulers to keep the superstitious and vulgar in awe.'[51] It was the sort of objection raised by deists and freethinkers. In reply the minister says, among other things, that God in himself is holiness and bliss, whereas the unrepentant sinner is just the opposite. Therefore the sinner is in an unholy, unblissful, i.e. wretched condition. Hell is nothing else but total wretchedness. Further: 'The dread of various torments after death hath been in all ages the strongest bulwark against the overflowings of secret ungodliness. The world cannot be ruled without his fear.'[52] The minister goes on to point out that everyone who calls Christ his redeemer acknowledges thereby that he is in need of redemption.

Fletcher had intended, in a fourth part, to answer the objections of self-righteous moralists and formalists; in a fifth to challenge their conscience and their experience; in a sixth to present the witness of the church; and in a seventh to answer further objections and give further guidance. These later parts were never produced. It is evident from Fletcher's plan, however, that he was greatly concerned to defend and expound the doctrine of sin as comprehensively as possible. He continued to work intensively on this theme, and in 1772 published a fully revised work on the doctrine of sin.

Basic preoccupations and lines of development in Fletcher's theology in the 1770s

In the first of his works which we discussed, Fletcher defended the experiential dimension of Christian faith, with reference to the inner witness of the Spirit in the heart of the believer, against the charge of 'enthusiasm' (fanaticism). In doing so, he stressed the rational nature of his own interpretation. The second work also dealt with the experiential dimension of faith, but now under the strongly mystical conception of a revelation of the Son of God in the heart of the believer. In the sermon discussed above, Fletcher clearly explained the character of salvation as an operation of divine grace, without any recourse to the Calvinist doctrine of predestination, and with an emphasis on good works as necessary fruits of faith. In the last of the four works discussed, the doctrine of sin was the central issue. It was on this theme, and in what he had to say about the inner witness of the Spirit, that Fletcher came closest to the thinking of Paul and Calvin. On the other hand, it should not be overlooked that in his understanding of the earthly existence of human beings as a sphere of testing and probation, as well as in his emphasis on promise and punishment, he was taking up early-Enlightenment themes.

This latter influence was also present in a concept which was not specifically dealt with in any particular work, but which is frequently to be found in the letters: the evidence of the *providence of God*. Statements about God's providence could already be found in the letters Fletcher wrote before his conversion, where he could attribute to divine providence the fact that he had been protected in life-threatening situations. It was, however, only in the context of crisis situations in life that he spoke in this way. He did not, for example, refer to God's providence in the matter of the choice of a family in which he could serve as resident tutor. His profound experience of sin and grace then changed his outlook. He no longer spoke of the divine providence only in crisis situations, but also in the most diverse issues and decisions of daily life. The fact that he was Vicar of Madeley was for him an infallible sign of the leading of the providence of God. In a pastoral letter to Miss Hatton, who had recovered from a first bout of illness, Fletcher wrote (alluding to a saying of Jesus in the Bible):

> If a sparrow falleth not to the ground, nor a hair from our head, without our heavenly Father's leave, it is certain, that higher circumstances of our life are planned by the wise and gracious Governor of all things. This kind of faith in providence, I find of indispensable necessity to go calmly through life, and I think too, through death also.[53]

The biblical text which says that not even a sparrow can fall to earth without our heavenly Father's involvement became the central text for Fletcher's observations on the providence of God, which he linked closely with the thought of godly training.

According to Fletcher, it is only faith in providence which makes it possible, even amid disappointments and in the face of illness and death, to trust that God turns all things to good – that, for example, disappointments only occur to prevent greater ones, or to bring about a greater blessing. This was not something that could be inferred from the course of events, but was an affirmation of the hope springing from faith. The importance which Fletcher attached to providence is clear from his statement that a person who follows the guidance of faith, in the measure given to him, and of providence, will be led in the right way. His faith in God's providence so encompassed all human activities that developments and conditions of human origin fell completely outside his range of vision. The questionable consequences of such an understanding are, from a modern standpoint, most clearly to be seen in the social field. Thus, for example, he could write to the poor in his parish, who had formed themselves into a society:

> I thank God, none of you are rich in the things of this world . . . May you know the happiness attending your state. It is a mercy to be driven to the throne of grace, even by bodily want, and to live in dependance on divine mercy for a morsel of bread.[54]

This is the only statement we have from Fletcher in the 1760s on the subject of poverty. The fact that in this early period he did not yet comment on social questions is attributable to his understanding of the providence of God. This in no way prevented him from seeking to relieve poverty in his parish, so far as it lay within his power. But his involvement in the social field in the 1760s was limited to charitable activity.

A further concern which, like the last, is mainly to be found in the letters, goes back to Fletcher's personal struggles with faith, and demonstrates to what extent those struggles left their stamp both on his approach to theological problems and on his theological development. At the start of his ministry in Madeley, Fletcher expressed the hope that at least after ten years he would be able to say: 'I am nothing – I have nothing – I can do nothing.'[55] This longing to realize his own nothingness grew out of his view of himself as a pharisee, whose whole being rebelled against God in haughty arrogance:

> . . . the leaven of the Pharisees sticks closer to me than to anybody else. My God humbles me daily, by making me see and feel that in me dwelleth no good thing, but the very reverse of all that is good. On Sunday evening, when the poor labours of the day are over, I have a more pungent sense of this than all the rest of the week. O what would I then give for the wings of a dove to fly from myself and be at rest.[56]

The wish to be nothing can find expression in the mystical concept of absorption into God, casting oneself from moment to moment into the 'bottomless abyss of divine faithfulness and mercy', as he once expressed it in words reminiscent of Lady Huntingdon.[57] The Countess's influence is recognizable in such turns of phrase. However, similar statements are to be found in letters to other addressees, though not to John and Charles Wesley. In writing to them Fletcher kept to the Pauline terminology of 'dying to oneself'. He corrected himself along these lines in one of his letters to Miss Hatton: 'I apprehend that an important step towards that conformity, is to become *nothing*; or rather to be, with St. Paul, to become in our own eyes *the chief of sinners*, and the *least of saints*.'[58] Over and over again we find the desire to cast himself upon the Lord, to claim no independent standing of his own. In his letters to the Countess this was expressed occasionally in another mystical concept, in the desire to sink into the depths of the divine love. In his letters to other addressees in the latter part of the 1760s he expressed himself more strongly in language influenced by Paul. In so doing he took up the biblical perception that the way to life leads through death, without incurring the danger of the dissolution of the personality. The recognition of his own nothingness was now expressed less in terms of sinking into the divine love, and more and more in terms of the expectation of fulfilment through the Holy Spirit:[59]

> Well, My Lady, if these bodies must fall a sacrifice to death and sin, we must in the strength of him that is the resurrection & the life, sell our lives as dear as we can, & do death & sin as much mischief as heavenly POWER will enable us. – Power from on high is what I want still. I blush to take up the pen to complain still to your Ladyship of my want of Power; I would lay it by, and hide my self, till I can testify an abiding day of pentecost. My unbelief runs some time so high that I doubt whether it will come before my dying day.[60]

We have already come across repeated references to the expectation of being *filled with the Holy Spirit*. This came later to be linked with an understanding of revelation in salvation history, the beginnings of which are discernible in the *Six Letters on the Spiritual Manifestation of the Son of God*. The first clear statements of it are to be found in a letter of 1770.[61] In the writings of the 1770s and 1780s, the different 'dispensations', as Fletcher called them, by which God's dealings with the human race are unfolded in the drama of salvation history, will be of central significance.

10

Fletcher as a Clergyman of the
Church of England

Swiss-born Fletcher saw himself as committed to the Church of England, its doctrine and its liturgy. He had to face up to accusations that he was a Methodist from opponents within the church. He also had to contend with Baptists, Quakers and Catholics, who made up about a quarter of the population of his parish. He was associated with the itinerant Methodist preachers in Shropshire, and with national and regional attempts to form unions of Anglican clergy who were close to Methodism. Fletcher's understanding of his role as a clergyman of the Church of England developed amid the tensions of the relationship between the state church and the Methodist movement within it.

Response to opposition within the church

In his early years in Madeley, Fletcher aroused opposition within the church from two sides: from his brothers in the Anglican ministry, and from members of his parish. From his response to their attacks, the main features of his position on the doctrine, ecclesiastical law and liturgy of the Church of England become clear.

During the first visitation by the diocesan archdeacon in 1761, a neighbouring clergyman delivered a sermon directed against Fletcher's preaching. Fletcher's written response was described in the last chapter. In it he held firmly to Holy Scripture and to the church's homilies and articles of faith. He was convinced that his preaching was in accordance with the church's doctrine, and he saw no need to distance himself in any way from its traditional teaching. From the way in which he refers to 'our' homilies and 'our' articles it is clear how strongly he felt himself to be an integral part of the church's ministry.

In his own parish Fletcher aroused opposition from some respected persons who wanted to charge him with contravening the 'Conventicle

Act'.[1] At the height of the controversy Fletcher wrote a letter for the attention of the bishop, but this letter has not been preserved. Fletcher later defined the basis of his preaching activity in this way: God's command to preach the gospel stood above every human regulation, and before the bishop had 'shackled' him with canon law, that same bishop had charged him, at his ordination, to seek out Christ's lost sheep.[2] Fletcher's basic argument is clear: the call to mission was part of the gospel, and he was convinced that this mission had also been entrusted to him by the church. There was no conflict between the word of Scripture and his basic commissioning by the church. But if an individual canon seemed to point in another direction, then it must be seen in relation to the commission as a whole, which was to be regarded as the superior norm. Thus Fletcher justified his apparently irregular behaviour by a critical scrutiny of ecclesiastical law.

In his use of *The Book of Common Prayer*, Fletcher seems, so far as our knowledge of it goes, to have adhered very strictly to the prescribed liturgy.[3] In the cover in which he kept his little notebooks of sermon outlines, he had written out some prayers which, presumably, he used regularly when preaching, both in Madeley and on his travels. These prayers agree almost word for word with those officially prescribed by the church. In his preaching activity, therefore, Fletcher made use of the written prayers of the church, and did not replace them with the kind of free prayer which was practised, for example, in the class meetings of the Methodist societies. The cover of the sermon booklets contains, among other things, two of the six altar prayers from *The Book of Common Prayer* which were read after the Lord's Supper, as well as a petitionary prayer which is in close verbal agreement with Canon 55. This latter prayer was used partly before and partly after the sermon in the post-Reformation period, but in Fletcher's day it was scarcely used at all. When Fletcher's Madeley congregation heard this prayer, or when he used it outside the worship of the church while preaching at Methodist gatherings, he was declaring himself a convinced, not to say high church, Anglican. However, his concern over the proper interpretation of some particular statements in the liturgy, on such questions as baptismal regeneration or hope for the dead, makes it plain that his attachment to the Church of England did not involve unthinking acceptance of all that church's traditions.[4]

When Fletcher appealed to the tradition of the Church of England, it was often in opposition to the church in its existing form. He would on no account abandon his characteristically Methodist convictions. His

radical understanding of the message of the Bible led him, especially in
the early 1760s, to be harshly critical of the clergy. At a meeting of
clergy in his garden, in the summer of 1761, he expounded Jeremiah
6.13f., and drew some parallels with the current state of the church.
There were many, he said, who preached the gospel, without knowing
which wounds it was meant to heal; there were many who spoke peace
to their soul, before they had received from God the peace which passes
all understanding. Bishop Latimer had uttered the same warnings in his
day, which had been a high point in the history of the church.[5] Fletcher's
attachment to the Church of England in no way excluded a critical
approach to it. On the contrary, it demanded such an approach.

Controversy with the Baptists

The first challenge from a group outside the church in Madeley came
from the side of the Baptists. The Baptists shared the fate of all dissenting groups. In the first half of the eighteenth century they declined
substantially. But in the 1760s and 1770s, influenced by the strong
Methodist movement, they began again to show signs of growth –
growth which was at its strongest at the beginning of the nineteenth
century. In the 1850s there must have been around two hundred Baptist
congregations in England, with some ten thousand members.[6] We do
not know how old or how big the Baptist congregation in Madeley may
have been. However, we have the impression of an active congregation,
which had been influenced by Methodism both in the style of preaching
and in the content of some of its utterances.

Around the turn of the year 1761/62 Fletcher was sent a ninety-page
document which was full of personal opinions and fallacies. Out of
concern for his society, he responded to the first twenty pages. He had
little hope of convincing the Baptists, however, since they were too
vehement and conceited to pay attention either to reason or to the
Scriptures. In their case Fletcher did not draw his arguments from the
tradition of the church, since he wanted to make his case to the Baptists
on grounds which they themselves could accept. Barely two years later
he again took up his pen to defend himself against a further attack from
the Baptists. Neither of his two replies is extant.[7] Although we have no
trace of the content of Fletcher's argument with the Baptists, the form
his reaction took is instructive. He answered their questions in writing.
He wrote a little book in which he set down his counter-arguments. In

other controversies too he followed the same procedure. Where such handwritten booklets exist, they always include a request to the reader to read the book as quickly as possible and then pass it on. Since the societies formed by Fletcher were most strongly affected by the controversies, these answers of his in booklet form must have been intended primarily for this circle. An example of such an answer is available from his controversy with the Quakers. Although the argument with the Quakers is better attested in the sources, the conflict provoked by the Baptists was the more intense.

Relations with the Quakers

Towards the end of the seventeenth century the Quakers were quite numerous. In the course of the eighteenth century, however, the number of members fell by about a half. The Quakers can be counted among the so-called 'old Dissenters', who underwent no change and received no impetus from the Methodist movement.[8] In and around Madeley, however, they occupied influential positions. The Darby family had built up Coalbrookdale, possessed a large landed property in Madeley, and was involved in wider partnerships in the coal and iron industries. Abiah Darby, the wife of Abraham Darby II, gave an account in her diary of her meetings with Fletcher.[9] The first entry was made as early as 20 January 1761. Soon after taking up his appointment in Madeley, Fletcher visited the Quakers for the first time. He asked them questions about their principles. They lent him some books. In the summer of 1762 Abiah Darby wrote a letter to Fletcher in which, among other things, she acknowledged that, under the hand of the Lord, he was performing a good service for the betterment of the people in his parish. She conceded that Fletcher was polite, even when their opinions differed. In November 1764 she attended – not for the first time – one of Fletcher's meetings: '. . . A great weight came upon me to go to the Meeting of the Priest of this Parish and his followers . . . Where I had been before at considerable distances of time.'[10] The result was an argument which lasted for many hours. The course and content of this discussion have been passed on to us by Fletcher in a reply he wrote and circulated in his parish, and especially to the societies concerned.[11]

Fletcher began his written response with a letter to Mrs Darby. It was the question of truth which had led him to engage in this dispute. By giving his answer in written form he wished to clear up the matter once and for all. In an introduction to his document, Fletcher described the immediate occasion of the objections which Mrs Darby had now raised for the third time. In consequence, he had called a meeting of parishioners on 22 November 1764. He had announced beforehand his intention to answer complaints made by Dissenters and Unbelievers against the Church of England. When Mrs Darby arrived, he had been engaged in expounding and defending the doctrine of the Trinity as it is contained in the Athanasian Creed, one of the three major confessions of the early church. Thereupon she had presented an exposition of the Trinity, protesting, however, to Fletcher's gathering, first that they ought to be more concerned with questions of practical duty than with such debates about the Trinity, and secondly that the Athanasian Creed was full of false statements about the Godhead. From Fletcher's description of the way the argument developed, it appears that Mrs Darby constantly raised objections couched in general terms, but, when questioned, was unable to substantiate them.

Fletcher felt strongly that it was his duty to defend the doctrine of the church against dissidents and unbelievers. The first two chapters of his written reply to Mrs Darby were devoted to the exposition of the Athanasian Creed. Further chapters dealt with matters in dispute between the Quakers and the tradition of the church: chapters three and four were concerned with the question whether both the written and the spoken word could be called 'the Word of God'; in chapter five various questions raised by Mrs Darby were discussed, especially concerning baptism and the Lord's Supper; and in chapter six Fletcher tried to demonstrate the basic error of the Quakers in relation to the means and forms under which God works. Fletcher based his argument mainly on biblical quotations. However, he also referred to the experience of contemporaries, and, on particular points, to the tradition of the ancient church as well. In many cases arguments were disposed of by reason alone, that is, by an exposition of their inner inconsistency.

At the end of the whole document Fletcher declared his readiness to change anything he might have misrepresented, and invited Mrs Darby to do the same. He wrote:

I hope the Reader by this Time laments with me the *bad* use that Mrs. Darby makes of a *Good* Understanding – How much better were it for her and [us] all, if instead of Quibbling & wresting the scriptures as these Sheets show she hath done, she wou'd Second my endeavours in promoting a reformation of Essentials in the parish with respect to Principles & manners.[12]

This seems to have brought to an end the controversy with the Quakers and their teaching. When Lady Huntingdon visited Fletcher in Madeley in 1767, Abiah Darby put her carriage at the Countess's disposal for the journey, and, at the Countess's request, paid her a visit. It seems that by this time generally friendly relations existed between Mrs Darby and Fletcher, with each recognizing the other's commitment in matters of practical piety.

Polemic against the Roman Catholics

Of quite another kind was Fletcher's controversy with the Roman Catholic Church, which was also represented in Madeley, and whose members Fletcher described as 'papists'. For Fletcher at that time the word 'catholic' always had the basic meaning of ecumenical-universal. The percentage of Catholics in the population of England was at first small, with a tendency to decline. However, towards the end of the eighteenth century there was a massive increase in the Catholic population. This was mainly a consequence of the influx of Irish Catholics, who came as a welcome workforce during the period of industrial expansion. However, there were already some Catholics in Madeley when Fletcher began his ministry there. Individual Catholics in Madeley Wood stirred up and spearheaded resistance to Fletcher. Fletcher's attitude towards the Roman Catholic Church was unequivocal: when, at the end of the 1760s, the 'papists' opened a church in Madeley, and two members of his congregation went over to Roman Catholicism, this is what Fletcher had to say on the subject:

> The Priest at Madeley is going to open his mass-house, and I have declared war on that account last Sunday, and propose to strip the Whore of Babylon and expose her nakedness to morrow. All the Papists are in a great ferment, and they have held meetings to consult on the occasion. One of their bloody bullies came to 'pick up', as he said, a quarrel with me, and what would have been the consequence had not I providentially had company with me, I know not. How far more their rage may be kindled to morrow I don't know.[13]

One of the leaders of the Catholics in this conflict seems to have been a person by the name of Slaughter, who in 1762 had been unsuccessfully sued by Fletcher in the ecclesiastical court, on the grounds of his conduct.

Among Fletcher's sermon outlines there is an exposition of I Timothy 4.1–3, in which he denounced all the errors and all the false teachings of the Catholic Church down the centuries. The Roman Catholic Church is identified with the figure representing the eschatological temptation to fall away from the true doctrine of Christ.[14] Fletcher's attitude to Roman Catholicism did, in fact, change over the course of the years. When he published a twelve-year-old sermon in 1774, he abandoned the identification of the double way of the pharisees (i.e. salvation by faith and works) with the 'papist way', and added a note to say that while it was true that the papists often fell into that error, it was also true that many had taught and lived scripturally: 'I would no more be a bitter Protestant, damning all the Papists in a lump.'[15]

Connections with the Wesleyan itinerant preachers in Shropshire

Fletcher's self-understanding as an Anglican can be more clearly understood in the light of his attitude towards the Methodist movement within the church, and particularly in his reaction to the first invitations to Methodist itinerant preachers. As a rule, the preachers did not begin their work in a new place on their own initiative. They waited for an invitation, and then decided either to accept or reject the invitation. When Fletcher came to Madeley, the Methodist members under Wesley's leadership numbered about twenty thousand. At that time there were no Methodist societies either in Fletcher's parish, or in the surrounding area. Fletcher, however, encouraged the formation of religious societies, and placed them under his own leadership.[16] In July 1764 John Wesley visited Madeley and Shrewsbury for the first time. In August 1764 Mather, one of Wesley's travelling preachers, received an invitation to 'Coalpit Bank', later known as Ketley Bank, but he was unwilling to follow it up without Fletcher's agreement. Fletcher was cautious. He withheld his consent, as he himself said, on the pretext that Hatton and he had already taken over this place, which was situated between their two parishes. Behind his caution lay the hope that the co-operation which had come about between himself and Hatton might be strengthened, but also – and especially – the fear that the appearance of Mather might cause an uproar, and damage the work that had already been done. Fletcher's fear may have had something to do with his knowledge of Mather from the latter's previous activities in the vicinity of Shrewsbury. He knew that for a time Mather had counted himself among the 'perfect', and had gathered around him a group of similarly minded people who had created a stir in the surrounding area.[17]

In the following year, 1765, for the first time, Wesley appointed Alexander Mather and William Minethorp as travelling preachers for Shropshire. It is not known whether he had spoken to Fletcher before doing so. When Mather took up his work in Shropshire in 1765, Fletcher's society in Wellington issued an invitation to him without Fletcher's knowledge. Fletcher allowed him to come, but expressed the hope that no damage would result from his visit. Presumably this first visit proved positive, as Fletcher had hoped, since the letter he wrote to Mather shortly afterwards invited him to share in a very precisely defined co-operative ministry. Fletcher had overcome his original reservations about Mather. He did not yet, however, go so far as to describe Mather's ministry as better and more effective than his own.[18] The common ground on which both the Methodist preacher Mather and the Anglican clergyman Fletcher based their actions was the promise of God's love in Jesus. Fletcher's invitation to Mather to work with him, arose, surprisingly, not from the fact that some day in heaven there would be no division between them, but because on earth here below he knew only one heaven: the love of Jesus. Fletcher wished thereby to avert any danger of competition. He issued an invitation which also affected the societies led by him in and around Madeley. He did not see the Methodists as another 'party', as an organization which would work against the Church of England. However, he drew a clear distinction between the societies he himself had built up in Ketley Bank (Wellington), Coalbrookdale, etc., where he welcomed an *occasional* visit from Mather or Minethorp, and the society in Trench (Wormbridge), which lay outside the jurisdiction of an English bishop, and where he desired visits from the Methodist preachers *as often as possible*.

Fletcher saw himself as deeply committed to the aims and objectives of the Methodist movement. But his letter did not amount to an integration of the societies or to a handing over of his societies to Wesley's travelling preachers. His letter had a dual purpose. On the one hand he wanted to let Wesley's travelling preachers know that they were welcome, and that they should carry on with their work in this new area, and to dispel in advance any antagonism, from his side or from theirs, by pointing to the task they held in common. On the other hand he wanted to prevent any misbehaviour on the part of the Wesleyan preachers, so as to avoid unnecessary conflict. Generally speaking, there was, among the people as well as among the clergy, a certain resistance to the intrusion of the Methodist preachers. The fact that we hear little of it in Fletcher's letters points to a relatively peaceful acceptance of them.[19]

Attempts to form unions, at national and regional level, of Anglican clergymen close to Methodism

Fletcher also cultivated contacts with like-minded clergymen of the Church of England. In the 1760s there were associations of such people both at regional and national level. The problems which arose in this area illustrate how Fletcher could see himself as Methodist and Anglican at one and the same time. There were at that stage about fifty ordained clergy of the Church of England who regarded themselves as sharing Methodist convictions. Most of them were influenced by Calvinism, and belonged more to the circle around Lady Huntingdon and Whitefield than to John Wesley. Soon after taking up his appointment in Madeley, Fletcher, who also maintained close contact with the Countess, got in touch with the 'gospel ministers', or 'evangelical clergy', as they called themselves.

In August 1761 he went to West Bromwich to visit Edward Stilling-fleet, who was chaplain to Lord Dartmouth. The Earl of Dartmouth was one of the politically very influential patrons of the Methodist cause. Towards the end of the 1760s he held high ministerial posts in the government. Fletcher invited Stillingfleet and his vicar, William Jesse, to Madeley, to preach from his pulpit. Stillingfleet's preaching, while Methodist in content, was strictly Anglican in its form. He hesitated to accept the invitation, because, according to Fletcher, he was afraid of behaving like a Methodist. At issue was the question of the authority of the church's statutes. In the event neither Stillingfleet nor Jesse came to Madeley. Fletcher then decided to visit Walter Sellon. Sellon had originally been a Wesleyan travelling preacher, then a teacher at Wesley's Kingswood School, and with the support of Lady Huntingdon had received episcopal ordination. He remained connected with John Wesley, who repeatedly urged him to leave his parish and work among the Wesleyan Methodists. We do not know when Fletcher undertook his journey to visit Sellon. However, in the summer of 1763, to Fletcher's great joy, Sellon came to Madeley. In June 1763 Fletcher had also received a visit from Mould and Riland, both of whom preached for him. The attempt at a pulpit exchange with Berridge in 1765 came to nothing, because of Berridge's resistance to the idea.

John Wesley had been pursuing for some time the plan of forming a union of evangelically minded clergy of the Church of England. Most of them had little contact with one another. A union would bring them closer together, enable them to join forces, and might become a nucleus for the renewal of the whole Church of England. A conversation with Lady Huntingdon strengthened him in this idea, and on 19/20 April 1764 he set out his proposals in a lengthy letter. He wrote two copies of the letter, and sent them to the Earl of Dartmouth and the Countess of Huntingdon.[20] In the letter Wesley traced the history of the Methodist movement, and lamented the loss which had come about through the withdrawal of ordained clergymen. The work had increased but so too had disunity. He listed around forty clergymen whom he had in mind for forming a union, among them Fletcher and people Fletcher knew as a result of his visits – Stillingfleet, Jesse, John Riland, Sellon and Berridge. The union would include all ministers who could assent to the following three essential points of doctrine: original sin, justification by faith, holiness of heart and life. Wesley's plan of union, however, required no other doctrinal agreement, and no agreement on matters of church order:

> Not an union in opinions: they might agree or disagree touching absolute decrees on the one hand and perfection on the other. Not an union in expressions: these may still speak of the imputed righteousness and those of the merits of Christ. Not an union with regard to outward order: some may still remain quite regular, some quite irregular, and some partly regular and partly irregular.[21]

Wesley expressed his positive understanding of the proposed union by means of a long list of questions, the gist of which was that, instead of passing judgment on another person's faults, it was most highly desirable to strengthen him in brotherly love. He was well aware of the human weakness which made such a union seem unthinkable, but, he said, 'with God all things are possible'. Wesley clearly understood that a union of this kind could only come about with the active support of Lady Huntingdon. He received from her a positive reply. In the middle of May he wrote back to her, and underlined how pressing the establishment of the union seemed to him. He was sick of disputing, he said, and his whole soul cried out for peace, at least with the children of God. He invited her, and all the clergy who had the opportunity, to take part in his annual conference in August, with a view to discussing his plan. At the end of July Lord Dartmouth received a letter from Wesley. Wesley ventured the opinion that the Earl was prejudiced against him, and that, after discussing the plan with other people, he had paid too much attention to the objections of third parties who were opposed to the union. In this second letter, Wesley proposed, among other things, the sending of an abridged version of the original letter to all the persons named in it, with a request that they would raise with him personally any objections they might have to such a union.

It is not known how or when Fletcher learned of the plan for the union. However, he expressed his interest in the scheme in a letter he wrote to Charles Wesley at the end of August. Fletcher was convinced that Lady Huntingdon could play a key role. If she could succeed in gaining the agreement of the other ministers, that would be a splendid thing. He himself supported the union plan, but was not able to take part in Wesley's conference. Fletcher personally solicited support for the plan. In June he travelled to Worcester for 'our little conference'.[22] We learn nothing more at this stage, but from a letter written in 1765, to which we shall later return, it appears that the 'little conference' referred to by Fletcher was a gathering of clergy from the wider region. It is highly probable that Wesley's plan for a union was discussed there. Stillingfleet, Lord Dartmouth's chaplain, would have been the one who reported on the contents of the plan. If this supposition is correct, the course of events leading up to Wesley's conference may be reconstructed as follows.

At this first regional gathering, there were strong objections to the plan for union, because of the idea of sending Wesley's travelling preachers into the parishes of evangelically minded ministers. Fletcher was given the task of communicating these objections to Wesley, and possibly brought them to his attention when he visited Madeley in July, but received no answer.[23] Fletcher and Hatton composed a letter to the Countess, asking her to bring their views to the attention of Wesley's conference, since they themselves were unable to attend and take part in it. Twelve clergymen participated in the Annual Conference of the Methodists, which began on 6 August. The problem over the sending of Wesley's travelling preachers into their parishes was raised, but Wesley turned a deaf ear to it. No agreement could be reached.

In spite of the failure of Wesley's conference, Fletcher tried to win over Stillingfleet to the plan of union. On Sunday 19 August he exchanged pulpits with Davenport, in whose church he preached in the morning. At midday he rode on to West Bromwich, where he preached for Stillingfleet before Lord Dartmouth and his house-congregation. Stillingfleet, however, continued to reject the plan of union. He demanded that Wesley should promise not to send any travelling preachers into the parishes of evangelically minded ministers. Fletcher himself had to recognize that a union could only be achieved if John Wesley accepted this restriction on his own activities. Wesley had stated earlier that he would not intrude into the parishes of evangelical ministers, but he was unwilling to give up his own work in cases where evangelical ministers were appointed to parishes in which Methodist societies already existed.[24] Thus Fletcher too met with failure on the question of the activity of Wesleyan travelling preachers in the parishes of evangelically minded clergy.

After the failure of the nationwide plan of union, in which John Wesley and, indirectly, the travelling preachers under his control would have been included, there soon came into being an alliance of evangelically minded Anglican clergy in middle England. It was a follow-on from the Worcester conference of 1764. Fletcher was involved in it. He informed Charles Wesley at the end of April 1765 that they had held a little conference of gospel ministers, which in future would take place four times a year. Six ministers had taken part: Davies, Baily from Pashur, Cook from Welland, Stillingfleet from West Bromwich, Riland, Hatton and Fletcher himself. Two other ministers, Biddulph and Talbot, must have withdrawn.[25] The rules by which the 'Worcester Conference' was organized were drawn up in 1765 and are still extant. To begin with, it was laid down that the meetings should take place every quarter in Worcester, and on each occasion should last from 10 o'clock in the morning until the midday meal at around 2 o'clock. New members could only be accepted with the consent of all the existing members. Every member, in order of seniority, would take on the leadership for a year, and would be required, among other things, to see that no disputes arose, and that the meetings should not be lacking in Christian love, peace and friendship. Seven themes on which the members could take counsel together were identified: (1) public preaching; (2) religious societies for the establishment and growth of faith and holiness in the respective parishes; (3) instruction in the catechism for children, and opportunities for the education of young people; (4) personal supervision of, and pastoral visits to parishioners; (5) sick visiting; (6) the leadership of one's own household; (7) special personal experiences. On each theme a series of questions was provided.

It was not by chance that these conferences took place in Worcester, and that they bore that name. Over a hundred years earlier, Richard Baxter had founded there the 'Worcester Association', which had provided a role model for groups of clergy. At that time larger meetings had taken place at quarterly intervals in Worcester, while smaller ones had been held monthly in several different places. In the new form, so far as we can gather from Fletcher, a circle of ministers seems to have met regularly from 1766 onwards. Fletcher mentioned in June of that year that he was travelling again to Worcester, and intended, on the return journey, to bring Davies back to Madeley to assist him, following a visit Davies had paid to him the previous year. A few questions and answers from the meeting in May 1767 are still preserved.[26]

In the meantime, at the national level, John Wesley tried once more to revive his plan for a union. Whitefield had returned from America in 1765, and had committed himself to renewed collaboration with the Wesley brothers. Thus a small circle, including the Countess, was formed in 1766. John Wesley also preached in the Countess's chapels. Wesley was encouraged by this new development, and on 15 October sent his original letter on the subject of a union of gospel ministers, with a short introduction, to around fifty ministers. He did not, however, discuss the dispute of 1764. The result was disappointing. Only three people, Richard Hart, Vincent Perronet and Walter Sellon, answered the letter. Nothing is known as to Fletcher's attitude to this development.[27] In the Conference of 1769 Wesley laid before his preachers a letter in which he finally drew a line under his plan for a union: 'Out of fifty or sixty to whom I wrote, only three vouchsafed me an answer. So I give this up: I can do no more. They are a rope of sand; and such they will continue.'[28]

In spite of this fresh failure of the attempt to form a union, the collaboration of the Wesley brothers with Whitefield and Lady Huntingdon went forward. However, while the leaders of the two streams in the Methodist movement thus found themselves working together, in the wider movement the rift between Wesley's travelling preachers on one side, and the 'gospel preachers' influenced by Calvinism on the other, grew ever wider and deeper. The disagreement between them shows up in the Worcester Conference. Early in 1768, John Wesley wrote a letter to Fletcher and made an allusion to the 'Worcester Conference'. Wesley had perceived that Fletcher was weary of the long, fruitless dispute. After a detailed, strongly negative, assessment of the Calvinistic gospel preachers, Wesley took up the question of lay preaching:

> As to the conference at Worcester on lay-preaching, do not you observe almost all the lay preachers (1) are connected with *me*? (2) are maintainers of universal redemption? Hinc illae lacrymae! [trans. 'hence these tears!']. These gentlemen do not love *me*, and do love particular redemption . . . For it is undeniable these quacks [Wesley's lay travelling preachers] cure whom we cannot cure, they save sinners all over the nation. God is with them, God works by them, and has done so, for near these thirty years. Therefore the opposing them is neither better nor worse than fighting against God.[29]

The dispute was no longer over the stationing of Wesley's travelling preachers, but over their lay status, on the grounds of which, in the view of many evangelically minded clergymen of the Church of England, they ought not to preach at all. Fletcher was in agreement with Wesley on the question of the eligibility of lay preachers. He was possibly the only person in the Worcester Conference who shared Wesley's opinion; in any case he was certainly in the minority.

Fletcher was, in terms of doctrine and liturgy, a true Anglican. He defended the Church of England vigorously against the attacks of Dissenters and against the growing influence of the Roman Catholic Church. He was influenced in his preaching by Methodism, which he defended as the recovery of the true, Reformation inheritance of the Church of England, in contrast with its present, visible form. A union of all clergy who were close to Methodism was therefore a pressing concern for him, since it would contribute to the renewal of the church. The union foundered, however, on the question of the observance of ecclesiastical law. So far as church order, and the form and method of preaching were concerned, Fletcher was in substantial agreement with John Wesley, and he maintained a critical distance from ecclesiastical laws.

11

Fletcher and the Methodists
(I: 1760–1770)

Fletcher's close connection with Methodism was already apparent. It was not limited to the Wesleyan wing of the movement, though that was where theologically he belonged. He wrote to his friend Charles Wesley in the autumn of 1760 that John Wesley, Thomas Maxfield and Lady Huntingdon received a letter from him every six months.[1] Particular tasks and challenges to which Fletcher had to address himself in the 1760s were connected with these three persons: with John Wesley it was the question of the leadership of the Wesleyan societies; with Thomas Maxfield, the dispute about perfection; and with the Countess, the foundation of the centre for theological training. In the pursuit of these issues, Fletcher's relations in the first half of the 1760s were predominantly with the Wesleyan wing, and in the second half predominantly with the Calvinistic wing in Methodism. Towards the end of the 1760s Fletcher was drawn into the growing theological tensions within the Methodist movement.

During the 1760s Fletcher maintained the closest personal relationship with Charles Wesley. It was only with him that he kept up a regular correspondence. The closeness was evident also in the contents of the letters, in which Fletcher wrote of his concrete, everyday experiences. However, only the letters to Charles Wesley from the first half of the decade are preserved. Those from the second half have presumably been lost, seeing that there is no indication of any intention to break off the relationship. Since Fletcher felt that he had these specially close personal ties with Charles Wesley, it was a particular sadness to him that Charles never visited him in Madeley. Over and over again Fletcher issued the invitation, and every time either something happened to prevent the visit, or Charles Wesley seemed to shrink from the journey. How much his correspondence with Fletcher meant to Charles Wesley is best illustrated in connection with Charles's plan to take on a parish. His brother

John knew nothing about it, but he asked Fletcher for his advice. This is clear evidence of the close, intimate relationship between them.[2]

John Wesley's request to Fletcher to take on the leadership of the 'United Societies'

The work of the Wesleyans, comprising the 'United Societies' and the Wesleyan travelling preachers, was entirely under the direction of John Wesley. There were only a few Anglican clergy, among them John Fletcher, who were close to Methodism. Fletcher was well known and widely respected, as a result of his having worked for several months in Methodist circles in and around London. However, Wesley's hopes of finding a competent co-worker were dashed when Fletcher took up the appointment at Madeley. Fletcher may have seen it as divine guidance, but Wesley had warned him against it in no uncertain terms: to settle down in a parish was to be caught in a snare of the devil. This warning, together with an extract from a letter to be discussed later, must be understood against the background of an earlier statement by Fletcher. When the question of ordination had arisen, Fletcher had designated John Wesley as his spiritual mentor, by whom the 'yes' or 'no' must be spoken. Wesley had no doubt inferred from this that his words of advice would continue to have decisive significance for Fletcher.

The step Fletcher took in accepting the parish of Madeley was incomprehensible to Wesley. In the summer of 1761 Wesley wrote him another letter, and again invited him to take up service with the Methodists. That in itself would not have been surprising. Totally unexpected, however, was the offer with which he hoped to gain Fletcher's collaboration. The only evidence for John Wesley's letter is to be found in a statement by Fletcher in a letter to Charles Wesley (written in French):

> Your brother [John Wesley] has finally done me the favour of writing to me. The main point of his letter is this: 'It is not right for you to be alone. You would do more good and gain more benefit from being among us. Come, then, and if you do not wish to be an equal partner with me, I will be ready to serve under you.'[3]

In serving with the Methodists, Fletcher's activities would be accompanied by greater blessing, and he himself would receive more blessing.

Such a comment from the mouth of John Wesley is understandable. However, the offer he attached to the invitation to work among the Methodists is most unusual: John Wesley, the leader of the 'United Societies', offered Fletcher joint leadership alongside himself, and was even ready to take second place and put himself under Fletcher! It has often been said of Wesley that he was an autocratic leader, who was unwilling to surrender any of his power. Yet it is clear that that is not altogether true. What moved John Wesley to make such an offer to Fletcher? Our sources have nothing to say on the subject. However, three factors must have come into the reckoning. First, John Wesley was already fifty-eight years old, while Fletcher was only thirty-two. If the Methodist work was to continue after Wesley's death, his eventual successor needed to be still young enough, by human standards, to hold office for a considerable time.[4] Fletcher was, in Wesley's eyes, intellectually the most capable among the younger generation of Methodists. And that was in effect the second factor: Wesley had a very high opinion of Fletcher, and of his attitude and capabilities. Fletcher was a clergyman of the Church of England, and was the very embodiment of the aspiration after a holy life. Thirdly, John Wesley had perceived that Fletcher liked to be independent. He therefore offered him collaboration on an equal footing, and was even ready himself to take second place, if Fletcher could thereby be persuaded to accept his offer.

In issuing his invitation, John Wesley overlooked the fact that taking over the leadership of the travelling preachers and societies was completely irreconcilable with Fletcher's self-understanding. The motive of humility was already evident in Fletcher's reaction to Charles Wesley's approach to him in the late 1750s, and it would play a decisive role when John and Charles renewed their approach in the 1770s. However, Fletcher did not mention this consideration in his reply to Charles Wesley in 1761. He dwelt only on the question of guidance under the providence of God. He said that he had told John Wesley that he would leave the parish ministry immediately if divine providence gave him an appropriate sign, but that he drew a distinction between John Wesley's pressing invitation and a divine command. He had come here in passive acceptance of the guidance of providence, and he would depart in the same way. To leave Madeley and take up Wesley's offer would be, in Fletcher's eyes, to act out of egoism and conceit. He was unable to discern, in Wesley's invitation, a sufficient sign of God's providence. When God wanted him to work among the Methodists, he would guide him in that way. But for the present his place was still in Madeley.

Wesley did not wish to abandon the idea of gaining Fletcher as his successor. Over and over again he stressed how highly he valued Fletcher's strong Methodist stance. This was made clear on his visit to Madeley in 1764, and also in a letter of February 1766, where he wrote: 'Unity and holiness are the two things I want among the Methodists . . . Why should we not give totum pro toto? I hope you will always love and pray for . . .'[5] During the 1760s, Fletcher too thought frequently about John Wesley's request, and although he had indeed declined the invitation in 1761 to take on the leadership of the whole movement, he had, as he later wrote to John Wesley, considered the possibility of accepting a position as Wesley's helper and co-worker.[6] But he had then been led by providence to help in the realization of a project of Lady Huntingdon.

Thomas Maxfield and the dispute over perfection

Around the end of 1760, a stir was caused in Wesley's societies in London by some members who claimed to have attained the state of Christian perfection. It is not known whether Fletcher had experienced the earliest beginnings of this outbreak of fanaticism in London. The first allusion to the perfectionist movement in his writings appeared in a letter written in November 1760. Thereafter, for a time, practically every letter he wrote to Charles Wesley contained references to the subject. Thus in early 1761 he had been informed by Maxfield that new witnesses to perfection in London numbered thirty-two. A year later, in 1762, a group of perfectionists led by Maxfield and Bell began to dissociate itself from Wesley. Fletcher was convinced that John Wesley had need of wisdom and determination if damage to the whole Methodist movement was to be avoided. Fletcher fully recognized that there was a genuine witness to Christian perfection, but that it needed to be clearly distinguished from errors. He was pleased with a writing of Wesley's which had helped many people in Wednesbury who had gone astray.[7] In the autumn of that year Fletcher had to check an arrogant misunderstanding of perfection in his own societies, and suspend two people from membership.

On the subject of the perfectionist movement, Fletcher raised a whole series of questions with Charles Wesley. For instance, whether among the three hundred witnesses there was not a single genuine one. He also raised the question of the appropriateness of Maxfield's preaching:

Crede quod habes & habes ['believe that you have, and you have'] is not very different from the advice of Christ: believe that you have the things for which you pray; the humility of the believer and the arrogance of the enthusiast pull this teaching to the right or to the left.[8]

Perfection was understood by the perfectionists, following the Latin maxim, in the sense of a perfection already bestowed on a person. The emphasis was on the promise made to believers. Neither a particular faith experience nor any ethical authentication was required. There was no definition of what perfection might entail. In the comments he made on the subject, Fletcher did not dispute the possibility of Christian perfection, for to do so would have been to set limits on divine grace. But the claim to perfection had to be subject to scrutiny. If perfection was not accompanied by Christian humility, it would lead to arrogance. Fletcher stressed repeatedly that humility and love are the two pillars on which Christian perfection must rest.

At the beginning of November 1762, shortly before his own arrival in London, John Wesley wrote a long letter to Thomas Maxfield. Fletcher knew nothing about this, but learnt through Ley what was taking place in London. He therefore wrote to John Wesley:

The corruption of the best thing is always the worst of corruptions . . . The nearer the parts that mortify are to the heart the speadier is an amputation to be resolved upon. You will say perhaps but what if the heart itself is attackt? then let the heart be pluckt out as well as the right eye . . . I have a particular regard for M-d [Maxfield] & B-l [Bell] both of them are my correspondents, I am strongly prejudic'd in favour of the Witnesses, and do not willingly receive what is said against them, but allowing that what is reported is one half mere exaggerations, the tenth part of the rest shows that spiritual pride, presumption, arrogance, unyieldingness, stubbornness, unteachableness, party spirit, uncharitableness, prophetic mistakes, in short every sinew of Enthusiasm is now at work in many of that body: nor do I fear it upon any bodies bare word. I have some of B-lls own letters to ground my fears upon. May I presume unask'd to lay before you my mite of Observation . . . Fear not, dear Sir, the Lord will take care of the Ark: tho' hundreds of Uzziah's should drop off, Most would return with Noahs Dove: Have faith in the word, and leave the rest to Providence. Deus providebit, is a comfortable motto for a believer.[9]

Fletcher proposed that a few unprejudiced persons should come together to define the distinguishing marks of enthusiasm. The perfectionists should be presented with their conclusions, first in love, then with the necessary firmness, and then, possibly, be excluded. Thus Fletcher advocated a clear testing of, and if need be separation from, the perfectionists.

Fletcher hesitated to send the letter, but, a week later, included it with a letter to Charles Wesley, with the request to send it on if he thought it was appropriate. We do not know whether or not Charles did so. In January 1773 John Wesley, with one or two persons whose names we do not know, held a conversation with Bell and two or three of his friends. He particularly wanted to correct Bell's error in prophesying the end of the world on 28 February. However Bell stood firmly by his opinion, and the tension among his followers grew. The result was the first secessions from Wesley's societies, and, in April 1763, the break between Maxfield and John Wesley.

The effects of the controversy were also noticeable in the vicinity of Madeley. Fletcher asked Lady Huntingdon to play her part in preventing 'enthusiasm' from spreading throughout the land. He also expressed to her his gratitude for the divine guidance that had led him away from London, so that he could not be overtaken by the fire of disunity and enthusiasm. In September 1763 Fletcher received a visit from two perfectionists, Bowen and Green, for whom, however, perfection meant only being fully justified. Fletcher therefore demanded that those who spoke of perfection should clearly define what they understood by it. In this way real progress might be made. He continued:

> The greatest hindrance seems to me to be *Crede quod habes & habes*, an inflamed imagination can ride far on this horse. Crede quod habes si sentis ['believe that you have, if you feel it'] or nunc crede quod habebis & habebis ['believe now that you will have, and you will have it'] seem to me to be the middle term between unbelief on the one hand, and imaginary faith on the other.[10]

In his response to Maxfield, Fletcher stressed the experiential dimension of faith. He was fully convinced of Maxfield's integrity and his desire to know and do the will of God. But he saw the danger of antinomianism in Maxfield's preaching. Fletcher was convinced that the whole controversy was a trial sent by God, and that in the end God would turn it into good. He wanted to write as plainly as he believed Maxfield could bear it. If Maxfield was shocked by his letter, that would be the will of God. He would rather lose a friend by 'honest plain dealing, than by unkindness'. Personal friendship must be able to withstand open controversy over the truth of the gospel.

For his part, Maxfield announced his intention of coming to visit Fletcher in Madeley. Fletcher was not unpleased with the idea, since he thought that Maxfield would perhaps pay more attention to him than to anyone else. But he asked Maxfield to delay his visit until the following spring. At first he received no answer, and did not know whether this was due to pressure of work or to annoyance. However, in the summer of 1764 there came a fresh request from Maxfield to visit Madeley. Fletcher agreed, firstly because he wished to see Maxfield preaching the gospel again as he had done in the past, and secondly because he himself 'loved peace like a catholic'.[11] At the beginning of 1765 Fletcher first received a visit from a man named Guildford, one of Wesley's travelling preachers, who described himself as perfect, but had his own idea of what that meant. Perfection did not by any means entail for him the 'recollection' so important for Fletcher.

In July 1765 Maxfield came to Madeley. He stayed there for two months. He no longer preached on perfection, and his activity appeared very helpful to Fletcher. After the first few weeks, Fletcher was even able to report how Maxfield was praised on all sides. Fletcher did not have the impression that Maxfield's teaching was antinomian, even though, earlier, danger had threatened from that side. Since Maxfield had become an ordained clergyman of the Church of England, his stay enabled Fletcher to make several journeys, even on Sundays. Thus he went to preach in Darlaston, in two churches in Staffordshire, in Tipton, with Stillingfleet in West Bromwich, and, in company with Sir Charles Hotham, in Bratby, where he met Lady Huntingdon. Fletcher discussed with Maxfield questions of faith and doctrine. Together they compiled a short credal confession. When at the end of 1766 Fletcher was parted for a while from his parish and his societies, he was again perfectly content for Maxfield to come and stand in for him.

John Wesley had visited Fletcher in the summer of 1764, but he did not come in the summer of 1765. Perhaps this had something to do with the fact that Maxfield was staying with Fletcher that summer. At the beginning of 1766, Fletcher again invited Wesley to Madeley. In the covering letter, he raised the subject of perfection. Fletcher wished to clarify how far perfection might be attainable in this life. He drew a distinction between the body and the will. The body, and all the powers of the soul which are dependent on it, could not attain perfection. This included, for Fletcher, not only the memory and the passions, but also the intellect. The will, however, which, according to Fletcher, was completely independent of the body, could gain perfection – and along with the will, the emotions controlled by it. It seems as though John Wesley, in his reply, was not entirely certain how he should interpret Fletcher's observations. He had the impression that basically Fletcher was coming to the same conclusions as himself. However, he proposed an amendment to Fletcher's distinction between body and will: all the faculties of the soul can only develop with the help of the bodily organs. In the course of this life, in Wesley's view, even the will was not something wholly independent of the body. If a person employed his faculties in the right way, that could only happen through the strength given to him by God. Only 'power from on high' could enable a person to think, speak or love rightly.

Fletcher had to abandon his hope of a public reconciliation and renewed collaboration between John Wesley and Maxfield: he concluded that they were not compatible. All needed to learn, he commented, what that word means, 'If anyone would be first among you, let him be the servant of all'.[12] He recognized that the controversy between Maxfield and John Wesley was not simply a question of theology, but also a question of authority. Thomas Maxfield no longer wished to be unconditionally subordinate to John Wesley, and every attempt at reconciliation was bound to founder on this question. The rapprochement between Fletcher and Maxfield also put Fletcher's relationship with John Wesley to the test. Fletcher greatly appreciated the fact that John Wesley did not, on that account, break off contact with him.[13]

The Countess of Huntingdon, and the founding of the theological college in Trevecca

'Madam, Conscious that few people can sympathize with me in so feeling a manner as your Ladyship, I shall make no apology for pouring out my complaints before you in this letter.'[14] Fletcher felt that he was understood by Lady Huntingdon, and described to her his situation in Madeley. A similar letter to John Wesley would no doubt have provided Wesley with an opportunity to point out to Fletcher that he would be able to give and receive more blessing by working among the

Methodists. The Countess, by contrast, had accepted Fletcher's entry into the parish ministry in Madeley, if at first reluctantly. Therefore she became, alongside Charles Wesley, a companion who shared Fletcher's joys and tribulations. The relationship between Fletcher and the Countess during the 1760s can be easily followed in the primary sources, though these consist entirely of letters written by Fletcher. None of the Countess's replies has been preserved. These letters are evidence of strong ties of Christian affection. They are *sui generis*. They are full of the praise of God, and marked at times by almost rapturous language.

Soon after Fletcher came to his parish, Lady Huntingdon offered him the services of a curate named Jones, so that he might be free to leave his flock if other duties called. Fletcher, however, declined the offer.[15] The Countess invited him to visit her, and preach for her again, but during the early years Fletcher found this impossible because of the pressure of work. Then in 1765 he asked the Countess to provide a stand-in for him, so that he could go and help with the preaching in Bath and other places. One of the reasons why Fletcher stressed, in his letters, the similarity of their preaching, was that on particular questions they thought differently. He told Charles Wesley in 1765 of a conversation he had had with Sellon and Lady Huntingdon. It had been a friendly conversation about perfection and the law. Clearly Sellon and Fletcher, who on these questions were in agreement with John Wesley, discussed with the Countess issues which were in dispute in the Methodist movement. It was because Fletcher was aware of the differences that he made a point of stressing their unity on essential matters.

At the end of 1764 Fletcher received a visit from Howel Harris, the (lay) leader of the Calvinistic Methodist revival in Wales. Harris had close contacts with Whitefield and Lady Huntingdon, but repeatedly advocated reconciliation and collaboration with the Wesley brothers. He led a fellowship with over a hundred members on a farm estate at Trevecca, in the parish of Talgarth, in Brecknockshire, South Wales. It seems that Harris was hoping to persuade Fletcher to become leader of a theological school at Trevecca. Fletcher, however, declined the invitation, again on the grounds that God's providence had placed him in Madeley, and that he would not dare to abandon his task without a special and clearly recognizable commission from his heavenly Lord. Fletcher noted appreciatively that Harris had placed him under no pressure, but had shown understanding of his position.[16] After Fletcher had turned it down, the project was in abeyance for a while. Instead, the

Countess invited Fletcher to undertake various evangelistic assignments. From 1765 onwards, therefore, he was often away from his parish for a few days or a few weeks at a time.[17] Different clergymen served the parish of Madeley during his absences.[18] Fletcher shared to the utmost of his powers in the evangelistic task of building up the church. He preached in Wesley's meeting houses, as well as in those of Whitefield and the Countess. He gave his services often alongside other clergymen, including Martin Madan, William Romaine and Whitefield. This collaboration happened along the lines of the union of evangelically minded clergy, for which John Wesley had hoped in vain. At the same time Fletcher was insisting to the Countess that he was most especially called to the work in his parish in Madeley.

> My unworthy services in Mr. Whitefield's Chapels have been attended with remarkable success. The shout of a King has been heard among us, and the glorious enquiry, 'What shall I do to be saved', is heard on all sides. Not unto us, O Lord, not unto us poor dust and ashes, but unto thy name must we ascribe the glory. In our own eyes we should ever be nothing, and Christ all in all – to his grace every good in us, or done by us, must be ascribed, and at his feet our labours in glory will be for ever laid, for He alone is worthy. I am overwhelmed with a sense of the goodness of God in making use of such a feeble instrument for good – and am at a loss how to express the infinite gratitude I owe . . .[19]

Many people came to faith through Fletcher's preaching. He himself only spoke of this in a very restrained way, and ascribed all the honour to Christ and the working of his grace. Whitefield expressed himself more positively: 'Dear Mr. Fletcher is become a scandalous Tottenham-Court preacher. I trust he will come down into your parts baptized with the Holy Ghost as with fire.'[20] Through his activities, Fletcher became known in wider circles. Thus in 1767 he was appointed one of the court chaplains to the young David Stuart Erskine, Earl of Buchan.

Lady Huntingdon did not abandon her plan for a college in Trevecca. She felt it was necessary to found an institution for theological training, to produce an ongoing supply of evangelically minded clergy for the Anglican Church as well as for her own chapels. In November 1767 she sent Fletcher her plan, together with the conditions for admission to the college. She wanted to admit only students who had been converted to God, and who were resolved to devote themselves wholly to God's service. They would have the possibility of studying for three years. During this time they would receive free training and maintenance, as well as one suit of clothing each year. At the end of their training they would be free to decide for themselves where they wished to serve. Since the planned college was to be open to both Calvinistic and Wesleyan Methodists, and since it was to be based only on the fundamental doctrines common to both streams, Fletcher saw the possibility of promoting, by his collaboration, peace and an ecumenical attitude between the two streams of Methodism:

> With regard to the superintendency of the College, or the examination of the candidates, I know myself too well to dream about it; nevertheless so far as my present calling and poor abilities will allow, I am ready to throw in my mite into the treasury that your Ladyship may find in other persons.[21]

Presumably the Countess's wish to entrust the oversight of the college to a clergyman of the Church of England was bound up with her aim of making it possible for men trained there to be ordained into the Church of England.

Putting the plan into practice was not easy. Lady Huntingdon sent a highly gifted seventeen-year-old called Easterbrook to Madeley. Fletcher was of the opinion that the young man might be able to take on the leadership of the school, but presumably that never came about. The Countess also asked Fletcher about the books which should be used in the school. Fletcher admitted that he was not sufficiently well acquainted with English literature, since he had studied abroad, and also, as a teacher, had mostly used foreign books with his pupils. He also argued that a plan of studies should first be drawn up: 'Grammar, Logic, Rhetoric, and Ecclesiastical History, and a little Natural Philosophy, and Geography, with a great deal of practical Divinity, will be sufficient for those who do not care to dive into languages.' He mentioned a few books which were known to him, and which he regarded as valuable, among them some by Puritan theologians:

> . . . and I would recommend them not to forget Watt's Logic and his History of the Bible by questions and answers, which seem to me excellent books of the kind for clearness and order. Mr. Wesley's Natural Philosophy contains as much as is wanted, or more. Mason's Essay on Pronunciation will be worth their attention. Henry and Gill

on the Bible, with the four volumes of Baxter's practical works, Keach's Metaphors, Taylor on the Types (printed at Trevecca), Gurnal's Christian Armour, Edwards on Preaching, Johnson's English Dictionary, and Mr. Wesley's Christian Library, may make part of the little library . . .[22]

In May Fletcher mentioned in a letter that Lady Huntingdon had found a tutor for Trevecca from Suffolk – a person who was not known to him. The opening of an institution for theological training seemed even more pressing when in March of that year six students were excluded from the University of Oxford because they had engaged in Methodist preaching. Whitefield wrote an open letter on the subject, and Sir Richard Hill composed his *Pietas Oxoniensis*, to which Fletcher would refer back in the theological controversies of the 1770s. However, the events in Oxford were not the main reason for the founding of the college in Trevecca. It had been planned for a long time; the course of events simply made it even more necessary.

John Wesley followed the plan for the college from a distance. He was doubtful about it, and wrote to his brother Charles:

I am glad Mr. Fletcher has been with you. But if the tutor fails, what will become of our college at Trevecca? Did you ever see anything more queer than their plan of institution? Pray who penned it, man or woman? I am afraid the visitor too will fail.[23]

Wesley visited Fletcher in Madeley in the summer of 1768, but left no account of their discussions. After various building modifications in Trevecca, the college was opened on 24 August 1768. Fletcher took on the oversight of it as President, on behalf of the Countess, although he would have preferred to be found among the students rather than among the leaders. He continued to be Vicar of Madeley, and travelled to Trevecca several times a year to carry out his duties as Visitor. From Madeley also came one of the first students at Trevecca. This was the 23-year-old Glazebrook, a miner, who had been one of the first converts under Fletcher's preaching.[24]

It is not clear who was first appointed as tutor. In the secondary literature we find the name of John Henderson, at that time an infant prodigy only twelve years old. Henderson's father, who was one of Wesley's travelling preachers, sent him to Kingswood School, where, at the age of eight, he was so far advanced that he even taught Latin. In

Fletcher's letters, however, we find neither the name of Henderson, nor any reference to the activities of two tutors. On the other hand, Fletcher did mention a person by the name of Williams,[25] who, according to him, had carried out his duties very well during the early months. After that, however, difficulties arose, and the situation deteriorated.[26] Fletcher put in a strong plea:

> I believe Mr. Harris will join me and the generality of the young men in entreating your Ladyship to set over this place, according to the first plan, a *grave, steady, experienced zealous* person who hath *parts activity & devotedness to God & his cause.*[27]

Fletcher also asked Charles Wesley whether he knew of a good tutor. Independently of this request, a person called John Jones presented himself. Fletcher was unsure whether he was the right man for the post, and asked him to gain some practical experience of the job before making up his mind.

In his first report on the college, after about three months, Fletcher wrote that he was not satisfied with the situation. He had issued a warning to each individual student: 'I told them that if things went on at this poor trifling formal rate I would advise your Ladyship to pick out half a dozen of the most earnest, and send the rest about their business, that room might be . . . for a better set.'[28] By April 1769 the situation had improved. The danger of formalism still existed, but the young men could see the danger for themselves, and were trying to avoid it. Relations with the students presented no difficulty to Fletcher. He went through them one by one, and reported on the state of their faith, and their progress in their studies. The development of personal faith was important for Fletcher, but he also looked into questions of social behaviour and pronunciation. His greatest problem was the cost of housekeeping. In financial matters too he wanted to exercise his superintendency satisfactorily.

Among those taking part in the first anniversary celebration of the college in August 1769 were John Wesley, Howel Harris, Shirley and Fletcher. Soon after that, the problem of finding a new tutor was resolved. Joseph Benson, who for three and a half years had been a teacher in the classical department at Wesley's Kingswood School, was to take the place of the existing tutor.[29] Benson visited Trevecca for the first time in January 1770. Fletcher therefore paid a further visit to Trevecca, shortly before his departure for Switzerland. During the early part of the year, while Fletcher was still abroad, Benson took up his post. Benson had first made Fletcher's acquaintance in some brief meetings during the latter's journeys to Bristol and Bath, but he was impressed by Fletcher's deep faith and by his sermons.

Growing theological tensions in the Methodist movement

Fletcher's activity as President of the college fell during a time of growing tensions within Methodism. The failure of Wesley's plan for a union was an indication of the differences which existed. From 1768 at the latest, disputed questions of doctrine and church order marked the discussions of the evangelically minded clergy of the Church of England in their Worcester conferences. John Wesley had heard that Fletcher was weary of the disputes at these gatherings, and in March 1768 wrote him a long letter which contained strong criticism of Calvinistic clergy. Wesley wrote:

> Some happy exceptions I allow; but, in general, do men gather grapes of thorns? Do they gather constant, universal self-denial, the patience of hope, the labour of love, inward and outward self-devotion, from the doctrine of Absolute Decrees, of Irresistible Grace, of Infallible Perseverance? Do they gather these fruits from Antinomian doctrine? or from any that borders upon it? Do they gather them from that *amorous* way of praying to Christ or that way of preaching His righteousness? I never found it so. On the contrary, I have found that even the precious doctrine of Salvation by Faith has need to be guarded with the utmost care, or those who hear it will slight both inward and outward holiness. I will go a step farther: I seldom find it profitable for *me* to converse with any who are not athirst for perfection and who are not big with earnest expectation of receiving it every moment. Now, you find none of these among those we are speaking of, but many, on the contrary, who are in various ways directly or indirectly opposing the whole work of God; that work, I mean, which God is carrying on throughout the kingdom by ἄνδρες ἀγράμματοι καὶ ἰδιῶται. In consequence of which His influence must in some measure be withdrawn from them.[30]

Wesley had the impression that Fletcher was associating too much with 'genteel' Methodists – an allusion to the Countess and her circle. He advised Fletcher to converse with people who were free from Calvinism and antinomianism: there was no need for him to be a hermit. Fletcher's reply to Wesley is not known. In fundamental matters, such as the calling of lay preachers and the emphasis on holiness, he was at one with Wesley. However, we may suppose that the tone of Wesley's letter surprised, not to say shocked, him.

The theological controversy of the 1770s began to take shape in the letter from John Wesley quoted above. Wesley gave an indication there that the doctrine of justification by faith needed to be closely guarded against antinomianism. Shortly after Wesley had written his letter, there appeared the document *Pietas Oxoniensis*, referred to earlier, in which Sir Richard Hill came to the defence of six students expelled from the University of Oxford. In this document Hill put forward the Calvinistic doctrine of predestination. Sellon replied to it, with a document in which he examined critically the arguments against the Arminian doctrine that Christ had died for all people. Fletcher thanked Sellon for this document, and wrote to him:

> I have inquired what the Calvinists think of them [Sellons writings], but I do not hear much about it. They choose rather to be silent; a sign that they have not any great thing to object . . . There are some disputes in L.H.'s [Lady Huntingdon's] College; but when the power of God comes, they drop them. The Calvinists are three to one. Your book I have sent them as a hard nut for them to crack.[31]

The controversial questions were thus discussed in the college in Trevecca. Fletcher even encouraged discussion by sending Sellon's book to Trevecca. But receiving power from God was for him more important than theological arguments. In this positive concern, Fletcher knew that he was at one with the Countess. He was able to continue to work with Calvinistically minded 'gospel ministers' in spite of differences in the interpretation of the doctrine of election. In so far as he was able, he hoped to lead the students at Trevecca to holiness of heart and life.

PART IV
THE TIME OF THE CONTROVERSIES
(1770–1777)

12

Wesley's Conference of 1770, and the Calvinistic Methodists

'Take heed to your doctrine. We said in 1744 "We have leaned too much toward Calvinism".'[1] This warning was uttered in 1770, when John Wesley and his lay travelling preachers came together for their annual Conference. They took counsel together to consider what could be done to revive the work of God in places where it had decayed. After giving guidance on a number of practical concerns, the Conference turned its attention to questions of doctrine, and referred back to the deliberations of 1744.

In 1744 Wesley had called his first Conference, which had devoted its time to questions of doctrine and church order. In the context of a discussion about the doctrine of justification, the Conference had debated the significance of works of repentance before justification, and of obedience after it, and had established that the notion of the 'imputation of the righteousness of Christ' was not to be found, in those terms, in Holy Scripture. Thus the Conference arrived at the conviction that, unknowingly, they had leaned too much towards Calvinism and antinomianism.

A year later, in 1745, it was admitted that the truth of the gospel lay very near both to Calvinism and antinomianism. The difference was no more than a hair's breadth. It would therefore be foolish and sinful to run as far as possible from these points of view simply because one did not fully agree with them. Methodists were close to Calvinism, first in ascribing all good to the free grace of God, secondly in denying all natural free will, and thirdly in excluding all merit from man, even for what he has or does by the grace of God. They were close to antinomianism, firstly in exalting the merits and love of Christ, and secondly in rejoicing evermore. It was stressed, however, that faith did not take the place of holiness or good works, but rather that both belonged together, as cause and effect.

The first two Conferences thus put in writing the main features of the attitude of Wesley and his co-workers to the Calvinistic Methodists. Two things must, however, be noted. First, the doctrinal statements in the conference minutes were extremely concisely formulated. Only one or two central statements were recorded, in catchword form. The counter-arguments of the Calvinists were not explained; nor was the Conference's own doctrinal position systematically established and developed. Secondly, the two streams in Methodism described themselves and each other as, respectively, 'Arminian' and 'Calvinistic'. But the Calvinism of the Calvinistic Methodists was not identical with Calvin's theology, any more than the Arminianism of the Wesleyan Methodists was identical with the theology of Arminius. Evidence of Fletcher's awareness of the difference is to be found at various points in his writings from the 1770s.[2] For a proper historical understanding of the controversies within Methodism, this distinction is of fundamental significance.

In the previous chapter we were able to see how, in the 1760s, a plan for union between the two streams of Methodism failed, and how the tensions increased. This is clear from a letter sent by John Wesley to Fletcher in 1768, warning him against long useless discussions with Calvinists. At the Conference in 1769 a disappointed Wesley finally drew a line under his attempt at a union of clergymen of the Church of England who preached justification by faith, comparing them to a rope of sand. During 1769 and 1770 there was an increase in theological writings and pamphlets which brought to public attention the difference between Arminian and Calvinistic Methodists.

The annual Conference of 1770

At the Conference of 1770, Wesley again addressed himself resolutely to the unity, growth and progress of his own societies. The consideration of the doctrinal questions began with the reference (quoted at the beginning of this chapter) to the Conference of 1744, which had detected too strong a leaning towards Calvinism. Now, in 1770, the conclusion reached in 1744 was interpreted as follows:

> 1. With regard to *man's faithfulness*. Our Lord Himself taught to use the expression. And we ought never to be ashamed of it. We ought steadily to assert, on His authority, that if a man is not 'faithful in the unrighteous mammon,' God will not give him the true riches.

2. With regard to *working for life*. This also our Lord has expressly commanded us. 'Labour' – ἐργάξεσθε – literally 'work' – 'for the meat that endureth to everlasting life.' And, in fact, every believer, till he comes to glory, works *for* as well as *from* life.

3. We have received it as a maxim, that 'a man is to do nothing in order to justification.' Nothing can be more false. Whoever desires to find favour with God should 'cease from evil, and learn to do well.' Whoever repents should do 'works meet for repentance'. And if this is not in order to find favour, what does he do them for?

Review the whole affair.

1. Who of us is *now* accepted of God?
He that now believes in Christ, with a loving, obedient heart.

2. But who among those that never heard of Christ?
He that feareth God, and worketh righteousness, according to the light he has.

3. Is this the same with 'he that is sincere'?
Nearly, if not quite.

4. Is not this 'salvation by works'?
Not by the *merit* of works, but by works as a *condition*.

5. What have we then been disputing about for these thirty years?
I am afraid, about words.

6. As to *merit* itself, of which we have been so dreadfully afraid: we are rewarded '*according to our works*', yea, '*because of our works*'. How does this differ from *for the sake of our works*? And how differs this from *secundum merita operum*, – as our works *deserve*? Can you split this hair?
I doubt I cannot.

7. The grand objection to one of the preceding propositions is drawn from matter of fact. God does in fact justify those who, by their own confession, neither feared God nor wrought righteousness. Is this an exception to the general rule?
It is a doubt, God makes any exception at all. But how are we sure that the person in question never did fear God and work

righteousness? His own saying so is not proof: for we know how all that are convinced of sin undervalue themselves in every respect.

8. Does not talking of a justified or a sanctified state tend to mislead men? almost naturally leading them to trust in what was done in one moment? Whereas, we are every hour and every moment pleasing or displeasing to God, according to our works; according to the whole of our inward tempers, and our outward behaviour.[3]

These doctrinal formulations were intended to clarify matters among the Wesleyan Methodists, but, once they were known about, they evoked misunderstanding and contradiction among the Calvinistic Methodists. The opposition between the two streams was most clearly in evidence at two points: on the one hand, in events in and around the college at Trevecca, and on the other, in the relationship between John Wesley and Lady Huntingdon and her circle.[4] In both areas Fletcher was drawn into the conflict, and forced to make clear where he stood. First, in the autumn of 1770 there arose disputes which had no obvious connection with Wesley's Conference in the summer. The memorial service following the death of George Whitefield was a contributory factor to them. Around the end of 1770, the anti-Calvinistic tendency of Wesley's Conference became known, but it was not until the beginning of 1771 that the contents of the conference minutes came to the attention of the circle around Lady Huntingdon, where they led to a storm of angry protest. Since the documentation of the events described in what follows is of varying quality, it is only partially possible to establish reasons, and to separate causes from effects.

A dreadful heresy?

Fletcher returned from his continental journey in the summer of 1770. At the end of July he wrote a letter from Madeley to the tutors and students at Trevecca. The theme running through the whole letter was: Christ is all in all; in Christ the believer finds his life, his very being, and all pride and vainglory are at an end. In conclusion, Fletcher expressed his intention to visit Trevecca before the anniversary celebration. Fourteen days after this letter, Wesley held his preachers' Conference. At the end of it he travelled to Bristol, whence he too originally intended to visit Trevecca for the anniversary. However, Wesley received from Lady Huntingdon a formal request that he should not attend, and went instead to Cornwall. The differences between Wesley and the Countess cannot be attributed to her awareness of the conference minutes.[5] Fletcher's letters suggest other possible conclusions.

Fletcher reported, in a letter to Charles Wesley in September 1770, that he had tried to set all prejudices aside. He emphasized that it was he and the students who had invited John Wesley to visit Trevecca. In other words, the Countess herself had not invited Wesley to the anniversary celebration, and so regarded his intention to come as self-invitation. Fletcher also reported that the Countess did not want her students to collaborate with Wesley's preachers in Brecknockshire. She was dismayed at Wesley's teaching on perfection, and was also afraid that, in the work in Bath, Charles Wesley would pursue only his own interests. Fletcher repeated this view in a later document on the events in Trevecca. He spoke of a split in the Methodist work in Brecknock and Hay, areas not far from Trevecca. The Countess had forbidden her students to preach for Wesley, and instructed them at all times to preach for Whitefield. All this had wounded his, Fletcher's, 'catholic senti-ments', and had separated his two friends, the foundress of the college and John Wesley, from one another. On account of the Brecknock split, an unfriendly, though he hoped well-intentioned, letter had been written by one of these persons, and it had been understood by the other as extremely offensive.[6] Fletcher saw himself at first in the role of a mediator between the Countess and John Wesley. If he became involved in the disputes it was in the hope of resolving them.[7]

George Whitefield died in America on 30 September 1770. Before his death he had expressed the wish that John Wesley should preach at a service of remembrance for him in England. Thus, in November 1770 Wesley led a service in the 'Tabernacle', Whitefield's meeting house in London. He brought together the basic teaching of Whitefield and of the Methodists as a whole under two heads: the new birth, and justification by faith. He stressed his points of agreement with the Calvinistic stream in Methodism, and made no reference to the doctrine of predestination. Followers of Whitefield reproached Wesley for having passed over the most important point of doctrine, and – when the minutes of the 1770 Conference became known – for having contradicted himself.

The doctrine of perfection had been a stumbling block for a long time. It was also a cause of tensions at the college in Trevecca. Joseph Benson, who had been working as tutor there since early in 1770, sided with Wesley in these arguments. He was strongly influenced by Fletcher and his expectation of a spirit-baptism, which he saw as confirmation of

Wesley's teaching on perfection. In November, Benson had to travel to Oxford, on account of some commitments there. The Countess wrote him a friendly letter in which she stressed how much he was missed in Trevecca, and recalled how Fletcher, on one of his visits, had had to shake the students out of their spiritual sleep:

> Dear Mr. Fletcher is come, and in that spirit that could move stones, and would let none of them [the students] sleep . . . Nothing but gospel power can make us hope, or rationally believe, any thing can stand long but upon that work for its foundation. To see or feel this to be the grand or positive need is our greatest want.[8]

Fletcher's central concern is again in evidence here. The letter is also a sign of the as yet unchallenged attitude of Fletcher and Benson. During Benson's absence, however, the conflict over doctrinal questions in Trevecca was intensified, under the influence of strongly Calvinistic circles, and this, together with unfounded accusations and intrigues, led at the turn of the year 1770/71 to Benson's dismissal from the post of tutor.

Fletcher was quickly informed of the situation through letters from Benson and the Countess, to both of whom he wrote back immediately. In his reply to Benson, he wrote:

> *If* the procedure you mention is (a fair copy of the [crossed out]) fact, and your letter is a *fair* account of the transactions and words that passed relatively to your discharge, that Great Lady has taken a false step. I write by this post to her with all possible plainness on the affair. *If* the plan of the college is overthrown, I have nothing more to say to it. I'll keep to my tent for one: The Servant of all I trust I shall ever be, the confined tool of any one party, I never was, I never will be.

And in the same letter Fletcher gave an extract from his reply to the Countess:

> Mr. Benson made a very just defence when he said he did hold with *me* the possibility of the Salvation of all, that mercy is offered to all, and yet may be receiv'd or rejected: If this is what your Ladyship calls Mr. W's [Wesley's] opinions *free will* and *Arminianism* and if 'every Arminian must quit the College' I am actually discharged also; for in

my present views of things, I must hold that sentiment, if I believe the bible is true, and God is Love.[9]

Fletcher's reply made it unmistakably clear: the original plan for the College had been abandoned, prejudices reigned supreme, mutual love had been grievously violated, and a spirit of partiality had triumphed. At the same time, however, Fletcher warned Benson to abstain from everything that might add fuel to the fire. In her response to Fletcher, the Countess said that his view of the events was not an accurate one. However, Fletcher held firm on three points: first, that he himself would resign from the office of President if every Arminian was required to leave the College; secondly, that in the future he would not be a member of any party, and would not abandon his commitment to anyone who feared God – especially not his commitment to John Wesley; and thirdly, that he could not interfere with anyone who was striving for perfection. To the surprise of the Countess and her circle, on doctrinal questions Fletcher took his stand clearly on the side of Wesley.[10]

Fletcher wanted to continue to be mediator and reconciler. He had supported the setting up of the College, because it had seemed to him to offer the possibility of collaboration between Arminian and Calvinistic Methodists. But if this basic assumption were to be abandoned, he would have to resign from office. As Fletcher understood it, there were two conflicting conceptions of the doctrine of redemption, but these did not exclude the possibility of collaboration. So far as the doctrine of perfection was concerned, the conflict arose, in Fletcher's view, from mutual misunderstanding, since the respective frames of reference were different: while the Countess laid more stress on the depth of the Fall, John Wesley's emphasis was rather on the power and effect of the recovery of the image of God; while the Countess spoke of free grace in a wonderful way, John Wesley insisted on the wonderful use we should make of God's grace. Fletcher said that on this account he could continue to love and respect both protagonists, even though, perhaps, each of them might accuse him of prejudice, because he did not see things exactly as they did.

On 20 February 1771 Fletcher set out for Trevecca. On his arrival he found all at peace. He preached on Sunday 24 February, but was oppressed by an unaccustomed heaviness. More than ever he was convinced that he was not in the right place, and that he must lay down the oversight of the College. He informed the Countess of his decision, and, on the following Wednesday, the students also. However, his high regard for the Countess and his love for the students caused him to waver in his decision. But the events which then followed strengthened him in his conviction that he ought to give up the presidency.

The Countess showed Fletcher a letter she had read out to the students, which in Fletcher's view would exclude all convinced Calvinists from the college in precisely the same way as, previously, Arminians were excluded. In addition, Walter Shirley, a clergyman closely associated with the Countess, had already announced that he would oppose before the whole world the doctrine of baptism with the Holy Spirit, that is, the expectation of a filling with the Holy Spirit which still remained outstanding after justification. With the support of Harris, he had told the students that the promise of the Spirit had been fulfilled in its entirety at Pentecost.[11] Now, therefore, Fletcher expressed fundamental misgivings about continuing to exercise oversight at the College. It was not to be expected that the students would follow someone they regarded as blind.

It was only during Fletcher's stay at Trevecca that Lady Huntingdon received, through Shirley, a copy of the minutes of Wesley's Conference. She was shocked at the contents, since, as she saw it, the Wesleyans had abandoned the central point of justification by faith. The heresy contained in the minutes was so dreadful that it must be publicly contested and every believer ought to be incensed against it. Fletcher admitted that the impression created by the minutes lent support to the Countess. He could no more excuse Wesley's unguarded language than the Countess's violent reaction to the doctrinal statements. He tried in vain to calm the storm. The Countess demanded of all the students that they should set down in writing their opinion on the disputed points of doctrine, and after a little delay this was done. She also let it be known that all who did not totally reject the views of the Conference would have to leave the College. As President of the College, Fletcher did not wish to evade the challenge. He defended the statements in the conference minutes by placing them in the context of Wesley's doctrinal opinions as a whole, and criticized only their unguarded and over-concise formulation. Finally he resigned irrevocably from the post of President of the College, and informed all the students of the step he had taken.

Fletcher informed John Wesley of the events at Trevecca:

The College will take quite a Calvinist turn, and an itinerant ministry will go out of it to feed the Church of God of that sentimental denomination. I strongly recommended them to set fire to the harvest of the Philistines, and not to that of their fellow Israelites who cannot pronounce Shibboleth in their way. My lady seemed quite disposed for peace last Friday; and she will write to you to beg you will explain yourself upon the Minutes, that she and the College may see you are not *an enemy to grace*, and may be friends at a distance instead of open adversaries . . . The points that will most stop the mouth of our friend are the total fall of man, and his utter inability to do any good of himself; the absolute necessity of the grace and Spirit of God to raise even a good thought or desire in the heart; the Lord rewarding no work, or accepting of none, but so far as they proceed from his preventing, convincing and converting grace; the blood and righteousness of Christ being the sole meritorious cause of our salvation, and the only spring of all acceptable works, whether we do them spontaneously from life or for more abundant life . . . I look upon Lady Huntingdon as an eminent servant of God, an honest, gracious person, but not above the reach of prejudice; and where prejudice misleads her, her warm heart makes her go rather too fast . . . My prayer is that you may fully disappoint them [opponents], by guarding the Gospel truth in your own heart and life and doctrine, as much from the legal as the antinomian extreme, between [which] it invariably lies.[12]

John Wesley replied to Fletcher's letter without delay. He repeated and confirmed the points which Fletcher had formulated as the basis of an answer to the Calvinists, and ended his letter with the counter-question: 'Who is there in England that has asserted these things more strongly and steadily than I have done?'[13] When, in June 1771, Wesley wrote a letter to Lady Huntingdon, he likewise stressed that for thirty years justification by faith had been his central concern. His statements in the minutes of the Conference of 1770 in no way contradicted the doctrine. Wesley saw a confirmation of his message in the large numbers of people who had come to faith, especially in recent days. God would not have borne witness to a lie. In the last section of the letter, Wesley expressed his esteem for the Countess, though by administering a word of caution to her he implied (no doubt unwittingly) his superiority to her.[14]

A little while later Wesley received an important letter from Fletcher, who began by describing his vain endeavours to overcome prejudices. He said that Lady Huntingdon had seen in Wesley's affirmation of the doctrine of justification by faith an ambiguity of which she disapproved, and she was astonished that he, Fletcher, had fallen for Wesley's deceptions. He had to warn Wesley, he said, that the struggle would draw in wider circles of people. Through Hatton he had learned of a printed circular letter by Shirley which was to be sent to all serious-minded clergy and lay persons in England. He himself had not received a copy of it, since he had forfeited his reputation as a 'real Protestant' by what he had written in Wales about the conference minutes. The circular letter described the minutes of Wesley's Conference of 1770 as a dreadful heresy, and called for a collective public protest to be made on the occasion of Wesley's 1771 Conference:

> Sir
> Whereas Mr. Wesley's Conference is to be held at Bristol on Tuesday the 6 August next, it is proposed by *Lady Huntingdon* and many other *Christian Friends (real Protestants)* to have a meeting at Bristol, at the same time, of such principal Persons both *Clergy & Laity* who disapprove of the underwritten Minutes; and as the same are thought injurious to the very *fundamental principles* of Christianity, it is farther proposed, that they go in a body to the said conference and insist upon a formal *Recantation* of the said *Minutes*; and in case of a refusal, that they sign and publish their *Protest* against them. Your presence, Sir, in this occasion is particularly requested: But if it should not suit your convenience to be there, it is desired that you will transmit your sentiments on the subject to such person as you think proper to produce them. It is submitted to you, whether it would not be right, in the opposition to be made to such a *dreadful Heresy*, to recommend it to as many of your christian Friends, as well of the *Dissenters* as of the *Established Church*, as you can prevail on to be there, the cause being of so public a nature.
> I am, Sir, your obedient Servant
> Walter Shirley.[15]

The Calvinistic periodical, *Gospel Magazine*, edited by Romaine, also published cutting comments on Wesley's conference minutes. Wesley felt it necessary to send to his preachers a short statement of his position, which, however, consisted in the main of rhetorical questions. Fletcher affirmed that he would support Wesley, on the basis of the evangelical principles which Wesley had personally attested to him, and invited Wesley to visit him in Madeley. Fletcher also planned to write to Shirley, with a view to Shirley's withdrawing his circular letter:

I write to Mr. Shirley to expostulate with him to call in his circular letter: He is the last man that should attack you. His Sermons contain propositions much more heretical and anticalvinistical than your Minutes. If my letters have not the desir'd effect I shall (probably) if you approve of them & correct them make them public for your justification. I find Mr. Ireland is to write to make you *tamely recant*, without measuring swords or breaking a pike with Our *real Protestants*. I write to him also.[16]

At the end of July John Wesley spent some time in Madeley. Probably Fletcher took advantage of this opportunity to show Wesley the letters he had written to Shirley in defence of the conference minutes. Possibly he handed them over to Wesley, so that he might publish them, if the need arose. A week later, Wesley's Conference began in Bristol. Both the Countess and Shirley recognized – probably largely as a result of Fletcher's reaction – that the circular letter had been too hastily and too arrogantly composed. They wrote accordingly to John Wesley, shortly before the start of the Conference. Shirley expressed the hope that the withdrawal of his circular letter would lead to the withdrawal also of the disputed doctrinal statements.[17]

On one of the days of the Conference, 8 August, Shirley, together with a few of his friends who had appeared on the scene, presented his case to the Conference. Wesley reported in his journal that the matter had been freely discussed for two hours, and he said that he believed that Shirley and his friends were now satisfied that he, Wesley, and his preachers were not disseminating false doctrine, but were sound in the faith. Shirley submitted a declaration which, after a slight alteration by John Wesley, was approved and signed by all the preachers present, with the exception of Thomas Olivers:

Whereas the doctrinal points in the Minutes of a Conference held in London, August 7th, 1770, have been understood to favour justification by works – Now, we, the Rev. John Wesley and others assembled in Conference, do declare that we had no such meaning, and that we abhor the doctrine of justification by works as a most perilous and abominable doctrine. And as the said Minutes are not sufficiently guarded in the way they are expressed, we hereby solemnly declare in the sight of God, that we have no trust or confidence but in the alone merits of our Lord and Saviour, Jesus Christ, for justification or salvation, either in life, death or the day of judgement. And though no one is a real Christian believer (and consequently cannot be saved) who doth not good works when there is time and opportunity, yet our works have no part in meriting or purchasing our justification from first to last, either in whole or in part.[18]

A few days later, Shirley wrote to John Wesley expressly acknowledging that the declaration had convinced him that he had misunderstood the sense of the statements made by the Conference of 1770, and that he wished to reaffirm his satisfaction with the way the declaration was formulated. It seemed that the conflict was thereby ended, and that the doctrinal questions had been clarified to the satisfaction of both sides. However, peace had not come to stay.

Calvinism in England

A few brief notes may help to shed light on the convictions of the Calvinistic Methodists, who were part of a richly varied tradition of Calvinistic thought in England. Though they regarded themselves as Calvin's heirs, their Calvinism did not correspond precisely with the beliefs of the Reformer. Two hundred years of church history had left their mark.[19]

It was under Calvin's follower in Geneva, Theodore Beza (1519–1605), that the doctrine of predestination first became the main content of, and the key to, the whole doctrinal structure.[20] Beza maintained that God sent Christ to deliver only the elect. We cannot probe into God's eternal decree in order to know for certain whether 'Christ died for me'. But good works are the consequences of salvation, from which we can infer Christ's work within us. Beza made use of the *syllogismus practicus*, the inference back from the works of faith to justification by faith.

William Perkins (1558–1602) proceeded to build upon Calvin and Beza, and founded an English stream within the Calvinist tradition (often known as Puritanism), which, within the predestinarian framework, stressed that one's own standing before God could be experienced and proved. This was the start of an experimental predestinarian tradition. Perkins's main concern was to show those who suffered from doubt and despair that it was possible to be sure of one's calling and election, and how this could be done. God's covenant is always, on the human side, bound up with a condition. The covenant of grace is conditional on our receiving Christ in faith, and repenting of our sins. Preaching must therefore begin with the law, in order to make plain to people their sin and the punishment due to it. Saving grace is a form of irresistible grace. Perkins stressed the dual action of grace: in the first operation of grace, the human will is passive. By grace it is renewed, so that a person can believe, do penance and obey. But this renewed will is too weak, unless it is backed up by the second, supportive operation of grace. Without this co-operation of grace and will, the person is again deprived of grace. With Perkins the accent lay on a second operation of grace. Faith does not, of its essence, imply assurance, but it leads to repentance, which, by way of the conscience, makes possible the inference of assurance. Thus the assurance of saving faith becomes itself a fruit of faith. We have assurance by inference from the repentance or sanctification of which we become aware in ourselves.

Paul Baynes (d. 1617) developed Perkins's line of thought further, in trying to distinguish more clearly between the temporary faith of the reprobate and the true faith of the elect. The will and desire to hate sin and to strive after the good became an infallible sign of election by God. True faith could be recognized by its fruits, especially repentance. There were different degrees of faith, and there could also be a 'winter of the soul', when all might seem dead, only to return to life at the appropriate time. Baynes thus reached the voluntaristic conclusions which characterized the experimental predestinarian tradition.

At the beginning of the seventeenth century, several Calvinists held a strongly voluntarist view of faith. Although by nature human beings were spiritually dead, and only the Spirit of God could change them, they preached as if people held their fate in their own hands: while the enabling power came from God, the act of faith was their own. On the basis of the fruits of faith, people could and should be sure that they belonged to the elect. Mostly it was taught that repentance preceded faith. Obedience became a condition of faith, and the law a reference point for one's own standing in relation to salvation. Common to all these proponents of a faith measurable by experience was the desire to help those in doubt by showing them a way to find assurance.

An exponent of this stream of Calvinist tradition in America, John Cotton, changed his view on the matter. He made an intensive study of Calvin, and, as a result, stressed that faith was a fruit of the Spirit, and that assurance belonged essentially to faith. There could therefore be no deliverance preparatory to union with Christ. Sanctification could not be regarded as evidence of justification. The doctrine of temporary grace must again be taken seriously. Faith preceded repentance, and depended on a free, unconditional, gracious promise. The law was fulfilled for those in whom Christ lived. In the wake of Cotton's preaching an antinomian controversy broke out. The controversy spread to England, reaching its peak at the beginning of the 1640s. Among the proponents of antinomianism were John Eaton (1575–1641), Tobias Crisp (1600–43) and John Saltmarsh (d. 1647). The doctrine of predestination was reinterpreted by them in the sense that saving faith is only the realization of what has already been accomplished from all eternity. This could lead to the assertion that the elect are justified before they believe. In God's eyes an elect person has no sin. The law can pass no judgment on such a person. In 1690 Crisp's sermons were republished, and unleashed a further controversy over antinomianism.

Several of the theologians who took part in the Westminster Assembly (1643–52) wrote against the antinomians. These Westminster theologians aimed, with their confession of faith, to emphasize the holiness of the Christian life, over against the threat posed by antinomian doctrine. The concept of preparation for grace was not followed up, but the idea of preparation was underlined, in that, on the road to salvation, the law was regarded as preparatory to the gospel, and repentance as preparatory to faith. Although repentance was not the ground for God's bestowal of forgiveness on human beings, nevertheless no one should expect forgiveness without it. The theory of temporary faith was of doubtful value. Justifying faith could be described both as a work of God and as a human act of faith. The covenant of grace made faith its only condition, but faith, for its part, would produce obedience to God's commandments. Saving faith could be found in different degrees, and could attain to full assurance. Faith and assurance did not belong essentially together. Certainty of acceptance could be found in the inferential judgment of the conscience. God would accept good works in Christ and reward them. Thus the theology of the Westminster Assembly remained predestinarian and voluntarist, recognizing the experiential nature of faith.

Calvinistic Methodism as represented by Sir Richard Hill

When the theological controversy broke out within Methodism in the 1770s, several persons became involved on the Wesleyan and on the

Calvinistic sides of the dispute. While Fletcher was foremost in taking up the argument on the Wesleyan side, Sir Richard Hill was a leading spokesman on the Calvinistic side. On the other hand, Walter Shirley, who had sparked off the conflict over the conference statements of 1770, had no more to say, after publishing his report on the 1771 Conference. Sir Richard Hill was the first to react to Fletcher's first *Check*, written in defence of the minutes of Wesley's Conference. For a short while, his brother, the Dissenting minister Rowland Hill, also engaged in the controversy.[21]

Sir Richard Hill insisted that it must be one thing or the other: a person was in a state either of rejection or of election; either under God's curse, or the object of his favour. One cannot prepare oneself for justification. And there is no faith which precedes justification. Where God, in his power, works upon the soul, it happens on the basis of the covenant which God has already made with that person. Christ's reconciling act brings effective and full reconciliation for those whom God loves. The curse of the law is done away. The law can pronounce no judgment on God's elect:

> Either Christ has fulfilled the whole law, and borne the curse, or he has not. If he has not, no soul can ever be saved; if he has, then all debts and claims against his people, be they more or be they less, be they small or be they great, be they before or be they after conversion, are for ever and for ever cancelled.[22]

All the sins of those who are beloved by God, whether past, present or future, are forgiven.

Justification does not necessarily include assurance of the forgiveness of sins and of peace with God, and so the means of grace must be sought. In every believer are to be found both the old and the new nature, flesh and spirit, which fight against each other. The elect person is not sinless, but does not fall from grace through committing sin – a point illustrated, for Hill, by the traditional example of King David and his adultery. God hates sin, but he does not hate his elect who commit sin. The object of what he does is always his own glory in the salvation of his elect through Christ Jesus: 'God's ways are past finding out . . . But he has always the same thing in view, namely, his own glory in the salvation of his Elect by Christ Jesus. This, Adam was accomplishing when he put the whole world under the curse.'[23]

Everything works together for good. Even a serious fall into sin can help to bring the elect person nearer to Christ. Hill was not wanting to encourage people to commit sin: one would not deliberately break one's leg, simply because one knew that there was a doctor who could heal it. Good works necessarily spring from a true and living faith. There can, however, be a 'wintertime' of faith, when these fruits are blown off by the violent winds of temptation and wickedness, and fall to the ground. God would, of his grace, reward the good works of his elect. With this understanding of Calvinism, Hill stood nearer to the antinomian tradition of such a person as Crisp than to the Westminster theologians.

Fletcher never accused his Calvinistic friends of being antinomian in practice. However, their principles seemed to him forcibly and inevitably to lead to antinomianism. Not without reason, he saw in them a revival of the theoretical antinomianism propounded by Crisp in the seventeenth century. He opposed this stream of tradition (as described above) with arguments including those of moderate Calvinists. Already in his first two *Checks*, Fletcher had attacked Crisp and his doctrine of final salvation, according to which an elect person could not fall from grace even through the most serious sins. Now he found the selfsame doctrine in Hill's writings. Over against this he insisted that committing sin could not bring greater glory to God. The Fall ought not to be attributed to the secret will of God. Any distinction between the hidden and the revealed will of God should be rejected, since in the last analysis the hidden will of God would cancel out his revealed will.[24]

The doctrine of the divine decrees, in which, before laying the foundations of the world, God had decided on the salvation or damnation of every single person, was, according to Fletcher, contrary to both Scripture and reason. As he moved on from criticizing antinomianism to criticizing the doctrine of final salvation, the doctrine of predestination also came under his scrutiny, and he broached the subject of the reverse side of the doctrine – the teaching on reprobation – which Hill consistently ignored. He thus reached the conclusion that the statements of his opponents could not credibly set forth either the loving kindness or the righteousness of God. In its extreme form, Calvinism was indistinguishable from fatalism. Fletcher could even draw a parallel with Roman Catholicism. The extremes met: 'Error moves in a circle; extremes meet in one . . . For although the one makes a great noise about *faith* and *free grace*, and the other about *works* and *true charity*, they exactly meet in *narrow grace* and *despairing* uncharitableness.'[25]

One could imagine, Fletcher wrote, that the devil himself might have thought out the doctrine of salvation held by this kind of Calvinism.

Fletcher drew a distinction between Calvin, moderate Calvinists, and the radical 'high Calvinists'. He referred occasionally to statements of Calvin that Christ had died for all, and, amidst all his criticism, found at least some words of appreciation for the 'moderate' Calvin:

> . . . and though I must do him [Calvin] the justice to acknowledge, that he seldom went the length of modern Calvinists in speculative Antinomianism, yet he made the matter worse by advancing many unguarded propositions about absolute decrees, and the necessary, final perseverance of backsliding believers.[26]

Fletcher saw 'high Calvinism' as the logically inevitable end-product of the doctrine of predestination, and therefore was able to say, in general terms, that Calvinism in its highest form led to antinomianism, Manichaeism and fatalism on the one hand, and to ungodliness, arrogance and despair on the other. Fletcher illustrated his view of the consequences of Calvinistic doctrine with concrete examples.[27] The pointing up of the statements of his opponents in this way made mutual understanding more difficult.

In Sir Richard Hill's view, Fletcher's presentation of the case was a scandalous defamation, and not in any way a fair account of his (Sir Richard's) own teaching. That was true, to the extent that Fletcher started out from an inner inconsistency in Hill's statements. On the one hand, Hill said that the salvation of the elect was settled and could not be lost, even through sin. That was the theoretical antinomianism of which Fletcher accused the Calvinistic Methodists, and which he vehemently denounced. On the other hand, Hill insisted that true faith could always be recognized by the good works it produced. If Hill was really serious about this, argued Fletcher, then he ought to abandon his doctrine of complete unconditional salvation and of a 'wintertime' of faith, and agree with him, Fletcher.[28] For his part, Hill failed to understand Fletcher's statements, did not accept his arguments, and condemned his teaching as Arminianism, Pelagianism, papism, etc.[29] He did not wish to attack Fletcher personally, but he was convinced that Fletcher's and Wesley's convictions were as far removed from those of the Reformers and the Puritans as the east was from the west.[30]

Fletcher, for his part, did not always recognize the controversial intention or the ambiguity behind the words used by Hill. But when

Fletcher, in his writings, gave his assessment of the state of the controversy, it sprang from his genuine concern to make progress towards
resolving the issues. In the course of the controversy he acknowledged
that he had learned from the Calvinists of the existence of an 'elective'
grace of God, though he had not taken on board the Calvinistic understanding of election. In his later writings he distinguished clearly
between moderate Calvinists and 'high Calvinists', and, equally,
between moderate Arminians and 'high Arminians'. He strove for
reconciliation between the moderates on both sides. They were, in his
view, less far apart than their doctrinal opinions might at first sight seem
to suggest. He wished to accept the concerns and affirmations of both
sides in so far as they conformed to Scripture, without subscribing to the
contradictions within their respective systems.[31]

13

The Controversies of the 1770s
and their Precursors

Movements diverging from orthodox Calvinism before the
eighteenth century

A glance at movements which diverged from orthodox Calvinism
should help towards a better understanding of the 'Arminian' position
of the Wesleyan Methodists in its historical context. The theologies of
Arminius the Dutchman, Amyraut the Frenchman, and Baxter the
Englishman represent variations in the heritage left by Calvin. At some
points they are clearly distinguishable from orthodox Calvinism.

Jacob Arminius (1560–1609) studied under Beza, among others, but
later rejected Beza's harsh teaching on predestination. For a while he
was an admirer of Perkins, but became dissatisfied also with Perkins's
treatment of predestination. His teaching on faith is not dissimilar to
that of the tradition initiated by Perkins, who, however, did not draw
from it all the same consequences as Arminius. Arminius was influenced
by the humanistic spirit of the Netherlands. For him, theology was not a
theoretical, but a practical science or field of learning, which affected
human behaviour. Arminius spoke of four divine decrees: (1) God's
sending of his Son as mediator and redeemer; (2) his decision to bestow
his favour on those who repent and believe, and to allow unbelievers to
remain in their sinful state; (3) his decision to provide, in sufficient and
effective measure, the means necessary for repentance and faith; (4) his
decision to save those who, as he knows from all eternity, will believe
and persevere, and to condemn those who, he knows, will not believe
and persevere. Arminius taught that Christ had died for all people, and
that he prayed even for those who were not among the elect. He interpreted Romans 9 as referring to the predestination not of individuals,
but of particular groups of people.

Arminius's understanding of the gracious activity of God was different from that of the Calvinistic tradition. Grace, he believed, could be resisted, and could be lost by those who fell away from faith. On the subject of David's sinful behaviour, Arminius argued that it did not prove the Calvinistic theory that an elect person could not fall from grace and that David would not have been lost even if he had not repented, since in fact David had repented. Arminius drew out clear consequences from his position, especially in his understanding of faith as obedience. He could describe faith as a threefold act of obedience, in repentance, belief in Christ, and adherence to God's commands. A believer is one who does not resist grace. What Perkins described as a twofold operation of grace, Arminius understood as a twofold operation of the Spirit: first, that a person may be able to have the will, may believe and may be converted; secondly, that he has the will, does believe and is converted. He differed from Perkins in that it was only with the second operation, involving human activity, that he spoke of a person as a believer. Arminius did not wish the human response to be understood as a meritorious work.[1] The evidence of assurance was, in his view, produced by the work of the Spirit, and by the fruits of faith, together with the conscience. Here again we find the *syllogismus practicus*.

After the early death of Arminius, the conflict with orthodox Calvinists over the doctrine of predestination went further. The disciples of Arminius, the Remonstrants, adopted five basic principles: (1) God has decreed that all who believe in his Son and who persevere in this faith will be saved; (2) Christ died for all, but only those who believe can rejoice in the forgiveness of sins; (3) a person must be born anew, through God's Spirit; (4) though indispensable, grace is not irresistible; (5) perseverance is possible by the help of the grace of the Holy Spirit, but the question whether it is possible to fall away from the life in Christ is left open.

Although Fletcher did not know Arminius's own writings, he knew, and quoted from, the works of three early Arminian theologians: Episcopius (1583–1643), Philip Limborch[2] (1633–1712) and Jean le Clerc (1657–1736). These men had developed and elaborated the teachings of Arminius. Their understanding of the Fall is important in our context: the corruption in human nature resulting from Adam's fall is not in itself of the nature of sin, but it has left all human beings inclined towards sin. People are responsible for their own deliberate acts and their consequences. The guilt of Adam's sin only becomes real when individuals acquiesce in their inborn weakness through their own transgression of the law. Humanity did not lose, through the fall of Adam, the possibility of being free to produce good deeds. But divine grace is the source of all that is good, and the means whereby it is developed and brought to fulfilment (Latin, *complementum*). Without God's grace nothing good can be thought, willed or carried out. John Locke (1632–1704) also belonged to the circle around le Clerc and Limborch. It was from these three, who all stressed the reasonableness of the Christian revelation, that the Dutch-English early Enlightenment emanated.

Another variation of Calvin's heritage arose in France, where the school of Saumur taught neither orthodox Calvinism nor Arminianism. It worked on the humanistic legacy latent in the French Reformed tradition, and attempted to follow its own middle way. One of its representatives was Moyse Amyraut (1596–1664). He took over the views of his teacher, Camero, who was an opponent of Beza. Amyraut continued what Camero had begun, and in the process, by contrast with his orthodox opponents, became engrossed in Calvin's writings, to which he frequently appealed. New developments, as compared with orthodoxy, were his understanding of history and his use of the knowledge principle. The human-historical side of God's self-revelation was examined. According to Amyraut, God could not be known in himself, but only through his works in history. In place of the orthodox two-pronged dialectic of covenant of works and covenant of grace, he introduced a three-stage progressive view of covenant of nature, covenant of law and covenant of grace. Each of these covenants, including the covenant of grace, is in the form of a hypothetical contractual relationship, which only becomes effective and binding when the appropriate condition is fulfilled. God's apportionment (French, *dispensation*) of punishment and reward takes place within the framework of his covenant agreement. In the three-stage historical sequence, the loving kindness of God is progressively revealed: he is seen as the good, the righteous and finally the gracious God. This action in salvation history is an accommodation of God to the human race, and reveals his pedagogical purpose for them.

Amyraut's emphasis on salvation history also affected his understanding of the Trinity, which he saw primarily not as immanent but as 'economic', by which he meant the outward working of the triune God upon creation. The three persons of the Trinity had each their 'revelation time', with regard both to the human condition and to the course of salvation history. With regard to the human condition, Amyraut held that the work of God the Father has its correlation on the human side in men and women as rational created beings, not yet stained by sin; that the work of God the Son has its correlation in those not yet freed from sin through the operation of the divine Spirit; that the work of God the Spirit has its correlation in those whom God has enlightened and made aware of their deliverance. With regard to salvation history, Amyraut identified the revelation of the Father in the epoch of the covenants of nature and law; the revelation of the Son as the first conditional economy of the covenant of grace, that is, as the universal-conditional will of God; and the revelation of the Spirit as the particular-absolute will of God.

Not only in the course of salvation history as a whole, but also in the covenant of grace itself, Amyraut drew distinctions between the three persons of the Trinity in terms of their work: the Father plans redemption; the Son carries it out; the Spirit applies it to human beings. The office of the Son and the office of the Spirit are related to each other as hypothetical and absolute covenant, as universal-conditional and particular-absolute will of God, as revealed and hidden will of God, as the sun and the capacity of human beings to see with their eyes. Because humans are completely incapable of good, God has to open their eyes. But Amyraut was not speaking of a natural, so much as of a moral incapacity for good, since, while on the one hand he could refer to incapacity in the moral and religious fields, on the other he was wanting to insist that people are not blocks of wood but rational beings who are morally responsible. Amyraut drew the conclusion that people are able to respond to grace, but are unwilling to do so because they are sinful.

In the universal covenant of grace, which is founded on the atoning death of Christ for all people, faith is required as the only condition. However, God, through his Spirit, creates in the chosen individual the faith which he demands. The Spirit brings enlightenment. He produces the capacity to recognize the light, i.e. Christ. He does not compel people, but convinces them. Since the will inclines towards what a person has recognized, enlightenment always has an effect upon the will. Election is a work of the Spirit. Election and rejection are a mystery. Election only becomes perceptible to a person later, when faith comes about. The universal and particular decrees of God become clear to people one after the other, and operate upon each other. The economy of salvation is an unfinished work, still moving towards its completion in history.

There are many parallels[3] to Amyraut in Fletcher's theology, but also clear differences[4] from him. It is uncertain whether Fletcher knew

Amyraut's writings. There is no explicit evidence for it, and in my opinion it is unlikely. Nevertheless an indirect influence on Fletcher by Amyraut cannot be ruled out. The role played by the theology of Saumur in the supersession of high orthodoxy by rational orthodoxy in western Switzerland should not be underestimated.[5] But, as a possible link with Fletcher, mention must also be made of Richard Baxter, who in many ways developed similar thoughts to those of Amyraut, and who expressed approval of the Frenchman in his Confession of 1655.

The name of the Englishman Richard Baxter (1615–91) has been mentioned several times already. Baxter was born in Shropshire, did not receive any university education, and after his ordination worked in various parishes in Shropshire until, in 1641, he came to Kidderminster in Worcestershire. In 1660, like hundreds of other clergymen, Baxter had to hand back his benefice and parish to the person who had previously held them. He declined the bishopric which was offered to him. Even before the Act of Uniformity came into force in the autumn of 1662, he preached his farewell sermon in London, and thereby openly declared himself to be a Nonconformist. Preaching illegally, and frequently suffering persecution, from then on he worked for a wider public through his writings. No other writer in seventeenth-century England published as much as Baxter. Basic to his work was the attempt to combine 'praxis', that is, the call for personal faith and personal holiness, with 'theory', that is, the pursuit of a rational, comprehensive body of doctrine, suited to people's need.

As a rule, Baxter distinguished between different laws, rather than different covenants. Over against the law of innocence, existing between God and Adam and demanding sinlessness in accordance with the law of works, stands the law of mediation, existing between God and Christ, according to which Christ dies as a man and so receives authority over the human race until the Last Judgment. God's way of deliverance for humanity consists, first, of the universally effective law of grace, which was given to Adam by God after the Fall, and which, as a positive law of grace, demands repentance and is accessible to the natural understanding, and, secondly, of the perfect law of grace, which is given to the Christian by Christ, and which, as a positive law of grace, demands repentance and faith in Christ, and depends on supernatural revelation.

God has created human beings with intelligence, will and practical ability. Human free will is directed by the intellect. God uses no compulsion, but exercises a moral authority over human beings by means of punishment and reward, as befits their status as the crown of creation. Towards God, the law of nature requires praise, prayer and worship; towards one's neighbour it requires honesty and submission to authority; towards oneself it requires contentedness and moderation. In the Fall, Adam's will obeyed the senses rather than the intellect, and broke out of its natural subordination to God. The Fall led to a moral inability to choose the good. Though it does not know it, the whole world owes to Christ the fact that, after the Fall, humanity was not punished by death. Creation and Fall belong to the realm of the natural understanding. The doctrine of human nature, the Fall and God's demand for conversion can be recognized by the intellect. The doctrine of redemption, by contrast, depends on biblical, supernatural revelation. The condition attached to the perfect law of grace is faith, repentance and conversion. By faith in Christ, one is placed under the lordship of Christ, and obedience is thus one's duty, though not a prerequisite for one's salvation. Those who never heard of the gospel are subject to the first form of the law of grace, which demands only repentance and conversion to God.

Baxter attached great importance to the Holy Spirit. Through the Holy Spirit God helps people to live in accordance with God's will. The Spirit is at work in history in different degrees. Only as much is required of human beings as, with the measure of the Holy Spirit granted to them, they are able to achieve. The Holy Spirit works towards salvation in three ways: (1) as preparatory, general grace in the whole world; (2) as special grace in individuals, bringing faith in Christ, repentance, conversion and thankfulness; (3) as habitual faith, that is, as resolute faith, established through praxis, leading to the sanctification of the life of the believer. The Holy Spirit does not overwhelm people, but makes them willing to obey God's commandments, by clarifying the reasons for them and the advantages attached to them, and making possible a rational consideration of them. People can hinder or assist the Holy Spirit, depending on the extent to which they obey his promptings. That does not exclude for Baxter the possibility that God might convert people by means of an unfailingly effective grace without their coming to Christ – in which case it would be the Father who drew them.

No one is condemned, apart from those who deliberately condemn themselves by rejecting salvation. Baxter declared emphatically that, in face of the righteousness of God, Christ really and truly achieved atonement for all people, and that no one should perish for want of an atoning sacrifice, but only for lack of faith. Corresponding to the work of the Holy Spirit described above, God leads people back to himself step by step. Alongside the revealed will of God, there is also the hidden will of God, whereby God chooses to bring people to faith even though their sensuous self-love opposes him. If God had not bestowed on some people the grace which unfailingly converts them, then all people would resist the gospel, and would be rejected by God. God's unfailingly effective grace is the victorious inner grace of absolute election.[6]

In his teaching on justification Baxter distinguished three stages: (1) our first justification, by which we find ourselves in a justified state; (2) our daily justification, as a continuation of this state, and a constantly renewed justification from the guilt of individual sins; (3) our final justification, by the verdict of the Judge. In the Last Judgment, though our good works are insufficient to satisfy the law of works, they are enough to guard us against the false accusation of impenitence. Faith should not push obedience into the background, and obedience is dependent on faith in Christ's fulfilment of the law of works. Not perfect, but sincere obedience towards God in Christ is a condition of our progress in a state of justification, and of our perseverance in it. Certainty of faith is not a constitutive part of justification before God, but it is the justification before our own conscience. A believer can therefore live and die without this justification of the conscience. Certainty of faith is always incomplete, but is worth striving for. Believers should not be tormented by anxiety, but should take care to fulfil their duties. They should not only be concerned about the state of their own soul, but should do good to many people. In Baxter's theology great importance is attached to sanctification. In opposition to the antinomian Calvinists (Crisp, Eaton, Saltmarsh) Baxter stressed the importance of the law even for believers.[7] Since he was frequently confronted by antinomians, especially in Cromwell's army, his writings were largely directed against these opponents.

In his stance in relation to other Christian viewpoints, Baxter drew a distinction between doctrine and praxis, and in his later writings gave more weight to praxis. It is characteristic of him that he regularly sought a middle way between extreme positions. He was convinced that the truth lay in the middle, and that often in the past conflicts had been waged over words. He also tried to follow a middle way in the disputes between extreme Calvinism and Arminianism, and in doing so showed similarities to the school of Saumur in his soteriology, though he did not follow Amyraut's interpretation of the Trinity in salvation history. Like Wesley, Fletcher was well acquainted with Baxter's writings. But despite his appreciation of Baxter, Fletcher took up his own independent theological positions.

The course of the controversies within Methodism over Antinomianism and Predestination[8]

> I rejoice likewise not only in the abilities but in the temper of Mr. Fletcher. He writes as he lives. I cannot say that I know such another clergyman in England or Ireland. He is all fire; but it is the fire of love. His writings, like his constant conversation, breathe nothing else to those who read him with an impartial eye.[9]

Such was the verdict of John Wesley on the best theological advocate of his beliefs, when, notwithstanding the agreement between Wesleyan and Calvinistic Methodists at the Conference of 1771, conflict had been rekindled.

Only a day after the 1771 Conference, Shirley heard that Fletcher's letters to him were in print. He asked Wesley not to go ahead with their publication. James Ireland supported this request, suggesting that Wesley might await Fletcher's decision. Wesley, however, was convinced that his doctrinal statements of 1770 ought to be defended and explained, and emphasized this in a letter to the Countess. He tried to appease the petitioners by saying that he had corrected the more harsh expressions, and he also shortened some passages. On Monday 12 August Wesley set out for Wales. Three days later Ireland received a letter from Fletcher asking him to do all he could to prevent the publication of the letters. Fletcher himself would be willing to sell his last shirt to cover the cost. He was nevertheless convinced that the doctrinal statements of 1770 needed explanation and justification, whether his letters were published or not. If they were published he would be obliged to see it as a necessary evil, since a defence was necessary, even though, in the changed circumstances, the form in which he had chosen to provide it was no longer appropriate. Ireland's intervention with the printer proved unsuccessful, and Thomas Olivers, Wesley's publisher, promptly announced that Fletcher's *A Vindication of the Rev. Mr. Wesley's minutes* was on sale. 'What a world! Methinks I dream when I reflect that I have written on controversy; the last subject I thought I should have meddled with.'[10] This cry of Fletcher's chimes in with the description of the author in the publication itself. The work appeared anonymously, but on the title page it read: 'by a Lover of Quietness and Liberty of Conscience'. Certainly that was Fletcher's original intention. He valued peace and freedom of thought. There ought, in his view, to be freedom of conscience among the Methodists over all that went beyond the generally accepted basic doctrines. But, as will be clear from what follows, Fletcher became more and more concerned to find a theologically acceptable consensus even on the disputed questions.

Fletcher's publication, which later became known as the *First Check to Antinomianism*, was made up of five letters to Shirley. The first letter gave a general overview of John Wesley's teaching. While not passing over the differences from the Calvinistic Methodists, Fletcher demonstrated that John Wesley totally assented to and preached the basic doctrines of Christianity: the Fall, justification through the merits of Christ, sanctification through the operation of the Holy Spirit, and the worship of the one true God, mysteriously differentiated as Father, Son and Holy Spirit. In the second letter, Fletcher explained Wesley's intention in formulating the doctrinal statements of 1770: they were directed against antinomianism, which was flourishing in Wesley's own societies. John Wesley's position was compared with that of a James among the disciples of Jesus, or a Baxter among Puritan theologians. Fletcher then turned, in the third and fourth letters, to particular points in the Conference's declaration. His exposition, in its general drift, followed the lines of the first statements of his views, as they had been expressed in his letter to Lady Huntingdon in March of the same year. But the defence now was more comprehensive, more informed, and more clearly presented. Fletcher defended Wesley's statements with arguments from Scripture, with general judicious, reasoned reflections, and with the experience of Calvinistic clergy. He interspersed quotations from Shirley's own sermons, which in part contained statements even more far-reaching than those in the minutes of Wesley's Conference. In the fifth and last letter, Fletcher criticized Shirley's overhasty and unlawful action in issuing his circular letter, and expressed the hope that his own letters would refute the criticisms made of John Wesley, expose the threat from antinomianism, and finally turn the unhappy split in the Methodist movement into an even greater union. Because of the timing, this letter could not mention the agreement achieved in the Conference of 1771.

Fletcher expressed, both to the Countess and to Shirley, his deep uneasiness that his defence of the Conference statements had appeared in conjunction with opposition to Shirley's circular letter, since this meant that an objective clarification was accompanied by comments of a personal nature. John Wesley recommended the Countess to read Fletcher's document. The first edition was so quickly sold out that, as early as September, a second, unaltered edition appeared. Fletcher once more tried to prevent it, but again his letter arrived too late.[11] Shirley, for his part, also published in September an account of the events surrounding the Conference of 1771.[12] The discussion of questions of fact became more and more overlaid with personal mistrust, directed now not only against John Wesley but also against John Fletcher. At the same time the breach between the Countess and Fletcher grew deeper.[13]

In Fletcher's view, Shirley's account contained a very important misinterpretation of the agreed statement of 1771. Shirley was of the opinion that the statement had ruled out, once for all, the doctrine of justification by the works of the law on the Day of Judgment. To counter such conclusions, Fletcher took up his pen again and wrote a sixth letter to Shirley. Two others followed in its wake, and all were finally published together. Thus there appeared, before the end of the year, Fletcher's second treatise against antinomianism.[14]

A Second Check to Antinomianism contained, in the first letter, a statement of the scriptural basis for the doctrine of a second justification according to works. This doctrine, Fletcher claimed, was agreeable to reason, and was also supported by tradition, including even that of the Calvinists.[15] He quoted Matthew Henry (1662–1714) and Whitefield, in his arguments against the antinomian teachings of Crisp and Saltmarsh. Christ would judge us according to our works, according to the measure by which our faith worked through love. However, the use of the unusual concept of 'justification according to works', in place of the more traditional 'judgment according to works', caused further misunderstandings on the Calvinist side. What Fletcher wanted to do was to distinguish between merit, which is due to Christ alone, and the evidence, which is to be seen in the fruits of faith, but his terminology was dangerous.

The second letter in the *Second Check* was directed at Shirley personally.[16] Fletcher thanked Shirley for maintaining the ties of friendship between them, and invited him to preach in Madeley on justification by faith. He also offered to share in a service of worship with Shirley, if he was staying in Shirley's neighbourhood. He wanted it to be clear to all the world that they could carry on a sensible, matter-of-fact controversy without renouncing brotherly love.[17]

In the third letter in the *Second Check*, Fletcher described in detail the different forms and causes of antinomianism. With an allusion to Crisp, Fletcher called the opposite of practical Christianity 'Antinomian Crispianity':

> It would shame the careless Remonstrants, and shew them how orthodox some Calvinists are in point of works, and it would confound the slothful Calvinists, and make them see how they have left *Practical Christianity* for *Antinomian Crispianity*.[18]

Fletcher referred his opponents to Bishop Hopkins and to D. Williams. He illustrated the antinomian threat with an exposition of the Last Judgment, according to Matthew 25. The danger now, he argued, was more from the side of antinomianism than from the side of work-righteous pharisees. In two footnotes, he sought to make it clear that he was writing against those who allowed themselves to be led astray into antinomianism by the unrestrained teachings of certain Calvinists, and not against moderate Calvinists. Among seventeenth-century theologians, Baxter was the one by whom Fletcher was most impressed. Baxter had succeeded, he believed, in seeing the right relationship between faith and works. He had been the 'John Wesley of the previous century'. When the controversy was over, Fletcher would like to read more of Baxter's writings. Beyond antinomianism, there were still other controversial theological themes claiming Fletcher's attention, and there were topics on which other people wanted him to write,[19] but all this had to be postponed, because a fresh opponent, Sir Richard Hill, had joined in the controversy.

At the end of 1771 there appeared a reply by Sir Richard Hill to Fletcher's *First Check*. The document took the form of five letters, which were written in a tone of high personal regard for Fletcher. Fletcher began to compose a reply to Hill's letters in January 1772, although the controversy was becoming burdensome to him. He could see no good in it, and it seemed to be making no progress. One night he dreamt he had clasped Lady Huntingdon's knees, begged for peace, and asked her to cast the cloak of love over all offences. He had been very happy in his dream, and hoped that it was a good omen. However, the dream was not so quickly fulfilled.

In April 1772 Fletcher's *A Third Check to Antinomianism* was published. Now for the first time the subject of election by God came up for discussion. Out of the controversy over antinomianism arose a parallel controversy over the doctrine of predestination. John Wesley was not unhappy about this development.[20] Fletcher not only attacked his opponent's predestinarian thinking, which in his view led to antinomianism, he also, in this *Third Check*, set out for the first time his own understanding of the gracious action of God, setting it in opposition to the so-called Calvinism of Hill. Fletcher again insisted that in their personal life both Hill and Crisp were exemplary. What he was attacking was their teaching. He, Fletcher, wanted to conduct the controversy in mutual love.

During those months, Fletcher had Jones as his curate, and this meant that he had more time left for writing. He was already wanting to address himself to a fresh issue,[21] when a further encounter with Richard Hill arose. Hill replied to Fletcher's *Second Check*, and added to his letters a postscript directed against John Wesley. This was followed a little later by his reply to the *Third Check*. The tone of Hill's writings was becoming sharper. The battle-lines between the two camps began to harden. Lady Huntingdon now demanded explicitly that Fletcher should not preach any more in her chapels. Richard Hill's brother Rowland also published a retort to Fletcher's *Check*. Since all these writings appeared within a short space of time, Fletcher decided to answer them all together. A fourth *Check* was written in the course of the summer and autumn, and published before the end of the year.

The new work was entitled *Logica Genevensis: or, A Fourth Check to Antinomianism*, and was divided up into thirteen letters. As so often, it turned out to be much more extensive than Fletcher had originally intended. In an introduction, Fletcher addressed himself to all sincere Calvinists in the Church of England, and asked them to take the trouble to read his *Check*. He had tried, he said, to present the issue impartially,[22] but it was not possible to paint a picture of the night without using dark colours. Fletcher's doctrine of a second justification on the Day of Judgment, in accordance with a person's works, stood in sharp contrast to that propounded by Hill, which spoke of final salvation, and the imputation of Christ's righteousness. When at some points in his writings Richard Hill was in agreement with Fletcher's opinions, Fletcher even employed Hill's concessions as arguments against him. He made greater use of the testimony of the church, in its liturgy, articles of faith and homilies. He answered the complaint that his doctrine was new, and that none of the Puritan ministers had taught it, by referring to the writings of the 'Westminster Divines', and even by quoting from his contemporary Madan, who was fundamentally and vehemently opposed to the teachings of Wesley and Fletcher.

From Hill's statements, Fletcher put together a satirical creed, which was constructed in the 'I' form, and which was designed to expose the errors in Hill's Calvinism. The eleventh letter was devoted, among other things, to Pauline texts on the relationship between justification by faith upon repentance and justification in accordance with the works of faith on the last day. In the two final letters, Fletcher went into the disputed concepts of 'imputed righteousness' and 'free will', and tried to establish what agreement had been reached, and what differences remained. The truth of the gospel, he maintained, lay between the two extremes, in a proper balance between 'solifidianism' and moral conduct.

Not long after its appearance, John Wesley spoke appreciatively of the good influence of the *Fourth Check*, saying that it had strengthened many people in the truth. In doing so, he was thinking principally of his own societies. From other quarters Fletcher had heard otherwise. Lady Huntingdon did not wish to meet Fletcher personally any more, but said that she prayed for him daily – which Fletcher gratefully acknowledged. He was also able to preach again in one of the Countess's chapels, at Ashby, where Glazebrook was minister.[23]

A week after Richard Hill had received Fletcher's *Fourth Check*, he published his reply, which was intended as a concluding blow against Fletcher's teachings, and also as an attack upon John Wesley. But the end of the controversy was not yet in sight. Once again Fletcher had to postpone his work on other theological writings. He was even urged to continue the controversy by the peace-loving Ireland, who was beginning to recognize the dangerous tendencies of 'Calvinism'. Fletcher therefore planned the draft of a *Check* which would be directed in equal measure against pharisaism and antinomianism. He wanted to ensure that his campaign against antinomianism would not be misinterpreted as leading to pharisaism. He asked his friend Charles Wesley to list and supply him with the various pamphlets which had been written against him. Much of what was circulating in London or Bristol was unknown and inaccessible to him in Madeley.

At the end of July Fletcher received from Richard Hill an offer which, though honourably meant, was based on false assumptions. Hill wanted to suspend the sale of his writings, and, for the sake of love and friendship, bury the controversy.[24] The offer seemed one-sided to Fletcher, since he would have to leave unanswered writings by Hill which had already been published and distributed. However, he made the proposition that Hill might read the manuscript of his reply before it went to press, and raise any objections he might have to it. This was declined by

Hill, who decided nevertheless to put a stop to the sale of his own writings. Thus, probably towards the end of 1773, Fletcher published the first part of the *Fifth Check*, in which he dealt with Hill's last writing and other tracts from the Calvinist camp. In *Logica Genevensis continued: or, the first part of the Fifth Check to Antinomianism* Fletcher once again criticized the irrelevancy, the lack of arguments and the inaccurate reproduction of quotations in the writings of his opponents. In an attempt to conduct the controversy in a constructive way, Fletcher again set out in an appendix the things which were generally agreed and the differences which, though they still remained, were already being overcome, as a result of concessions by his opponent. The second part of the *Fifth Check* appeared in March 1774, and was intended as a reply to Berridge's *The Christian World Unmasked*. While criticizing the writer's incautious language, which might lead the reader into antinomianism, Fletcher sought to bear in mind the positive content of Berridge's statements.

Whilst Calvinistic writings replete with accusations and defamations were descending on Fletcher and his writings, he and the Countess, in a private exchange of letters, had achieved a measure of reconciliation.[25] But Fletcher wished to avoid a public meeting with the Countess until she had read his latest publication:

> Lady H. (entre nous) gave *me leave* to see her privately, I declined as not conscious to have done anything to make her ashamed of giving me leave to wait upon her openly, she then consented I should see her before all the world, but I have declined doing it till she has seen my *Scriptural essay* (which the calvinists will call *popery unmasked*) and my scales. *This favourable turn* is under God owing to a few arguments by which I have tried to (persuade [crossed out]) convince her that *derived worthiness* in believers perfectly agrees with Christ's *original merit*.[26]

In the middle of 1774 there appeared the first part of the *Equal Check to Pharisaism and Antinomianism*. The origins of this paper went back more than a year. In it, Fletcher was not arguing against a controversial document by the opposition, but setting out his own mediating theology. It was an attempt at a compromise between the two streams in Methodism. Fletcher was aware that he might come under attack, not only from Calvinists but also from Arminians. He hoped that, with two or three further writings, he might be able to bring the controversy to a close. Although he no longer regretted having been drawn into the controversy, he did not want always to have to spend half his days writing.

Fletcher began his *Equal Check* with a historical discussion of the meaning of faith and obedience and the harmony between them, beginning with Cain and Abel and continuing down to the present day. Then followed the sermon on Romans 11, written in 1762, to which we referred earlier. He published the sermon with remarks in parentheses, and with a commentary in footnotes. This in turn was followed by an essay on the amazing reward for works performed under the covenant of grace, supported by biblical quotations. The conclusion consisted of an essay on truth, which was intended to be a 'reasoned defence of the doctrine of salvation by faith', and which was dedicated to Lady Huntingdon. With this essay, Fletcher sought to dismantle the walls of division and to bring about reconciliation:

> Exceedingly sorry should I be, if the testimony which I have borne to the necessity of *good* works caused any of my readers to do the worst of *bad* works, that is, to neglect *believing*, and to depend upon some of the external *faithless* performances, which conceited Pharisees call 'good works'; and by which they absurdly think to make amends for their sins, to purchase the Divine favour, to set aside God's mercy, and to supersede Christ's atoning blood . . . I design in general to prove, that true faith is the only plant, which can possibly bear good works; that it loses its operative nature, and dies when it produces them not; and that it as much surpasses good works in importance, as the motion of the heart does all other bodily motions.[27]

Fletcher insisted that faith and works belonged essentially together, and set out in detail the different stages in God's action in revelation, to which he had already referred in the earlier *Checks*. It was this last part of Fletcher's teaching that John Wesley, who read with satisfaction and recommended everything that Fletcher wrote, found specially valuable:

> Mr. Fletcher has given us a wonderful view of the different dispensations which we are under. I believe that difficult subject was never placed in so clear a light before. It seems God has raised him up for this very thing – 'to vindicate eternal Providence
> And justify the ways of God to man'.[28]

Wesley was well aware of the difference between Fletcher's style of

argument and his own: while he himself wrote briefly and adduced just
a few weighty arguments, Fletcher presented his case in detail, with
much supporting evidence, and did not fail to answer possible objections in advance. The only thing Wesley missed in Fletcher's writings
was that they did not sufficiently point out and attack the 'charms of
Calvinism', by which so many people had been captivated.[29]

After Sir Richard Hill had withdrawn from the controversy and put a
stop to the sale of his books in 1773, the rumour spread that he had
retracted his teachings. He therefore published, probably towards the
end of 1774, the three letters which he had written privately to Fletcher
a year previously, offering to bring the controversy to an end. He felt
obliged to allow the sale of his books to be resumed. But he no longer
wanted to go on disputing, because he found the controversy distress-
ing. However, as an appendix to his latest publication he added a 'Creed
for Arminians and those who are perfect', which he himself had composed. This 'creed' was, as it were, a repayment in kind for Fletcher's
corresponding satire against the Calvinists in his *Fourth Check*, though
he did not support his case with appropriate quotations from his opponent. Fletcher did not wish to let this false creed rest. He composed a
creed of his own in reply, and published it in 1775.

Fletcher's creed was entitled: *The fictitious and the genuine Creed:
being 'A Creed for Arminians', composed by Richard Hill, Esq. to
which is opposed, A Creed for those who believe that Christ tasted
death for every man.* Fletcher decided to answer the second part of
Hill's 'Creed for those who are perfect' in a separate pamphlet, which
also appeared in 1775. In a postscript, Fletcher added that the controversy had been of benefit to him in many different ways, since he now
understood the gospel better and more clearly. In a personal letter to
Charles Wesley, Fletcher wrote:

The Lord is wonderfully gracious to me: and what is more to me than
many favours, he helps me to see his mercies in a clearer light. I have
so far leaned to calvinism as not to dare to be thankful in years past,
for mercies which now make me shout with joy. Calvinism has taught
me to call them *common* mercies, as I made as little of them as the
apostates do of the blood of Christ, when they call it a *common*
thing. But now the calvinian veil begins to rend, and I invite you and
all the world to praise God . . . O how I hate that delusion which has
robbed me of so many comforts. I hope I shall have yet a blow at the
very heart of it before I die.[30]

By the end of 1774, before the publication of the creed, there appeared the second part of the *Equal Check*: *Zelotes and Honestus reconciled: or, the second part of an Equal Check to Pharisaism and Antinomianism. Being the first part of the Scripture-Scales to weigh the Gold of Gospel Truth, – To balance a multitude of opposite Scriptures, – To prove the Gospel-Marriage of Free-Grace and Free-Will, and restore primitive Harmony to the Gospel of the Day.* In every controversy, Fletcher sought to build bridges of reconciliation. He continued to do so in the second part of the *Equal Check*. In the 'Scripture-Scales' it became very clear that Fletcher wanted to be a biblical theologian. The beginnings of it had been evident in the *First Check*, when Fletcher referred to apparently contradictory Scripture quotations, whose inner coherence needed to be recognized. Now, in the 'Scripture-Scales', he meticulously and methodically gathered together words of Scripture which contradicted various doctrinal statements. He had no standard method of doing this. Often he would set individual biblical verses over against each other. The passages concerned could come from the most widely differing books in the Old and New Testaments. In some places, Fletcher undertook to expound whole disputed passages, such as Romans 9 and Ephesians 1 on the doctrine of election. The second part of the 'Scripture-Scales' appeared in June 1775: *Zelotes and Honestus reconciled: or the third part of an Equal Check to Pharisaism and Antinomianism. Being the second part of the Scripture-Scales.* By this means Fletcher hoped to lead Zelotes, the antinomian solifidian, and Honestus, the pharisee, from their extreme paths to the balanced way of his Scripture-Scales. He concerned himself ever more strongly with the subject of reconciliation, although it was he who, in defence of John Wesley, had started off the controversy, and his writings were being sold by Wesley's travelling preachers.

In the autumn of 1775 there appeared the work which had been begun long before, and many times laid aside: Fletcher's treatise on Christian Perfection, of which he had written to Charles Wesley in 1771:

I am busy about my 3rd & last Check which I trust will be the most useful. I want both your prayers and advice. I shall introduce *my*, why not *your* doctrine of the Holy Ghost, & make it one with your brothers perfection. He holds the truth, but this will be an (addition to it [crossed out]) improvement upon it, if I am not mistaken. In some of your *pentecost hymns* you paint my light wonderfully. If *you do not recant* them [a humorous allusion to the Calvinistic Methodists, who had retracted their writings after Fletcher had quoted from them] we shall perfectly agree.[31]

Thus appeared *The Last Check to Antinomianism. A Polemical Essay on the twin Doctrines of Christian Imperfection and a Death Purgatory.* This treatise did not follow on from the concern with reconciliation in the *Equal Check*, but was, rather, a continuation of the original *Checks to Antinomianism*. During its long period of gestation, the work had grown to over three hundred pages. Even John Wesley offered a restrained criticism of the length of the book. By contrast, he pointed with approval to the concisely framed creed from the beginning of 1775,[32] and the concluding part of the *Last Check*, with its 'Address to the Perfect'. In this book Fletcher quoted more copiously than elsewhere from John Wesley's publications on the subject. He was concerned to make clear the extent to which they agreed, since the stress Fletcher laid on being filled with the Holy Spirit could lead to differences, as in fact John Wesley had already pointed out in connection with the *Equal Check*. John Wesley had recognized and warned Fletcher that he occasionally overlooked the fact that even the so-called 'babes in Christ' had received the Holy Spirit, though not yet in such full measure as 'fathers in Christ'.

The theological controversy over antinomianism and predestination did not, however, come to an end with the appearance of the *Last Check*. After John Wesley had repeatedly expressed opposition to the writings of Augustus Toplady, Toplady composed a reply, to which, this time, Wesley offered no response. Instead, Fletcher took over the pen, since Sir Richard Hill had recommended Toplady's disputed book as a masterly work. Fletcher's paper, *An Answer to the Rev. Mr. Toplady's 'Vindication of the Decrees'*, appeared finally in 1776. The position he took was different from that of Wesley's previous criticisms of Toplady, and held closely to the principles set out in the 'Scripture-Scales'. Fletcher refuted, point by point, every argument he could discover in Toplady's writing. In a postscript he announced that he would shortly publish his reply to a very recently issued new work by Toplady. The publication was delayed, but finally appeared in 1777 as *A Reply to the principal arguments by which the Calvinists and the Fatalists support the doctrine of absolute necessity: Being remarks on the Rev. Mr. Toplady's 'Scheme of Christian and Philosophical Necessity'*. Both of Fletcher's writings against Toplady took issue with the notion of necessity. The sharp logic of his arguments exposed Toplady's false conclusions, yet at the same time, through the use of illustrations, remained comprehensible even to uneducated readers.

But Fletcher's real aim, to which the last two writings in the theological controversy were dedicated, was to pave the way to reconciliation. He completed them with great difficulty, because his tuberculosis had by this time brought him to the brink of death. James Ireland arranged to bring the opponents in the controversy together before Fletcher died, as it was feared he would. At the end of 1776 Fletcher visited Berridge, and at about the same time a meeting took place with Shirley, Rowland Hill and other Calvinists. Fletcher urged them to promote peace in the church. He had also received a friendly letter from Lady Huntingdon, and was again in correspondence with her. He was thus able to write to Ireland that the world seemed to him to have become a world of love. His conversations with leading Calvinistic Methodists encouraged Fletcher to complete and publish his last two works.

First, in 1777, appeared a short tract which bore the marks of the new atmosphere of reconciliation: *The Doctrines of Grace and Justice, equally essential to the pure Gospel: with some remarks on the mischievous divisions caused among Christians by parting those doctrines. Being an introduction to a plan of reconciliation between the defenders of the doctrines of partial grace, commonly called Calvinists; and the defenders of the doctrines of impartial justice, commonly called Arminians.* Against the background of church history, Fletcher showed how the two doctrines had fallen apart, and stressed the importance of an equal balance between the grace and the righteousness of God. Cranmer had achieved this, he maintained, at the time of the Reformation. The controversy provoked by John Wesley in 1770 now seemed to lead to the happy goal of confirming the early Christian evenly balanced gospel.

The second tract bore the title: *The Reconciliation: or an easy method to unite the professing people of God, by placing the doctrines of grace and justice in such a light, as to make the candid Arminians Bible-Calvinists, and the candid Calvinists Bible-Arminians.* Here Fletcher sought to present unifying, truly evangelical doctrine, and he set out his own understanding of election and rejection.[33] He dedicated his tract to James Ireland. He was convinced that he had found the way back to the heart of scriptural truth, which had been abandoned by rigid Calvinists and Arminians, but which could be endorsed by moderate Calvinists

and Arminians. He showed Arminians where they could learn from
Calvinists. He urged the two streams in Methodism to be reconciled on
this foundation, and to carry out their task together in love and unity.
He referred to Wesley's plan of union in the sixties, and on the basis of
it proposed the foundation of a 'society for the promotion of unanimity
and tolerance among Christians'. In concrete terms, his plan included
pulpit exchanges and shared communion services between moderate
Arminians and Calvinists. His failing health, however, did not permit
him to take an active part in the realization of his idea. But he still tried
to act as mediator between Lady Huntingdon and John Wesley. Even
during the time of his convalescence on the Continent, he used his letters
to promote reconciliation: 'The heavenly dove loves no selfishness. My
tract was not contrived to please but to reconcile parties; party people,
therefore, will never like it. And neuters are seldom valiant in the cause
of peace.'[34] Fletcher confirmed to the Countess in 1777 that he would
not withdraw any of his writings. He was convinced that the controversy had been necessary. He had recognized that the 'Arminians' held
only a part of the truth, and that the doctrine of the 'Calvinists' also
contained a part of the truth. Thus he discovered a balanced understanding of the gospel, a mutual interplay of grace and righteousness. In
these last two writings Fletcher sought to summarize the gains acquired
from the theological controversy.

The way in which Fletcher sought to reconcile the two streams in
Methodism is instructive. He did not try to formulate a new, common,
as it were 'all-Methodist' body of doctrine. He recognized, rather, that
both sides, with their own special emphases, were stressing part of the
truth, and expressing it within a particular doctrinal framework. Each
of these dialectical structures, however, ran the danger of concealing or
even denying the truth of the gospel through a wrongly understood
systematization. Fletcher recognized implicitly that biblical truth is
always received and communicated with particular accents, and
through particular thought-forms, which can be neither ignored nor
abolished. Rather, they must be examined to see what aspects of truth
they contain, and thus regarded as of value.

The effect of Fletcher's writings is hard to determine. No research has
been done into it. Provisionally, the following observations may be
made. On the one hand, the writings were published and read within the
framework of Wesleyan Methodism and, as a result of its great expansion, not only during Fletcher's lifetime, but throughout the whole of
the nineteenth century. Their influence was therefore very widespread.

This applies both to England and to America, both to the main stem and to the side-branches of the spreading tree formed by the proliferation of Methodist churches. For many decades, Fletcher's works were required reading in the studies programme of would-be Methodist preachers. Their effect on the Holiness Movement of the nineteenth century and the Pentecostal Movement of the twentieth is to be seen precisely in the special link between the doctrine of perfection and the gift of the Holy Spirit.[35] Whether Fletcher's writings encouraged the moralizing tendency in nineteenth-century American Methodism is, however, in my view, questionable.[36] On the other hand, the effect of Fletcher's writings should not be overestimated. Reconciliation between the Calvinistic and Wesleyan streams in Methodism was not achieved, and his writings were hardly likely to win the assent of those on the Calvinistic side.[37] Fletcher's mediating theology did not become the basis for greater mutual esteem between Calvinistic and Wesleyan Methodists, nor an incentive for the development of a similarly motivated, moderate Methodist theology on the part of the Calvinists. The continuing division between the two streams in Methodism is illustrated by the fact that at the end of 1777, as a riposte to the Calvinistic periodical *Gospel Magazine*, John Wesley founded his own periodical, the *Arminian Magazine* – a very provocative title to Calvinist ears.

The political controversy of the 1770s over American Independence

In 1775 the armed struggle between American settlers and British troops broke out. Only a brief outline can be given here of the long history leading up to this event. The deeper reasons for the conflict were not simply of a commercial nature, but arose from differences in the social and political environment. The British lived in a richly traditional, orderly society. Their political system, based on constitutional monarchy, was stable. It was considered to be well balanced, and had been tried and tested. The British looked back with horror on the troubles of the seventeenth century. With regard to the colonies, they saw themselves chiefly as a trading nation. Their supremacy in trading and the superiority of British naval power went hand in hand. Britain conducted a trading policy which aimed at maintaining the most stable possible mutual balance of interests. In the American colonies, by contrast, the traditional British social system did not apply. What counted was not a person's inherited social status, but individual effort and success. Laws and government regulations were generally felt to be contrary to individual interests. The colonists called England their homeland, and George III the best of all kings. But at the same time England was far away, and their attention was mainly directed towards their own concerns. Thus the interests of the British Empire and its trade were opposed to the colonists' own interests and desires for expansion.

Around the middle of the 1770s, the dispute over the status of the American colonies began to create huge waves in England too. In the autumn of 1775, John Wesley, who had earlier spoken out against the taxation of the American colonies by the Parliament in London, issued a pamphlet in which he defended the legality of the taxes. Within a few months the pamphlet attained a circulation of between 50,000 and 100,000 copies, and provoked an equally powerful reaction. In many places Wesley met with anger and resentment, since public feeling was being stirred up against the Government. One of the many retorts to Wesley's pamphlet came from Caleb Evans, a Baptist minister from Bristol. Startled by the vehemence of the dispute, Fletcher, contrary to his original intention, felt obliged to hurry to Wesley's assistance. He sent his manuscript to Lord Dartmouth, who at that time was still Secretary of State for the American colonies, so that he might offer his advice as to whether publication was wise. Lord Dartmouth could see no reason for preventing it, and John Wesley was convinced that publication should take place immediately. Fletcher's pamphlet appeared at the beginning of 1776: *A Vindication of the Rev. Mr. Wesley's 'Calm Address to our American Colonies'*. Evans at once composed a reply, to which Fletcher responded in turn with a second political pamphlet, which went to press in May: *American Patriotism farther confronted with reason, scripture and the constitution . . .*

In agreement with John Wesley, Fletcher proposed a day of public repentance and fasting. By royal proclamation at the end of October, 13 December was declared a general fast day. For this day Fletcher published a third, short pamphlet, which, in the main, arose out of an excerpt from his second pamphlet: *The Bible and the Sword: or, the appointment of the general fast vindicated: in an address to the common people.* Fletcher's second pamphlet was submitted by Lord Dartmouth to the Lord Chancellor, who was also responsible for ecclesiastical appointments, and who officially made known his approval of it. Fletcher's earliest biographers report that he was asked whether he wished for advancement in the church. The reply he is reported by the biographers to have given is in harmony with Fletcher's lifestyle and inner disposition: he is said to have answered that he was in need of nothing but more grace.[38] 'I have unaccountably launched into Christian Politics, a branch of divinity too much neglected by some, and too much attended to by others.'[39] Fletcher explained, at various points in his writings, why he was now concerning himself with political questions. The gospel, he believed, led to the observance of a strict ethical code, which included, for example, obedience towards the authorities, and the payment of taxes. Just as the government afforded the protection of the secular sword, so the church should afford that of the spiritual sword. Fletcher wanted, as he put it, to fight with spiritual weapons. He wanted to find answers to political questions from the standpoint of the gospel, and above all to argue his case with words from Scripture. He quoted from many Old Testament texts. He also hoped in this way to convince the American settlers, many of whom paid attention to Scripture. Fletcher was convinced that the conflict between Britain and the American colonies could not be settled by force of arms. By a military victory, which Fletcher regarded as possible, Britain would gain nothing but more mistrust, and would be accused of tyranny. If reconciliation could not be achieved now, early in 1776, or by the summer, then the struggle should be continued only with spiritual weapons and arguments.

At the centre of the theological dispute was, of course, the question as to where the source of political power lay. Fletcher's opponents advocated the new theory of the 'social contract', according to which power was given to a government on the basis of the consent of the governed.[40] Fletcher opposed this theory, which had had some influence in England from the time of the early Enlightenment, with great determination. Over against it he set the traditional argument that all power was given by God. He drew a distinction between the electoral choice of the people, which puts a government in office, and the fundamental granting of authority to rule, which God alone can confer. Fletcher did not dispute the power of the people to overthrow their king, but rather their right to do so. On the other hand, he emphasized that a government could not carry out its functions without the support of the majority of the people. The agreement of the people did not, he maintained, create governmental power, but it did make possible the exercise of it.

Fletcher hoped for a reconciliation with the American colonies. He urged attention to their need for parliamentary representation and protection from arbitrary decisions, and supported negotiation with them over taxation procedure, though the government was not legally obliged to negotiate. Fletcher's final, mediating request to the king was expressed in the form of a comparison. The comparison shows, on the one hand, what conclusions Fletcher drew from the principle that the king's authority is given to him by God, and, on the other, how, with this idealistic view, he overlooked the fundamental difference between God and an earthly king in a constitutional monarchy: as God's grace does not detract from the divine sovereignty, so, he claimed, a gracious act on the part of the king would not impair the royal sovereignty. The royal sovereignty and grace seemed to Fletcher so heavily imbued with a divine quality that he could foresee no other outcome than the conversion of the rebellious colonies and mutual reconciliation.

Alongside Fletcher's theological arguments about the source of authority, he often made statements of a legal nature, verging at times on legal briefing. He was acquainted with the constitution and details of the English electoral system, and he drew comparisons with the political troubles of the seventeenth century. He described himself as a republican by birth and upbringing, who, however, through his own experience and by his own free choice, had come to prefer the sensible, moderate form of the British monarchy, and the balance of powers in the two houses of the British Parliament. Fletcher rejected both extreme monarchism and extreme republicanism. Here too he sought to pursue a middle course. He valued the well-balanced nature of the British constitution, and shared with John Wesley an unswerving loyalty to the crown, in a politically turbulent age.

Fletcher opposed the absolute right to possess property urged by his opponents. He argued that it was not only God who had a right over our property, but also the government, which had to care for the common good of society. Private interests, even in questions of property, should be subordinated to public well-being.[41] It might become necessary for the government to use armed force to protect the public good. Since all authority was given by God, however, government and king were answerable to God for their actions. The authority granted to them by God needed to be exercised in accordance with God's law, which would lead to peace in the community and to the general good. If this accord were not guaranteed, Fletcher would offer passive resistance to the measures concerned, or to the government and the king.

In line with corresponding remarks in Wesley's writings, Fletcher also addressed himself in two places to the question of slavery. In his first article, he reproached the American settlers for their blindness: there were many among them, he said, who would cry 'Tyranny! Slavery! Theft! Murder!', when they were required to pay small taxes, although as slave-owners they must know only too well what real tyranny and cruel bondage were. In his second article Fletcher made his reproach more radical: through the slave trade, the British Empire was saddling itself with a grave injustice. The blood of the slaves was crying out to heaven. If Britain did not repent and change its ways, God's wrath would fall upon the nation. Against this background, Fletcher proposed fasting and prayer as signs of repentance and conversion. All fasting must have as its objective the removal of evil, outside us and within us.

14

Fletcher's Dispensational Theology

The account of Fletcher's theology which follows is based upon his contributions to the controversy over antinomianism and predestination, and upon a treatise on the doctrine of sin, which appeared in 1772. Fletcher's theology is here displayed in its more mature form.[1] The account deliberately draws on Fletcher's own thought-forms and language.[2] We turn first to the grounds on which he based his arguments – to the significance and mutual relationships of Scripture, reason, tradition and experience. In the light of the question which was central to the Calvinistic controversy, and of Fletcher's two basic axioms, the territory over which his theology ranged becomes plain. The themes of creation, the Fall, initial salvation and free will lead into soteriology, and show what Fletcher regarded as the typical 'human state of probation'. Thus human existence in the world and before God comes into view, and the relationship between faith and works is outlined. In Fletcher's thought, the themes raised in this process are not just set alongside each other, but, as it were, held together in an inner unity by overarching statements which make up the doctrine of God. The twofold arch, on the one hand the action of the trinitarian God in history, and on the other (closely connected with the first) the election and rejection of human beings by the gracious and, at the same time, righteous God, influences all the statements held together under it. The chapter ends with some observations on the doctrine of judgment according to works, and on Fletcher's mediating position in relation to the starting point of the controversy.

The formal methods of argument

In the 1760s, Fletcher used four categories of argument: Scripture, tradition, reason and experience. He took over this fourfold basis from John Wesley, and in doing so revealed the extent to which he had been influenced by the Dutch-English early Enlightenment. In his writings from the 1770s, Fletcher argued in part explicitly from these categories. An interesting and important shift, which had begun to manifest itself even in the 1760s, now became apparent: Scripture and reason became the main categories, with experience and tradition following on behind them. This shift can be seen particularly clearly in Fletcher's treatise on the doctrine of sin. In the 1760s he had planned a treatise which was to have been based on all four categories. The completely new treatment of the subject, which appeared in 1772, described itself typically as *An Appeal to Matter of Fact and Common Sense: or, a rational demonstration of man's corrupt and lost estate.* Fletcher wanted to show the reasonableness of the revealed doctrine, thereby responding to the challenge of his time, which looked for reasonableness in doctrinal statements. The early influence on Fletcher of reasonable orthodoxy, his acquaintance with the high esteem in which reason was held in the Anglican tradition, and the effect upon him of John Locke's early Enlightenment understanding of reason, were all reflected in his formal methods of argument.

Scripture and reason are the standards by which a doctrine must be measured. Fletcher appealed to the Reformation. The Protestants had at that time declared, he maintained, that reason held an important place in matters of faith, and that all such matters could and should be decided by Scripture, understood rationally and in accordance with the context.[3] Fletcher wanted to measure his teaching, and also that of his opponents, by Scripture and reason. He did not admit his opponents' claim that, unlike him, they understood things in a spiritual manner, unless they could support their teachings by sound human understanding, or by the Scriptures.

Scripture was, for Fletcher, the basic norm in questions of faith. It had been brought home to him strongly, through his work on the essay on truth, that the means whereby the Spirit of God speaks is the word. The word of truth meets us in Scripture. So, he believed (in harmony with the Calvinistic tradition), it is the one Spirit of God who manifests himself in the word of Scripture and in the personal experience of the believer. The divine authority of Scripture can, however, be demonstrated to critical contemporaries by means of rational arguments. Critical and historical investigations by godly scholars are useful and helpful for bringing to light the clarity and unanimity of the witness of Scripture.[4] The simple quotation of passages from Scripture does not provide sufficient proof. Scripture needs to be properly interpreted. If the literal sense of a passage is not applicable, then it must be understood in a figurative sense.

In the interpretation of Scripture, the believer has to rely on the use of reason. Reason is absolutely necessary for the right understanding of Scripture. However, reason cannot make statements on faith independently, without reference to Scripture. Thus there could be, for Fletcher, no situations of conflict in which reason stood over against his understanding of faith. Reason served faith in two ways. On the one hand, it led to the point at which one would be ready to recognize biblical teaching as sensible and reasonable. Because the opponents of Fletcher's doctrine of sin appealed to reason, they ought to be made aware, in the name of reason, of the truth of the biblical teaching on sin. On the other hand, faith needed to be reflected upon and accounted for rationally. There was, though, a tension in the concept of reason. Fletcher could say that reason was a beam of the light that lightens everyone coming into the world – that reason was a reflection of the eternal Logos. A similar definition could have been offered by Locke and reasonable orthodoxy. Over against it, however, stood other, more numerous, statements by Fletcher, in which his radical doctrine of sin found expression: reason is afflicted by the corruption in human nature, and devotes itself to the service of corruption, so that true reason is as rarely to be found as true piety. There was, for Fletcher, a happy medium – an albeit narrow pathway, along which reason and revelation went hand in hand. In seeking to follow this pathway, Fletcher was making an unspoken appeal from the corrupt reason of his critical contemporaries to reason enlightened by revelation.

Fletcher often used the category of reason to describe logical reflections by means of which he could test the soundness of his opponents' methods of argument. He exposed with irony ridiculous error which sought to pass itself off as truth. In his treatise on the doctrine of sin, reason was presented as the means whereby what the understanding had assimilated through the senses could be judged, and conclusions drawn from it. This was a reflection of Locke's epistemology. In so far as the conclusions of reason could claim universal validity, Fletcher, in conformity with the age, would speak of 'common sense'. In this context, Fletcher could also refer to the category of experience, to facts and sound human understanding, which, however, could only be applied in relation to universal basic human experiences.[5] In other respects, the recourse to experience had amazingly little place in the development of his argument.[6] Experience was, for Fletcher, an unsafe means of resolving unsettled questions, and he therefore never based his argument primarily upon it.[7] Rather, it is the conscience that takes third place, after Scripture and reason. In his statements about the significance of the law for the believer, Fletcher particularly invoked a person's conscience as the deciding factor. However, the conscience too is affected by the corruption of human nature as a whole, and its decisions are therefore unsafe, since in part it does not react at all, while in part it reacts too sharply and too often.

Statements from tradition occupied much space in Fletcher's writings. Nevertheless tradition as an independent factor had no place in Fletcher's own arguments. He referred to tradition only for his opponents' sake, for apologetic reasons. He wanted to counter the claim that he was teaching completely new, hitherto unheard of, things. In his quotations he based himself mainly on the Fathers of the first centuries, on the Reformers, and on seventeenth-century Calvinists who stood in the experimental predestinarian tradition. The latter were particularly welcome witnesses in Fletcher's eyes, because, with their Calvinistic background, they counted rather as among his opponents. From many of them he took quotations which supported his position, but he did not overlook the elements in their theological thinking which conflicted with his own. Fletcher found himself most closely drawn to Richard Baxter, who had been in the previous century what John Wesley now was in the eighteenth century. Except in the *Last Check*, he did not quote particularly frequently from John Wesley, whose teaching he had set out to defend, although the essential closeness between them is obvious. He once remarked that he did not wish to follow John Wesley any further than Wesley followed Christ. The continental Reformers were mentioned only infrequently.[8] In his writings Fletcher often made use of works on church history and the history of doctrine, and of collections of texts, all of which provided him with quotations.[9] In addition, he could quote from philosophers such as Hobbes and Locke, or contemporaries like Voltaire and the French *encyclopédistes*. Sometimes he would be in agreement with them, while at other times he would be quoting them as the voices of perceptive unbelievers.

Fletcher's arguments contained many pictures, illustrations, stories and comparisons. He used these devices both to expose the flaws in the apparently plausible arguments of his opponents, and to illustrate what he himself meant. He knew the danger that lay in making inappropriate comparisons. He used symbolic pictures and stories with the deliberate intent of setting his statements within the framework of an easily understood, everyday experience of the world. This style made for greater clarity. Fletcher wanted to make his writings accessible not only to the educated, but also to plain men and women in his parish and in the Methodist societies. Occasionally he combined his theological expositions with sermon-like interjections and applications to particular groups of people among his readers. In the last analysis, even his theological writings were meant to awaken, promote and strengthen faith.

The basic question in the theological controversy, and the two fundamental axioms

Fletcher began the theological controversy because, in common with John Wesley, he gave an important place to human responsibility in the process of salvation. The controversy flared up over the basic question of the relationship between faith and works. 'Solifidianism' was, for Fletcher, only another word for antinomianism. The dominant antithesis in his theology lay not in the tension between law and gospel, but in that between sin and grace. The problem of determining the relationship between God's dealings and human activity was the central issue in the controversy. Out of it arose such themes as the Fall, free will, predestination, the saving work of Christ, etc. In the course of the controversy, there was a shift in the way the basic question was treated. In the earlier writings, human existence before God held the centre of the stage. In the later ones, Fletcher increasingly took the doctrine of God as his starting point for discussing the human condition.

Already in the *First Check*, Fletcher established two axioms which he saw as the basis of John Wesley's understanding of the gospel:[10]

> As a consequence of the doctrine of General Redemption, Mr. W. [John Wesley] lays down two axioms, of which he never loses sight in his preaching. The first is, that ALL OUR SALVATION IS OF GOD IN CHRIST, and therefore OF GRACE; all opportunities, invitations, inclination, and power to believe, being bestowed upon us of mere grace; – grace most absolutely free; and so far I hope that all who are called gospel-ministers agree with him: but he proceeds farther, for secondly, he asserts with equal confidence, that according to the gospel dispensation, ALL OUR DAMNATION IS OF OURSELVES, by our obstinate unbelief, and avoidable unfaithfulness: as we may *neglect so great salvation*, desire to *be excused* from coming

to the feast of the Lamb, *make light of* God's gracious offers, refuse
to occupy, bury our talent, and act the part of the slothful servant; or
in other words, *resist, grieve, do despite to*, and *quench the Spirit of
grace*, BY OUR MORAL AGENCY.[11]

These axioms reappeared either implicitly or explicitly in all the writings
which followed. They defined Fletcher's thinking. Taken together, the
two axioms guaranteed the balance of the gospel. Fletcher's aim, which
he achieved especially in the *Equal Check*,[12] was to do justice in his
writings to both aspects. The 'Scripture-Scales' rested entirely on
these two axioms. What 'solifidians' and 'moralists' respectively had
developed, with exclusive reference to one or other of the two axioms,
was, according to Fletcher, marvellously held together in the gospel.
Gospel preaching on one of the axioms needed to beware of contradicting the other, either directly or indirectly. The two axioms could
also be demonstrated by statements on free grace and free will, and in
this way their apparent contradictoriness could be explained.[13] The
territory over which Fletcher's theological thought ranged thus becomes
apparent. Although the word 'axiom' signifies a self-evident truth,
Fletcher saw in many parts of his theological approach a corrective to
tradition.[14] He remained true to the two axioms even when his theology
was fully developed.

Creation, the Fall, initial salvation and free will

God has created this world in accordance with his perfect plan.
Creation can be divided up into inanimate nature, the plant world, the
animal world, and, at the highest level, humans, who are rational,
independent beings. This gradation reflects God's wise purpose as
creator. He created human beings with free will. Human free will is part
of what it means to be made in the image of God. Adam owed his free
will to the grace of God in creation. In his original state of innocence,
Adam was bound to God in faith. Faith in this context is understood as
an unbroken trust in God and a firm observance of his will. Such faith in
God was necessary for Adam. It was faith in God as creator, lawgiver
and judge. God gave Adam the law of innocence, which required perfect
obedience, which made no allowance or provision for any act of transgression, and which was combined with the promise of reward or, as the
case might be, with punishment. Adam had a natural and a spiritual life.

The latter consisted in the empirical knowledge of the creator, and in uprightness and true holiness. Human beings were the moral and supremely marvellous images of God. They were thus rational and free creatures, who knew and loved their creator. In his observations on creation, Fletcher was strongly influenced by early Enlightenment thought.[15]

Adam, however, was disobedient, and fell into sin. The Fall was not only moral disobedience, but rebellion against the authority of God. The root of sin lay in Adam's lack of faith. Through the Fall, Adam lost God's favour and his likeness to God. He became a vessel of wrath. He lost his knowledge of, and love for, God. Fear and dismay took the place of love. Adam also lost his conjugal love for Eve. Obstinacy and recrimination took its place. In no way does sin have its origin in God. If the endowment of human beings with free will did not contravene the wisdom and goodness of God, then the sin of those human beings, acting freely on their own initiative, cannot impugn the divine perfection. It is not right to say: 'God has allowed sin', or: 'all that is, is good, because overall it serves a great end'. On the contrary, God has forbidden sin, and threatened it with punishment, while not absolutely preventing it, so as not to deprive human beings of their freedom of action. By his sin, Adam brought down the just curse of God on himself and on everything which had been created for him. The consequences of the Fall are to be seen not only in the corruption of human nature, but in the whole creation. The suffering and groaning of all creatures – like the death which is the consequence of sin – is not testing but punishment. In conformity with Reformation tradition, Fletcher interpreted the Fall, not just as disobedience (as it was for the early Enlightenment), but as unbelief and rebellion against God.

Fletcher's understanding of original sin can, then, be seen as an attempt to do justice to the tradition of the Reformation and the early Enlightenment.[16] Along with a fresh understanding of God's saving activity in Christ, this led to the doctrine of initial salvation, which was, I believe, a unique interpretation.[17] The whole human race is contained in Adam's seed: '. . . *all have sinned* in him [Adam], who was all mankind seminally and federally collected in one individual.'[18] In Adam all people have sinned. If God had not shown himself gracious, the whole human race would have died in Adam's seed. The punishment would have come upon it, like the sin, without any personal awareness or personal decision. It would have been God's just punishment. However, in the event that the human race should fall into sin, God had made provision for its restoration through Jesus Christ.[19] Thus, as through Adam's sin condemnation came upon all people, so through the righteousness of Christ justification is made available for all.[20] All people received this indescribable blessing because they were in Adam's loins when God created him. The blessing in Christ exceeds the curse in Adam, since humanity's new status under the gospel is more favourable than that of Adam in paradise. No one will be condemned by God for the original corruption which we sustained in Adam's seed:

> Every anti-calvinist may, and I for one, do believe, that *in every man born into the world* and considered according to the first covenant, original corruption (not Adam's transgression) *deserves* God's wrath and damnation at the hands of a holy and righteous God; without dreaming that any man shall be ever damned for it: seeing that, according to God's mercy and goodness displayed in the second covenant, Christ *the second Adam*, is come *to taste death for EVERY man*, and to be *the Saviour of ALL men*; so that for his sake, *the free gift is come upon ALL men to* justification of life.[21]

Fletcher called this salvation, which in Christ is offered to everyone, 'initial salvation'. This means that there is unconditional justification for little children, dependent neither on faith nor on works. Initial salvation is not tied to baptism either, but baptism is performed in the church on the basis of the initial salvation granted, in Christ, to all people. Fletcher laid particular stress on three things: this original grace of God in Christ is given to *all* people; it is *saving* grace;[22] it operates without our help, i.e. it is *irresistible*. This last aspect of it is precisely what distinguishes it from all other operations of divine grace. These statements about initial salvation have far-reaching consequences. Fletcher was well aware of them. He drew out the consequences above all in the framework of his understanding of the operation of the triune God in history.

Fletcher's understanding of original sin and initial salvation combined two features. First, under the influence of Methodism, he adopted Pauline statements about the sin which embraces all people, and about the redemption of all through the death of the Son of God on the cross. Secondly, in order to interpret and explain these convictions, he made use of concepts which, in the wake of the early Enlightenment, had come to be regarded as fundamental: the personal responsibility and free will of each individual, as well as the centrality of history.

For the moment, however, we are still concerned with the implica-

tions of the doctrine of original or initial grace for individual men and
women:

> But the moment we allow that the blessing of the second Adam is
> as general as the curse of the first: that God *sets* again *life and
> death* before every individual, and that he mercifully restores to all a
> capacity of choosing life, yea, and of having it one day more
> abundantly than Adam himself had before the fall, we see his good-
> ness and justice shine with equal radiance, when he spares guilty
> Adam to propagate the fallen race, that they may share the blessings
> of a better covenant.[23]

Fletcher was postulating a free will which, following the Fall, was
naturally only capable of evil, but which, thanks to the grace of God
given to all people, was now capable of good.[24] Free will was no longer
indebted, as for Adam, to the creative grace of God, but now, for all
people, to God's redeeming grace. The freedom of the will does not
detract from free grace, since free will has its basis in free grace. Neither
does human freedom of action deprive God of the honour due to him.
There is no place for self-glory or pharisaical pride, since all that is good
and well-pleasing to God is the outcome of God's grace. The human will
can be convinced but not compelled, otherwise it ceases to be free will.
Fletcher criticized those who argued for a radically unfree will just as
much as those who argued for a radically free will. Both groups were
contradicting the basic double axiom on salvation and condemnation. If
free will rises up against free grace, it becomes arrogant, and no longer
knows its proper place.

Thus it is true, on the one hand, that human beings are conceived in
sin. They are by nature corrupt. There is no natural innocence, even for
the newborn. A person can have no natural power to remain innocent.
On the other hand, in Christ God has given to all people freedom to
choose the good. He will not restrain this freedom by necessarily effective, irresistible grace. If the outcome of God's word depended on God
alone, the truth would always lead to deliverance. But human beings
can put up a resistance. They can decide against grace. The corruption
in their nature leads them to personal rebellion against God. They
willingly consent to sin. Even children as young as ten experience their
own corruption. Human beings see God as an intruder. They flee from
the divine doctor and his bitter medicine. It is only when they see on one
side their own imminent ruin and on the other redeeming love that they

can submit to the painful, judicial direction of God. It is painful and bitter to have to abandon every thought of meritorious works of their own, and see themselves as sinners before God, dependent on his grace alone. The grace of God in Christ, which from our side finds expression through faith in Christ, is the original and only meritorious ground of our salvation.

In his doctrine of sin and grace, Fletcher, as he himself had recognized, differed not only from his Calvinistic opponents, but also from Pelagianism. His doctrine of sin shows that he was not only influenced by, but also at variance with, early Enlightenment thinking. His criticism of the Calvinistic doctrine of predestination applied also to the doctrine of original sin with which it was linked. In the light of the latter, it was not reasonable to believe that a person could justly be condemned by God. A personal judgment upon us by God can only be right if we personally and deliberately commit sin. If a particular kind of action were compulsorily imposed upon us, it would no longer be a moral action: 'When you begin at *Sin*, you can never ascend higher than *Free-will*: and when you begin at *God*, you can never descend lower than *Free-will*.'[25] Morality can only exist where we are freely allowed to decide between good and evil. It is illuminating that a quotation from Locke appears at this particular point in Fletcher's writings.[26] Thus while Fletcher drew on early Enlightenment thought, he also diverged from it, as his treatise on the doctrine of sin particularly shows. The total corruption of human beings, whose will is only made free to choose the good through the grace of God in Christ, is heavily stressed. Corruption cannot be overcome by education. It is total, and embraces a person's every faculty. Against the kind of criticism of tradition and Scripture which was being made in the name of reason, but at the same time influenced by it, Fletcher sought to reinterpret and to validate the Pauline doctrine of sin.

The trinitarian dispensation of God's grace in history, and the doctrine of election and rejection associated with it

Fletcher developed his doctrine of grace in a trinitarian/salvation history perspective in which each person of the Trinity had a particular time and function. He spoke of the 'dispensations' of God. It was only in his later writings that he gave attention to the unity of the triune God in his revelation in history, and to the nature of God as the three in one.

During the theological controversies of the 1770s, the trinitarian dispensation of God's grace in history and the related 'economic' doctrine of the Trinity held centre stage.

All truths can promote understanding, but only religious truths exercise a direct influence on the will. Jesus Christ is the truth, saving truth. He is the Word of God. Living, saving faith relates to the truth, to Christ, as its cause and its object. The truth which saves is one. But it is revealed to people in different measure. Thus Fletcher defined faith not as an explicit christological confession, but in more general terms as 'believing in saving truth from the heart, for inward and outward righteousness, according to the measure of light revealed to us'. The definition was framed so widely because initial salvation is granted to everyone through Christ's redemptive act, and in every nation those who fear God and work righteousness are saved. God does not require us to believe what he has not revealed to us. Fletcher was here taking up a basic concept of the early Enlightenment,[27] and interpreting it in the framework of his economic understanding of the Trinity.

Neither people who lived before the birth of Christ, nor the heathen who have not yet heard the gospel, are fundamentally excluded from salvation. God has revealed himself to different people at different times in different measure. To make this clear, Fletcher employed two different sets of distinctions. The first set related to groups of people. He distinguished three, sometimes four, groups: heathens, Jews, Christians – with the Christians often subdivided into babes in Christ and mature Christians.[28] The other set related to the operation of the triune God. Fletcher distinguished three dispensations: of the Father, of the Son and of the Spirit. In these dispensations God acts in a sustaining, a redemptive, or a convicting and sanctifying way. What at a lower level remains hidden to knowledge becomes plain at a higher level. Both sets of distinctions can be applied to history as a whole and to an individual person. Thus, on the one hand, historically, the dispensation of the Father is given to everyone.[29] The dispensation of the Son was promised to God's people in the Old Testament, and found fulfilment in the life, death and resurrection of Jesus Christ. The dispensation of the Spirit was promised to the disciples of Jesus, and found fulfilment after Pentecost. On the other hand, in relation to individuals and their growth in faith, the Father can draw people who believe in him as Creator to the Son as their redeemer. Christ can fill those who believe in him as redeemer with the fullness of the Holy Spirit.

Fletcher's trinitarian dispensation of God's revelation in history was formulated with reference to the minutes of Wesley's Conference of 1770.[30] It must, however, be regarded as his own achievement. John Wesley saw it as a valuable contribution towards resolving the controversy, and towards a better understanding of the biblical message.[31] Fletcher took as his principal biblical text the parable of the talents in Matthew 25, and interpreted it in the sense that God had given one talent to the first, the heathen; two talents to the second, the Jew; and five talents to the third, the Christian. Fletcher's reference points were not, as a rule, the different covenants made by God,[32] which, taken as a whole, were a sign of God's elective grace. He preferred to use the concept of covenant in establishing the contrast between the covenant of righteousness, or works, and the covenant of grace. The former was God's covenant with Adam before the Fall. The latter is the covenant which God has made with the whole human race. When, therefore, the Old Testament speaks of the establishment of different covenants, it is a question of different stages in the revelation of the one covenant of *grace*, which God has made with humanity in Christ. Neither in terms of promises nor in terms of moral demands, therefore, is there any fundamental opposition between the Old and New Testaments. The law given to Moses on Sinai cannot be equated with the Adamic law. It is rather a version of the law of Christ, which embraces both promise and punishment. By means of his teaching on the threefold dispensation, Fletcher was drawing attention to the activity of the triune God in its historical stages.[33] If the dispensation of the Spirit represents the last and highest stage, that is because of the special office of the Spirit, who guides people into all truth:[34] God is; God is love; God is mine in Christ. Fletcher described his trinitarian-dispensational understanding of God's revelation as 'my key and my sword'. He used this key also for the understanding of the Pauline doctrine of election and rejection.[35] He recognized that he differed from the Arminians, in that he taught the free, elective grace of God. He acknowledged that his theological opponents had made him aware of the biblical witness to God's elective grace. His interpretation, though, differed from that of Calvin and the Calvinistic tradition, and found its place within the dispensation of God's covenant of grace in history.

In his criticism of the Calvinistic position, Fletcher maintained that one attribute of God cannot be cancelled out by another. So, for example, God's wisdom, which confers freedom of action on human beings, cannot be annulled by appealing to his omnipotence. God's attributes, such as his holiness, wisdom, righteousness and grace, must

all be given equal weight. This applies in particular to the two central
attributes of God, his grace and his righteousness, in which Fletcher's
two basic axioms are reflected, and which must both be brought to bear
in equal measure.[36] Fletcher's 'Scripture-Scales' and his last writings in
the theological controversy were wholly devoted to this issue: sovereign,
discriminating, free grace can be found in a good God, because goodness can dispense free, unearned gifts; sovereign, discriminating,
free wrath, however, can never be found in a righteous God, because
righteousness can never inflict free, undeserved punishments.

On this basis, and in opposition to tradition, Fletcher did not understand election as an absolute, unconditional action of God, deciding on
a person's salvation without reference to that person. However, he was
in harmony with the predestinarian tradition in believing that election is
not conditioned by God's foreknowledge of a person's obedience or disobedience. God's choice is always based on his free, undeserved grace.
On the basis of the initial salvation offered, in Christ, to all people,
without any contribution on their part, Fletcher understood divine
election within the framework of his salvation-history perspective of the
dispensations. He distinguished two kinds of election, or rejection,
by God. In both cases the free, undeserved grace of God worked in
harmony with his educative wisdom. In one case the starting point for
Fletcher's reasoning was the *grace* of God; in the other it was God's
righteousness.

On the one hand, election and rejection mean sharing, to a greater or
lesser degree, in the *grace* of God, as the parable of the talents shows.[37]
Fletcher developed this in his exposition of Romans 9, in which, among
other things, he explained the words 'Jacob have I loved, but Esau have
I hated', in the light of parallel passages, as a way of expressing the
'more' and the 'less' of divine love.[38] It is a matter of election by the
sovereign, distinguishing grace of God, which shows partiality and
imposes no preconditions. The reverse side is a rejection which –
contrary to the Calvinistic understanding – does not exclude people
from salvation, but leaves them at a lower level in the process of revelation.[39] This process of election and rejection has an individual as well as
a social aspect, since it can relate to an individual person as well as to
that person's membership of a social group (family, town, nation). For
Fletcher the Bible is full of witnesses to this kind of election in God's
dealings with the world.

On the other hand, as a second aspect of God's activity in electing
and rejecting people, there is the retributive *righteousness* of God,

which is impartial and conditional.[40] It is conditional because it is bound up with our obedience or, as the case may be, disobedience. In his grace, God rewards our obedience. The reverse side of this election is a just rejection of those who wilfully despise and wantonly forfeit the grace and glory of God. Conditional election and rejection in accordance with people's deserts is dealt with by Fletcher mainly within the framework of 'judgment according to works'. But we shall return now to the first manner in which God's election and rejection operates, and try to understand it in the context of the threefold dispensations of God the Father, the Son and the Holy Spirit.

Jesus Christ died for all. From God's side, no one is excluded from eternal salvation, not even those people who are not able to hear the message of Christ. The reference here is to the pagans, who in terms of the parable of the talents have received only one talent. Their faith is not explicitly directed towards Christ, and carries with it no assurance of forgiveness. It can, however, be saving faith, since they know that God is, and that he will judge this world righteously. They are not condemned, even if they cannot have the experience of Christians that 'the love of God is shed abroad in our hearts through the Holy Spirit'. They stand under the general dispensation of the Father.[41] If they live uprightly, in accordance with the light that has been revealed to them, and do not bury their talent, they will gain eternal salvation. Fletcher pointed to the example of the Roman centurion Cornelius, who feared God and did right, and was therefore pleasing to God.[42] He compared God's Spirit, who reveals God to us, with the wind. As every person has had experience of the wind, so too has everyone been touched by the Spirit of God. Where, when and how strongly the wind will blow is not, however, within a person's control. The Spirit of God moves in the same way, where he will, bestowing more talents on one person than on another.

More talents have been given to Jews and Christians than to pagans. To the Jews the Messiah was promised; to the Christians he appeared.[43] Under the dispensation of the Son they have been illuminated by a clearer light. It would be madness for them to want to remain at the lower stage. The abundant measure of the grace of God has been revealed. It is true now, for all those to whom the good news of Christ has been preached, that whoever believes is saved, while whoever does not believe is condemned. If a person rejects the truth revealed to him by God, he has delivered himself up to judgment. The person to whom the gospel of Jesus Christ is preached, is called to decision, since the gospel reveals to him his own sin and the grace of God. Therefore Fletcher added to his treatise on the doctrine of sin an appendix bearing as its title the question: 'What must I do to be saved?' He wanted to lead the reader to true repentance, which included genuine sorrow for sin.

The source of such human sorrow is not so much a fear of judgment, as a recognition of God's holiness combined with the recognition of oneself as a sinner. This leads individuals to recognize that it is God's grace alone which sustains them, and which allows them to wait and struggle until the love which appeared in Jesus Christ shines out on them personally. The genuineness of the sorrow is evidenced not by its length and intensity but only by the fact that it drives us from our own apparent righteousness to Christ. Repentance is not a subordinate part of some judicial process. Fletcher, however, drew the attention of any person seeking salvation to three things. First, such a person should examine Scripture, in order to discover the corruption in human nature. Secondly, Fletcher uttered several warnings to those who repented: they should not, for example, join a superficial company, or confuse the covenant of works with the covenant of grace in such a way as to want to do for themselves what must be God's doing. Thirdly, he urged that they should be convinced not only of their own original and actual sin, but of their unbelief. Those who are convinced of their unbelief are not far from faith. Now above all it was important to know nothing but Christ, and him crucified. Even the smallest measure of God-given trust would begin to draw the soul to Christ and unite it with him. Through faith Christ takes up his abode in people's hearts. The believer has experienced forgiveness of sins and is a new creation. The believer knows then that the essence of the Messiah is love. In this context Fletcher warned against the false humility which considers that one is not yet sufficiently humble. Jesus teaches us true humility. We should not hope to achieve humility apart from him.

Fletcher's observations in 'What must I do to be saved?' make clear his independent approach in recognizing a mutual interaction of the divine and the human. This also finds expression in his conception of faith. Faith is at one and the same time a free gift of God and our own most noble work. For Fletcher it was not only possible but necessary to say both things. Faith is a gift of God. God enables us to believe. But we are rational, responsible creatures, who have to deal with God's gifts. Faith is a gift of the redemptive grace of God, just as breath, movement and food are gifts of the creator God – gifts which on our own responsibility we make use of and put to the proof in our actions. Otherwise the call to faith would be asking the impossible of a person. Of course faith is first of all a humble, passive receiving, and only after that a joyful, active giving. One must separate the act of faith and the fruits which grow from it, so as not to wish to see the fruits before the tree has been planted.

The two inseparable fruits of faith are the assurance of the forgiveness of sins and true holiness, which together constitute the righteousness which is effected by God through faith. The former of these, the assurance of forgiveness, points to the latter, holiness, or the combination of faith and love. The first was treated by Fletcher mainly within the framework of repentance and conversion, the second in the context of sanctification and the Last Judgment. Because of the nature of the theological controversy, it was the second, the linking together of living faith and obedient love, that received more attention in Fletcher's writings. In harmony with the twelfth of the Thirty-Nine Articles of the Church of England, Fletcher insisted that 'good works spring out necessarily of a true and lively Faith'.[44] He made use of pictures to help him present this combination as a living interaction. So, for example, he compared faith and works to the beat of the heart and the blood in the arteries. As the pulsating life of the body is extinguished just as much by the stopping of the heartbeat as by the severing of the main artery, so too can the life of faith be destroyed both by unbelief and by the failure to perform the good works awakened by faith. To the maxim (current also among the Calvinists): 'Use grace and have grace', Fletcher added the corollary: 'Misuse grace and lose grace'. God, who is merciful and holy, demands of us both faith and obedience. Obedience allows the truth to reign, so that a human being is a human being, and God is God.

The gospel lives by a harmony between living faith and loving obedience similar to that between breathing in and breathing out.[45] Against this background, Fletcher was also able to reinterpret Calvinistic teaching on the imputed righteousness of Christ. Faith is a powerful, life-giving, justifying, sanctifying, triumphant, liberating grace. In so far as this faith originates from Christ and contains the power to act in an upright manner, through it Christ is imputed to us as righteousness. Whoever continues in faith to the end will be saved on Judgment Day, because true faith produces righteous fruits. It is a comforting evangelical doctrine that the person who perseveres in obedient faith cannot fall from grace.

Fletcher stressed very strongly the connection between faith and morals, but he developed no ethical system of his own. In his observa-

tions directed particularly towards individuals, love, as the fulfilling of
the law of Christ, becomes the central content of works of faith, and the
standard by which they are judged, as we shall see in the section below
on the dispensation of the Spirit. In his writings on the political controversy, Fletcher defended the traditional ordering of society.

The dispensation of the Son does not bring God's work of salvation
to an end. It is followed by the dispensation of the Spirit. John the
Baptist already drew attention to the person of Christ and to Spirit
baptism. Fletcher did not dispute that every person under the dispensation of the Son also stood under the influence of the Holy Spirit.
Following a gentle criticism by John Wesley he corrected himself on this
point.[46] But he drew a distinction between, on the one hand, pious Jews
in the Old Testament and babes in Christ, and, on the other hand,
mature Christians. Only the last of these live in the unbroken presence
of the Holy Spirit, in the full assurance of faith. They have experienced
the baptism, that is, the fullness, of the Spirit. The greatest of all the
promises in which we can share in this life and before the second coming
of Christ has been fulfilled in them. Whether a believer in Christ receives
the fullness of the Spirit depends on God's choice. In the early church,
even after Pentecost, not all believers lived in Christian perfection.

Nevertheless, believers can put their trust in the promise made by
Christ. Fletcher urged Christians not to seek to reach perfection through
their own works, but through a living faith. They should look forward
to perfection in three ways: in faith, just as they are, and always.
Fletcher left open the question as to how perfection is attained, whether
instantaneously, or gradually. There is a growth in grace and love which
both precedes and follows baptism with the Spirit.

Fletcher did not understand filling with the Holy Spirit as the
bestowal of spiritual gifts. In common with tradition and the general
belief of his time, he limited such gifts to early Christianity. Fletcher's
special concern was with the fruit of the Spirit, especially with being
filled with perfect love. The dispensation of the Spirit brings the inbreaking of Christian perfection already in this life:

> If *Christian Perfection* be nothing but the *depth* of evangelical
> repentance, the *full* assurance of faith, and the *pure* love of God and
> man, shed abroad in a *faithful* believer's heart by the Holy Ghost
> given unto him, to cleanse him, and to keep him clean *from all the
> filthiness of the flesh and spirit,* and to enable him to *fulfil the law
> of Christ,* according to the talents he is intrusted with, and the

circumstances in which he is placed in this world: – If this, I say, is *Christian Perfection*, nothing can be more absurd than to put off the attaining of it till we die and go to heaven. This is evident from the descriptions of it which we find in the New Testament.[47]

Fletcher fitted into his salvation-history pattern the doctrine of Christian perfection which had come to him from Wesley. In doing so, he hoped to contribute to a better understanding of John Wesley's teaching. He believed himself to be at one with the hymns of Charles Wesley and with the tradition of the Anglican Church, especially with its liturgy.

The doctrine of Christian perfection, or perfect love, was as central for the Wesleyan Methodists as it was disputed by the Calvinistic Methodists. Fletcher tried to explain his understanding of it in the *Last Check*. Absolute perfection can only be attributed to God. Even Christ in his manhood did not know this absolute, unending perfection. Everything that exists is, in comparison with God, imperfect. But in all God's works there is a gradation. The perfection of an archangel is different from that of an angel, and different again from that of a human being. Christian perfection must also be distinguished from that of Adam before the Fall. It is no longer possible for any person to fulfil the covenant of works in unbroken obedience. Christian perfection, like any other form of perfection, must be measured against the revelation given: that is to say, it must be distinguished from the perfection which might be attained by Jews under the revelation given to them.

Christian perfection, since it is not absolute perfection, grows in grace and love. Perfect wisdom and knowledge are withheld from human beings, but not perfect love according to the measure of the revelation given to them. Fletcher therefore distinguished between deliberate and unintentional sins, between disobedience and ignorance. His understanding of Christian perfection was built essentially upon this distinction, which was rooted in early Enlightenment thought. As Fletcher understood it, in Christian perfection a person is so filled with the Spirit of God as no longer to commit sin, in the sense of deliberate sin. Grace now dwells in such a person. Our indwelling sin is the pride which dwells in us, i.e. our rebellion against God. In Christian perfection this is done away with.[48] Sin makes us proud, not humble. We become more humble as our life becomes more holy and obedient. Fletcher distinguished between the indwelling sin, which is done away with in Christian perfection, and the fundamental possibility and danger of sinning, which is still present even in perfection. Perfection is not –

any more than the life of faith – a state in which one can haughtily imagine oneself to be secure. On the contrary, Christian perfection is characterized by the deepest humility, since it allows us to experience in the most radical way our dependence upon God. A person who no longer obeys the Spirit of God is repossessed by high-handedness and sin, and transgresses God's law.[49] All perseverance in perfection has its foundation in the blood of Christ and is firmly attached to obedience to God's will. Whoever lives in perfection fulfils the law of Christ.

The gospel too has its law. The greatest privilege of this evangelical law, however, and the fundamental difference between it and the law of the Garden of Eden, is that it knows repentance and conversion. The law of Christ is fulfilled in love. Being filled with the Holy Spirit makes it possible for a person to live in perfect love. Love is the greatest gift of God. Fletcher preferred to call Christian perfection 'perfect love'. He expounded the meaning of love as, in particular, the love of individual Christians for God and for their fellow human beings. Christian perfection is particularly directed towards the will, which is the essential moral power of the soul. It leads one along the way of the cross, since it involves following the Lord, who does not so much advertise himself by spiritual signs as prove himself in temptation and suffering. In Christian perfection, the positive aspiration of the mystics is attained and transcended: Christ in us.[50] According to Fletcher, the mystics often fell into the error of withdrawing into passivity, instead of loudly praising the operation of the grace of God, and doing good. Life under the dispensation of the Spirit, too, is not without its promise: in his abundant grace God has promised the return of Christ, and our reward in eternal life.

In Fletcher's *Last Check*, in my opinion, there were two overlapping, yet distinct understandings of perfection, which, in the process of argument, were directed towards different ends. (1) Perfection must be attained in order that one may be accepted at the Last Judgment. The Christian must achieve holiness on this earth, and must be renewed in the image of God. Against the Roman Catholic idea of purgatory after death, and against the Calvinistic idea of a purification in death (described as 'death-purgatory'), Fletcher argued that a person should not hope for any supplementary operation of grace in death. Perfection, in the sense of moral perfection, had to be attained here and now. (2) Perfection is not an absolute concept, and does not signify a condition or state, but, corresponding to the dispensation under which one finds oneself, is a relative concept, signifying a relationship – the relationship between God and a human being, in which the person concerned lives wholly filled with the love of God. This filling is promised to the justified and born-again Christian. Perfection, in the sense of religious/spiritual perfection, is a gift of God's grace which has been promised, and which is worth striving for. As he responded to counter-arguments, Fletcher, in my opinion, leaned ever more strongly towards the second of these understandings, which was the one that fitted in with his trinitarian/dispensational standpoint.[51] In this second view, which Fletcher developed increasingly, the nature of Christian perfection as promise moved more strongly into the foreground. At the same time he continued to maintain that whether the fullness of the Spirit was bestowed on the believer depended on the elective grace of God.

Judgment according to works

Every person must appear before the judgment seat of God, and God judges all according to their works. It is a judgment according to the evidence of works of faith, in conformity with the revelation granted to the individual. In the judgment, faith, understood in the sense of Hebrews 11.1, is done away with. Faith gives way to sight. God will then judge us, not according to our faith, but according to the evidence of our works, according to obedient love. God will judge the world in Christ. It is not a judgment before angels and human beings, since God alone sees into people's hearts. Judgment according to works embraces not only our words and deeds, but also, and most importantly, our thoughts, wishes and disposition, which first and foremost determine our deeds. People will be judged in accordance with the revelation granted to them. Even pagans, who do not bury the one talent they have received, but who fear God and do right, will be saved.[52] Similarly those who have come to faith in Christ will be saved, if they have a living, i.e. an obedient and steadfast, faith which has borne fruits. The judgment, or, as Fletcher could also describe it, the final justification according to works,[53] does not nullify the significance of the merit available solely through the death of Christ, but rather confirms its fundamental significance, and along with it justification through faith in Christ. This is clear also in the case of little children and mentally handicapped persons, who cannot produce the fruits of faith and who are therefore saved through the sacrificial death of Christ alone. On the other hand, all the good works of a believer who falls from faith become worthless. The judgment constitutes a barrier set up by God to avert an antinomian misunderstanding of faith. Faith without works is dead.[54] Fletcher claimed not only the support of the epistle of James and the Sermon on the Mount for his statements, but also that of the Pauline and Johannine literature.

Human works are good, if they are founded on the truth. Christ is the truth. Pharisaic self-righteousness can never lead to good works. Nor can there be any good works which are meritorious in themselves. Every good work is founded primarily on the grace of God, and only secondarily on a person's obedience.[55] God's judgment is gracious, in that he does not demand of us what he has not first given to us. It is just, in that God judges all people, without respect of persons, in accordance with what he has given to them. Those who stand under the Christian revelation have the privilege of knowing the law of Christ as an evangelical 'law of freedom', or 'law of faith', which embraces repentance and forgiveness, and only imposes on us what God makes it possible for us to fulfil.[56]

In the strict sense, merit attaches only to Christ's work of salvation. But in a derived sense, even in the Bible, it is possible to speak of the merit and worthiness of human works. The reference then is always to good works performed through faith. Corresponding to this, we have the promises and threats which are attached to the fulfilment of the law, and the reward and punishment of human works before the judgment seat of Christ. Both are a spur to human obedience. Love would indeed be the supreme motive for obedience, but it can only be effective in so far as the believer is filled with the Holy Spirit. Thus Fletcher reinterpreted, within the framework of his doctrine of grace, the promise and threat of punishment which in the early Enlightenment were bound up with the emphasis on law.

In the judgment, God rewards our good works. This, however, is to be ascribed only to the elective grace of God, and not to any entitlement to reward on the human side. In his abundant grace, God rewards the fruits of the grace he himself bestowed upon us. The believer is thus doubly blessed. As some stars in the firmament shine more brightly and others less brightly, so it is in God's eternal kingdom.[57] The person who dies in a state of initial salvation, and who has no chance to perform good works, will achieve a correspondingly smaller measure of glory. On the other hand, the person who buries his talent, i.e., neglects the grace given to him, is punished. This is the just judgment of God in his wrath. Punishment, however, is not the essential, primary work of God, but his strange work.

Although, with his doctrine of judgment according to works, Fletcher laid the emphasis upon human obedience, he did not countenance any kind of self-righteousness. Both at the beginning and at the end stood the grace of God in Christ. Every good work is grounded in the grace of God. All self-esteem is excluded. People cannot, therefore, appear before God trusting in 'their' good works, but only in God's abundant grace which has made them capable of good works.

Theology of the centre

As we saw, underlying Fletcher's theology were two axioms which were meant to make salvation and damnation comprehensible: God's free grace and human free will. In one of his later writings, Fletcher linked the two axioms together in the following way:

> Our first talent or degree of salvation is merely of God's Free-grace in Christ, without any work or endeavour of our own: and our eternal Salvation is originally, capitally, and finally of God's Free-grace in Christ; through our not neglecting that first talent or degree of salvation. – I say, through our not neglecting, &c. to secure the connexion of the two gospel-axioms, and to leave Scripture-room for the doctrines of remunerative Justice. The second Gospel-axiom bears up the doctrines of Justice, and extirpates the doctrine of Free-wrath. It is the following proposition, which, I believe, no candid bible-christian will deny. Our eternal damnation is originally and principally of our own personal FREE-WILL, through an obstinate and final neglect of the first talent or degree of salvation.[58]

When the starting-point for Fletcher's argument was, as in this quotation, the doctrine of God, he based the second axiom on the righteousness of God, rather than on human free will. He could then attach equal importance to the two axioms, understanding them as referring to the grace and righteousness of God, and so avoid giving the impression that God and human beings were of equal significance.

The notion of the freeing of the human will through the redemptive grace of God makes comprehensible the concept of a righteous judgment of God for believers and unbelievers. Over and over again Fletcher insisted on the sole merit of Christ. If he could speak of trusting in repentance, faith, hope, charity and perseverance, it was only in a secondary sense, as deriving from God's saving act in Christ:

I trust ONLY and SOLELY in GOD as the first and capital CAUSE, and in CHRIST as the first and capital MEAN, of my present and eternal SALVATION: but besides this PRIMARY trust, I have a thousand INFERIOR trusts. Take a few instances. I have a sure trust and confidence, that the Bible will further me in the way to eternal salvation, more than the Koran: – baptism, more than circumcision: – the Lord's supper, more than the Jewish passover: – the house of God, more than the playhouse: – praying, more than cursing: – repentance, faith, hope, charity and perseverance; more, far more than impenitence, unbelief, despair, uncharitableness, and apostasy.[59]

From the very beginning of the controversy over antinomianism and predestination, Fletcher was aware of the legitimate concerns of both Calvinistic and Arminian Methodists. He thought of himself as a reconciler between the two parties, since the truth lay between the extremes. He saw it as his task to defend both free grace and believing obedience. He presented his understanding of the gracious activity of God in the framework of a trinitarian economy of salvation.

Even if Wesley – and with him all Arminian Methodists – were theologically closer to him, he understood himself as the man in the middle. His last piece of work in the context of the theological controversy bore the characteristic title: 'Reconciliation'. He called for reconciliation between the moderate representatives of both sides, the 'Bible-Calvinists' and the 'Bible-Arminians', and portrayed the operation of the triune God as love. He thus announced a central theme, which was to occupy him during the years that followed: 'God is love. Let us be like our Father who is in heaven.'[60]

15

Fletcher and the Methodists
(II: 1770–1777)

Towards the end of the 1760s Fletcher had often moved in Lady Huntingdon's circle, but the controversy over antinomianism and predestination led to a public breaking off of theological relations with the Calvinistic stream in Methodism. Fletcher's activity as a minister in the Methodist movement was thenceforward limited almost entirely to the Wesleyan stream. In the 1770s he no longer spoke of taking part in the gatherings in Worcester where, towards the end of the 1760s, he had engaged in long discussions with evangelically minded Calvinistic ministers. It appears that the Worcester conferences became a purely Calvinistic affair. Fletcher's friend, Ireland, who was anxious to effect a reconciliation, attended a Worcester conference in 1773, and sought to put in a good word for Fletcher. Fletcher expressed his appreciation of his friend's unsuccessful attempt in the following words: 'I thank you for having dared to speak a word for me at Worcester, but the stream of prejudice ran too high for you to stop it: it was drowning yourself without saving your friend. It is good to know when to yield.'[1] We learn nothing from later letters of any reconciliation with the circle of Worcester ministers.

   As our description of the course of the theological controversy showed, Fletcher's relationship with Lady Huntingdon was, nevertheless, interrupted only briefly. In 1773 he was permitted to preach again in one of her chapels, and at the beginning of 1774 he reported that they had reached agreement on doctrinal questions. Around the turn of the year 1776/77 Ireland brought together some of the opponents in the controversy, and from three extant letters written by Fletcher to the Countess in the course of 1777 we learn, among other things, that she had invited him to spend a period of convalescence with her. Fletcher's longing for reconciliation and agreement between Calvinistic and Wesleyan Methodists as a whole did in fact come to nothing, though, in a narrow circle around Fletcher, an understanding was reached between some leading exponents who were able to pick up the threads of their former friendship and mutual respect. But during the period 1770–77 it was Fletcher's relations with the Wesleyan Methodists, and his position among them, that came to the fore.

A close relationship continued to exist between Fletcher and Charles Wesley. Among those with whom he corresponded regularly, Fletcher now included Joseph Benson, whom he had come to know and appreciate especially at Trevecca. Since Benson shared Fletcher's understanding and expectation of a baptism with the Holy Spirit as the beginning of Christian perfection, they were very close to each other in their spiritual outlook. This subject dominated their correspondence after Benson's dismissal from Trevecca. When Benson expressed the wish that Fletcher might be the first of the two of them to be filled with the Spirit, Fletcher responded with a biblical picture: he hoped, he said, that God would allow them, like Joshua and Caleb, either to die together or to enter the Promised Land together. The exchange of letters also covered such questions as the possibility of Benson's ordination, a mission in America, and, finally, the position of the Methodists within the Anglican Church. But before we embark upon the last of these questions, another exchange of letters calls for discussion.

John Wesley wishes to choose Fletcher as his successor

In the 1770s, the Wesley brothers again tried to persuade Fletcher to undertake some responsibilities within the Methodist movement as a whole. In 1771/72 Charles Wesley invited Fletcher to London, to work among the Methodists there. Fletcher thanked him for the invitation, but observed that he had received no call to stir people up *at present*.[2] As he saw it, his place continued to be at Madeley, and he was committed to the theological controversy.

John Wesley had great trust in Fletcher. By now Wesley was close on seventy years old. He wondered where he might deposit his papers, and saw Fletcher as the most suitable person.[3] Ten years earlier he had asked Fletcher to take over the leadership of the whole movement, but had received a negative reply. His plan to bring together into a union the Methodist preachers and the evangelically minded clergy of the Church of England had not materialized. Wesley knew that he could hold the Methodist societies and preachers together in a unified body for as long as he lived, but what would happen after that? In 1769 therefore he had stipulated that after his death all the preachers should meet in London and elect a group to take on the leadership. But he became more and more convinced that such a leadership group would not be able to undertake the task alone, and that it would be necessary for an Anglican clergyman to preside over the work.

So at the beginning of 1773 John Wesley wrote again in the clearest terms to Fletcher, and called upon him to become his successor. He was expecting that the theological controversy would soon come to an end, and wanted to take advantage of what he saw as a favourable opportunity to persuade Fletcher to leave Madeley. He began his letter by describing the expansion of the work, and explained that it was necessary for it to be under the leadership of *one* person, and that that person should be initiated into the leadership *before* his, Wesley's, death. The qualifications required in such a person would be many and varied, but Wesley wrote with complete conviction:

> But has God provided one so qualified? Who is he? *Thou art the man!* God has given you a measure of loving faith and a single eye to His glory. He has given you some knowledge of men and things, particularly of the whole plan of Methodism. You are blessed with some health, activity, and diligence, together with a degree of learning. And to all these he has lately added, by a way none could have foreseen, favour both with the preachers and the whole people.[4]

In his letter Wesley anticipated Fletcher's objections, and argued that though Fletcher did not yet possess the grace and the gifts necessary for this office, God would equip the person he chose. Finally Wesley urged Fletcher not to spend time conferring with other people, but to come and share the work with him.

Like his brother John, Charles Wesley was also convinced that Fletcher was the right man for the job. So, even before John's letter to Fletcher, Charles had written: 'There is all reason to hope J. F. [John Fletcher] will succeed J. W. [John Wesley].'[5] Both brothers hoped that they would be able to call John Fletcher to be John Wesley's successor in the leadership of the whole Methodist movement. Fletcher, however, did not allow himself to be induced into giving a positive answer. He wrote:

Rev. and dear Sir,
I hope the Lord, who has so wonderfully stood by you hitherto, will
preserve you to see many of your sheep, and me among them, enter
into rest. Should Providence call you first, I shall do my best, by the
Lord's assistance, to help your brother to gather the wreck, and keep
together those who are not absolutely bent to throw away the
Methodist doctrines and discipline, as soon as he that now letteth is
removed out of the way. Every help will then be necessary, and I shall
not be backward to throw in my mite. In the meantime you sometimes need an assistant to serve tables, and occasionally fill up a gap.
Providence visibly appointed me to that office many years ago. And
though it no less evidently called me hither, yet I have not been without doubts, especially for some years past, whether it would not be
expedient, that I should resume my office as your deacon; not with
any view of presiding over the Methodists after you; but to ease you a
little in your old age, and to be in the way of receiving, perhaps
doing, more good.

After referring to his financial situation, which would enable him to
work among the Methodists without remuneration, and to his concern
for the theological college at Trevecca, he continued:

But being shut out there, it appears to me, I am again called to my
first work. Nevertheless, I would not leave this place, without a fuller
persuasion that the time is quite come. Not that God uses me much
here, but I have not yet sufficiently cleared my conscience from the
blood of all men. Meantime I beg the Lord to guide me by his
counsel, and make me willing to go any where or no where, to be any
thing or nothing. Help by your prayers, till you can bless by word of
mouth, Rev. and dear Sir, your willing though unprofitable Servant in
the Gospel.[6]

While Wesley was stressing the need for Fletcher to be initiated into the
work at once, so that he might mature and be equipped for the great
task, Fletcher's own wish was to be a co-worker, if Charles Wesley, as
John's successor, needed support. Behind this lay differing views on
Fletcher's standing among the Methodists. While John Wesley wanted
to nominate Fletcher as his successor, Fletcher wanted at the very most
to be in the second rank, supporting Charles as John's successor, or
working with him as his helper. Because Fletcher could not see himself

as leader of the Methodist movement, he could not appreciate the urgency with which John Wesley wanted to take him away from Madeley to be his co-worker. Fletcher was not able to recognize Wesley's call as the call of God.[7]

It was a serious and pressing concern of John Wesley to find a successor. He could conceive of no more suitable person than John William Fletcher. In spite of Fletcher's negative reply, Wesley persisted in his call to him. He visited Fletcher in Madeley in the summer of 1773. A little while later he wrote him a letter in which he expressed the great satisfaction he had derived from their meeting, and added that they ought to spend more time together, working at their common task. Wesley insisted that it might be too late if Fletcher only stepped into the breach when he, Wesley, had died. He alone could introduce a successor, who would then be accepted by the Methodists. Now, when the *Checks* had made Fletcher known and respected, would be the providential time. John Wesley offered a pulpit exchange with Richardson. Contact with the Methodists would arouse Fletcher's interest, and make him ready for the task:

> And till something of this kind is done you will not have that στοργή [trans. 'love', especially in the sense of parental love] for the people which alone can make your labour light in spending and being spent for them. Methinks 'tis pity we should lose any time. For what a vapour is life! Could you not spare a few days to be with us at the Conference? Probably it would be a means of strengthening you.[8]

Fletcher, however, did not find the inner freedom to leave Madeley, either to visit the Methodist societies with Wesley, or to travel again with Ireland to the Continent. As we shall see, he was awaiting a new, deeper experience of being filled with the Holy Spirit.[9]

Following John Wesley's visit to Madeley, Fletcher said in a letter to Charles Wesley how amazed he was at John Wesley's good health. He would outlive both of them, he thought. Fletcher was convinced that his task lay in taking John Wesley's part in the theological controversy. Wesley confirmed this to him in a letter written at the beginning of October, in which he also took up Fletcher's idea of working as a helper:

My Dear Brother

I think you judge exactly right. I believe you are in your place. God
has undoubtedly given you to me for an Assistant & has directed you
to that very path, wherein you may at present most effectually assist
both me, & those who are connected with me. I cannot advise you to
leave Madeley, no not for one Month, till you have finished the
several tracts you mention, none of wch [which] appear to me to be
unnecessary . . .[10]

This letter made both points: on the one hand Wesley expressed his conviction that at Madeley Fletcher was in the right place for composing
the necessary theological tracts; on the other hand he made it very
clear that undoubtedly Fletcher had been given to him by God as his
'assistant', and that his place in Madeley was only justified by his
participation in the theological controversy. Wesley avoided the word
'successor' in his letter, and spoke rather of an 'assistant'. As a rule
assistants were reliable itinerant preachers who exercised a supervisory
and leadership role within a region. Wesley would have liked to see in
Fletcher a regular and not just occasional helper in matters of leadership. In the same letter Wesley mentioned a severe cold, and urged
Fletcher to undertake daily exercises to maintain his health. Fletcher
again, weighed down by concern for John Wesley's health, answered
with the request that Wesley should not overwork. There was a
difference, he said, between sparing oneself for one's own sake or the
sake of the world, and sparing oneself for the sake of God's cause and
that of the church.

In Methodist circles the rumour began to spread that Fletcher would
be accompanying John Wesley on his travels. In February 1774 Fletcher
received a letter from a Methodist, thanking him for his *Checks*
and expressing the hope that the rumour about Wesley and Fletcher
travelling together would prove to be true. Benson too had heard of it,
but received from Fletcher the reply that the information was groundless, though 'groundless' was preceded by the word 'almost'. In the
summer of 1774 John Wesley again journeyed to Madeley, where he
preached four times in a day and a quarter. Fletcher formed the opinion
that Wesley's health was continuing to improve, and that the odds were
ten to one on Wesley's surviving him. A year later, however, at the
beginning of July 1775, Fletcher heard from James Ireland that John
Wesley was at the brink of death in Ireland. Fletcher wrote without
delay to Charles Wesley. His whole letter was devoted to thoughts on

life and death, and to the question of the future leadership of the Methodist societies:

> The Methodists will not expect from you your brother's labours, but they have (I think) a right to expect that you *will preside over* them wh[ile?] God spares you in the Land of the living. A committee of the oldest and steadiest preachers may help you to bear the burden, and to keep up a proper discipline both among the people and the rest of the preachers; and if at any time you should *want my mite of assistance*, I hope I shall throw it into the treasury with the simplicity and readiness of the poor widow, who cheerfully offered her (next to) nothing . . . Should your brother be called to his reward, I would *not be free to go to London* till you and the preachers had settled all matters. My going just at such a time would carry the appearance of a vanity which I abhor. It would seem as if I wanted to be some body among the Methodists.[11]

In this crisis situation Fletcher's own attitude was clearly evident: Charles Wesley should take on the overall leadership, and a few of the preachers should be ready to assist him in it. Fletcher thus stood firmly by John Wesley's plan of 1769. He wanted to offer his assistance only when Charles Wesley and the preachers had arranged everything, and called upon him. Fletcher shrank from taking the initiative, and himself accepting a leading role.

Only ten days later Fletcher could report with relief that John Wesley's constitution was so much better than his own (which had greatly worsened) that Wesley was likely to outlive him. He, Fletcher, would make no plans to help fill the gap when 'that great tree', John Wesley, fell.

The plan for a Methodist daughter-church

The serious setback in John Wesley's health intensified discussions about the future of the Methodist movement. For a long time Benson had been concerned about the standard of the education and training available for the Methodist preachers. Now he formulated a plan which included the testing of all preachers. Those who were competent and blameless should be appointed to their duties through the laying on of hands by John and Charles Wesley and Fletcher, as well as by other ordained ministers. Less well-educated preachers should receive additional training at Kingswood. Blameworthy preachers should be admonished and, if necessary, dismissed. Benson first submitted his proposals to Fletcher, who then forwarded them to John Wesley. In commenting on them, Fletcher emphasized that while ordination of the Methodist preachers would certainly establish their unity, it would at the same time have the effect of separating them, in large measure, from the state church, which the Methodists were called to permeate like leaven.[12] Benson had the opportunity to present his concerns, especially over the testing of the character and work of each individual preacher, to the Conference held in August 1775. Wesley noted in his Journal that the preachers would now be tested more meticulously than ever. He gave no indication, however, whether the question of ordination had been dealt with.

Benson's proposals and the apparent imminence of John Wesley's death led Fletcher to the conviction that the time had come for Wesley to ensure the continuance of the work after his death by giving it an institutional framework and a constitution. On 1 August 1775, the opening day of the Conference, Fletcher remembered the assembled preachers in his prayers of intercession. He felt impelled to put his thoughts about the future of the Methodists down on paper. The result was a long letter to Wesley in which he set out his view of the future status and constitution of the Methodist societies. The letter reached Wesley only after the Conference was over.

> I love the Church of England, I hope, as much as you do. But I do not love her so as to take her blemishes for ornaments . . . These specks could with care be taken off, and doing it in the circle of your influence might, sooner or later, provoke our superiors to godly jealousy and a complete reformation.[13]

Fletcher's proposals concentrated on relations with the Church of England. He proposed the setting up of a general society, which would embrace all the Methodists in Great Britain, Ireland and America, would be a daughter-church of the Anglican Church, and would not deviate from the Church of England in anything but the church's obvious shortcomings in doctrine, order and hierarchy. This Methodist daughter-church would defend the Anglican Church against all unfair attacks by the Dissenters:

> That this society shall be the Methodist church of England, ready to

defend the as yet unmethodized church against all the unjust attacks of the dissenters – willing to submit to her in all things that are not unscriptural – approving of her ordination – partaking of her sacraments, and attending her service at every convenient opportunity.

A document should be published containing the articles of faith, liturgy and homilies of the Church of England with the necessary corrections. As needing correction, Fletcher mentioned only general 'Pelagian, Calvinistic and papistical' blemishes. The Wesley brothers and other representatives should address a petition to the Archbishop of Canterbury, asking that the step that was being taken should not be regarded as a schism, and that bishops should be able to ordain all Methodist preachers who fulfilled the canonical requirements of the church.

Fletcher went on to say, in his letter, that if this request were not granted, the Wesley brothers would be obliged to take an irregular, though not unevangelical, step, and themselves ordain suitable preachers. Ordained preachers should exercise oversight over a wider area. The Conference should, moreover, have the power to dismiss both ordained and unordained preachers. How unlikely it was, in Fletcher's view, that the bishops would accede to the request for ordination, was demonstrated by the ninth point in his letter, where he proposed that after the death of the Wesley brothers the authority for ordination should be in the hands of three to five of the most reliable Methodist ministers, who would then take over Wesley's responsibilities. It was further proposed that confirmation – at present the prerogative of the bishops – should be carried out by John Wesley or his successors, and that only confirmed persons should be admitted to Holy Communion. Kingswood School should have a new function, similar to that suggested for it by Benson. Point 13 brought together the things that should be required of Methodist preachers:

That the grand plan upon which the Methodist preachers shall go, shall be to preach the doctrine of grace against the Socinians – the doctrine of justice against the Calvinists – and the doctrine of holiness against all the world. And that of consequence three such questions as these be put to the candidates for orders at the time of ordination:

I. Wilt thou maintain with all thy might the scripture doctrines of grace, especially the doctrine of a SINNER's free justification merely by a living faith in the blood and merits of Christ?

II. Wilt thou maintain with all thy might the scripture doctrines of justice, especially the doctrine of a BELIEVER's remunerative justification by the good works which ought to spring from justifying faith?

III. Wilt thou preach up Christian perfection, or the fulfilling of the law of Christ, against all the antinomians of the age; and wilt thou ardently press after it thyself, never resting till thou art perfected in humble love?

Perhaps to keep the work in the Church it might be proper to add:

IV. Wilt thou consider thyself as a son of the Church of England, receding from her as little as possible; never railing against her clergy, and being ready to submit to her ordination, if any of the bishops will confer it upon thee?

Overall it becomes clear that Fletcher was concerned to give the Methodist movement a place *within* the Church of England. His whole plan was based, on the one hand, on the not unjustified anxiety that after Wesley's death the Methodists might separate from the Church of England, unless a clear legal framework and obligation existed, and, on the other hand, on the hope that the reformation of the Church of England would receive a fresh impetus from the proposed Methodist 'daughter-church'. The difficulties in Fletcher's plan were obvious, however, seeing that he was trying to claim for the Methodists the protection of the Church of England, while at the same time speaking of corrections to its articles of faith, its liturgy and its homilies, and of ordination by the Wesley brothers. He was thereby showing his readiness to countenance a break with the way in which the bishop's office in the Church of England was traditionally exercised. His conviction was that the Methodists should remain sons and daughters – albeit wilful ones – of the Church of England.

The action John Wesley was to take seven years later, in 1784, when he was again faced with similar questions (relating, however, not to the Methodists in Great Britain and Ireland, but to those in America where political independence had been won), would show a certain resemblance to Fletcher's plan. But we know of no direct response to the plan either from John or from Charles Wesley. When John Wesley wrote to Fletcher fourteen days after the Conference, he mentioned the thorough testing of every preacher, but not the proposal in Fletcher's letter for the setting up of a Methodist 'daughter-church'. He urged

Fletcher, who was still busily engaged in producing documents related to the theological controversy: 'When you do not write, you must travel. I think the sooner the better. Sit still till I die, and you may sit still for ever.'[14] This exhortation appeared repeatedly in Wesley's letters to Fletcher over the following two years. He hoped to take Fletcher with him on his travels, so as to initiate him into his future task as leader of the Methodist movement.

John Wesley wishes to persuade Fletcher to become involved in the travelling ministry

Fletcher consistently declined to be nominated as Wesley's successor. At the beginning of 1776, however, when the end of the theological controversy was in sight, he showed for the first time a readiness to accompany Wesley on his travels. He wrote to John Wesley:

> Rev. and dear Sir
> I received last night the favour of yours from Bristol. My grand desire is to be just what the Lord would have me be. I could, if you wanted a travelling assistant, accompany you, as my little strength would admit, in some of your excursions; but your recommending me to the societies as one who might succeed you (should the Lord call you hence before me) is a step to which I could by no means consent. It would make me take my horse, and gallop away. Besides such a step would at this juncture be (I think) peculiarly improper, and would cast upon my vindication of your minutes and address such an odium as the calvinists have endeavoured to cast upon your address [John Wesley's document on the political question of the American colonies]. It would make people suspect that what I have done for truth, and conscience sake, I have done it with a view of being what Mr. T- [Toplady] calls the Bishop of Moorfields [alluding to Wesley's headquarters]. We ought to give as little hold to the evil-surmisings and rash judgments of our opponents as may be. If nevertheless providence throws in your way a clergyman willing to assist us [*sic*!], it would be well to fall in with that circumstance.[15]

Once again Fletcher showed the caution that was so typical of him. But at the same time he indicated the possibility of his accompanying John Wesley on his travels. In a letter to Benson he gave an indication of the wider background to this change. He wanted to break the chains which

bound him to his parish. A young clergyman had offered to take over
the parish as his curate. Fletcher now felt freer, and wanted to be completely led by God. A first journey, in the spring, proved impossible
because Fletcher was still occupied with his second tract in the political
controversy. Once he was certain that the young curate, Greaves, would
remain with him in Madeley, his travel plans became firmer. But by this
time his state of health had seriously deteriorated. He was coughing up
blood from time to time. A journey that had been planned for July could
not, therefore, take place. Fletcher was staying instead at a sanatorium
in Bristol, with Ireland. There he had a meeting with Wesley, who
wanted to take him on a journey to Cornwall. From his own experience
Wesley was convinced that nothing would improve Fletcher's health so
much as a long journey. The doctor, however, would not give his
permission. After a while, therefore, Fletcher returned to Madeley.
There another doctor gave him to understand that he was not suffering
from consumption, but that his illness and weakness were of nervous
origin, and were the result of overwork and exhaustion, and prescribed
other remedies for him. Fletcher's state of health then improved, and in
September he was able to resume preaching.

In October 1776 Fletcher travelled once more to Bristol. Then,
contrary to his original intention, he undertook a long journey with
John Wesley. They first set out together for London. From there the
journey extended to Norfolk, with visits to Oxfordshire and
Northamptonshire on the way. At the end of November they returned
to London. Wesley had the intention of continuing his journey with
Fletcher, but Fletcher's friends refused to allow it.[16] Fletcher's state of
health deteriorated very rapidly in London. He stayed first with
Greenwood at Stoke Newington, then later moved to be with Ireland in
Bristol. For the whole of the following year his health was so poor that
his friends would allow him neither to return to Madeley nor to join
Wesley in his travels. On two days in August 1777 Fletcher visited
Wesley's Conference and his preachers. This event left an incomparably
profound impression on all who were present. Apparently they all burst
into tears, and John Wesley prayed earnestly and with great assurance
that Fletcher should not die, but proclaim the works of the Lord.

16

Vicar of Madeley
(II: 1770–1777)

The period from 1770 to 1777 was marked, in the life of John William
Fletcher, by the theological and political controversies in which he took
part. Throughout the whole of this time, however, he was and remained
Vicar of Madeley. It is astonishing to realize how active he was both in
his parish and in his societies. Three of his writings from this period
were closely connected with his parish work. When he was away from
his parish he wrote letters to his congregation and, especially, to the
religious societies. Since, in his correspondence at this time, he had less
to say than in the 1760s about incidents and experiences in Madeley, it
is harder to get a picture of his parish work and its development. For
example, it is known only that from time to time he had a friendly
minister by his side – not for how long he was able to count on such
help. Fletcher often received visits, especially from Methodists. His
activity was affected on the one hand by his expectation of the outpouring of the Holy Spirit, and on the other by increasing illness which,
towards the end of this period, led to longer spells of absence from his
parish.

Three parish-related writings from the 1770s

Outstanding among those of Fletcher's writings which will be dealt with
in this chapter is the one on the doctrine of sin. This treatise had a long
pre-history. In 1766 Fletcher had written, as a test-piece for a larger
work, a dialogue between a minister and a parishioner on the doctrine
of sin. This test-piece remained unfinished.[1] Fletcher had done further
work on the subject in a different form. In letters written in 1770 and
1771 he referred frequently to his 'book', by which he meant his new
work on the doctrine of sin. The manuscript was completed in 1771,
but Fletcher suddenly decided to put off the printing of it. He wanted to

revise it again, and had it sent back from Bristol to Madeley. Then the manuscript got lost. It was found several weeks later in the side-room of a public house in Madeley where the boatman had left it. In the course of the year 1772 Fletcher frequently begged Charles Wesley to check and correct first the manuscript and then the printed version. He wanted to dedicate his book to the well-to-do members of his parish in Madeley, and therefore it had to be neatly produced. It appeared in 1772 under the title: *An Appeal to matter of fact and common sense: or, a rational demonstration of man's corrupt and lost estate.* The dedication began with the words:

> To the principal Inhabitants of the Parish of Madeley, in the County of Salop.
> Gentlemen,
> You are no less entitled to my private labours, than the inferior class of my parishioners. As you do not choose to partake with them of my evening instructions, I take the liberty to present you with some of my morning meditations . . .

The work went through countless editions, and after Fletcher's death was translated into other languages. The first edition was immediately sold out in Methodist circles in Bristol and London. Several months later Fletcher complained that he himself had not set eyes upon a single copy.

We have already gone into Fletcher's basic teaching on the doctrine of sin in our presentation of his theology. We return to *An Appeal . . .* in this chapter not only because of the dedication, but also because of the way in which Fletcher chose to set out its contents. He based his exposition of the consequences of the Fall, and the curse that had fallen on creation, on descriptions of the life of the residents of Madeley and the surrounding area. It was contrary to reason, he argued, to suppose that a good and just God had created the world to be as people were experiencing it. Human experiences needed to be interpreted in the light of the curse which lay over the whole creation. Fletcher mentioned, for example, a famine which, for several years, had caused the poor to riot and plunder.[2] He gave a forceful description of working conditions in the mines, in the dragging of the barges, and in the foundries. Fletcher was well acquainted with these workplaces and with the world his parishioners lived in. And he was also able to describe the curse which lay upon the rich man who wanted to revel in his wealth:

View that corpulent epicure, who idles away the whole day, between the festal board and the dozing couch. You may think that he, at least, is free from the curse which I describe: but you are mistaken: while he is living, as he thinks, a life of luxurious ease and gentle inactivity, he fills himself with crude humours, and makes way for the gnawing gout and racking gravel. See even now how strongly he perspires, and with what uneasiness he draws his short breath, and wipes his dewy, shining face; surely he toils under the load of an undigested meal.[3]

Fletcher wanted to convince his readers that since the fall of Adam a curse lay over creation, and every human being was a sinner in need of redemption through Christ.

Fletcher's descriptions of working conditions did not lead on to fundamental reflections on society or social relations. Nevertheless through his descriptions, and through the way he chose to dedicate the book, he made it clear that for him the situation was totally different from what God willed. He was in no way indifferent to the fate of the poor. Rather, with an uncommon radicality similar to that of John Wesley, he was ready to share with them all that he had. So, for example, he described to his patron Ireland how he had preached and at the end shared out such provisions as he had. And he urged the same life-style on others: 'Do not eat your morsel by yourselves, like selfish, niggardly people; but whether you eat the meat that perisheth, or that which endureth unto everlasting life, be ready to share it with all.'[4]

Two other short tracts, arising out of actual situations, appeared in the course of 1773. One of them bore the title *The Penitent Thief*. It was about John Wilkes[5] who, in accordance with the laws current at that time, was to be condemned to death for housebreaking and theft. Through his sister, who worked at the vicarage as a maidservant, Wilkes asked Fletcher to make an appeal for clemency on his behalf. Instead of putting in a plea for him, Fletcher wrote him a letter telling him of the promise that Jesus could forgive his sins, as he had forgiven the penitent thief hanging by his side on the cross, and urging him now likewise to confess his sins and to ask God for forgiveness. For Fletcher the law of the land and sentences passed in accordance with it had to be fully respected. Soon after this letter was written, Wilkes's sister went, with a friend, to Stafford, to be with her brother during his last days in prison. The two women recorded their conversations with Wilkes in a diary. They talked earnestly with the condemned man. John Wilkes

began to pray, and, after a mighty struggle, he experienced the forgiveness of his sins. He went to the place of execution praising God, his
redeemer. Fletcher added to his account of these events extracts from
the church's liturgy, and Bible quotations on the subject of repentance.
He compiled these texts, as he expressly said, not just for a condemned
evildoer, but also for the true churchgoer. The liturgy of repentance
applied to both, since churchgoers ought not to adopt an attitude of
pharisaic disdain, and distance themselves from criminals. Both criminal
and churchgoer are sinners before God.

The second tract from 1773, *A Dreadful Phenomenon*, concerned an
earthquake in Madeley. On 27 May, for a quarter of an hour, tremors
and movements of the earth occurred, and the waters of the Severn rose
and overflowed the adjoining land as the river changed its course. Nine
hectares of land were destroyed. Rises and falls of over ten metres were
recorded. Fletcher described the newly formed landscape in detail. But
he was not writing only about the forces of nature. His main aim found
expression in the sermon which he preached before a large crowd on the
following day, and which he subsequently had printed. He insisted that
the first moral cause of the natural catastrophe was human sin and
God's admonitory righteousness. He explicitly included the first argument from his new work on the doctrine of sin: if God, who is good and
who has created everything good, sends disturbing natural catastrophes,
this can only be seen as his way of drawing attention to his displeasure
over the way people are living. Fletcher preached on Numbers
16.30–34, and drew a comparison between the behaviour and fate of
the company of Korah and that of members of his own congregation. In
several places he stressed that God is love, and that punishment is his
strange work:

> God is *Love*, rather than vindictive *Justice*: Nor hath he *any pleasure
> that the wicked should die.* Hence it is, that the *ministration of
> righteousness,* or righteous mercy, *exceeds in glory.* Nevertheless,
> says St. Paul, *the ministration of condemnation is glorious. The
> wrath of man worketh not the righteousness of God*; yet, when that
> wrath is wisely over-ruled, or justly punished, it turns to God's
> praise. Every rational being *must* then answer the end of his exis-
> tence, by glorifying the Author of it one way or another. We *must* all
> reflect honour upon our Master, either as a gracious Rewarder of
> those that diligently seek him, or a just Punisher of those that obsti-
> nately offend him. Thus, while the blessed shew forth in heaven the

praises of his Holiness and *Mercy*; the Wicked in hell display those of his Holiness and *Justice*.[6]

For Fletcher it was a sign of the mercy of God that the natural catastrophe had claimed no human lives. All the more, then, should it be a warning to the unrepentant. This call to repentance and conversion was characteristic of Fletcher's preaching.

The expectation of the outpouring of the Spirit

The earthquake in Madeley gave rise to reflections on the work of the Spirit. From the 1760s the expectation of the outpouring of the Spirit had been a central theme in Fletcher's thought. Three days after the earthquake he wrote to his friend Charles Wesley:

> This awful *accident has not the effect* one could naturally expect. I fear the people in these parts are gospel hardened. Some of the gentlemen of my parish had the courage to stand upon the ruins and among the chasms, putting their bottle one to an other while I preached: One of them was the owner of the ground. I see nothing will do for us but a day of pentecost: without it we shall live and die jews, and our neighbours heathens. O for faith to pray, till the Lord answers by fire and pleads by the sword of his spirit with all flesh.[7]

In Fletcher's opinion the earthquake should have led people to repentance, and this did not happen – not, at least, in sufficient measure. Fletcher ascribed the fact to a hardening of hearts. Such a hardening, he believed, could only be overcome by the Spirit of God. The expectation of a new Pentecostal event was, therefore, for Fletcher, an expression of his conviction that only God could bring people to salvation. The Spirit would lead the unrepentant, the 'heathen', to repentance, and believers, the 'Jews', to Christian perfection. Fletcher had said something similar two years earlier. He had, he said, in the previous six years, experienced only one revival in his parish. He nowhere described the event, but he observed that those who called Jesus their Lord did not seem to have the power of the living God with them and in them. Fletcher was longing for God's Word to take effect. He feared that, although much had been heard of the gospel, the poor stinking Lazaruses remained quietly in their graves. For this reason it was necessary that God should pour out

his Spirit. This expectation had not only a personal dimension, but also
an ecclesiastical one: Fletcher lived in hope of the appearance of a
Pentecostal church: 'I want to see a Pentecost-christian church [an]d if it
is not to be seen at this time [on] earth, I am willing to go and see tha[t]
glorious wonder in heaven.'[8] And in another place he wrote:

> Let us join the few, who *besiege* the throne of grace, and not give
> over putting the Lord in remembrance, till he has raised himself
> a *Pentecost Church* again in the earth; I mean a Church of such
> believers as are all of one heart and one soul.[9]

Fletcher looked for this outpouring of the Spirit also in his personal life.
He was convinced that God would create something new. When in
1773 Ireland invited him to go on another continental journey, Fletcher
replied:

> My spiritual circumstances are what I must look at. I am brought to a
> point: like a woman with a child, I must have a deliverance into the
> liberty of a higher dispensation, and I tremble lest outward things
> should hurt me. The multiplicity of objects, circumstances, and
> avocations, which attend travelling, is as little suited to my case, as to
> that of a woman with child.[10]

Fletcher subordinated everything to the hope of being filled with the
Spirit of God. Life is short; the time must be redeemed. Most of all,
Fletcher went on, he would like to spend his life in prayer. That a person
should have to attend to outward concerns seemed to him no more than
a necessary evil. But the tasks he saw before him, both in his parish in
Madeley and, on top of that, in the wider Methodist movement, prevented him from deciding to withdraw into a contemplative way of life.
Fletcher's ideal of perfect love naturally involved not only love for God
but also love for one's neighbour, and to that extent was a social, as
well as an individual, concept. He held the conviction that this ideal
could only be attained as a gift of God. Unlike Wesley, however, he was
of the opinion that ultimately he must seek it along the path of stillness
and withdrawal from involvement with the world. In Fletcher's case it
was practical demands rather than theological perceptions which led
him to outward involvement. An example of his tendency to regard outward things as a threat is a statement in one of his letters to Charles
Wesley:

God make us faithful to our convictions, and keep us from the snare of outward things. You are in danger from musick, children, poetry; and I from speculation, controversy, sloth &c &c. Let us *watch* against the deceitfulness of self and sin in all their appearances.[11]

In his personal life and in his theological works Fletcher was greatly preoccupied with the question of the outpouring of the Spirit. It is highly probable that around 1776/77 he was working on a tract on this subject under the title *An Essay on the Birth of the Spirit*, in which he intended to demonstrate the connection between Christian perfection and the filling, or baptism, of the Spirit. The document has not been preserved, but in the secondary literature it is often confused with the sermon on the new birth which appeared in the 1750s.[12] In 1778, however, Fletcher drew Mary Bosanquet's attention to his manuscript which, when he went on his second continental journey, he had left behind in London. Miss Bosanquet handed the manuscript over to Joseph Benson. Both of them expressed reservations that Fletcher might have set the standard for Christians too high. When Fletcher returned to England in 1781 he again insisted, in a conversation with a Methodist travelling preacher, on the importance of the expectation of the filling of the Spirit, without which the Methodists would become slothful believers.[13]

Fletcher's activity in the parish despite increasing illness

As early as 1773 Fletcher's health problems increased. If he had to preach more frequently, he had trouble with his voice. His parishioners noticed how abnormally quickly he had aged. Occasionally he informed Charles Wesley in general terms of various difficulties and trials in his parish, without, however, giving concrete examples. The things that concerned him at the literary level in the theological controversy rarely found expression in his sermons, unless the text on which he was preaching directly demanded it. Preachers from the Countess of Huntingdon's Connexion were active in the societies around Madeley, following invitations from the Baptists. Fletcher clung to the word of the apostle Paul: 'so long as Christ is preached'.

In 1774 two of Fletcher's principal opponents in Madeley died:

The opposition of my parish is stunned by the death of 2 of the greatest enemies I had; One our great Nabal who was kill'd as he came home from a midnight revel by a fall from his horse. The other who was shot with a mortification thro' [his] bowels by drinking a cup of perry: The very man who pu[t] his bottle to the others at the Bir[ches].[14]

Nevertheless trials and difficulties increased. In spite of everything, Fletcher stuck to his duties as Vicar of Madeley. He was not convinced that God had called him to any other work. He even declined a request to become tutor to the son of his former pupil, Hill, commenting laconically: 'I thought he had had enough of me.'[15]

In answer to a question from Benson, Fletcher expressed his opinion on the exposition of Scripture by women in the societies.[16] The issue was becoming ever more pressing within Methodist circles. Fletcher replied that, while he would not encourage it, he would not absolutely dissuade anyone from doing it. The arguments on which he based his opinion were: (1) God was not bound by a person's gender, any more than by robes, time, place or age; (2) in Acts 2.18 'handmaidens' as well as men were mentioned as having received the gift of prophesying, and prophesying was closely related to preaching. However, Jesus had not called any women to be apostles, and had not entrusted any woman with the preaching of the gospel. Fletcher thus saw the task of women rather as fulfilling a secondary, helping and supporting role, in the manner of Mary Magdalene, Priscilla or Phoebe. Probably he was not confronted by this question within his own societies, though he did meet it in his encounters with the Quaker Abiah Darby, who both prophesied and preached.

Fletcher tried to see everything in the light of Jesus Christ. In 1772 he wrote to one of the sons of Vincent Perronet, Charles, who was ill, on the subject of the life of faith. The likening of what is seen to the shadowy and transitory, and the contrast between the seen and the unseen, is a theme we shall often come across in the 1780s:

By faith we see things visible as temporal, fading; as a showy cloud that passes away. By faith we live upon the *invisible, eternal* God: we believe that *in him* we live, move, and have our being: we begin to feel after, find, and enjoy our ROOT; and insensibly we slide from *self* into *God*, from the visible into the invisible, from the carnal into the spiritual, from time into eternity . . . Oh! My friend, let us rest more upon the *truth as it is in Jesus*, and it will make us more abundantly free, till we are free indeed; free to *suffer* as well as to *triumph* with him. Of late I have been brought to feed more upon Jesus as *the truth* . . . All out of him are but shadows. All *in him* are blessed sacraments, I mean visible signs of the fountain, or little vehicles to convey the streams of inward grace.[17]

Because Fletcher saw the grace of Christ at work everywhere, he believed himself called to make all people aware of it. He expressly pointed out to his parishioners, for whom he was pastorally responsible, how they were indebted to God for themselves and their life. He paid particular attention to those who were sick. He visited them. Through regular contact and earnest conversations, he sought to lead his parishioners to a firm faith. In 1776 Alexander Benjamin Greaves came as Fletcher's curate. When Fletcher knew that, on account of his illness, he was going to have to be away from his parish for a long time, he asked the Bishop of Hereford to ordain Greaves to the priesthood. During his absences from Madeley Fletcher remained in correspondence with his congregation, and especially with the societies. When he returned to Madeley for a short time in the late summer of 1776, he did not at first take on any responsibilities. But he had difficulty in accepting the loving care of his parishioners for him. He thought their solicitude was excessive, and found it harder to bear than the harsh words he had had to take in connection with the theological controversy. During his absences his parishioners were always enquiring after his state of health. They brought along a horse, and once even a post-chaise, to make the return journey easier for him. Before going away to recuperate in 1777 Fletcher burnt personal documents, since he was not able to take them with him:

> Before I left Madeley, as I was not sure of returning there again, and was obliged to put my keys into the hands of strangers, I thought it advisable to destroy my loose papers; among them were a variety of letters from my friends, and as my weak state of health and the short time I had to prepare for my journey, did not permit me to sort them; Yours, My Lady, shared the common fate.[18]

This is the reason for the almost complete absence from the archives of letters written to Fletcher.

Charles Wesley expressed his prayer for Fletcher's healing in a poem, the first verse of which reads:

Jesus, thy feeble servant see!
Sick is the man beloved by Thee:
    Thy name to magnify,
To spread Thy Gospel-truths again,
His precious soul in life detain,
    Nor suffer him to die.[19]

During his convalescence Fletcher stayed either with Ireland at Brislington near Bristol, or with Charles Greenwood at Stoke Newington. It was on one of these visits that Ireland succeeded in persuading Fletcher to agree to have his portrait painted.[20]

When Fletcher found that he was unable to be in Madeley over the Christmas period in 1776, he wrote a long letter to his parishioners. This is one of the few surviving letters addressed to the whole parish, and not to members of the societies only. Fletcher made an urgent appeal to his readers to accept Christ:

> . . . may the eye of your understanding be more and more opened to see your need of a Redeemer; and to behold the suitableness, freeness, and fulness of the redemption, which was wrought out by the Son of God, and which is applied by the Spirit, through faith. The wish which glows in my soul is so ardent and powerful, that it brings me down on my knees, while I write, and, in that supplicating posture, I entreat you all, to consider and improve the day of your visitation, and to prepare in good earnest, to meet, with joy, your God and your unworthy pastor in another world . . . I beseech you, by all the ministerial and providential calls you have had for these seventeen years, harden not your hearts. Let the long suffering of God towards us, who survive the hundreds I have buried, lead us all to repentance. Dismiss your sins, and embrace Jesus Christ, who wept for you in the manger, bled for you in Gethsemane, hanged for you on the cross, and now pleads for you on his mediatorial throne.[21]

Fletcher's ardent desire was to be joined to all his parishioners, in the deepest love, in the presence of God, for all eternity. When people objected that he ought not to make such a fuss about their souls, he replied that he had in fact concerned himself too little about their spiritual interests, and that he hoped to do better if he was granted health again. Fletcher was convinced that he had preached the truth to his congregation. His inadequacy consisted, as he saw it, not in his having preached a false gospel, but rather in his having preached with too little resolution, fidelity and urgency. While his letters to his parishioners were marked by the call to conversion and faith, those to the societies were mostly concerned with the exhortation to progress along the way of faith. In the centre of the political parish, at Madeley Wood, Fletcher had a house built, bearing the major part of the cost himself.[22] The house was to serve as a school for children by day, and as a meeting place for adults in the evenings.

'They forbid my writing, but I will write to the last.'[23] Friends and doctors forbade Fletcher to write or to speak, but he disregarded their warnings. He was already terminally ill by 1776. Early in 1777 he claimed that death had lost its sting. He still looked forward to being filled with the Spirit, while praising God for all that he had received in the past and was continuing to receive day by day, and trusting him for all that he had not yet received. Above all he laid emphasis on the compassionate mercy of God. He was not impatient, and had no doubts about his salvation. He did not fear death, but did not long for it either:

To fear it [death] would be, in my circumstances, mistrust of God's mercy and Christ's saving power; to desire it would be forgetting that it is a punishment, and that the sword of divine justice ought to be reverenced and not rushed upon. Nevertheless, blessed be God, I long to depart and to be with Christ out of the noise of a sinful world, and the mistakes of an imperfect church; . . . thanks be to divine mercy I find that my Saviour stands between me and all doubts, fears, pains and temptations. He knows my weakness; and therefore keeps my enemies at arm's length, bese[e]ch him my Lady to shew me the same favour and more abundantly till he has finished the work of faith in me with power and endewed me with all that *power from on high* we have so often pray'd for together.[24]

A man whom Fletcher had visited when he, Fletcher, was seriously ill, reported that he had expected to see him with one foot in the grave, but had found instead a man with one foot in heaven.

Doctors and friends advised Fletcher to travel to the Continent again, in order, perhaps, to recuperate in a warmer climate. At the end of 1777, when he was again feeling a little stronger, Fletcher consented not to return to Madeley, but to start out on the journey with Ireland. So in December 1777 he took his leave of England, not knowing whether he would ever return. One of the last to visit him, on the evening before his departure, was John Wesley.

PART V

CONVALESCENCE AND FINAL YEARS

(1778–1785)

17

Convalescence in Nyon

Following the advice of his doctors and friends, in 1777/78 Fletcher went off again to the Continent.[1] Eight years earlier he had made a similar journey with Ireland, and had visited his home town, Nyon. Now he was to stay there for three whole years. Throughout this time he was conscious of his links with his parish in Madeley, and was always hoping to return there.

Looking back to the first continental journey in 1770

When Fletcher had gone off on his journey with Ireland in 1770 he had been in good health. Together they had visited the Protestants in France, where Fletcher had also preached. Their journey had taken them to Naples and Rome.[2] Both on the journey and in his home town of Nyon Fletcher had left behind a great impression.[3] Several years later, a German pastor from Lausanne, Magister Stroehlin, who was trying to convince someone that people whose Christian faith and life were not mere show did actually exist, pointed to Fletcher as an example. Stroehlin described how Fletcher's first sermon in Nyon had so impressed not only well-disposed, virtuous people, but also worldly minded ones, that from all sides the preacher was adjudged to be a truly apostolic man. Children had been brought to him to be blessed. People had surrounded him in the street, in order to hear his prayers. He had shared his income with the poor. It was completely amazing, Stroehlin reported, how great an influence he had exercised in so short a time. He did not remember ever having heard so much good of a single person. It was, however, precisely this unanimous praise from so many people that had seemed so dreadful to Dutoit, the mystic, that he had deliberately refused to meet Fletcher in 1770.[4] But during Fletcher's second stay in Nyon, from 1778 to 1781, a meeting between them did take place. Thus began one of Dutoit's few friendly relationships with a pastor.[5]

The second stay in Nyon, 1778–1781

When he travelled to the Continent in 1778, Fletcher, who by this
time was forty-eight years old, was seriously ill. Surprisingly quickly,
however, he gained strength. The mild climate of southern France
helped to improve his health. Soon he began to preach, wherever he was
invited. His brother, Henri Louis de la Fléchère, collected him from
Montpellier in March or April 1778, and travelled with him, and
probably Ireland too, to Nyon. Fletcher took short rides out from
Nyon. In May he journeyed to Macon, where he took leave of Ireland,
and then returned to Nyon by steep mountain ways. Great exertions
(such as he had to make on this journey, when he was obliged for a
while to go on foot because the horses were scarcely able to pull even
the empty coach up the hill), or a severe bout of coughing, had the effect
of bringing back all the symptoms of his consumption. The second
winter in Nyon, 1779/80, was extremely cold, and Fletcher had to
move, on account of his sister's marriage, into what was for him an
unhealthy house. This again greatly weakened him. The three years
from 1778 to 1781 were thus marked by repeated rises and falls in his
state of health.

On one of his early rides out, Fletcher discovered in Morges some
relatives of the Perronets in Shoreham. Another group of relatives had
laid claim to an inheritance of between six and seven thousand pounds,
which should probably have gone to the Shoreham Perronets, and the
Reverend Vincent Perronet's son, William, had come to Switzerland in
the hope of clarifying the situation. The son stayed for a while with
Fletcher in Nyon, then went on to Lausanne. The settlement of the
inheritance took longer and ended less successfully than had originally
been hoped. This also delayed Fletcher's return to England, since he
wished to travel back with Perronet. The result was that Fletcher spent
almost three full years in Nyon. During this time he was also involved in
difficulties within his own family. He did not provide factual details of
the problem in his letters, but it most likely concerned an incident with a
nephew who tried by armed force to extort a large sum of money from
Fletcher's eldest brother. Fletcher, suspecting that something untoward
had taken place, intervened at the risk of his life, and brought the
attempt at extortion to a satisfactory conclusion.[6]

> The ministers in the town of my nativity have been very civil. They
> have offered me the pulpit; but I fear, if I could accept the offer, it

would soon be recalled. I am loath to quit this part of the field without casting a stone at that giant, Sin, who stalks about with uncommon boldness. I shall, therefore, stay some months longer, to see if the Lord will please to give me a little more strength to venture an attack.[7]

In July Fletcher described what he had begun to do, and the difficulties which were arising as a result of his activities. He spoke highly of the ministers in Nyon, but they were not accustomed to his new style of preaching:

The day I preached [in the church], I met with some children in my wood walking or gathering strawberries. I spoke to them about our Father, our *Common Father* – . . . I outrode them, but some of them had the patience to follow me home, and said they would speak with me; but the people of the house stopt them, saying I would not be troubled with children. They cried and said, *They were sure I would not say so, for I was their good brother*. The next day when I heard it, I enquired after them, and invited them to come to me; which they have done every day since. I make them little hymns which they sing. Some of them are under sweet drawings, yesterday, I wept for joy, on hearing one speak of conviction of sin, and joy unspeakable in Christ which had followed, as would do an experienced believer in Bristol. Last Sunday I met them in the wood: there were 100 of them, and as many adults. Our first Pastor has since desired me to desist from preaching in the wood, (for I had exhorted) for fear of giving umbrage; and I have complied from a concurrence of circumstances which are not worth mentioning: I therefore meet them in my Father's yard.[8]

Fletcher extended this work with children, so far as his state of health allowed. One minister in Nyon gave him the opportunity of using the church to give instruction to any children who wished to come. This permission was withdrawn, however, at the time of the official visitation in May 1779. In any case the room in the church had reminded the children too much of school, so that they were no longer coming so regularly or in such great numbers. Fletcher was convinced of the need to give religious instruction to children from an early age, since religion and morality were very closely connected. But for Fletcher, by contrast with too many of his contemporaries, the motivation for working with children lay, primarily, not in concern for their moral instruction, but in the love of God for all his fallen creatures.

In a letter written in September 1778 Fletcher described a journey with his brother Henri Louis in the Jura mountains. On the French side they met three wandering missionary preachers, and were impressed by their preaching. In the same letter Fletcher reported that he had preached once more in the church, and also once in a prison yard before two thousand people who had come to see the execution of a con- demned prisoner. The governor would not, however, allow him to accompany the condemned man to the scaffold. Fletcher planned to stay in Nyon through the winter and, whenever possible, express his opposi- tion to the use of mercenaries, which he attacked with a verse from Voltaire. He had spoken with Dutoit, among others, about writing an appropriate tract, but in view of a possible public outcry he had to abandon the idea of publication.

In 1779 difficulties with the political authorities became more acute. The lieutenant colonel forbade the ministers to allow Fletcher to hold classes for instruction or exhortation in their parsonages, on the grounds that these houses belonged to the government. From now on Fletcher held his meetings in the house of his brother, Henri Louis. A few younger women and four or five older ones, as well as a young pastor, met regularly. Fletcher's exhortations were centred on the love of God, our creator and redeemer:

> The truths I chiefly insist upon, when I talk to the people who will hear me, are those which I feed upon myself as my daily bread – 'God our Maker and Preserver, tho' invisible, is *here* and every *where*. He is our chief good, because all beauty and all goodness centers [*sic*] in and flows from him. He is especially *Love*, and love in us, being his image, is the sum and substance of all moral and spiritual excellence – of all true and lasting bliss. In Adam we are all estranged from love and from God; but the second Adam, Jesus, Emmanuel, God with us, is come to make us know and enjoy again our God as the God of love and the chief good. All who receive Jesus, receive power to become the sons of God &c &c.[9]

Fletcher had read with great satisfaction the *Apology* of Samuel Lutz, the pietistic pastor in Yverdon at the beginning of the eighteenth century. He was convinced that he too ought to address himself to his fellow countrymen in print, seeing that he had no opportunity to preach. At first the possibility of preaching had been open to him in Nyon, so far as the state of his health would allow. For this he had been indebted to the ministers of Nyon, who had taken him under their wing. But on the occasion of the visitation of 1779 he was accused of belonging to a sect (unnamed), which was everywhere spoken against. The discussion went on for a long time, and was so exhausting for Fletcher that he had to leave the meeting. The matter ended in peace, and he was invited to supper. A week later there took place the so-called Colloquy of Nyon, in which the ministers of Nyon and the surrounding area came together. In the report on the Nyon visitation, the conversation with Fletcher was not mentioned, but the minister who had been in charge of it raised the question of disregard for the sanctity of Sunday, especially at harvest time. The reference must have been to one of Fletcher's denunciations. The Colloquy of Nyon considered such disregard to be so serious that the matter ought to be brought to the attention of a superior body – the ministers' assembly in Morges. This assembly composed a letter to the civil authorities, describing disregard for the sanctity of Sunday, whether by staying away from worship or by performing everyday tasks, as a growing evil at every level of society. But in their letter the assembled ministers also expressed uncertainty about the step they were taking, since they would be accused either of saying nothing about anything, or of being ridiculous pedants. They asked the authorities for a word of clarification. At the same time the ministers' meeting in Morges was also considering requesting the authorities to ban gambling and a lottery which were taking place in Nyon on Sundays.[10]

In 1779 Bridel, the minister of Crassier, was elected president of the Colloquy of Nyon. His predecessor, who had already been trying to restrict Fletcher's activity, died soon after Bridel's appointment, and the new president then took up his pen and wrote a letter to Fletcher which started off a long controversy.[11] Bridel felt obliged to ensure that the orders and instructions of the authorities were observed. His letter was a declaration of loyalty to the authorities, and was meant to provide him with a defence if at any time they reproached him for tolerating Fletcher's meetings. Bridel began his letter by expressing his high regard for Fletcher's origins, his extraordinary gifts, his religious knowledge, his love for others and his zeal. But he then went on to say that, while he was neither a bigot nor inclined to persecution, he had been given to understand that Fletcher was holding special meetings in barns. He was asking him to remember, he said, that the rules for holding services of

worship had been clearly laid down by the authorities, and that everything should be done, as the apostle Paul had said, in an orderly fashion.
Bridel went on to say that, over the last century, the authorities had
issued various regulations against such conventicles; that except in times
of persecution the church was the only place where services of worship
should be held; that even a resident minister was not permitted to
exercise any public functions other than those conferred on him by
official instructions; that such gatherings as those which Fletcher had
been holding were dangerous, because they could give people an
aversion to the regular service of worship and the ministers; and that
people attended such meetings out of curiosity rather than enlightened
and genuine interest. Praise, prayer and instruction were good motives,
but one altar should not be set against another altar, nor one service of
public worship against another such service. If he was filled with zeal for
the glory of God, Fletcher could make use of the pulpits which the
ministers would at any time make available to him.

In his reply Fletcher first took up the positive part of Bridel's letter,
and stated that he had already preached once, and in doing so had given
his support to Bridel's pronouncements against the profanation of
Sunday and against gambling. In other parts of his reply he assured
Bridel and the ecclesiastical and civil authorities of his loyalty. Bridel
should not, he said, cast doubt on this unless he had convincing
evidence. Since Bridel had had copies of his letter to Fletcher circulated,
so that not only the ministers' assembly in Morges but also the authorities had knowledge of it, Fletcher, for a time, considered publishing his
reply as well, but there are no positive indications that this actually
happened. In a second response to Bridel's letter, Fletcher took up the
basic question as to whether a minister can and should take the gospel
everywhere. If this important duty were to be neglected, and if its
neglect would result in a decrease in godliness in his native land, then
Bridel must excuse him, Fletcher, for attaching so much importance to
the question. The public responsibilities of ministers ought not to be
restricted to two or three hours a week, since that would lead to the
extinction of all godliness among the people.

In a third letter Fletcher explained the circumstances under which he
had come to Nyon early in 1778. He said that the first minister in Nyon,
Guichard, who had known him for thirty-six years, had immediately
offered him his pulpit, but the poor state of his health had, for the most
part, prevented him from preaching. Instead, with the permission and
under the supervision of the two ministers in Nyon, he had instructed

the children in the church. This action had been prohibited by Pastor Raffinesque, the person who had carried out the visitation in Nyon, but Fletcher justified it with several quotations from the *Berner Synodus* – a Reformation document from 1532, which had been officially reprinted by the Berne authorities in 1735 and sent to all ministers. Fletcher held the document in high esteem, and would even have liked to translate it into English. In his letter he went on to explain how it came about that he had expounded the Word of God in a barn in Eysin.

It emerges from further letters written in reply to Bridel that, in the presence of the governor, the lieutenant colonel had forbidden Fletcher to preach from the pulpit. The governor was probably under the impression that Fletcher had been banished from England. The prohibition must have been imposed in the late summer of 1779. Fletcher asked whether he was to attribute the ban to the fact that, in his preaching, he had urged the authorities to insist that the laws against the profanation of Sunday should be observed. In doing so he had said nothing other than what Bridel had written to him, and what, so he had heard, the venerable ministers of the Morges assembly had demanded in a petition to the authorities. Thus Fletcher skilfully demonstrated the correctness of his conduct, which he went on further to support by detailed argument. A subsequent letter dealt with the question as to whether card-playing by Christians should be condemned in principle, or only (as Bridel thought) when carried on to excess. Fletcher advocated the former view. He listed many personal and social leisure activities which were edifying, including religious arts. In card-playing, by contrast, time was killed, and money which ought to be used for more important things was won and lost. All true Christians should be convinced that any surplus money ought to be shared with the needy members of the great 'family of the Lord'. Fletcher underlined his arguments with references to the *Berner Synodus*, to a sermon by Crousaz, a professor at the Academy in Lausanne, and to an official decree.

Despite the prohibition mentioned above, a young minister continued to put his house at Fletcher's disposal twice a week, and other ministers took part in the gatherings. In the autumn of 1780 Fletcher mentioned again that the lieutenant colonel had forbidden him to preach. He had, however, continued his exhortations three times a week in a private room, so long as his health had permitted. The ministers had informed him that he would be able to preach if he accepted re-ordination in the Waadt district, and, indeed, that if he did so the assistant minister in Nyon would offer him his post. A young pastor from Geneva, who was tutor to Fletcher's nephews, seems to have written so effectively in his defence in the summer of 1779 that the ministers at least no longer wanted to put any hindrances in the way of Fletcher's activity. Nevertheless the official prohibition was not lifted. Fletcher's effectiveness therefore continued to be limited to the small gatherings, to which adults as well as children came. A meeting which was held in the house of Fletcher's brother Henri Louis continued to exist even after Fletcher's return to England. Since his opportunities for speaking were so restricted during his stay in Nyon, Fletcher applied himself mainly to his written works.

The attachment to Madeley and the return to England

Hardly had Fletcher arrived in Nyon before he was wanting to return to his parish in Madeley and to his English friends. He was reckoning on a stay of no more than a few months in Nyon. In his letters he encouraged his deputy Greaves in his work. Both in prayer and in his letters he remained constant in his attachment to his parish in Madeley. He paid special attention, however, to the religious societies:

> My dear companions, let us be *consistent*: let us seek first the kingdom of God and his righteousness, and all other things, upon your *diligent, frugal, secondary endeavours*, shall be added unto you. Let us live daily, more and more, upon the free love of our gracious Creator and Preserver, the grace and righteousness of our atoning Redeemer and Mediator, nor let us stop short of the powerful, joyous influence of our Comforter and Sanctifier.[12]

Fletcher urged the members of the societies to live in love and unity. He illustrated their spiritual calling with allusions to their secular occupations as workers in mines, blast-furnaces and river-boats:

> Dig hard in the gospel for hidden treasure. Blow hard the furnace of prayer with the bellows of faith, until you are melted into love, and the dross of sin is purged out of every heart. *There is a river that maketh glad the city of God*: it is the grace that flows from his throne. Jesus is the vessel, the heavenly ark: get together into him, and sweetly sail down into the ocean of eternity. So shall ye be true miners, furnacemen, and bargemen.[13]

Meanwhile, in March 1779, John Wesley had visited Madeley. He compared the people in Madeley Wood to those in his beloved Kingswood. He found out, however, that Fletcher's strenuous efforts to enforce discipline had not had as good results as might have been expected. There were already signs of difficulties with Greaves in the exercise of his ministry. The precise circumstances are unclear. We have no information from the period from May to December on what was happening in Madeley. At the end of the year Greaves seems to have suffered an attack of consumption, and Fletcher urged him to take care of himself. Fletcher also indicated that he had received letters from his parish which were not very good.

On top of this disturbing news came financial worries. The new meeting house which Fletcher had had built in Madeley Wood turned out to have cost more than had been planned. He had to meet debts of £200. In addition, his stipend never reached the £50 which, instead of the more usual £40, he had promised to Greaves as payment. Now he wanted to send to England immediately a sum of £50 which he had set on one side for the publication of a book in Switzerland. He was ready to sell part of his inheritance so as to be able to settle his debts, but, because of a shortage of money in the Waadt district, he could only have sold it at a loss. He considered renting out his parsonage in order to find the money. In the autumn of 1780, however, he learnt that his friend James Ireland had paid the greater part of what was owing. He wanted to take at least £100 with him when he returned to England so that he might either pay off what remained of the debt or repay part of what he owed to Ireland. Before his return to England he borrowed some money from his sister Anne.[14]

Fletcher took an interest in political developments, especially the American colonies' War of Independence, in which France and Spain had also become involved. 'I beg you will not fail, when you have opportunity, to recommend to our flock, to honour the King, to study to be quiet, and to hold up, as much as lies in us, the hands of the government by which we are protected.'[15] He thought that even if England lost America and the islands of the West Indies, not an ear of corn less would grow in Great Britain. He hoped that material loss might lead to moral improvement, since wealth led only to luxurious living and arrogance.

Over and over again the return journey to England was delayed. Even the deadline that had been set for the autumn of 1780 went by. Perronet had not yet been able to sort out his inheritance, and Fletcher had lost the manuscript of one of his new works, and so had to rewrite it. In addition, his illness flared up again. Fletcher asked Greaves to be patient, and again urged him to give special care to the young and those who were sick. He made plans to return to England early in 1781 with Ireland, who was spending the winter months in southern France. Ireland pressed for the journey to take place in the middle of February. Fletcher would travel via Lyons to join Ireland in the south of France, and they would then make their way back to England together via Paris.

> I need not be urged to return: brotherly love draws me to Madeley, and circumstances drive me hence . . . I wish I could contribute to shake the dry bones in my parish; but I have no confidence in the flesh; and what I could not do, when I was in my strength, I have little prospect of doing now that my strength is broken . . . I thank you for your view of the iron bridge. I hope the word, and the faith that works by love, will erect a more solid and durable bridge, to unite those who travel together towards Sion.[16]

The departure was delayed a little further because of disturbances in Geneva, but in March 1781 Fletcher left his home town of Nyon, after a stay of three years. William Perronet, who was ill and weak, had to be left behind in Lausanne. The sudden return of wintry weather, and overexertion in riding and preaching, damaged Fletcher's health. From Montpellier, on one occasion, he rode out into the Cévennes and preached in the open air to about two thousand French Protestants. It is said that in Paris it was only thanks to his being confused with Ireland that he avoided being arrested for his activity as a minister.[17] In April Fletcher crossed the Channel and returned to his English friends.

18

Later Writings in French (1779–1785)

After the first of Fletcher's writings known to us appeared in French in the 1750s, all the publications which followed were in English. During his long stay in England, however, Fletcher continued to take an interest in what was happening on the Continent. Among other things he sent for the writings of Voltaire. The utterances of this great philosopher of the French Enlightenment aroused in him both interest and aversion. On his second continental journey he reported to the Wesley brothers on his impressions of France:

> Materialism is not rare, Deism and Socinianism are very common; and a set of Free-thinkers, great admirers of Voltaire and Rousseau, Bayle and Mirabeau, seem bent upon destroying Christianity and government . . . If we believe them, the world is the dupe of kings and priests. Religion is fanaticism and superstition. Subordination is slavery and tyranny. Christian morality is absurd, unnatural and impracticable; and Christianity the most bloody religion that ever was. And here it is certain, that by the example of Christians *so called*, and by our continual disputes, they have a great advantage, and do the truth immense mischief. *Popery will certainly fall in France, in this, or the next century*; and I make no doubt, God will use those vain men, to bring about a reformation here, as he used Henry the Eighth to do that work in England: so the madness of his enemies shall, at last, turn to his praise, and to the furtherance of his kingdom . . . If you ask, What system these men adopt? I answer, that some build on Deism, a morality founded *on self-preservation, self-interest,* and *self-honour*. Others laugh at all morality, except that which being neglected *violently* disturbs society; and external order is the decent covering of Fatalism, while Materialism is their system.[1]

For Fletcher the new philosophical currents failed because they were typical of a way of thinking which imagined it could get along without

God and divine revelation. That is apparent also from his comment on the deaths of Voltaire and Rousseau, from which he drew the following double warning:

> God deliver us from self [with reference to Rousseau] and Satan [with reference to Voltaire], the internal and external fiend; The Lord forbid we should fall into the snare of the Sadducees, with the former of those two famous men [Voltaire], or into that of the Pharisees with the latter [Rousseau].[2]

Over against the contemporary French philosophy of a Voltaire or a Rousseau, Fletcher sought to set his own understanding of true philosophy. During his stay in Nyon he often worked on his French writings from morning until late at night. *La Louange* appeared in print in Nyon in 1781. A second enlarged edition in French appeared in England in 1785, under the title *La Grace et la Nature*. A third later writing in French was *The Portrait of St. Paul*, the origin of which went back to Fletcher's stay in Nyon between 1778 and 1781, but which was not published until after his death, in an English translation.

La Louange – *'Praise'*

La Louange, a poem based on Psalm 148, was written during Fletcher's stay in Nyon and was a revision of an earlier poem which has not survived. It appeared in print in Nyon in 1781. Fletcher did not regard himself as a gifted poet. Nevertheless he published this work, partly because his friends pressed him to do so, but partly also because he wanted to encourage poets to apply their art to the service of virtue and godliness. He wanted to demonstrate the difference between the false philosophy of the modern 'philosophizers' and true wisdom.[3] He drew attention to this difference in the long explanatory notes which accompanied the poem. The whole poem is divided into fourteen cantos in which particular themes from Psalm 148 are developed. In the process Fletcher ranged far wider than the psalm itself, weaving into his poem other words from the Bible and complete biblical narratives. The beginning of the poem, the opening stanzas, might equally well have been written by a deist, marvelling at the beauty of the universe. Yet even in the first canto it is clear that it is not just a supreme being but the triune God who is here being praised. Fletcher was calling the reader to true godliness and virtue.

In the third canto, which was dedicated to philosophers and clergy, Fletcher defied the spirit of the age by placing the Pauline doctrine of redemption at the centre. He wanted to speak not only of virtue, but of human sin and human redemption by God. The attention of the philosophers was drawn to their wise predecessors in antiquity, and to the difference between creator and creation. Only arrogance can imagine that it discerns the depths of God. Fletcher was not content simply to argue against philosophy. He wanted above all to address the philosopher as a human being, and to point out his need of the Saviour. Pascal was for him the very model of a person who was both a Christian and a philosopher.[4] In his notes on this part of the poem Fletcher faced up to the issues of materialism, of the difference between the operation of grace and fanaticism, of the doctrine of the Trinity, and of the doctrine of redemption. He compared quotations from foolish philosophy – especially from the writings of Rousseau – with quotations from true wisdom. He wanted to defeat the modern 'philosophizers' with their own weapons, while calling on reason, experience and facts as witnesses in support of his own statements. In addressing the clergy, he pointed out the significance of redemption and the new birth for the attainment of true virtue and godliness. Otherwise, he argued, preaching is reduced to moralizing talk which, in face of the power of sin, cannot change people. Paul was offered as an example, in both his life and his teaching.

The cantos which followed contained exhortations to praise God addressed to princes and the government, to the poor, the sick and the afflicted, as well as to those who were suffering for righteousness' sake. In a note about the last category, Fletcher stressed that it was always a mark of true Christians that they did not persecute others but were themselves persecuted, by both unbelievers and pseudo-Christians. Christianity was not a religion which led to fanaticism and the persecution of others. Such things resulted from the behaviour of arrogant pseudo-Christians. In succeeding cantos God was praised and human beings instructed by animals, plants and inanimate creation. Here too the praise of God and redemption were closely connected with each other. Thus, for example, the list of domestic animals included the cockerel, whose crowing, following Peter's denial of Christ, was to be interpreted not directly as praise of God but as a call to the sinner to repent. In the canto on the tiger and the lion, Fletcher acknowledged Voltaire's concern over the unjust condemnation of Calas and Sirven, and, taking up a verse from Voltaire's *Henriade*, he spoke out against the use of mercenaries in Switzerland. In other footnotes he contrasted the philosophy of Newton or Locke in England, or of the Bernese scholar Haller, with that of Voltaire in France and of Hume in England.

Through his poem Fletcher wanted to invite everyone to praise God and to live in virtue and godliness. It is surprising, therefore, that at the end of the poem an 'I' – undoubtedly Fletcher himself – says he will express his praise only in silence, because he would not like to besmirch heavenly praise with his own sinfulness. From a literary point of view it seems probable that underlying the 'I' sections of the poem are parts of Fletcher's earlier draft. These 'I' sections are to be found at various places in the poem, and most of them are also included in the revised second edition, which appeared under the title *La Grace et la Nature*. The surprising twist at the end of the poem thus leads to the conclusion that, even at this later stage in his life, Fletcher had not been able to overcome the tension, not to say the disjuncture, between his commission as a preacher of the gospel (which would naturally lead him to praise), and his understanding of himself as the least and most unworthy of all sinners. He recognized the operation of the grace of God in all created things, and he invited all creatures to praise God, but when he looked at his own life he could see only his sinfulness and God's righteous judgment, with the result that, in this poem, he seemed to be denied admission to the choir of worshipping creatures. Yet in his letters he could urge others to break out of a silence which might be regarded as ingratitude: 'O! for this matchless love, let rocks and hills, let hearts and tongues break an ungrateful silence . . .'[5]

There were three questions Fletcher was not able to go into in the footnotes to *La Louange* because they were too detailed. He referred to an article on gambling, which was probably never published. A second note, on the connection between doctrine and morality, appeared posthumously, in the context of *The Portrait of St. Paul*. A third, on the arms trade, was probably included in his pamphlet on the peace agreement of 1783, and from there found its way into the second edition of his poem.

La Grace et la Nature – *'Grace and Nature'*

Fletcher gave further attention to his poetical work even after his return to England. The second, enlarged edition appeared in England in 1785 under the title *La Grace et la Nature*, and was dedicated to the Queen of Great Britain. Fletcher included in it, among other things, an extra

foreword on evangelical, rational 'mysticism'. By that he meant a form
of speech which expressed its content in pictures, animals, personifi-
cations, allusions, similes, etc. He compared his work with that of poets
and writers from ancient times until the present. He felt that he was
particularly guided by the biblical form of narration. There were, he
said, many scripture passages – such as, for example, the discussion of
Jesus with Nicodemus on the new birth – which could be clearly understood only in a derived, spiritual sense. Fletcher believed that simple
people in particular would be better able to hear the truth by means of
such a mode of expression. Evangelical mysticism would bring the deep
things of theology within the reach of simple people. Fletcher's positive
mysticism was deeply influenced by his pneumatology.[6]

La Grace et la Nature contained twenty-four cantos, in place of the
original fourteen. The notes too had been substantially expanded. The
main message had changed, in this second edition of the poem, from the
praise of God to the instruction of men and women, and their turning
back to God. The rearrangement of some of the cantos in the second
edition led to a clearer construction. The cantos were in some instances
shortened and in others lengthened. Many verses were revised or recast,
and in many places we find an adaptation to English circumstances. The
most extensive enlargements occurred in relation to the Paris peace
treaty of 1783, which was celebrated in four cantos. Here Fletcher
presented in revised form what he had published a year earlier in three
parts under the title *Essai sur la Paix de 1783, Dédié à l'Archevêque de
Paris*. In it he spoke out strongly against the inhuman war trade and in
favour of peace, which Christian kings who called upon the same Lord
ought to promote and preserve. Fletcher drew a distinction between
wars which were necessary for the defence of one's country and for the
freeing of the oppressed, and excesses in war, which he strongly condemned. The high value which he placed upon peace had to be understood against the background that many people in England were under
the impression that too many concessions had been made. Fletcher
admitted that the peace treaty demanded sacrifices, but he was hoping
now for a fresh blossoming of trade between the peoples. The last canto
in this interpolated poem dealt with the return of the Prince of Peace,
Jesus Christ, and the effects of his reign.

The Portrait of St. Paul

In the third canto of *La Louange* philosophers and clergy had together
been invited to praise God. The work *The Portrait of St. Paul*, which
was not published by Fletcher himself, but which appeared posthumously in an English translation, was addressed to the same two
groups of people – the first two parts to the clergy, the last part to
philosophers.[7] John Wesley read this work immediately after it
appeared in 1790. For several decades it had an enduring influence on
the Methodist travelling preachers. It had its origin in Fletcher's stay on
the Continent, and it arose in response to lukewarmness and to the
effects of the radical Enlightenment which held sway there. Fletcher also
made several references to Ostervald. The work consisted of three parts.
In the first main part Fletcher drew the portrait of the true Christian and
of the evangelical clergyman, by contrasting the exemplary traits of Paul
in the first subsection with the picture of the lukewarm, contemporary
minister in the second. The second main part dealt with the doctrines
which an evangelical clergyman ought to promote. The third main part
was devoted to the connection between doctrine and morality, and was
essentially an attempt to come to grips with contemporary philosophy.

In the first main part the character of a true Christian and the duties
of a good minister were looked at from similar points of view. Fletcher
wanted to address himself to both groups of people. Since he regarded a
concrete example as more effective than rules and regulations, he
described the moral character as it was to be seen in Paul. Not every
believer was called to be a clergyman, and not every clergyman was
called, like Paul, to found new churches, but all Christians ought, in
accordance with their situation, to be filled with the godliness of the
apostle. In his introduction Fletcher mentioned various situations in
which Christians, including women, might find themselves, and various
tasks which might be allotted to them. His aim in writing was to present
Paul as an overall pattern for the orthodox confessor of the faith as well
as for an immature Christian and a sincere deist. The moral character of
Paul was unfolded in forty sections. Because there were so many
sections, many of the thoughts were repeated. Fletcher laid particular
stress on the fact that Paul had experienced and known God not only as
creator, but also as redeemer. For Paul, repentance and a living faith
were at the heart of Christian devotion. From them sprang humility and
love, two essential distinctive marks of Christian faith. Paul was called
to the work of an apostle, and he surrendered himself totally to his

Lord. He carried out his duties with all his might. He knew how to divide his time between preaching and prayer. He defended the truth, and never sacrificed it to a false understanding of love. He was patient even in trials and temptations. He was ready to seal the truth of the gospel with his blood. Biblical texts on the life of the apostle furnished the material for the forty sections. The weight of what Fletcher had to say lay, admittedly, less on the moral character of Paul than on the moral lessons which every minister and Christian could draw from it.

Fletcher painted a picture of the apostle as he was able to see it – a picture that he had for a long time taken as a pattern for his own life.[8] He quoted biblical texts in support of his understanding of the ministerial office, just as he had done in his discussions with other ministers in and around Nyon. He emphasized the great importance of repentance and the life of faith for every evangelical minister. He explained how the call to the ministry could be discerned. He stressed the need to struggle for one's flock, both in public preaching and in private prayer. In the section on marriage he spoke more positively and with much greater understanding than he had previously done of the value of marriage for a minister. Fletcher contrasted the lukewarm minister and the false apostle with the example set by Paul. In doing so he made use of quotations from Bishop Massillon, from Pastor Roques and from Ostervald. He responded to several criticisms of the use of Paul as an example. His actual disputes with the ministers of the assembly in Morges were reflected in these responses, as, for example, in his condemnation of the writing down and delivery of sermons in a theatrical manner, or of the limiting of all ministerial activity to the Sunday sermon.

In the second main part of the work Fletcher turned his attention to the doctrines preached by an evangelical minister. In his statements he distanced himself from a contemporary understanding which gave pride of place to the existence of a supreme being and exhortation to a virtuous life, and avoided all talk of grace or redemption, through fear of irrational 'enthusiasm':

> The minister of the present age, being destitute of Christian piety, is neither able to preach, nor clearly to comprehend, the truths of the Gospel. In general, he contents himself with superficially declaring certain attributes of the Supreme Being; while he is fearful of speaking too largely of grace or its operations, lest he should be suspected of enthusiasm. He declaims against some enormous vice, or displays

the beauty of some social virtue. He affects to establish the doctrines of heathen philosophers: and it were to be wished, that he always carried his morality to as high a pitch, as some of the most celebrated of those sages. If he ever proclaims the Lord Jesus Christ, it is in but a cursory way, and chiefly when he is obliged to it, by the return of particular days. He himself continues the same through all seasons! and the cross of Christ would be entirely laid aside, unless the temporal prince, more orthodox than the minister, had appointed the passion of our Lord to be the preacher's theme, during certain solemnities of the church.[9]

Fletcher saw what is revealed in the Old and New Testaments as being summed up essentially in the Decalogue and the Apostles' Creed. He set out four central points for preaching: (1) true repentance towards God; (2) living faith[10] in our Lord Jesus Christ; (3) the hope which the Holy Spirit pours into the hearts of believers; (4) Christian love, which is the abundant source of every good work. Once again Fletcher explained his understanding of the 'dispensations', by the help of which he analysed the biblical message. Theological statements were always seen in relation to their outworkings in a person's godliness and morality. Revelation proved itself true in personal experience.

Fletcher began his treatment of repentance by establishing why all people are sinners and need to be born again. He described how a minister leads people to repentance by helping them to recognize their depravity. Every sin can be traced back to failure to observe the commandment to love God and one's fellow human beings. Fletcher used quotations from the *Berner Synodus* to describe the extent to which human sinfulness is expressly revealed in the cross of Christ. He warned against superficial, pharisaical repentance. The necessity of repentance ought not to be preached apart from the proclamation of the forgiveness of sins through faith in Jesus Christ, otherwise sinners are being thrust without hope into an abyss:

> To shew the necessity of repentance, without publishing the remission of sins, through faith in Jesus Christ, would be to open a wound without binding it up. It would be leading sinners to the brink of a tremendous gulf, and cutting off all possibility of their retreat. But nothing can be more contrary to the intention of the faithful minister, than to sport with the miseries of man, or *ultimately* to aggravate his distress.[11]

The statements in the subsection on living faith consisted almost entirely of biblical quotations. In order to illustrate how little a contemporary minister preached such faith, Fletcher included a conversation between two neighbours, based, probably, on his experiences in Nyon. In the subsection on hope, Fletcher emphasized the need, in the face of a world characterized by sin and death, for a firmly based hope, not directed towards things that are transitory. For the believer Christ is not only the object of faith but also the source of hope. A fourth subsection dealt with Christian love:

> If the evangelical pastor proclaims *repentance, faith and hope*, it is with a view of leading sinners to that *christian charity*, which is justly esteemed the crown of every grace. In preaching *repentance*, he lays the axe to the root of every corrupt tree. In publishing evangelical *faith*, he plants the tree of life. When he proclaims the hope of the Gospel, he causes that tree to put forth a beautiful blossom: but when he preaches Christian *charity*, he calls forth the rich fruit from every vigorous branch.[12]

Love for God and love for one's neighbour belonged, he maintained, inseparably together. The person who, in faith, has recognized that God is love, can do no other than love in gratitude, because God has first loved us.

To the charge that he was preaching new doctrines, Fletcher responded with quotations from the *Berner Synodus*, and with references to the Second Helvetic Confession, to the French Protestants' confession of faith, to the *Confessio Augustana*, and to the articles of faith of the Church of England. The remaining arguments of the second main part of the work were devoted to the unfolding of the trinitarian revelation of God in salvation history, under the covenant of grace. Under the dispensation of the Father, the outward bodily manifestation of the Son for the forgiveness of sins was promised. Under the dispensation of the Son, the full manifestation of the Spirit for the sanctification of believers was promised. Under the dispensation of the Spirit, the return of Jesus Christ for the glorification of the saints was promised. Fletcher described the unfolding of the gracious dealings of God in history. More strongly than in the 1770s he stressed the *unity* of God's trinitarian activity. At *all* times the Father, the Son and the Holy Spirit were working together to bring to completion the salvation of the sinner. It is only at the historical level and in human perception that the manifestations of the Son and the Spirit are differentiated:

There never was a time, in which the Son and the Spirit were not occupied in completing the salvation of believers, but there was a time when the Son became manifest upon the earth, making a visible display of his astonishing labours: and then it was, that his particular dispensation had its commencement. So likewise there was a time, when the Holy Ghost, more abundantly shed forth by the Father and the Son, began to work his mysterious operations in a more sensible manner: and at that time commenced the particular dispensation of the Spirit, which serves to perfect the dispensation of the Son, as that of the Son was given to perfect the dispensation of the Father.[13]

Fletcher was seeking to establish a clear distinction between the believer's being filled with the Holy Spirit and the claims of religious 'enthusiasts' and fanatics. Believers who are filled with the Holy Spirit do not brush reason aside, but are guided by the biblical testimony, observe the means of grace, fit in with the church's order, and distinguish themselves by the gifts of love, by true devotion and not simply by outbursts of feeling.

In the third main part of the work, dealing with the connection between doctrine and morality, Fletcher took issue with philosophy, that is, with the deism of the Enlightenment, rather than atheism proper. He had two objects in view. He wanted to defend doctrines, or 'truths', derived from the Christian revelation against the charges that they were contrary to reason and that they had had bad ethical consequences. The Christian revelation was being seen as contrary to reason and morality, both in its essence and in its import. For all his criticisms of Rousseau and Voltaire, Fletcher was still able to recognize moments of truth in their writings. The existence of a supreme being, and, in a restricted sense, the providence of God and the reality of a future judgment, were presumed by Fletcher to be undisputed, and generally acknowledged as reasonable. But he criticized the superficiality of the deist conception of God, and tried to point out the sense of the classical Christian doctrines. Before speaking of the defectiveness of philosophical knowledge, he first admitted that many Christians gave the philosophers grounds for just criticism:

It must, however, be confessed, that many christians have afforded philosophers too just a subject of scandal, by continually opposing *faith* to *reason*; as though, in order to be possessed of the richest christian grace, it were necessary to renounce that noble faculty, which chiefly distinguishes us from the brute creation. Like the great Apostle, we may rationally oppose *faith* to *sense*; but we can never, without the highest indiscretion, oppose it to *reason*.[14]

Fletcher argued that philosophical teachings on natural religion and morality were not capable of producing true love in the heart, since they failed to recognize the reality of sin. If the philosophers took the existence of God and of a just judgment seriously, then they must recognize their sinfulness. Good, moral, commandments were to be found both in the Koran and in the works of modern philosophers, but these had been fashioned from Christian tradition. Fletcher went on to say that doctrines exercise an important influence on people's ethical behaviour. They make one's duties plain. He then asked what influence the doctrines of the gospel had had on people's lives, and explained it in the light of the Apostles' Creed. In general terms he pointed to the usefulness of these doctrines – a procedure which must be seen in the light of his normal apologetic practice.[15] Because the believer is aware of the Fall and of redemption, the doctrines of the gospel are superior to 'philosophy'. They are better able to embrace the truth, and lead a person to a better moral outlook. Fletcher referred to evidence for the character of the early Christians. Obviously if faith has no effect on the life of a Christian, then it is no more than the faith of a hypocrite. Many of these apologetic arguments were already to be found among representatives of the Dutch-English early Enlightenment and reasonable orthodoxy, whose work was known to Fletcher. This was not, however, true of the emphasis on the Fall and on redemption which were central to Fletcher's line of argument.

In a subsection, Fletcher dealt with the charge of Rousseau and his followers that although there were many excellent truths in the gospel, it also contained irrational, obscure and foolish things. If these latter elements were removed, they said, they would be able to accept the gospel. In his response to this, Fletcher took 'gospel' to mean the totality of God's saving revelation in Christ, and not, as Rousseau understood it, simply the four Gospels. As was his custom, Fletcher began his answer indirectly, with a comparison: if we insisted on first fully understanding and discerning everything that we use every day and live by, then we would have to cease to live. But it would be irrational to acknowledge, on the one hand, that the natural sciences have their impenetrable mysteries, while insisting, on the other, that on no account should there be any such mysteries in religion. It was perfectly possible,

he argued, to be in a state of humble faith and active love, without
having sounded the depths of all spiritual mysteries:

> For the *practice* of solid piety, it is by no means necessary, that we
> should be permitted to fathom the depth of every spiritual mystery.
> It is enough, that fundamental truths are revealed, with sufficient
> perspicuity, to produce in us that faith, which is the mother of
> charity.[16]

Fletcher offered essentially three explanations as to why the revelation of the gospel and the doctrines based on it have their veiled
and mysterious side. First there was God's wisdom in nurturing us.
Secondly, as a consequence, there was the fact that God has placed us in
a state of probation: we are called to the obedience of faith. Thirdly, and
most importantly, over and above this, there was the need to recognize
the contrast between the creator and his creation, between the finite and
the infinite.

At the end of this third main part of his work Fletcher again set out
his understanding of the revelation of the triune God in history, in order
to refute the argument of Rousseau and Voltaire that, since the gospel
had only existed for eighteen hundred years, it could not be binding on
everyone. Jews, Mohammedans and pagans are also saved, he argued, if
they live in accordance with the revelation that has been given to them.
Fletcher distinguished, therefore, between two kinds of deists: the
humble, who, in accordance with the enlightenment they have received,
seek salvation; and the arrogant, who wilfully and consciously reject
the gospel that has been revealed to them. Wise Socrates must thus
be distinguished from present-day conceited philosophers. Fletcher
ended the third main part with an exposition of the Parable of the
Talents, and with a quotation from the ancient Christian writer
Lactantius, on the influence of the gospel and of philosophy on human
renewal.

Fletcher's defence of the Christian faith, here as in the preceding
poetical works, was based on the conviction that natural morality is
superseded by revealed morality, since the latter alone takes the Fall and
redemption as its starting point. It is thus only through revelation that
philosophical knowledge becomes true wisdom. Revelation cannot be
comprehended by reason in a way which resolves all mysteries. It has its
mysterious side, but, when rightly understood, is not contrary to reason.
We must follow the path of faith in accordance with the revelation given

to us, and grow in knowledge as we do so. True Christianity, for Fletcher, was in no way fanatical Christianity, such as the philosophers of the Enlightenment feared, but, on the contrary, it was characterized by humility and love.

19

Fletcher and the Methodists
(III: 1781–1785)

Fletcher was fifty-two years old when he returned to England from the Continent. On his return, he went first to London, where he preached in Wesley's 'New Chapel'. Then he spent a few days in the Bristol area with Ireland. One of John Wesley's preachers sought Fletcher out in Brislington. His report of their meeting was full of respect and admiration. Fletcher appeared to him as a person no longer bound to earthly things, but one who conversed constantly with God, while at the same time taking the utmost interest in, and offering praise for, all the visible signs of God's activity in the world.[1] This one encounter typified the radiance which Fletcher shed over the Methodists during the last years of his life. For many, Fletcher was the outstanding example of a sanctified life.

> I would do something in the Lord's vineyard, but I have not strength. I can hardly, without over-doing myself, visit the sick of my Parish: I was better when I left Switzerland, than I am now . . . He [Greaves] will go when I can get some body to help me: could you spare me brother B- [Bailey]? It would be a charity. Unless I can get a Curate zealous enough to stir among the people, I will give up the place: it would be little comfort to me to stay here to see the dead bury the dead.[2]

So wrote Fletcher to John Wesley, a few months after his return. He was most seriously concerned, first, about problems in his own parish, and with his curate, Greaves. He was astonished to find how little living faith there was in his parish. He himself was again in a very poor state of health, and was unable to carry on the work alone. Greaves had made repeated complaints about the work in Madeley, and had expressed his intention of leaving the parish, but he still remained there.

At the end of May Fletcher wrote a long, unequivocal, letter to Greaves, in which he pointed out the inconsistency between Greaves's complaint that there was too much work and too many inconveniences for him in the parish of Madeley, and the fact that he nevertheless continued to stay there and function as curate. Fletcher was still in need of a curate, but it had to be a person who was able and willing to take over the work completely. He declined to reappoint Greaves, since Madeley, he said, was not the right place for him. Ireland was prepared to provide a curate, and to pay him, since Fletcher needed rest and care. Around the end of July, Bailey arrived, and Fletcher was therefore able to leave his parish and go to Cross Hall. Only a month later, however, Fletcher returned to Madeley, because Bailey had to go to London for his ordination. Greaves came back temporarily, but with him came fresh problems. Fletcher would have liked to keep Bailey, whom he valued highly, in Madeley, but Bailey's return to his former post in Kingswood was urgently awaited. Fletcher had therefore to manage without a curate.[3]

'My dear Polly'

Cross Hall, to which reference was made above, was closely connected with a particular name and event: the marriage of John Fletcher to Mary Bosanquet. When he began his ministry in Madeley Fletcher had, for several days, been considering the possibility of marrying. The same thought had been in his mind some years later. Each time the person concerned was Mary Bosanquet. According to the testimony of Fletcher himself and of Charles Wesley, he first expressed his affection for her and his intention to marry her in 1781.[4] For her part, Mary Bosanquet had said in 1768, when she thought her companion, Sarah Ryan, was close to death, that she felt she might be called to marry Fletcher.[5] Fletcher, however, seems never to have known of her thoughts on the subject.

In the 1770s Mary Bosanquet was very worried about Fletcher's health, and in 1776 she invited him to her house so that she might care for him. Fletcher thanked her for the invitation shortly before his departure for the Continent, and admitted that he too had had similar thoughts.[6] They began to exchange letters on the subject of Christian perfection, but the correspondence was interrupted when one of the letters got lost on the way. When Fletcher recovered his health on the

Continent, his friends there wanted him to marry: 'I have been so well, that my friends here thought of giving me a wife; but what should I do with a *Swiss wife* at Madeley? I want rather an English nurse.'[7]

When Fletcher returned to England he came across the mislaid letter on Christian perfection, and answered it immediately. It was in a further letter, which reached Mary Bosanquet on 8 June (but which has not been preserved), that Fletcher must have expressed for the first time the affection which he had felt for her for over twenty years, and which he hoped might lead to the establishment of a closer bond between them.[8]

Who was this woman, whom Fletcher had known for so long, and who was the only one he would consider marrying, if ever he were to take such a step? Mary Bosanquet was ten years younger than Fletcher. She was from a well-to-do family, and she came into contact with the Methodists very early on. She sought out the Methodists, against her parents' wishes, especially during her stays in London. It was there that she must have met Fletcher for the first time. At the age of twenty-one she received an allowance from her parents, and left home. She developed a close friendship with Sarah Ryan. In 1763 she went with Sarah Ryan to Leytonstone, where her family had property. There she started Methodist meetings. Along with Sarah Ryan she belonged to that first generation of Methodist women who also preached in public. To the end of her life she remained one of the most important female figures in Methodism. Her house soon became a home for poor people and orphans. In consequence Mary Bosanquet fell into financial difficulties. When her father died, she received the income from a fortune of £4,500 which was held in trust for her. In 1768 Mary Bosanquet moved with her whole 'family' to Yorkshire, where she took over an estate at Cross Hall. But the hopes she had had of balancing her financial budget were disappointed. She found herself obliged to give up her labour of love for poor people and orphans. It was at this point, early in 1781, that Fletcher's letter reached her. During the month of August Fletcher stayed with Mary Bosanquet at Cross Hall. They decided to marry, but before doing so wanted to seek the advice of the friends they had in common, as well as the approval of Mary's relatives.[9]

In September, Bailey, who was standing in for Fletcher in Madeley, had to go away, and Fletcher was obliged to return to his parish. He also had to inform his new housekeeper that she would have to go back to London since he was planning to marry Mary Bosanquet.[10] Fletcher and his bride-to-be, his dear 'Polly', now engaged in an

intimate correspondence. His changed attitude towards marriage came
out clearly in the letters:

> My first, my best, and most generous friend . . . Surely a human
> creature *alone*, is but *half* himself. And yet how many, for want of
> having made the comparison, glory in their loss! I will do so no more.
> I will glory in Christ Jesus, and in the dear member of his mystical
> body his Providence has so remarkably appropriated to my help and
> comfort.[11]

Fletcher's love-letters show his anxiety as to whether his bride-to-be
really would give her consent, but also this 52-year-old's joyful antici-
pation of their life together. At the time they were still waiting for
answers from friends and relations.

Fletcher wrote to John Wesley by the end of August. The beginning of
the letter shows clearly how difficult it had been for Fletcher to bring
himself to discuss this personal matter with John Wesley during the
summer months. He related how he and Mary Bosanquet had reached
the conviction that God was bringing them together. He then hesi-
tatingly asked for John Wesley's approval, not of the marriage, but of
an intimate exchange of thoughts, by letter and by word of mouth,
between two persons who felt affection for each other or were intended
for each other.[12] The answer came in the middle of September. John
Wesley characteristically took note of the uncertainty in Fletcher's
enquiry, and replied cautiously that a correspondence accompanied
by watchfulness and prayer would not cause any problems. Other
responses from friends, including Ireland, turned out to be very positive,
and Fletcher therefore concluded that, though Wesley had said very
little, he was nevertheless not against the relationship, while the other
letters spoke the language of his own heart. After the friends had given
their approval, Mary Bosanquet's relatives were approached. The attitude of her uncle, Claudius Bosanquet, was particularly important, since
he was responsible for the administration of her inheritance. Fletcher
sent him a curriculum vitae, gave his reasons for wanting to marry
Mary, and put a figure on his own total assets of £2,000.[13] In his letter
to Mary Bosanquet's brother, he admitted that he had held back from
marriage in earlier years partly because of the wealth of his bride-to-be.
By her gifts and her devotion, however, she was well equipped for the
work of a minister's wife in a parish. Mary Bosanquet's relatives, like
their friends, agreed to the marriage.

Fletcher spent the rest of the year 1781 at Cross Hall. This was made possible by a pulpit exchange with John Crosse, a clergyman from Bradford. Fletcher had promised to make another journey to Nyon with Ireland, but, for understandable reasons, he decided not to go. More quickly than expected, a buyer was found for the Cross Hall property, and the financial problems were resolved.[14] It is possible that Lord Dartmouth had helped to bring financial matters to a satisfactory conclusion.[15] On 12 November 1781 Mary Bosanquet and John William Fletcher were married in Batley church. John Wesley congratulated them on their marriage. He wrote to say that he would not have wanted to see Mary Bosanquet joined in marriage to any other person than John Fletcher. In his characteristic way he urged them to lead a carefully regulated life from their first day together in Madeley, such as had been the custom in the earlier extended family in Leytonstone.[16] Charles Wesley wrote to Mrs Fletcher:

> Yours I believe is one of the few marriages that are made in heaven. Better late than never – My friend had thoughts of proposing to you (I am his witness) 20 years ago: but he bore false witness against himself, that he then sought not you but yours . . . I sincerely rejoice that he has at last found out his Twin-soul, and trust you will be happier, by your meeting thro' all eternity . . . When I heard of your marriage I said – It will be adding 2 or 3 years to his life. Many will rejoice if it should be a Dozen.[17]

Limited activity among the Wesleyan Methodists

Anyone glancing at the records of the Conference of 1781 would find the following surprising entry:

> Q. How are the Preachers STATIONED this year?
> A. As follows: – 1 *London*, John Wesley, Charles Wesley, John Fletcher, Thomas Coke . . .[18]

The rumour that Fletcher was to leave Madeley spread like wildfire. Fletcher, however, returned to Madeley. He was married, and no longer had a curate to call on. Both factors bound him even more strongly to Madeley. There could be no question of his leaving the parish. During that conference year, to the best of our knowledge, Fletcher never worked among the Methodists in London. His name did not appear in the list of stations in 1782.

In his first letter to John Wesley after returning from the Continent Fletcher had indicated that he would give up his parish in Madeley if he could not find a competent curate. He had not made any explicit reference to the alternative of working alongside John Wesley. He had also shown interest in the situation of the Methodist societies in America, and had had some thoughts about the increasing laziness and self-satisfaction among believers:

> Another [reason for the spiritual decline] yet may be, the judging of the greatness of the Work by the numbers; which I fear, misleads Mr. **** himself. And so long as he firmly believes Methodism flourishes and increases, it will be almost in vain to offer, or administer remedies to remove declension.[19]

As far as he could, Fletcher sought by exhortation and example to awaken people from their slumbers. His activity during his stay in Yorkshire in August 1781 stemmed from this concern. Fletcher took part in the Conference which was meeting in Leeds at that time. He and Thomas Coke were members of a small group to which Wesley looked for advice. In his *Journal* Wesley commented favourably on one of Fletcher's sermons during the Conference: 'I desired Mr. Fletcher to preach. I do not wonder he should be so popular, not only because he preaches with all his might, but because the power of God attends both his preaching and his prayer.'[20] From other reports we know that Fletcher chose to preach on the great promises of God, to expound his dispensational view of the Trinity in salvation history, and thereby to stir the Methodists into action. His participation in the meetings of the Conference led to the hope that he might now work entirely with the Methodists. Charles Wesley was convinced that a great responsibility lay on Fletcher for 'gathering up the wreck' – that is to say, for holding the Methodist movement together after the death of its leader. In his view Mrs Fletcher should limit her husband's workload, so that he might go on living for a long time. She tried to do so, but with variable success.

In 1782 John and Mary Fletcher received an invitation from the Methodists in Dublin, but because of a deterioration in John's health, and the lack of a curate, they at first declined it. The Dublin Methodists repeatedly renewed their invitation. In spite of John's ever-worsening state of health the Fletchers finally decided to undertake the journey, and set out in August 1783. They stayed in Ireland for seven weeks. John preached, and, together with his wife, visited Methodist classes. They held prayer meetings, and exhorted the faithful. Fletcher's activity was not limited only to Methodist meeting houses, but he preached in various places, both in English and French. The visit turned out to be an unforgettable event for the Dublin Methodists. During and after the visit there was evidently a revivalist awakening. A little episode throws further light on Fletcher's inner disposition during this journey: before he left them, the people of Dublin wanted to present him with a gift of twenty-five guineas, to cover his travelling expenses. Fletcher was unwilling to accept the gift under any circumstances, but they pressed him so hard that he finally accepted the money, on condition that he could do with it whatever he chose. To the astonishment of the Dublin Methodists he immediately handed the money back, saying that he had heard that they were in urgent need of support for their benevolent fund. On the return journey from Ireland, Fletcher accompanied two friends to Bristol, where he stayed for a few days, preaching in various places. One hundred and fifty-one members of the Methodist society in Dublin signed a letter of thanks to the Fletchers, who continued to maintain contact by letter with individual Dublin Methodists.

Further invitations to work among the Methodists were declined by Fletcher, but he took great interest in the progress of the Methodist movement. He welcomed and supported Coke's plans for the establishment of a missionary society, but declined to go to London himself. Often it was only with difficulty that he could care for his own congregation.

> . . . I make just shift to fill up my little centry [sentry] box, by the help of my dear Partner. Had we more strength we should have opportunity enough to exert it . . . Your great stage of London is too high for people of little ability and little strength . . .[21]

Contacts between Fletcher and Calvinistically inclined 'gospel ministers' continued into the 1780s, but not with the intensity they had had in the 1760s. Source material is scanty. For example, there are no letters to Lady Huntingdon from these later years, when she and the preachers connected with her had finally separated from the Church of England and registered their meeting houses as Dissenters.[22] The little we know, however, leads to the conclusion that Fletcher continued to value his relationship with his erstwhile opponents in the theological controversy, and thus sought to strengthen the bond of love between them. But his more far-reaching 'plan of reconciliation' from the 1770s could never be put into effect.

The Conference of 1784

It was not until 1784 that Fletcher again took part in one of the annual Conferences of the Methodists. He preached on several days, and assisted Wesley in the distribution of the Lord's Supper. His greatest contribution, however, lay in the resolution of the dispute between some of the preachers and John Wesley. In February 1784 Wesley had drawn up a legal document constituting the 'Conference of the people called Methodists'. According to this document, the Conference consisted of one hundred preachers nominated by John Wesley, including four ordained ministers: John and Charles Wesley, Thomas Coke and James Creighton. At that time, however, there were already 161 preachers in full connexion with Wesley, and a further twenty-two on probation. Most of those who were excluded felt themselves to have been passed over, or feared that, after the death of the Wesley brothers, the 'legal hundred' would exercise hegemony over the Methodist movement. Fletcher himself was not one of the hundred. His name had appeared on the list of preachers only in 1781. As a personage well known and respected among the preachers, who, however, was not a member of the 'legal hundred', he could act as mediator. It was largely due to him that the gulf between the dissatisfied preachers and John Wesley was bridged. He preached two impressive sermons in which he earnestly urged his hearers to show mutual love and acceptance, and spoke of John Wesley as father and the preachers as Wesley's children. One of the preachers described Fletcher's work of mediation in the following terms:

> Never, shall I forget the ardour and earnestness with which Mr. Fletcher expostulated, even on his knees, both with Mr. Wesley and the preachers. To the former, he said, 'My father! they have offended, but they are your children!' To the latter, he exclaimed, 'My brethren! my brethren! He is your father!' and then, portraying the work in which they were unitedly engaged, he fell again on his knees, and with fervour and devotion engaged in prayer. The Conference was bathed in tears, many sobbed aloud.[23]

John Wesley referred in his *Journal* to Fletcher's exertions in the cause of reconciliation.

It was within a smaller circle during the same Conference that the question of the future of Methodism in America came up for discussion. John Wesley was planning the ordination of preachers for independent America, as it had now become, as well as the publication of a shortened version of the *Book of Common Prayer* and the articles of faith of the Church of England, for the use of American Methodists. The action John Wesley proposed was similar in many respects to the plan put forward by Fletcher in 1775, but with two important differences: it was now a question of making provision for a country which had become independent of the motherland both constitutionally and ecclesiastically; and in this particular situation Wesley declined to make further representations to the bishops. The role played by Fletcher in the discussions remains – like much else connected with Wesley's ordinations – obscure. Such evidence as we have from third parties suggests that Fletcher was probably drawn into the debate, and advised Wesley to strive for the persons concerned to be ordained by bishops, adding that if Wesley was obliged to perform the ordinations himself he should draw up appropriate legal documents.

Fletcher's own relationship to the Methodist movement was also discussed in the 1784 Conference. When all the preachers were undergoing the annual examination of their character and service, Fletcher wished at first to leave the room, as one who was not involved. He said that he was only prepared to be present during the examination on condition that his name was read out with all the others. When Fletcher's turn came, an elderly preacher rose and said:

> I have but one thing to object to Mr. Fletcher: God has given him a richer talent than his humility will suffer him duly to appreciate. In confining himself to Madeley, he puts his light, comparatively, under a bushel; whereas, if he would come out more among us, he would draw immense congregations, and would do much more good.[24]

Fletcher answered by referring to the closeness of the bonds between himself and his congregation, to the extent of the work in Madeley, to the difficulty of finding a suitable curate, and to his own health problems. Yet the voice of that elderly preacher from the floor of the Conference was not without its effect. Fletcher asked that after his death Madeley might become part of a Methodist circuit, and expressed his willingness to be included in the conference minutes among the retired preachers. His name did not, however, appear in the 1784 minutes, though it was included in 1785. He was designated a helper in the Chester District.

Charles Wesley, the 'old, useless friend', as he now often described himself, was still convinced that Fletcher should take on the leadership of the movement after the death of his brother and himself. He wrote to Fletcher shortly before the Conference of 1784, when he felt that his own death was imminent:

> I trust y[ou] are reserved (after mine and my B[rother]'s departure) to gather up the Wreck. Be sure the Sheep will be scatter'd. All the beasts of the forest are watching for them. – Many will find shelter among the Moravians. Many will turn to the Calvinists – Baptists – Presbyterians & Quakers. Most, I hope will return [*sic*!] to the bosom of their Mother the Church of E. [England]. Not one but several new Sects will arise: *And Methodism will be broken into 1000 pieces.* It is impossible for you to know *now* or to divine or conjecture *what you are intended* for.[25]

Fletcher was still convinced that the providence of God had not yet called him to be a travelling preacher. He had the advantage, he wrote in a letter to Ireland, of having his place of work outside his very doors, so that he only needed to take a single step from the pulpit to his bed, and from his bed to the grave. His wife, too (he said), was convinced that she was called to a settled life. He went on to say:

> If I had a body full of vigour and a purse full of money, I should like well enough to travel about as Mr. Wesley does, but as Providence does not call me to it, I readily submit. The snail does best in its shell: were it to aim at galloping like the race horse, it would be ridiculous indeed.[26]

But it was precisely this snail-like existence that was incomprehensible to Wesley. Early in 1785 he invited Fletcher to the following Conference, and asked him directly whether he did not stay too much at home. In a letter to his brother Charles, John Wesley expressed himself even more clearly: 'About once a quarter I hear from Mr. and Mrs. Fletcher. I grudge his sitting still; but who can help it? I love ease as well as he does; but I dare not take it while I believe there is another world.'[27]

In this letter at least,[28] John Wesley failed to recognize that the life of the Vicar of Madeley, in one of the first areas to be undergoing industrial development, and especially when that Vicar's name was Fletcher, was no cosy, comfortable existence. In the last years of his life, considering his bodily weakness, Fletcher had often devoted himself to his ministerial duties with far more energy than was good for him.

20

Projected Theological Works

The doctrine of the Trinity and Christology: projected response to Priestley

Back in the 1770s Fletcher had been urged to defend the doctrine of the Trinity against a Socinian Quaker, but he had been unable to do so because of his involvement in the antinomian-predestinarian controversy, which was continuing to make fresh demands upon him. In 1782 Joseph Priestley's *The History of the Corruptions of Christianity* was published. Priestley was a scientist, and a theologian of the English Enlightenment, who contested the divinity of Jesus and became a leading representative of the Unitarians. In the work mentioned above, he included the divine Sonship of Christ and the triunity of God in his list of irrational and pernicious doctrines. Various newspapers and magazines reported on the publication, and made Priestley's ideas known. Fletcher very soon became aware of it. In the autumn of 1783 he was urged by the Wesley brothers to write a response to Priestley: 'My brother very much wishes you woud [*sic*] answer Dr. Priestley (his last book I presume) & says the Dr. is afraid of you. Ask consent of the Lord & follow it.'[1] In March 1784 John Wesley visited Madeley, and read through Fletcher's letters to Priestley. Wesley wrote in his *Journal* that there was hardly another man in England so well fitted to answer Priestley as Fletcher. In the same year Henri Louis de la Fléchère also wrote to say how important it was to respond to Priestley's writings. He advised his brother to proceed in an indirect manner, so as to settle the matter more quickly. Shortly afterwards Fletcher received a letter from his erstwhile opponent Richard Hill, begging him to take up the debate with Priestley as soon as possible. Both Calvinistic and Wesleyan Methodists pressed for an early publication.

John Wesley wrote to Fletcher again in the spring of 1785, stressing the importance of responding to Priestley's document:

I have very little hopes of doing any good to either Deists or Socinians. But it's worth all our labour to prevent their doing mischief – at least, more than they have done already. For this reason I look upon everything with a jealous eye which prevents your answering Dr. Priestley. He is certainly one of the most dangerous enemies of Christianity that is now in the world. And I verily think *you* are the man whom God has prepared to abate his confidence.[2]

It was because of all these requests that Fletcher continued to work on his response to Priestley, so at the end of his poem *La Grace et la Nature*, when it appeared in 1785, the publication of the first part of a work in defence of the divinity of Christ was announced. Fletcher died, however, before the document was ready to go to press. His wife discovered separate parts of the manuscript, but did not know whether, or by whom, they were meant to be published. In 1787 the task of dealing with them was entrusted to Benson, who published the larger connected sections of Fletcher's manuscript, expanding them in some places. In what follows we shall discuss only the sections written by Fletcher in this two-part work, *A Rational Vindication of the Catholic Faith: being the first part of a vindication of Christ's Divinity; inscribed to the Rev. Dr. Priestley*, and *Socinianism Unscriptural: or the Prophets and Apostles vindicated from the charge of holding the doctrine of Christ's mere humanity: being the second part of a vindication of his Divinity; inscribed to the Rev. Dr. Priestley*.[3]

In the Introduction Fletcher lamented the fact that there were people who gave their assent to the Trinity, yet lived immoral lives. Such people provided an excuse for those who assented only to some doctrines, attacking the ones which were distinctively Christian, but who nevertheless led moral lives, and so could give the impression that their attacks against a particular doctrine were motivated by virtue. In his first letter to Priestley, Fletcher began the battle for truth by pointing out the provenance of Priestley's thoughts, and their connection with the denial of the union, in human beings, of mortal body and immortal soul.[4] He argued, briefly, that some of the quotations from the church Fathers produced by Priestley were saying precisely the opposite to what Priestley intended. These quotations in fact confirmed the doctrine of the Trinity. Fletcher made it quite clear that the battle was about fundamental articles of faith. Priestley might indeed have wanted to acknowledge the divinity of the Father, but the testimony of the Bible was that God could only be known in his Son, Jesus Christ, and by the power of the Holy Spirit. Fletcher identified three main arguments in Priestley's work: first, that the doctrine of the Trinity was irrational; secondly, that the doctrine of the divinity of Christ had no basis in the Old Testament; and thirdly, that it received no support from the New Testament either. Fletcher was leaving aside a fourth argument, concerning the support of the church Fathers, since enough had already been written on that subject.

It is clear from Fletcher's response that on both the doctrine of the Trinity and Christology his arguments deviated from reasonable orthodoxy in content as well as form.[5] Certainly he shared its view of reason. But the doctrine of the Trinity was not, for him, an obscure article of belief whose origin should not be speculated upon;[6] rather, it was derived from divine revelation and could and should be explained and accounted for. For Fletcher, Christology had not arisen out of the earthly activity of Jesus. The rational-historical basis for the Messiahship of Jesus in the prophecies of the Old Testament, the teaching of Jesus, the miracles of Jesus and the consequences of his coming was not valid.[7] Fletcher did not speak of the Messiahship of Jesus, but rather of the divinity of Jesus Christ. His detailed expositions, both in Christology (pre-existence, participation in the work of creation, manifestations in the Old Testament, mediatorial role)[8] and in the doctrine of the Trinity (unfolding of the distinction between Father, Son and Spirit in the Godhead),[9] showed clear parallels with the teaching of Calvin.

The first part of the published work, *A Rational Vindication of the Catholic Faith*, that is, of the divinity of Christ and the triunity of God, contained four chapters. Here, as in earlier writings, Fletcher sought to base his case on reason and Scripture. In the first chapter he dealt with misunderstandings and false teachings surrounding the doctrine of the Trinity. The existence of a supreme being, he said, was acknowledged even by deists, since it could be inferred from nature. But God's essential being is hidden from humans if God does not reveal it to them. Christians too, he continued, affirmed the unity of God. To that extent all true Christians are 'unitarians'. They uphold God's unity against all forms of polytheism. But they differ from Jewish or Socinian Unitarians, who restrict God the Father to an unfruitful, solitary unity, to the extent that it is no longer possible to speak of a father. Fletcher therefore dubbed them '*Disuniters*, *Dividers* of God, and *Manglers* of the Divine Nature'.[10] Once again Fletcher identified two extremes, which he wanted to avoid:

Man is not only prone to leave the narrow way of truth, but to run from one extreme to the other. When the Divine *Unity* was chiefly revealed, mankind madly ran into Idolatry: The Creator was forgotten; almost every creature was deemed a God. But since the Creator has revealed, that, in the Unity of the Divine Essence, there are *three Divine Subsistences*, human perverseness starts back from that glorious discovery, – and the Philosophers of this world, under pretence of standing up for the Divine Unity, and for the dignity of the Father, refuse divine honours to the second and to the third Subsistence, without which the Deity cannot exist, and the Father can be no Father.

Hence it appears, that *Idolatry* and *Impiety* are the two precipices, between which the Christian's road lies all the way to heaven . . . Dr. Priestley supposes that we are fallen into the former; and we fear that he and his admirers rush into the latter. Let us see who are mistaken. It is one of the most important questions that was ever debated. Either we are *Idolaters* in worshipping that which by nature is not God, or the Socinians are *impious* in refusing divine worship to that which is really God; and what is more dreadful still, they worship a mangled notion of Deity, and not the God revealed to us in the sacred Scriptures.[11]

In his second chapter, Fletcher exposed the irrationality and inconsistency of Priestley's arguments, by playing off two of Priestley's writings – *Disquisitions on Matter and Spirit* and *History of the Corruptions of Christianity* – against each other. In the former, Priestley admitted the limitations to which the human understanding is subject in making statements about God. In the latter, he maintained the rationality and comprehensibility of statements about God, arguing that one must choose between threeness or oneness in God.[12] In his third and fourth chapters, Fletcher introduced a large number of Bible passages from the Old and New Testaments in support of his arguments for the pre-existence of the Son of God and his role in creation, for the divinity of Jesus Christ, and for the Trinity.

The second part of the published work, *Socinianism Unscriptural*, contains a collection of eight letters left by Fletcher. They were mostly concerned with the question as to whether the Messiah of Old Testament expectation was a mere man. Fletcher's approach, as in the first part of the work, was again characterized by the fact that the starting point for both his thinking and his argumentation was the doctrine of the Trinity. He did not try to deduce the doctrine of the Trinity from the biblical testimony. Rather, he sought to demonstrate that only the doctrine of the Trinity, and the divinity of Jesus Christ which went with it, could make possible a rational understanding of the biblical testimony. The first two letters were principally concerned to show that the manifestations of God in the Old Testament were appearances of the pre-existent Son of God:

> The same Scriptures, which inform us, that *No man hath seen God* (the Father) *at any time, but* that *the only begotten Son, who is in the bosom of the Father, hath declared him,* (John I, 18), teach us nevertheless, that *God appeared* to several of the Patriarchs, and sometimes even in a *human* shape. Hence it follows, that we must either reject St. John's declaration above quoted, or admit, that he who thus appeared, is the *Son, the Logos,* who *was in the beginning with God and was God.*[13]

In a further letter, Fletcher described the three predictions, to Adam and Eve, to Abraham and to the sons of Jacob, all of which pointed to a divine redeemer and judge. These predictions found confirmation in the prophets. Fletcher repeatedly linked up Old Testament prophecies with the testimony of the New Testament, since he was convinced that they were in agreement. Essentially, therefore, he expounded Old Testament passages in the light of the New Testament.[14] He also cited a whole range of Messianic prophecies in which divine attributes appear. Thus, he maintained, the Old Testament itself bore witness to the divine glory of the Lord Jesus Christ.

There then followed two letters on the testimony of the evangelists and apostles to the divinity of Christ. By the fact that Priestley was forced to deny the inspiration of the biblical writers, Fletcher argued, he (Priestley) was indirectly admitting that those writers affirmed the Lord's divinity. Fletcher did not set about trying to prove their inspiration. Instead, he described the witness of Holy Scripture. The same is true of the final letter, where Fletcher went on to discuss the writings of Paul. One of Fletcher's main arguments was again the inconsistency of Priestley's statements. For example, he explained I Corinthians 8.4, 6, on which Priestley based his case, in this way:

> What appearance is there that St. Paul, having begun his Epistle by pointing out *our Lord* as the object of our adoration and prayers,

would contradict himself in the middle of that very Epistle? If you do not believe that he wrote by *divine inspiration*, you should at least allow that he wrote with *common sense* . . . If you insist that this expression εἶς θέος *one God*, which is applied to the *Father*, necessarily excludes the Son; it will follow by the same unscriptural rule, that this expression εἶς Κύριος *one Lord*, which is applied to the Son, necessarily excludes the Father, and thus to rob the Son of his *supreme Divinity*, you will rob the Father himself of his *supreme Lordship*! So true it is that unitarian overdoing, always ends in *undoing*; and that our Saviour spake an awful truth, when he said, *he that honoureth not the Son, honoureth not the Father*![15]

The letter ended abruptly. The normal conclusion was lacking. Fletcher's efforts to compose a response to Priestley's work remained fragmentary. Their posthumous publication, substantially enlarged by Benson, led, especially in the Methodist societies, to a strengthening of the 'Catholic faith', over against Enlightenment influences.

God, the Three-in-One, is love: from Fletcher's notebooks

Neither the doctrine of the Trinity, nor the interpretation of the Johannine sentence 'God is love', were new aspects of Fletcher's thought, which had not been in evidence before the 1780s. Both of them were present in the 1760s, and received stronger emphasis in the 1770s, in letters as well as in theological writings.[16] Fletcher's expectation of the outpouring of the Holy Spirit had made him well aware, early on, of the significance of the doctrine of the Trinity and of love. At first he laid emphasis mainly on the revelation of the Trinity in salvation history. In the last years of his life he was increasingly concerned with the unity of the triune God, and with the nature of God as love:

> Mercy, righteousness, peace and joy be multiplied to dear Lady Mary, and to all, who are dear and near unto her, from the Father of mercies, through the Son of his boundless love, and through the Spirit of infinite love, which the Father breathes continually towards the Son, and the Son towards the Father! So prays John Fletcher.[17]

Such thoughts are expressed in all Fletcher's writings and letters from the late 1770s and early 1780s. Especially remarkable, however, are the reflections he recorded in his little notebooks.[18] Here he was able to write down important thoughts from his quiet times of devotion and prayer. The notes are undated. They are included at this late stage in the biography because similar thoughts appear frequently in other works of Fletcher from this period. Here we can only deal with a few salient thoughts from the booklets. Some of the notes revolved around the three concepts of unity, distinction and union/reunion; others around the contrast between shadow and truth. They contain very frequent references to love.

Unity – distinction – union/reunion: this triad forms the heading at the beginning of one of the two notebooks. For Fletcher, the triad, rooted in God's being and reflected in the creation and redemption of humanity, embraced the essence and the operation of the divine love:

> Divine Love is a Union between God, as a lover, & the Soul, as his Love. he that is joined to the Lord is one Spirit (I Cor 6,11) – This Love-union hath 3 parts.
>
> I. UNITY. A primitive & original Unity containing all. This is the ground of Love. Represented, By the Father in heaven, Adam, alone in Paradise, And Man without a new birth on earth[.]
>
> II. DISTINCTION, without which the endearments of love cannot take place. Represented by the eternal generation of the Son, the extracting Eve from Adam, & the new birth of C[hrist] form'd in believers.
>
> III. UNION & REUNION of the two into one. This is love consummate. The Spirit of Love & bliss the produce of unity rising into distinction & reuniting again in love. This is represented by the H[oly] G[host] proceeding from the Father & the Son & as it were making them one again in the Mystery of the Trinity. By the Marriage of Adam & Eve in Paradise when twain became one flesh again. And 3.ly By the Love shed abroad in the regenerate soul in consequence of its new birth.[19]

This basic statement, with reference to the trinity of God, is expressed in different ways, and particularly related to the image of marriage:

> The Godhead in the father is divine love in the fountain. The Love Spring of eternity. – The Godhead in the son is divine love in the *birth*, or *image*, the love birth of eternity. – The Godhead of the

H[oly] G[host] is divine love in its marriage union, between the love
Spring & the love birth. The Love-Union in eternity. God being love
is compleat in eternity, by being within himself a birth & a marriage,
w[hich] two include all beauties, sweetnesses & blessednesses, all the
beautiful sweet & blessed fruits of love. How glorious a type of the
trinity is marriage.[20]

Fletcher spoke of the trinity of God as a living reality, which can be
experienced and is experienced. What he says about it demonstrates an
amazing grasp (for the eighteenth century) of the essence and
significance of the divine Trinity. The same could be said of Charles
Wesley's *Hymns on the Trinity*. The fact that the one God must be
Trinity was based, for Fletcher, on his being a living God:

If the supreme Unity [God] is the Supreme life it must be a trinity.
Life cannot be without society, nor society without distinction.
Solitude & the loss of distinction is the horror of death. Life is a
reflexion upon itself. An unity going forth into an image of itself, by
an union with itself in a compleat circle.[21]

The unity of the triune God now found much clearer expression than
in earlier years. In the *Checks*, a trinitarian/salvation-history perspective, in which a particular dispensation was assigned to each person of
the Trinity, was dominant. The danger thus arose that the unity of
operation of the triune God might be lost sight of. In the spiritual notes
from the later years of Fletcher's life, the living and life-creating unity of
God moved back into the centre:

Trinity.
God is a living unity. An unity without variety is dead. – A perfect
unity hath all variety in it – This unity and this variety are one by the
unity, distinct by the variety – As they are one & distinct there arises
from these two a third which is the union of both . . .

The Father is the supreme unity, the Godhead in its fountain – The
Son is his express image rising up out of the father, and abiding in the
father. The generation of the son is eternal, ever perfect, ever in act,
never to come, never past.

The third person is call'd Love proceeding from the other two,
because he is the union & fellowship, the mystical marriage and

heavenly kiss of the other two. The godhead embracing and conversing with itself.[22]

A contrast which found expression in many of Fletcher's thoughts was that between the visible, which is only shadowy, and the true, which is invisible. This contrast appeared in letters from the middle of the 1770s.[23] With this concept Fletcher sought to express the mystery of creation, and the relationship between the creator and his creation.[24] He stressed the separation between God and humanity, between the eternal and the temporal.[25] But, on the other hand, he spoke of God as the sole, inner, hidden substance of the world, and of created beings as the 'outer side of God':

> Man tho' the noblest part of the creation is but the image of God, divided from God himself. God is the only inward, hidden substance of all things, of the soul & body of man. Man perish'd by overvaluing himself instead of passing thro' the glory of the image inward to the tree of life the substance of glory itself as it is God. Creatures are the outside of God, in them we rest thro' idolatry. thus when men knew God in this outside they glorify'd him not as God. they worship'd the circumference, the garment. We must look at God in Christ beyond & thro' all things.[26]

Fletcher expressed it in a paradoxical form:

> God is all in all. Yet he is nothing of all. No creature is any thing at all of him or to him. He divinely comprehends and fills all creatures, yet he so transcends them all that they are less than nothing to him. He is above all, yet one in all, one with all, all in one, the only truth of all.[27]

Of the world, therefore, Fletcher wrote: 'This world is a mystery[,] a veil drawn before God's glory.'[28] And on human aspirations: 'The sensual man hunts shadows[,] the rational man pictures[,] the Christian substance.'[29]

Fletcher liked to speak of human beings as made in the image of God. In doing so he wanted the God-likeness, as well as creation, to be understood in terms of christology:

> The Lord Jesus is the 1st and supreme image of God, the first born of

every creature, the root, head, the pattern of every creature especially mankind . . . All is made in Christ as the eternal universal image of God, by him as the power & pattern, for him as the image [later amended to 'glory'] that is to be seen in all.[30]

Our Lord as he is a man is not a single but universal man, he took not on him any particular person but the human nature to subsist in the nature of God. He is *magnus*, the other *parvus* Adam. St. Paul calls him heavenly the other earthly man. he is not a branch nor the root alone but the whole tree of mankind in the spirit. he is the spiritual & heavenly man. Christ is the universal eternal image of God, & the first born image of every creature in particular both for kinds & individuals in this sense he is the *Truth* the original copy to w[hich] every thing is a transcript, the essential *word*, w[hich] expresses all things. In him was life & the life was the light of men. Our Saviour is our first and best life the original draught of our persons. these life[-]images in him are our light of righteousness beauty glory, nor can we rest till we rest in our original self in Christ.[31]

Not only redemption, but also creation, must be understood in the light of Christ and his role as mediator. It was precisely in his Christology that Fletcher broke through his otherwise negative evaluation of the visible and created as shadowy and concealing. At one point, in the context of observations on the resurrection of Christ, he arrived at a theologically fruitful statement: 'Humanity is not as a cloud to the sun of the Godhead but as a Crystal that reflects its beauty.'[32]

In a sermon draft probably from the 1780s we read:

. . . our sins will never turn away the heart of Christ from us, for they brought him down from heaven to die in our place; and the reason, why iniquity separates between God and our souls, is because it turns our eyes from him, and shuts up in us the capacity of receiving those beams of love, which are ever descending upon and offering themselves to us.[33]

Fletcher's statements about the being and activity of God culminated in love. In the *Checks* he had been concerned to find a balance between biblical statements on the justice of God and on the grace of God. His 'Scripture-Scales' were evidence of the attempt to reconcile the concerns of Bible-Arminians (justice) and Bible-Calvinists (grace). In the spiritual notes this endeavour took second place to the basic conviction that God is love, and that all statements about God must be developed from this one essential affirmation:[34]

> God is Love, fury is not in him. His heart is Love, wrath is the work of his hand his strange work. It is without him, as a cloud on the Sun. A vizor on his face. Fury in God is love by the opposition hightend to a flame to consume vanity & sin . . . God's power is equal to his will & his will is love.[35]

Fletcher could even celebrate the inadequacy of any comparison: 'It is not so natural to fire to burn, the Sun to shine, as it is to God to communicate himself in his love and loveliness.'[36]

The goodness and wisdom of God, like his providence, are understood in terms of his love. Fletcher never wearied of insisting that the love of God underlay its apparent opposite:

> God is love, the principle by w[hich] God manages war with his enemies is love not hatred on his part. It is a love strife seeking to consume the enmity of things and convert all into one love as fire . . .

> I [God] am all sweetness; the effect is from the subject I work on.[37]

God alone is good, and whatever is good in creation is so only by virtue of its union with God and its likeness to him:

> There is none good but one, that is God. See goodness in the appearance of God. God is good alone other things only by their union with him & likeness to him . . .

> The essence of God is Goodness – of Goodness Love. Goodness in Creatures is as an accident [in the sense of what is not characteristic of created things].[38]

Fletcher's understanding of the being and activity of God as love clearly burst the bounds of early Enlightenment statements. In connection with both the Holy Spirit and Christ, he insisted on God's redemptive and sanctifying activity. It is the Holy Spirit who enables us to participate in Christ:

We are made partakers of C[hrist] by the indwelling & operation of
his spirit in us . . . The H[oly] G[host] is given to us to be ever with us
and in us – He brings the father & son to us with all their train to sup
& lodge with us. – He shedeth abroad the love of God.[39]

Fletcher repeatedly described the redemptive work of Christ as love:

Love is a mutual union. Christ having made himself the centre &
Circle of all created & uncreated fulness by love attracts man's spirit
to himself. by love gives forth himself to live again in man. Thus man
is fill'd with all the fulness of God, by the manifestation of his
Saviours Love. The receiving of this Love into ourselves is Scriptural
faith . . .

Justification is a love look, and sanctification a love token . . .

Justification is the coming to an immense estate[.] Sanctification is the
improving it & knowing daily more of the unsearchable treasures.[40]

The comforting promise is also rooted in the love of God:

Say not I am unworthy unlovely – This love is free[,] the sun shines
upon wilderness, it brings loveliness, garments feasts, beauty
strength. It will form a bride out of nothing – out of a contrariety. It
will be a new creation & a continual preservation. Holiness is the
spiritual chastity of the soul to her heavenly Bridegroom. The
commands of the father are beams of love which obedience receives
& reflects back into the heart of God. – Joy is love flaming – it's the
laughter of the divine love in our Spirits.

God looks no more upon old things, nor should believers.[41]

Faith and love are closely bound together:

Faith draws all from God by J[esus] C[hrist] & charity carries all to
God by the same channel.[42]

In his exposition of the commandment of love Fletcher explained love
for oneself as love for that new self, which the person who has been
born again in Christ now has. On the relationship between promise and
demand, he no longer emphasized their mutual connection, but rather
the dependence of the latter upon the former:

There are many Precepts & duties in the gospel, but these depend upon the promise not the promise upon them. All evang[elical] graces are the Children of the promise. This like the Jer[usalem] above is free & the mother of all good perform[ances].[43]

Fletcher could sum up the loving relationship between God and the human race in the terse sentence: 'When we know God altogether lovely – when we know him as *love* we cannot help loving him.'[44]

21

Sanctified Life and Service

Christian perfection and a sanctified life

. . . Last Wednesday evening, He [God] spoke to me by these words, *'Reckon yourselves, therefore, to be dead indeed unto sin; but alive unto God through Jesus Christ our Lord'*. I obeyed the voice of God: I now obey it; and tell you all, to the praise of His love, – *I am freed from sin*. Yes, I rejoice to declare it, and to be a witness to the glory of His grace, that *I am dead unto sin, and alive unto God, through Jesus Christ*, who is my Lord and King! I received this blessing four or five times before; but I lost it, by not observing the order of God; who has told us, *With the heart man believeth unto righteousness, and with the mouth confession is made unto salvation*. But the enemy offered his bait, under various colours, to keep me from a public declaration of what God had wrought.[1]

In her account of a meeting of a Methodist 'band' in August 1781, Mrs Rogers quoted this testimony, given by Fletcher. He expressed the content of his experience in mainly biblical language. Thus he described the experience of perfect love without using the term 'Christian perfection'. Mrs Rogers also reported on one of Fletcher's sermons, in which he emphasized the connection between his experience and faith in Jesus Christ. He had pointed out that salvation carries the promise that Christ has won for us both forgiveness and sanctification. According to Mrs Rogers' account, the following inferences could be drawn from Fletcher's experience: perfection is a gift of God's grace, which is bestowed instantly; it is not characterized by a higher moral standard, but by a deeper relationship with God, which then has moral consequences. Fletcher gave the experience both a christological basis, relating it to Romans 6, and a pneumatological one, relating it to Acts 2. The claim to be free from sin was made against the background of a definition of sin which included only intentional and conscious sins, and which attached particular importance to the motivation underlying both thoughts and actions. This is also clear from the corresponding concept of love, as the driving force behind thoughts and actions. 'Perfect love' defined what was meant by being 'filled by the Spirit'. Like every other gift of God's grace, this too could be lost, if one buried one's talent in the ground.

Fletcher's conviction of Christian perfection came at the time when he was preparing for marriage. He remarked, however, that he had had the experience four or five times before, but had not borne witness to it. One must therefore exercise caution in trying to establish a closer connection between the developing relationship with Mary Bosanquet and the experience of Christian perfection at Cross Hall, although the two things happened at the same time and in the same place. Changes in Fletcher's view of marriage and in his understanding of perfection can be detected during the time of his stay in Nyon. These changes not only happened concurrently: they were also related to one another. Whereas in the 1760s Fletcher had decided that marriage was not for him, by 1778–81, when he was in Nyon, he was considering the possibility of marrying on his return to England.[2] And whereas in the 1760s he had – like Thomas à Kempis – understood the perfection for which he was striving as union with Christ the Bridegroom, thus excluding the possibility of his marrying, in *The Portrait of St. Paul*, composed in Nyon, he could speak positively of marriage, not now seeing it as a restriction on perfection. He no longer understood married love as something which competed with and threatened one's love for Jesus.[3] The changes in his view of marriage and in his understanding of perfection thus reacted mutually upon each other.

It is undeniable that Fletcher underwent a deep experience of purification, or sanctification. This is confirmed both by the testimony of third parties[4] and by Fletcher's own statements.[5] Charles Wesley, who, unlike his brother, was not convinced that human beings could experience the grace of perfect love in this life, questioned Fletcher about his experience. Unfortunately Fletcher's reply has not been preserved. The report of Mrs Rogers gives the impression that Fletcher had now attained Christian perfection, the highest stage in the Christian life, beyond which there could be nothing 'more'. Yet the draft of a letter from Fletcher to John Wesley contains an interesting correction. Fletcher first wrote that he had claimed to have entered into the glorious liberty of the children of God. However, he subsequently corrected his draft to say that he had claimed a degree of the glorious liberty of God's

children.[6] This correction expressed more clearly the thought of the
need for growth, and the connection with the prior and subsequent
operation of the Holy Spirit. In the few remaining pieces of evidence
from Fletcher's last years, the expectation of a still-awaited, greater
filling by the Holy Spirit again took centre stage: 'The Lord has indeed
blessed me with a Partner after my own heart – dead to the world, and
wanting, as well as my self, to be filled with all the life of God.'[7] The
testimony of 1781 was not thereby retracted. Rather, it was taken
up into the overall recognition that there was on earth no 'fullness'
beyond which nothing 'more' was possible. In his treatise on Christian
perfection in 1775 Fletcher had already insisted not only that it was
possible to experience filling by the Spirit repeatedly, until it had a
permanent effect on a person's fundamental orientation, but also that
the situation could never arise in which further growth was impossible.
This was confirmed in his own experience. He did not, however, get
around to recognizing that this meant that the whole question of
Christian perfection needed to be theologically thought through and
explained afresh.[8]

For decades Fletcher had struggled against the arrogance of his ego.
He regarded his own self as of no account. A brief statement in a letter
written in 1782 summed the matter up: '. . . when self is forgotten *as
nothing* before God, you put self in its proper place.'[9] This conviction
continued to determine the direction in which his devotion to God led
him. Under the revelation of the Spirit, the command to love God and
one's neighbour thus came to require a greater love for one's neighbour
than for oneself. Fletcher saw this exemplified in Paul, who wished himself accursed for his brothers' sake.[10] He remained imprisoned in an attitude of disparagement, often even distrust, of his own self. In the last
years of his life, however, the struggle against the arrogance of his own
ego took second place to the sense that the presence and activity of God
outshone everything earthly. No created thing should usurp the place of
the Creator. But what was the proper place of created things? At this
point Fletcher's understanding of what creatureliness meant remained
problematic. For him, everything earthly could only be shadowy.[11] A
shadow ought not to regard itself as having substance. Fletcher insisted
that everything visible is shadowy nothingness, and that God is all in all:

> And who are we, my Lady, that we should not be swallowed up by
> this holy, loving, living Spirit, which fills heaven and earth? If we
> could exclude him from our hearts, we might vilely set up *self* in

opposition to him, who is all in all. But whether we consider it or not, there he is, a true, holy, loving merciful God. Assent to it, my Lady; believe it, rejoice in it. Let him be God, *all in all*; your God in Christ Jesus; your brother, who is flesh of your flesh, bone of your bone; your surety, who payeth all your debt, in whom the Father was reconciling you and us unto himself, and in whom we are accepted. What an ocean of love to swim in – to dive into! Don't be afraid to venture, and to plunge with all yours.[12]

The expectation of a new Pentecost continued to characterize Fletcher's outlook in the final years of his life:

With respect to the great pentecostal display of the Spirit's glory, I still look for it within and without; and to look for it aright is the lesson I am learning. I am now led to be afraid of that in my nature, which would be for pomp, shew, and visible glory. I am afraid of falling by such an expectation into what I call a spiritual judaizing; into a looking for Christ's coming in my own pompous conceit, which might make me reject him, if *his* wisdom, to crucify *mine*, chose to come in a meaner way . . . But *my* Jerusalem! Why it is not swallowed up of the glory of that which comes down from heaven is a question, which I wait to be solved by the teaching of the Great Prophet, who is alone possessed of Urim and Thummim.[13]

What had at first been regarded as a final filling with the Spirit was superseded by the expectation of an even greater fullness. To the very end, Fletcher's life was set in the biblical tension between fulfilment and promise, where the final goal of sanctification, or perfection, is never reached. John Wesley's observation was very apt: 'And in his highest fervors of divine love, he always acknowledged his want of more.'[14]

Activity in the societies, and pastoral letters

Fletcher had failed to find a new curate in the summer of 1781, and he decided, following his marriage, to give up the search for one. His hope was that, in spite of the poor state of his health, he would now be able to carry on the work on his own. His wife, in fact, took on many tasks in the parish, mainly among the women and in the religious societies, though Fletcher alone remained responsible for carrying out specifically clerical duties.[15]

When John Wesley visited Madeley in the spring of 1782, John and Mary Fletcher told him of the difficulties they were having in persuading the people to join in society. After his sermon, Wesley urged upon the congregation the need to meet together for fellowship. Around fifty men and fifty women indicated their willingness, and were duly divided up into small groups. A year later, Mrs Fletcher could report that over and over again people were finding assurance of faith. There was close co-operation with the Methodist preachers in the area. The preachers visited Madeley, and worked in the various societies. John Wesley came to Madeley again in 1784. In that same year Fletcher received a visit also from Charles Simeon, who was a Fellow of King's College, Cambridge, and who later became one of the leading figures among the evangelicals in the Church of England.[16]

Fletcher's correspondence gives further insights into his pastoral care for others. A clergyman who had known him in the past, and who was wrestling with the question of the assurance of faith, asked his advice. Another clergyman asked him what he thought about house-visiting. Fletcher was convinced of the value of such visits, even to unbelievers. In that way one could feel their pulse, and break down prejudices. In the 1780s, two new names appeared from time to time in his correspondence: those of Miss Loxdale and Lady Mary Fitzgerald. Both of them had only recently come to faith in Jesus Christ. In the face of attacks from other people, Fletcher assured Miss Loxdale of her salvation. In his view there were two kinds of striving for faith. In the one kind, God's Spirit within a person was very active, while the person concerned was almost passive; in the other kind, the person was very active, and the help of God's Spirit practically imperceptible. Anyone who, like Miss Loxdale, was in a state of bodily weakness, should seek to reach the Kingdom of heaven in the former manner, since she could not attain it through the power of a praying and striving faith, such as many people had. In this way Fletcher was seeking to counter the notion of a single unified scheme of conversion which did not correspond to the needs of the individual. In later years Miss Loxdale became one of the leading female figures in the Methodist movement, and in 1811 she married Thomas Coke. In his letters to Lady Mary Fitzgerald Fletcher often stressed the fact that the two of them were bound together by the suffering which had befallen them – suffering in which faith could be tested and patient hope and perfect love could be exercised. He described the sufferings of Christ on the cross, and quoted from Thomas à Kempis. The thought of the endless and boundless love of God would dispel all preoccupation with self, and all temptations.

In 1783 Fletcher heard of the illness of Charles Greenwood, in whose home he had been cared for during his own serious illness. He invited the whole family to come to Madeley in the spring to recuperate.[17] But before the spring arrived his friend and benefactor had died. Fletcher was torn between grief for the loss of Greenwood and joy over the fact that he had died in full assurance of salvation. A year later, in a letter to the widow, Fletcher expressed his sense of indebtedness in one of his characteristic comparisons:

> Here is my humbling case; I wish to requite your manifold kindnesses, but I cannot; and so I must be satisfied to be ever your insolvent debtor. Nature and grace do not love it. Proud nature lies uneasy under great obligations, and thankful grace would be glad to put something in the scale opposite to that, which you have filled with so many favours. But what shall I put? I wish I could send you all the bank of England, and all the gospel of Christ; but the first is not mine, and the second is already *yours*.[18]

In 1785, two years after Greenwood's death, came that of one of the great old pillars of Methodism, the Revd Vincent Perronet of Shoreham. He was ninety-two years old. Charles Wesley led the memorial service, though he felt that this duty should rather have fallen to Fletcher.

Communal disturbances broke out in 1782. In a letter to Charles Wesley, Fletcher reported only briefly – but severely – on the mine-workers' rising:

> The colliers began to rise in the neighbourhood: happily the cockatrice's egg was crushed, before the serpent came out. However, I got many a hearty curse from the colliers for the plain words I spoke on that occasion.[19]

The unrest was sparked off by a poor harvest and the resulting scarcity of provisions in the autumn of 1782. In October there were uprisings in the area of Wednesbury and Stourbridge. In order to prevent their spreading to Shropshire, a meeting took place of the leading figures in the coal and iron industries, together with landowners, judges and a few clergymen (Fletcher among them). They agreed to reduce the number of ale-houses and take action against the excessive consumption of

alcoholic drinks, and to buy in from Liverpool supplies of flour and
rice, which would be sold cheaply to those poor families who took no
part in the disturbances. Each of those present accepted responsibility
for part of the cost. It was also probably the shortage of flour which
led to the project for installing a steam engine of the most modern kind
to power their own mill.[20] Fletcher supported these proposals. How
far he actually played a leading part in the implementation of these
decisions must remain an open question, in view of the lack of source
material. Handwritten documents suggest, however, that some months
later Fletcher was pursuing plans which went beyond the emergency
measures described above. He wanted to set up an association of people
who would seek to bring current laws to bear against any persons who
artificially caused a shortage of provisions or who made an existing
shortage worse. Any legal costs should again be shared out. The poor
should then know that the rich were seeking to alleviate their sorry
plight with all the legal remedies at their disposal.[21]

It is uncertain whether Fletcher was able to put this plan into effect. It
reveals, though, how he sought to resolve social problems within the
framework of the existing order. From his own income he gave as
much as he could to the poor. He urged the poor to be obedient to the
authorities and to their employers. But equally he urged the authorities
and employers to meet their obligations. Any social problems which
arose could, Fletcher believed, be resolved within the framework of the
social structures already in place. His approach was able to produce
positive results in his own time and situation, because Shropshire was
an area where industrialization was developing within an entrenched
'patriarchal' society (in the wider sense of the term). In this respect
Shropshire differed from more densely populated industrialized areas
where the support of an established social order, balancing the rights
and duties of each social stratum, was lacking. By demanding of
committed Christians at all levels a stricter observance of their responsibilities, Fletcher hoped to resolve social problems within, and with the
help of, the existing order and existing legislation. Fundamentally he
never questioned these things. In social praxis his theological understanding was governed by the principle that all power has been given by
God. By this means he was able, on the one hand, to legitimize the existing order as God-given, and, on the other, to relativize wealth and
power as simply held and exercised in trust.

Fletcher's pamphlet *Three National Grievances*[22] also sheds light on
his attitude on social questions. This document, of which only the

manuscript is extant, was printed in the winter of 1783/84, and possibly distributed, during the parliamentary session, to all the members of both houses of Parliament. Charles Wesley also expressed his support.[23] Fletcher focused on three evils: the increasing tax burden, the hardship of unequal taxation, and the continually increasing tax on the poor. He treated the first of these in greatest detail.

The high national debt made a reduction in taxation impossible, even though the war of American Independence had come to an end. Fletcher attacked first the tax on alcoholic drinks, tobacco and tea. He produced many price comparisons, and examples of smuggling. The rate of taxation was so high and smuggling could flourish so easily that such honest dealers as remained were being ruined, while the smugglers, and especially those who controlled them, were able to make huge profits. Many seamen were thus going astray, and no longer engaging in fishing, since smuggling was more profitable.[24] Meanwhile the customs officials were leading a comfortable life, and not bothering about their responsibilities. To remedy the situation, Fletcher proposed that taxation should be reduced by half, and that smuggling should be suppressed by effective laws and reliable officers. The state would thereby gain increased revenue.

The second part of the pamphlet, on unequal taxation, described this particular evil from the point of view of the honest consumer, as compared with the person who bought smuggled goods. Unequal taxation, it said, was a much greater evil than unequal representation in Parliament. Only a small part of the population kept aloof from handling, selling or buying goods that might have been smuggled. The Methodists belonged to this minority, since their 'General Rules' required them to have nothing to do with goods on which duty had not been paid.

The third part dealt with the increasing number of poor people who were in need of support. Fletcher traced this back mainly to the public houses, where all the money was wasted on drink, and where the misery of many families originated. This was where the neglect of children began. There were already too many authorized public houses, as well as an even larger number of unauthorized private vendors. Many proprietors of public houses were also involved in organizing cockfights and bull-baiting, and could only survive by promoting alcohol addiction. Honest, respectable proprietors were, unfortunately, becoming increasingly hard to find. With his observations on the subject of the sale and consumption of alcohol, Fletcher was addressing one of the

great problems of his day. He signed his submission with the pseudo-
nym 'Philanthropist'. Through his pamphlet he had tackled three
current evils which were a source of concern to honest people, and
which at that time were also under discussion in Parliament. Whether
his pamphlet helped towards overcoming these evils must remain an
open question. There is no record of any reactions to it. As far as the
public houses were concerned, Fletcher attempted to secure the closure
of the worst ones in Madeley. The fact that in the last two years of his
life he had a churchwarden who supported him in this struggle suggests
that he achieved some success.

In his last years in Madeley, Fletcher concerned himself especially
with the work among children and young people. He wanted to set up
Sunday schools in his parish. In a letter written in Nyon, before his
return to England, he had confessed to a teacher that he himself would
have chosen that occupation if he had not become a clergyman. He
regarded the education of young people as a most important and urgent
task. When the idea of Sunday schools arose, it was seized upon by the
Methodists in many places. Fletcher was supported in Madeley by the
Quakeress Abiah Darby. In order to discover whether it was worth-
while to set up such schools, Fletcher launched a pilot project. Within a
short time he gathered together 300 children. Each of them was given a
little song book. With the help of neighbours, the children learnt the
songs enthusiastically. When Fletcher observed that the number of
children was continuing to rise and that they were ready to learn, he
made proposals for the setting up of Sunday schools on an official basis.
The better-off residents in the parish helped to meet the cost of teaching
staff and maintenance. Thanks to this support it was possible to build a
school- and meeting-house in Coalbrookdale. Fletcher proposed
separate classes for boys and girls in each of three places – Coalbrookdale, Madeley and Madeley Wood. The Sunday schools were intended
for those children who had to work during the week, and whose education had been neglected. The children were to learn to read and write,
and to be taught the fundamentals of morality and godliness. Fletcher
was convinced that the source of depravity, both in his parish and
throughout the area, lay in the profanation of Sunday and in the
immorality which resulted from the neglect of children's education.
Parts of Fletcher's drafts of a manual of instruction for the teachers, of a
collection of prayers, and of the first part of a catechism, are still in existence.[25] A great love for neglected children preoccupied Fletcher and
many of his contemporaries. But Fletcher was still rooted in his own

time, and his attempts at raising morality and godliness did not, therefore, involve tackling underlying social conditions, such as child labour.

Final illness and death

In 1783 there was a fever epidemic in Madeley. At the end of 1784, in a letter to a man who was probably still quite young, Fletcher wrote that, while unable to sleep during the night, he was praying for the man. Even then many young people in the parish were still dying. In 1785 Fletcher formed the intention of taking part in the Methodist Conference, if such was God's will. A fever epidemic broke out again, and Fletcher wrestled in prayer as to whether he should go to London for the Conference or not. He came to the conclusion that he was called to stay in Madeley.[26] Mrs Fletcher's brother wrote to her in May to say that he was glad that she and her husband were still in good health. Those who were ill, he said, would certainly be grateful that they had not been abandoned in their time of need.[27] At the beginning of July, Fletcher trembled for the life of his dear wife, for she had caught the disease. He was soon able to write:

> I hope the worst is over, but her weakness will long preach to me, as well as my own. Dying people, – we live in the midst of dying people. – O let us live in sight of a dying, rising Saviour, and the prospect of death will become first tolerable and then joyous.[28]

On Thursday 4 August Fletcher arrived home late in the evening. He had caught a cold. On the Friday and Saturday he was very weak. Nevertheless he still went out of the house for part of the day. By Saturday evening he was suffering from a high fever. His wife asked him to let a lay preacher take a service on Sunday in the open air, but Fletcher was convinced that it was God's will that he, as an ordained priest, should hold a communion service in the church. The service lasted for several hours, and at times Fletcher scarcely had strength enough to stand. After the service he immediately took to his bed. The fever was again in evidence, though not as high as on the previous day.

Fletcher slept a great deal, but his strength ebbed away. Mary Fletcher wrestled in prayer for her husband's recovery, but had little hope of it. On the Wednesday there came to him such a revelation of the text 'God is love' that he was scarcely able to describe it. His wife reported:

On Wednesday . . . he told me, he had received such a Manifestation
of the full Meaning of that Word, 'God is Love', as he could never be
able to tell. 'It *fills me*,' said he, 'it *fills me* every Moment. O Mary,
my Dear Mary! *God is Love*! Shout, shout aloud – Oh! it so fills me, I
want a Gust of Praise to go to the Ends of the Earth.'[29]

On the Thursday Fletcher's voice became weaker. On the Friday his
wife noticed that his body was covered in spots. On the Saturday after-
noon the fever seemed to have subsided. Although no one had told him
which day of the week it was, to the surprise of those who were standing around he asked a clergyman who was present whether he was
ready for the next day's service. On the Saturday evening the fever
returned, and from time to time a severe shortness of breath became
apparent. Finally, with his eyes open, Fletcher fell into a kind of sleep.
After the evening service on the Sunday, many of the poor people who
had come from more distant places did not want to go away. They were
given permission to pass by the door of Fletcher's bedroom and take a
last look at their beloved pastor. During the night of that Sunday, 14
August 1785, John William Fletcher died, at the age of fifty-six. The
funeral service took place three days later. It was led by the one who for
many years had been Fletcher's friend and colleague in Shropshire, the
Revd Mr Hatton.

On 6 November 1785 John Wesley held a memorial service for
Fletcher in London, and preached on the text: 'Mark the perfect man,
and behold the upright! For the end of that man is peace' (Ps. 37.37).
The sermon appeared in print, with a foreword which began as follows:
'It was a consciousness of my own inability to describe in a manner
worthy of the subject such a person as Mr. Fletcher . . .'. Wesley ended
his sermon with the words:

> To conclude. Many exemplary men have I known, holy in heart
> and life, within fourscore years. But one equal to him I have not
> known – one so inwardly and outwardly devoted to God. So
> unblameable a character in every respect I have not found either in
> Europe or America. As it is possible we all may be such as he was, let
> us endeavour to follow him as he followed Christ.[30]

The periodical *Monthly Review*, which did not as a rule report very
favourably on the Methodists, wrote:

Mr. Fletcher was one of the most considerable among the Methodist ministers of the Wesleyan division. We have long been acquainted with his good character; and we firmly believe that the high encomiums here [in Wesley's sermon] passed on him were justly merited in their fullest extent.[31]

All the extant testimonies of friends and acquaintances are in agreement. Only some Calvinistic friends expressed criticism of the passionate side of Fletcher's character, tending sometimes towards hardness, which he had occasionally displayed in the early years. Nothing is known of Charles Wesley's reaction. At that time he was still involved in controversy with his brother over the ordinations John had carried out, his state of health was poor, and possibly he was the one most deeply affected by the early death of his younger fellow-pilgrim. Charles had thus been obliged to bury his last hope that Fletcher, rather than Thomas Coke, whom he did not value very highly, would take over the leadership of the Methodists after John's death. John Wesley wanted to include an elegy by Charles in his biography of Fletcher, but Charles never wrote it. Probably he could find no words to express what he felt on the death of his friend.

From August to November 1786 John Wesley was working on his life of Fletcher. It was the only biography he ever wrote.[32] He wished to present, as a shining example to the Methodist people, the man who himself never wanted to be talked about. John Wesley compared Fletcher with Gregory Lopez and Monsieur de Renty, persons of whom he thought very highly, and indeed elevated him above them. Thus, against his will, John William Fletcher became the saint of Methodism.

EPILOGUE

An Evaluation of the Life and Work of John William Fletcher

In a brief evaluation of the life and work of John William Fletcher, mention must again be made of four points which were of crucial importance: his Swiss origins and their effects; his life of faith; his theological work; and his relationship to Methodism.

1. Swiss origins and their effects

The first main part of this biography was devoted to Fletcher's early life in Switzerland. There we saw how he was influenced by his uncle Théodore Crinsoz de Bionens, and also noted the fundamental and far-reaching effect upon him of reasonable orthodoxy, the form in which the Dutch-English early Enlightenment had come to fruition within the church. These influences were in evidence in Fletcher's earlier years, before his conversion, and they were still discernible in his latest writings. Such influence was not, however, without interruption. His conversion, under the Methodists, cut deeply into it. At this stage he stressed that the capacity of the intellect was limited in consequence of the Fall. Nevertheless he was still convinced that the Christian religion needed to be reasonable. Since he clung to the early Enlightenment concept of reason, he was able, unlike the sceptics among his contemporaries, to achieve a synthesis between reason and revelation.

Fletcher's life-changing experience of sin and grace led immediately, in many areas, to a sharp break with his past: for example in the decisive contrast between sin and redemption, and in the emphasis upon the new birth and the operation of God's Spirit. In many areas, however, as he came to terms with his new experience and with the biblical message, a change occurred in his understanding of faith. This involved overcoming both a purely ethical striving for perfection and a one-sided emphasis upon the disciplinary aspect of God's dealings with us. His thinking became more and more imbued with the conviction that God's essential nature was love.

The manner in which Fletcher was affected by his theological past also changed with the passage of time. In his early years as Vicar of Madeley, he laid all the emphasis upon the break with the past. At that time he disputed with the clergy around him who had not come under the influence of Methodism. He insisted on the complete contrast between the biblical and the contemporary views of humanity and their respective understandings of redemption. In the last years of his life, his writings increasingly turned to criticism of Enlightenment philosophers and their followers in French-speaking countries. Now he was concerned not so much to emphasize the contrast, as to reproach them for the lack of reason in their arguments. He put before them his own understanding of the reasonableness of Christianity, which, precisely because it was a religion of revelation and redemption, was able to interpret human experience in a more reasonable way.

Like John Wesley, Fletcher did not recognize a simple opposition between Methodism and Enlightenment. The differences between early Enlightenment, deism and scepticism must be kept in mind. Fletcher wished to present Christianity as both scriptural and reasonable, and in his writings he drew upon Enlightenment thought while at the same time attempting to set limits to it.

2. *The life of faith*

The sovereignty of God, his providence and his omnipotence, were important themes in reasonable orthodoxy. Under its influence, Fletcher sought to lead an exemplary life, in accordance with the commandments of God. As a result of the preaching of the Methodists, however, he came to see himself as a self-righteous sinner. The sovereignty of God the Judge affected him at every level of his being. He experienced God as the one who was free to condemn him or to re-create him for new life.

It is not enough, however, to understand Fletcher's conversion as a shattering of his own moral endeavours. The particular point of his experience consisted not in the forgiveness bestowed on human beings in their imperfection and sinfulness, but rather in the overcoming of the power of sin and the opening up of the possibility of perfect obedience. The question of the graciousness of God was, for Fletcher, subsidiary to the main question as to the possibility of living here and now a sanctified life in which sin was overcome. He thus saw the new birth as the decisive breakthrough. The Holy Spirit was no longer simply enlightenment, but a mighty power, able to bring about this new birth in human beings. For Fletcher there was no such thing as grace which counted people as righteous but did not also make them righteous. Forensic justification could only be declared in so far as a person became new. The object of the life of faith was a sanctified life. Fletcher's surrendering of his life in a covenant with God illustrated this.

Fletcher's anxiety over his acceptance by God and his doubts as to his standing as a Christian, even after his conversion, were rooted in this understanding of God's redemptive activity. His striving after Christian perfection and the fullness of the Spirit was similarly an expression of his longing to overcome the power of sin. His struggles for faith were closely linked with his theological understanding of the biblical message. Within the framework of his experience and his knowledge of the redemptive activity of God, his conscience could only find relief when he could establish with certainty that the fruits of faith were present in him. The liberating joy of the salvation bestowed on him could not break through until he attained the longed-for filling with the Holy Spirit, Christian perfection. And even this experience would not be final, but would release a fresh, though now confident, hope and expectation. The hope of being filled with the Holy Spirit was a permanent feature of his life after his conversion.

It was a testimony to the seriousness, the genuineness and the depth of his struggles for faith that this one-sided understanding of conversion in terms of being made new should lead, towards the end of his life, to what to all his contemporaries seemed an almost superhuman holiness, expressed in his humility, his patience under suffering, and his love. Fletcher wanted his path of discipleship to be marked by the cross of Jesus Christ. It was his firm conviction that whoever wished to reign with Christ must also suffer with him. This work of renewal took place in a person whose tendency to pride, anger and passion was well known, and whose nature was once compared by his friend Charles Wesley to that of a stubborn mule.[1]

After his life-changing experience of sin and grace, Fletcher acquired a fresh understanding of the Holy Spirit as the power which effected justification and the new birth, and which gave people the assurance of their acceptance by God. This corresponded closely to Reformation thought. But in addition Fletcher exhibited – especially in his pastoral letters – a strain of Jesus-mysticism, which at times explicitly echoed

that of Thomas à Kempis. This Jesus-mysticism was uppermost precisely at the points where no discernible witness of the Spirit was to be
found in his experience. During his crises of faith, and in his pastoral
care for persons in the grip of temptation, he gladly embraced thoughts
of Jesus-mysticism. In later times, when he was no longer in doubt
about the operation of the Spirit in his own life, Jesus-mysticism rather
lost its meaning for him and gave way to a stronger emphasis on the
unity of God's trinitarian operation: 'I will not rest in the first
Comforter, so as to slight that *other Comforter*, who is to abide with us
for ever. I want not only to see Jesus altogether *lovely*, but to feel Him
altogether powerful and wise . . .'[2]

In a strange way, Fletcher's urge to press forward, striving after
redemption and sanctification, was offset by a passive readiness to be
led by the providence of God, together with a feeling of his own
insignificance. John Wesley saw this tendency towards withdrawal as a
sign of the dangerous influence of mysticism on Fletcher – an influence
which he also saw at work in his brother Charles.[3] Fletcher, for his part,
admitted to Charles Wesley that he was seeking to follow a middle way
between 'driving Methodism' and 'still mysticism'.[4] He said this in
connection with his hope of perfection. His life, however, showed that
he did not exactly find this middle way. The clash between the two
opposites coloured his whole life. It is seen at its sharpest in the contrast
between, on the one hand, Fletcher's statements about the clergyman's
responsibility as watchman, and his earnest prayer (often continued
throughout the night) for God's cause – as though everything depended
on the watchman's faithfulness – and, on the other hand, his waiting for
God's leading in his life, and his declarations that he himself was good
for nothing, and that God could get on just as well without him.
Fletcher wanted to do his duty with all his might, yet always felt himself
to be an unprofitable and unworthy servant of God, whose uselessness
was plain, and who would rather be unknown to the world than
famous. This paradox remained a constant feature of Fletcher's life of
faith.

3. *Theological work*

Every assessment of Fletcher's theological writings must take account
of the fact that he was largely self-taught. During his student days
in Geneva he may indeed have breathed in the new theological
atmosphere, but he did not study theology. Not until he was in England

did he begin to devote attention to the development of theology. From the very beginning, he saw himself as completely committed to the Bible. He supported his arguments with an abundance of biblical texts. Systematically, however, much still remained obscure, and at times even dangerous. It was not until the theological controversies of the 1770s that Fletcher was able to handle both the underlying questions in Methodism, and theological traditions in general, in a deeper, more comprehensive way. Development is clearly discernible both in his thought processes and in the content of his theological writings. In his theological work and in his grasp of the biblical message, he was on the move his whole life long.

Fletcher became the leading theologian of the Wesleyan Methodists in the controversy over antinomianism and predestination. He had not sought controversy with his Calvinistic brothers and sisters, but he did not shrink from it. He did not shirk his responsibility at this point. In his theological work he was never beset by scruples as to his own unworthiness and inadequacy: a sure sign that he saw this as his appointed task! He regarded himself as committed, in this work, to both truth *and* love, because both are grounded in God: Christ is the truth, and God, the three-in-one, is love. Fletcher was convinced that it may become necessary in the church to do battle for the right understanding of truth. But – unlike many of his adversaries – he wanted to do so in love, i.e. not calling into question his opponents' salvation, and to work towards reconciliation.

Fletcher's theology overall showed, unmistakably, signs of the influence of John and Charles Wesley, but also a search for further elucidation and systematization. He was not content to stick with the immediate controversial questions about the way salvation may be appropriated, but went on to expound the doctrine of God. For him, the whole human race stood under God's covenant of grace in Jesus Christ, and all people would be judged in accordance with the particular measure of revelation granted to them. Fletcher sought to trace through history the work of the triune God for human salvation. In this he took issue very strongly with the Calvinistic doctrine of predestination, and the biblical texts on which it was based. While John Wesley warned the members of his societies against thinking about predestination, Fletcher on their behalf undertook to do precisely that. He sought to rethink and understand the doctrine of election afresh, within the framework of his concept of salvation history. His explanation of the dispensations of God has had its impact upon Methodism in many different ways. By contrast, his interpretation of the biblical witness on election and rejection has left hardly a trace. Through his scriptural exegesis, Fletcher wanted to prepare the way for a reconciliation between Calvinistic and 'Arminian' Methodists. His opponents, however, never trod that path.

Fletcher's theology did not stem from any opposition between law and gospel. Indeed, he expressly denied that there was any such opposition. His theology was governed, rather, by the interplay of sin and grace. That it could be framed in this way was the outcome of both his own biographical development, and the imprint upon him of the Wesley brothers. It must not, however, be forgotten that a positive evaluation of law is also to be found in some of the streams of tradition originating from Calvin, as well as in the Dutch-English early Enlightenment. But Fletcher and the Wesleyan Methodists interpreted the law directly from the gospel as the law of grace, as the hortatory and demanding side of God's promise. Hand in hand with this evaluation of the law, and with the stress upon the conquest of sin as the central task, went also the emphasis upon sanctification.

Since Fletcher, after his conversion, was concerned above all to expose human sinfulness and to present Christ as redeemer, his theological output in the 1770s was characterized by the image of the scales. He wanted to give equal, balanced emphasis to the justice of God and the grace of God, since otherwise either antinomianism or pharisaical works-righteousness would be the result. He developed an 'economic' doctrine of the Trinity, but in doing so stood in danger of neglecting the unity of the triune God in his operation in the world. In his later writings in French, and in his little notebooks from the 1780s, he laid greater emphasis on this unity. He stressed the triunity through which God's nature as the living God finds expression. In the 1780s it was not the balancing of God's justice and his grace that governed Fletcher's doctrine of God, but rather the characterization, not only of the activity of God but also of his very essence, as love. So, in line with Charles Wesley's hymns on the Trinity, Fletcher arrived at a creative new perception of the basic conviction: God, the three-in-one, is love.

4. Relationship to Methodism

Through Methodism Fletcher became aware of the central significance of sin and redemption in the biblical message and in his own life. To the end of his life he remained bound to the Methodists by a deep debt of gratitude. A specially close friendship existed between him and Charles

Wesley. As a vicar in a Church of England parish, he regarded himself as completely committed to Methodism, and, equally, as a Methodist, he regarded himself as committed to the Church of England. The church's parochial system, and Wesley's system of travelling preachers, were, as he saw it, two legitimate and by no means mutually exclusive ways by which Methodism might be spread. For Fletcher, Methodism served to promote the further reformation of the Church of England. Methodism, it seemed to him, was charged with the task of bringing about renewal within the state church. As the vicar of a local parish, Fletcher sought to work towards that renewal. The formation of societies in and around Madeley also served the same purpose. At one stage, the Worcester Conference provided a basis on which similarly minded clergy from the region could be brought together. But differences within Methodism on questions of doctrine and discipline put a stop to hopes of further co-operation there.

Fletcher leaned towards the Wesleyan form of Methodism. Doctrinally he was in agreement with Wesley, and he condoned the transgression of church order by Wesley's system of travelling and lay preachers. But at first he also had a good understanding with Lady Huntingdon and the circle of Calvinistic Methodists connected with her. The plan for the college for preachers in Trevecca seemed to him to offer a suitable way of promoting peace and furthering mutual understanding. He saw himself as mediator between the two streams. It was the attacks on John Wesley from the Calvinistic side which brought him to the point of unequivocally supporting Wesley, and also of setting forth the theological convictions which they held in common. But the very controversy was to help towards reconciliation and the bringing together of 'biblical Calvinists' and 'biblical Arminians'. Apart from the split of the 1770s, Fletcher occupied a mediating position between Calvinistic and Wesleyan Methodists peculiar only to him and to Howel Harris – to a limited degree probably also to Charles Wesley. When, in the 1780s, the clergy and societies connected with Lady Huntingdon went over to the ranks of the Dissenters, Fletcher had to give up all hope of reconciliation.

Fletcher's relationship with John Wesley was characterized by mutual esteem. It was not, however, without its tensions. Wesley could not understand Fletcher's disinclination to travel; Fletcher was unable, either in 1761 or in 1773, to recognize as a call from God Wesley's invitation to be his successor. Wesley expressed his approval of Fletcher's ministry as Vicar of Madeley on only one occasion; at only one point did Fletcher work – without hesitation and without any sense of his own inadequacy – for and with the Wesleyan Methodists, and that was in his theological writings. Wesley's constant aim was to persuade Fletcher to leave Madeley. It was the considered judgment of both John and Charles Wesley that Fletcher ought to take over the direction of the whole enterprise. John Wesley was convinced – quite rightly – that Fletcher would only be able to exercise the leadership role such an appointment would require of him if he consented to be prepared for it during Wesley's lifetime and in association with him. Fletcher's refusal was based, not on any lack of respect for him among Wesley's travelling preachers, but partly on his own self-assessment (he could more easily see himself sitting at the feet of a fellow-Christian than standing at the head of the growing Methodist movement), and partly on the fact that the circumstances were very different from those attending his engagement at the theological level. He felt no sense of direct personal involvement, and therefore could not see any pressing reason for complying with John Wesley's request. Not until the end of the theological controversies of the 1770s did he now and again contemplate at least accompanying John Wesley on his travels. He always expressed his readiness to step into the breach if called upon in an emergency. But such an emergency never arose: John Wesley outlived him by six years. John William Fletcher, the leading figure of the second generation in Wesleyan Methodism, predeceased both John and Charles Wesley.

Notes

1. *Childhood and Background*

1. J. Gilpin, *Arminian Magazine*, 1792, 644f.

2. On the dating, see P. Streiff, Dissertation, 22. (The only certain date is that of his baptism on 19 September 1729.)

3. Father: Jacques de la Fléchère (1678–1756); Mother: Suzanne Elisabeth Crinsoz de Colombier (1693–?); further details on the family in P. Streiff, Dissertation, 21f.

4. Letter to John Wesley, 24 November 1756, and letter to Charles Wesley, 10 May 1757.

5. The language and form of expression are here clearly marked by his conversion experience.

6. Letter to Charles Wesley, 10 May 1757.

7. Letter to H. L. de la Fléchère, 11 May 1755 (with a comment by his brother on an event in the life of the twelve-year-old John William).

8. M. Fletcher, *De la Fléchère*, 2.

9. J. Wesley, *Fletcher*, 7–11.

10. See the quotation at the beginning of this chapter.

11. Among other things, the Consensus Formula defended the verbal inspiration of the Hebrew Old Testament text even down to the vowel points, against the rising biblical criticism, and, against universalist soteriology, affirmed that God sent Christ as mediator only for the elect.

12. No pietistic circle is known to have existed in Nyon.

13. Crinsoz de Bionens was a brother of John William's mother. More details on the family tree in P. Streiff, Dissertation, 21–2 and 33–4.

14. See chs 3 and 5 below.

2. *A Career in the Church or in the Army?*

1. There is no evidence of the matriculation in Geneva of the eldest of the three brothers.

2. J. Vernet, *Traité de la vérité de la religion chrétienne*.

3. Letter to Charles Wesley, 10 May 1757.

4. 'A dix huit ans je me jetais dans l'enthousiasme . . . Je consacrais à la lecture des prophètes et de quelques livres de dévotion, le temps que je pouvais dérober à mes etude' (*sic*) [trans. 'At the age of eighteen I plunged into enthusiasm . . . I devoted to the reading of the prophets and some books of devotion the time I was able to steal from my studies']. Letter to Henri Louis de la Fléchère, *c.* 1754–55. This 'enthusiasm' is related to speculation about the apocalyptic significance of numbers. A few years later Fletcher came to take up an explicit position in relation to the work of his uncle Crinsoz de Bionens; this is evidence for long previous study of it.

5. M. Fletcher, *De la Fléchère*, 4.

6. Letter to Cl. Bosanquet, 22 September 1781.

7. Draft of a letter to M. de Luc (?), undated (before 19 December 1782).

8. Normally one entered the lowest, eighth class at the age of seven or eight.

9. Letters to John Wesley, 24 November 1756, and to Charles Wesley, 10 May 1757. The sequence of events is given in the letter of 22 September 1781 to Cl. Bosanquet, but only in an imprecise and abbreviated form.

10. J. Gilpin, *Arminian Magazine*, 1792, 644.

11. On 13 January 1750, in the Treaty of Madrid, Spain and Portugal fixed the frontiers of their possessions in South America. It is probable that the project preceded the conclusion of this treaty.

12. Did his uncle wish to obtain a position for his nephew before he resigned? Nothing more is known.

13. Lausanne, Archives cantonales vaudoises, P. Campiche 282 (15 June 1750).

3. A Private Tutor Interested in the Methodists

1. On the dating, cf. P. Streiff, Dissertation, 53f. On the history of the Hill family, cf. B. Coulton, *A Shropshire Squire*.

2. Letter to his father, 7 March 1752 (translation from French).

3. Ibid.

4. Letter to his father, December 1752 (translation from French).

5. Further details on the Hill family in Barbara Coulton, 'Tutor to the Hills', 94ff.

6. '. . . Après vous avoir souhaité de même qu'à toute la famille ce qui peut contribuer à votre sanctification et à votre vrai bonheur, dans ce prochain renouvellement d'année . . .' [trans. '. . . After having wished you and all the family whatever may contribute to your sanctification and your true happiness in the coming New Year . . .']. Letter to his father, December 1752. It was not only Methodist preaching that defined the goal of life in terms of the twin concepts of 'holiness and happiness', but also forms of

piety influenced, as was reasonable orthodoxy, by the Dutch-English early Enlightenment.

7. 'Qui a jamais blamé les premier Chrétiens de s'être flattés, que l'apparition de l'Antichrist, sa destruction et la venue de notre Sauveur étoient proches, si cette idée toute chimérique qu'elle étoit les faisoit triompher du monde, et de la chair, en fortifiant leur esperance, et en leur faisont (*sic*) révétir l'esprit de Martyre, esprit qu'on n'aura jamais si l'on s'endort dans une dangereuse sécurité. Soyons donc toujours prets à en voir approcher l'accomplissement avec une Conscience pure, et un coeur détaché du monde, persuadés que rien ne peut surprendre ni ébranler le fidèle, dont le désir ne tend qu'à déloger de cette Chair pour être avec Christ' [trans. 'Who has ever blamed the first Christians for deluding themselves that the appearance of the Antichrist, his destruction, and the coming again of our Saviour were close at hand, when this idea, fanciful as it was, made them triumph over the world and the flesh, by strengthening their hope and making them assume the spirit of martyrdom – a spirit one will never have if one falls asleep with a dangerous sense of security? Let us then always be ready to see the promises fulfilled, having a pure conscience, and a heart detached from the world, in the conviction that nothing can surprise or shake the believer whose only desire is to leave this flesh in order to be with Christ']. Letter to his father, 7 March 1752.

8. Cliff College, Calver, Fletcher MSS No. 7, 'Volume of notes written variously in French, Greek, English and Latin'.

9. Letter to Charles Wesley, 10 May 1757.

10. Ibid.

11. Mrs Hill had become a friend of Charles Wesley's wife, Sarah Gwynne, and thus had direct knowledge of the Methodists, according to Barbara Coulton in her article 'Tutor to the Hills', 97. However, Fletcher does not say in his letter that Mrs Hill pointed him in the direction of the Methodists, as the inclusion of her name in the above-mentioned article suggests. Fletcher writes only 'a Lady', although his letter is addressed to Charles Wesley. Mrs Hill's influence should therefore not be overestimated. Cf. also the quotation at the beginning of ch. 5.

12. See the two letters to the class leader Mr Edwards, 19 October 1756 and undated, c. September–October 1758.

13. The term 'Wesleyan' was not used in John Wesley's lifetime, but it is employed in these pages to distinguish Wesley and the people in connexion with him from the Calvinistic wing of Methodism. It is preferred to Wesley's own term, 'Arminian', since Wesleyan Arminianism was not identical with the original seventeenth-century Arminianism.

14. It is known that V. Perronet also, in his early years, studied Locke with diligence and enthusiasm, cf. A. W. Harrison, 'The Perronets', 42. On the theological convictions dominant in the Anglican Church at that

time, and how they differed from those of the Methodists, cf. also Jeffrey S. Chamberlain, 'Moralism, Justification and the Controversy over Methodism'.

4. From Hell to Heaven

1. Letter to his brother Henri Louis, *c.* 1754–55.
2. Fletcher admitted to a change in his behaviour. On this point my interpretation in P. Streiff, Dissertation, 73, needs to be corrected.
3. J. F. Ostervald, J.-A. Turrettini and J. Vernet all wanted to attack deism. But in doing this, they drew on the support of early Enlightenment theological sketches, and thus built a bridgehead from which, in the name of reason and natural religion, one could move on to deism.
4. Letter to his brother Henri Louis, *c.* 1754–55 (translated from French).
5. Letter to Charles Wesley, 10 May 1757.
6. 'Tu crois en Dieu, en J. Christ, tu es Chrétien, tu ne fais tort à personne, tu ne t'es jamais anyvré, tu n'as jamais souillé la femme de ton prochain, tu t'acquites en gros de tes devoirs, on te dit même que tu le fais avec exactitude, tu vas à l'Eglise, et tu pries plus regulièrement que bien d'autres; quelque fois même tu parois le faire avec beaucoup de ferveur, tranquilise toi; Jesus Ch[rist] est mort pour les pécheurs, et son mérite suppléera à ce qui te manque' [trans. 'You believe in God, and in Jesus Christ, you are a Christian, you do wrong to no one, you have never been drunk. you have never defiled your neighbour's wife, you discharge all your duties, indeed it is said that you do so scrupulously, you go to church, and you pray more regularly than many others; sometimes you even appear to do it with much fervour, so set your mind at rest: Jesus Christ died for sinners, and his merits will supply what you lack']. Letter to his brother Henri Louis, 11 May 1755.
7. The diary published by Mrs Fletcher mentions January 1755, but the details in the letter of 10 May 1757 to Charles Wesley point to the six winter months of 1753–54; on the dating, cf. P. Streiff, Dissertation, 85f.
8. M. Fletcher, *De la Fléchère*, 5f.
9. The dream is found in J. Fletcher, *Works* (1877) IX, 440–2.
10. M. Fletcher, op. cit., 8.
11. Ibid., 10.
12. The description of Fletcher's conversion is based on the following three sources:
    – A diary-type description in M. Fletcher, *De la Fléchère*, 5–12;
    – Letter to his brother Henri Louis, *c.* 1754–55;
    – Letter to Charles Wesley, 10 May 1757.
A detailed analysis of the sources and their interrelationship, as well as

the reasons for dating the conversion in 1754, may be found in P. Streiff, Dissertation, 76–90.

13. F. W. Macdonald, *Fletcher*, 36f.

14. James H. Hodson, 'Fletcher's Covenant', 57–61.

15. After my own researches for my dissertation, I came across various details and references to sources. I caused a great deal of work for those responsible for the Methodist Archives in Manchester in tracking down these details, yet they were unable to locate the original or any translations in the places cited in the literature. Whether the original of the Covenant is extant, and if so where, remains an open question.

16. Cliff College, Calver, Fletcher MSS No. 7: 'Volume of notes written variously in French, Greek, English and Latin'.

17. John Wesley, *Works* 20, 203 (25.12.1747) and *Works* 21, 23 (6.8.1755).

18. Letter to his brother Henri Louis, 11 May 1755, 16 (translated from French).

19. Ibid., 25.

20. Ibid., 21.

21. Fletcher later made an intensive effort to understand the working of the Holy Spirit. He always starts from the conviction, then generally accepted, that the special gifts of the Spirit (e.g. I Cor. 12 and 14) were given only in the time of the apostles. The gifts of the Spirit, he believed, were even dangerous for those whose humility was not deep enough to receive them. By contrast, the fruit of the Spirit (cf. Gal. 5.22f.) should benefit every Christian, since without it religion is only an empty performance.

22. Letter to his brother Henri Louis, 24 February 1756, 64 (translated from French).

23. Letter to his brother Henri Louis, 11 May 1755, 52 (translated from French).

5. Private Tutor and Anglican Clergyman

1. Letter to his brother Henri Louis, 11 May 1755, 60 (translated from French).

2. Ibid., 55.

3. For information on the illness of 1756, see Barbara Coulton, 'Tutor to the Hills', 98.

4. Cf. detailed evidence in P. Streiff, Dissertation, 118f.

5. Letter to Richard Edwards, 19 October 1756.

6. 'A Letter on the Prophecies', J. Fletcher, *Works* (1808) IX, 431–50.

7. I only discovered this connection, so important for the development of Wesley's own position, after completing my dissertation on Fletcher.

8. Cf. the detailed argument in P. Streiff, Dissertation, 108f.

9. Letter to his brother Henri Louis, 24 February 1756.

10. Letter to John Wesley, 26 May 1757.

11. The fullest treatment of the subject is to be found, interestingly, in the letter of 6 September 1777 to V. Perronet. On Perronet's expectation that Methodism had been chosen by divine providence to bring in the impending Millennium, cf. A. W. Harrison, 'The Perronets'.

12. Further information on Fletcher's views on eschatology in P. Streiff, *Dissertation*, 117f.

13. Letter to John Wesley, 24 November 1756.

14. See N. Sykes, *Church and State*, 163f., 171, also C. Fabricius, *Corpus Confessionum*, 17/1 for the relevant canons of the Church of England.

15. Barbara Coulton, 'Tutor to the Hills', 98.

16. Letter to John Wesley, 24 November 1756.

17. C. Fabricius, *Corpus Confessionum*, 17/1, Canon 34.

18. Letter to Lady Huntingdon, 28 October 1760. In view of the accusations of negligence often made against eighteenth-century bishops, it is useful to know that the canonical conditions were indeed applied. One wonders also whether this is connected with the fact that Fletcher's relations with the Methodist movement were known, and those responsible therefore wished to test this candidate with particular care.

19. On the whole matter, cf. W. R. Davies, 'Georgian Ordinations'; also Barbara Coulton, 'Tutor to the Hills'. Only Macdonald's still widely neglected biography mentions Fletcher's appointment as assistant priest in Madeley.

20. J. Wesley, *Works* 21, 89 (20.3.1757).

21. Cf. also Barbara Coulton, 'Tutor to the Hills'.

22. Letter to Charles Wesley, 26 December 1758.

23. J. Telford, *Two West-End Chapels*, 32ff.

24. (A. C. H. Seymour,) *The Life and Times of Selina Countess of Huntingdon* I, 231.

25. Letter to Charles Wesley, 26 December 1758.

26. J. Wesley, *Works* 21, 164f. (after 9 September 1758).

27. J. Fletcher, *Works* (1807) VIII, 426–32 and first in J. Fletcher, *Letters* (1791), 427–35; original 'The Test of a New Creature' in Methodist Archives, Manchester, MAW Fl Box 36. The original gives the date 'Bristol, Sep: 1758' and the subtitle 'Being queries proposed to some supposed perfect in love'.

28. Earlier, and thus as Fletcher's first publication, there appeared in 1758 a writing known only from its title: 'A Christmas-box for Journeymen and Apprentices', cf. J. Wesley, *Fletcher*, 36f.

29. On further connections between Methodism and Huguenots in London, cf. G. E. Milburn, 'Early Methodism and the Huguenots'. Cf. also, on the influence of the 'French Prophets' on the beginnings of Methodism,

C. J. Podmore, 'The Fetter Lane Society'.

30. Fletcher describes the difference between the moral improvement of the pharisee and the rebirth of the Christian as follows: 'Quelques degrés de grâce prévenante, de la raison et de la réflexion suffisent pour la première; mais il faut pas moins pour la seconde que *le baptême du St. Esprit*, et une participation réelle à la mort et à la résurrection de Jésus' [trans. 'A few degrees of prevenient grace, of reason and of reflection will suffice for the former; but for the latter nothing less is needed than *the baptism of the Holy Spirit*, and a real participation in the death and resurrection of Jesus']. J. Fletcher, *Régénération*, 33.

6. What Am I Good for?

1. Letter to Charles Wesley, 15 November 1759 (original in French).

2. 'J'ai vécu en solitaire plus que jamais depuis votre départ, il me semble que je suis *inutile pondus* sur cette terre, je voudrois me cacher; je tremble quand le Seigneur me fait la grace de me voir moi meme, je tremble de paroitre pour ne faire que deshonorer sa cause' [trans. 'I have been more lonely than ever since your departure. It seems that I am a useless burden on this earth, and I would like to hide away. I tremble when the Lord is so gracious as to see me as I am; I tremble to think that I appear to do nothing but dishonour his cause']. Letter to Charles Wesley, 22 March 1759.

3. Letter to Charles Wesley, 24 October 1759.

4. 'Heureux si un orgueil subtil ne se déguisoit pas dans mon coeur sous ces dehors d'humilité: heureux si ce serpent dangereux ne se cachoit pas sous ces fleurs et ne se nourissoit pas de leur suc' [trans. 'Happy if a subtle pride was not disguising itself in my heart under this outward appearance of humility; happy if this dangerous serpent was not hiding under these flowers, and feeding on their juice']. Letter to Charles Wesley, 29 September 1759.

5. Letter to Charles Wesley, 19 July 1759 (original in French).

6. Letter to Charles Wesley, 18 February 1758.

7. Letter to Charles Wesley, undated, *c.* April 1759 (original in French).

8. Letter to Charles Wesley, 15 November 1759 (original in French).

9. (A. C. H. Seymour,) *The Life and Times of Selina Countess of Huntingdon* I, 236.

10. Letter to Charles Wesley, 26 December 1758.

11. Letter to Charles Wesley, 4 September 1759.

12. Letter to Charles Wesley, 4 September 1759 (original in French).

13. 'Methodist' is to be understood as making specific the general term 'Church', meaning the Church of England, not as denoting an independent entity contrasted with it. It means the Methodist part of the Church of England.

14. Cf., on the details of the development, P. Streiff, *Dissertation*, 150ff.

15. Charles Wesley, *Journal* II, 232.

16. See Barbara Coulton, in 'Tutor to the Hills', 100. She also gives further background information on the gift of benefices.

17. Letter to Charles Wesley, 14 September 1760.

18. Letter to the Countess of Huntingdon, 28 October 1760.

19. J. Wesley, *Fletcher*, 40, cf. ibid., 66f.

7. *Vicar of Madeley, Shropshire*

1. Letter to the Countess of Huntingdon, 19 November 1760.

2. For this whole section cf. Barrie Trinder, *The Industrial Revolution in Shropshire*.

3. Although this forge must have been close to the estate of the Hill family, in which Fletcher served as private tutor, its construction had nothing to do with them.

4. Fletcher, *Works* (1806) II, 38f.

5. Cf. P. Streiff, *Dissertation*, 175f.

6. Letter to the Countess of Huntingdon, 19 November 1760.

7. Letter to the Countess of Huntingdon, 6 January 1761.

8. M. Fletcher, *De la Fléchère*, 14.

9. 'sa brutalité et son Atheisme le font rire de la crainte des hommes et de Dieu; je doute si l'Angleterre peut produire un monstre si complet de son age: Il a justement 18 ans' [trans. 'his brutality and his atheism cause him to scoff at the fear of men and of God; I doubt whether England could produce another such monster at his age: he is just 18 years old']. Letter to Charles Wesley, 12 October 1761.

10. Letter to Charles Wesley, 12 October 1761.

11. Letter to John Wesley, 22 November 1762.

12. The Rev. Mr Hatton. Cf. P Streiff, *Dissertation*, 183f.

13. As, for example, in L. Tyerman, *Wesley's Designated Successor*, 105, where 1762–65 are described as 'three quiet successful years'.

14. Letter to the Countess of Huntingdon, 10 September 1763.

15. A visit had been planned for 1762, but Wesley must have changed his itinerary at short notice and returned to London; cf. letter to Charles Wesley, 22 August 1762.

16. John Wesley, *Works* 21, 481 (21–22 July, 1764).

17. Letter to the Countess of Huntingdon, 10 February 1769. This letter was not known to me when I prepared my dissertation.

18. Letter to George Whitefield, 18 May 1767.

19. Letter to the Countess of Huntingdon, 19 November 1760.

20. Letter to Charles Wesley, 9 September 1763 (originally in French).

8. The Quest for Empowerment and Effectiveness

1. Letter to James Ireland, 13 January 1770.
2. Letter to Charles Wesley, 10 August 1770 (originally in French).
3. Letter to the Countess of Huntingdon, 19 November 1760.
4. Letter to George Whitefield, 18 May 1767.
5. Letter from Miss Brain to John Fletcher, 6 January 1770.
6. Cf. the list in P. Streiff, Dissertation, 219f., and the sermon referred to in ch. 5 above.
7. J. Fletcher, *Works* (1877) VIII, 348 (Sermon on I Cor. 2.14).
8. Letter to the Countess of Huntingdon, 5 November 1766.
9. P. Streiff, Dissertation, 223f., also contains a rudimentary analysis of the sermon outlines. For a complete picture, a more thorough evaluation of the manuscripts would be necessary.
10. Letter to Miss Hatton, 2 June 1765.
11. Cf. J. Gilpin, *Arminian Magazine*, 1793, 59f. and 170ff.
12. J. Wesley, *Fletcher*, 67. The extract quoted is from a paragraph in which Wesley expressed his conviction that Fletcher ought not to have taken on the parish of Madeley.
13. Letter from John Pawson to M. Mayer, 29 September 1772, in Bowmer and Vickers (eds), *The Letters of John Pawson* Vol. I, 15. Pawson's letters were first published in 1994. The letter quoted shows for the first time the reaction of a hearer to Fletcher's preaching style.
14. Letter to the Rev. P. Dickenson, 29 March 1785.
15. Letter to Charles Wesley, 20 September 1762.
16. The foregoing quotation, and many other examples of pastoral counselling, show a certain affinity with the *Imitatio Christi* of Thomas à Kempis; cf. also P. Streiff, Dissertation, 225–7.
17. Letter to Miss Hatton, 1 November 1762.
18. Letter to Miss Hatton, 3 August 1763.
19. Letter to Miss Hatton, 5 March 1764.
20. Letter to Miss Hatton, 2 June 1765.
21. Letter to Miss Hatton, 17 July 1766. The expression 'dear Messias' used in this letter also indicates a fusing of mystical and early Enlightenment concepts.
22. Letter to Miss Hatton, 9 January 1767.
23. Letter to James Ireland, July 1766.
24. Letter to James Ireland, 30 March 1767.
25. Letter to James Ireland, 30 July 1768 (after the death of Miss Hatton, but before that of Ireland's daughter).
26. Sermon-note booklet 'Spiritual Extracts', Methodist Archives, Manchester, MAW Fl Box 20.

9. Theological Convictions

1. L. Tyerman, *Wesley's Designated Successor*, 180. (This is in connection with the explanation of the grounds for Fletcher's resignation as head of the theological seminary at Trevecca, cf. ch. 11 below.)

2. Letter to Miss Hatton, 1 November 1762, quoted in ch. 8. Cf. also the letter to Rev. Mr Hatton, 4 August, 1762: 'May the Lord Jesus convince us daily more and more, by his Spirit, of sin in ourselves, and righteousness in him!'

3. Cf. below, letter to Rev. Mr Prothero (1761), and the sermon on Rom. 11.5–6, of 18 April 1762.

4. Cf. the letter to Miss Hatton, 8 August 1765.

5. The following suggestions about the time limits of Fletcher's Calvinistic phase go beyond the observations made in P. Streiff, Dissertation, 235.

6. Cf. the questions put to Charles Wesley in connection with Hervey in letters of 19 July 1762 and 3 June 1764, and see the section below on 'The Appropriation of Salvation'.

7. For the difference between Calvin and Calvinian on the one hand, and the later Calvinistic tradition of the sixteenth to eighteenth centuries on the other, cf. chs 12 and 13 below. Cf. also, on the doctrines mentioned, the end of this chapter, and ch. 20.

8. Cf. further below in this chapter.

9. M. Keller-Hüschemenger, *Die Lehre der Kirche*, 102.

10. J. Locke, *An Essay concerning Human Understanding*, IV, 19.4.

11. Cf. such writings as John Toland, *Christianity not mysterious* (1696), and Matthews Tindal, *Christianity as old as the Creation; or, the Gospel a Republication of the Religion of Nature* (1730).

12. Cf. Henry Dodwell Jr, *Christianity not founded on Argument; and the true Principle of Gospel-evidence assigned* (1742).

13. This coincides with the predominant approach to sin and redemption in Fletcher's thought, which has no room for the concept of a pure, unsullied natural religion. Cf. also John Wesley's correction to Locke's *Essay concerning Human Understanding* in Sermon 70, on I Cor. 14.20, in J. Wesley, *Works* II, 587ff. (written in 1781).

14. 'Experimental' does not mean, for Fletcher, experimental in the modern sense, but rather refers to the 'experience-dimension', to the fact that something can be experienced.

15. J. Fletcher, *Works* (1877) IX, 404–32.

16. Ibid., 410.

17. Ibid., 414.

18. Ibid., 425.

19. Ibid., 428.

20. Letter to the Countess of Huntingdon, 24 November 1767.

21. First published in 1791. Quotations below are taken from J. Fletcher, *Works* (1807/16), VII, 317–73.

22. Still in 1774 Fletcher could speak of a possible middle way between Sandemanianism and enthusiasm: cf. his letter to J. Benson, 20 March 1774. On Sandemanianism and the Glassites cf. Derek B. Murray, 'The Social and Religious Origins of Scottish Non-Presbyterian Protestant Dissent'. Soteriologically we are presented with a rationally focused Calvinism, for which any emphasis on the experiential nature of faith represents a deviation into pharisaical justification by works. It thus becomes an unintentional testimony to the influence of the Enlightenment within the orbit of Scottish Calvinism (cf. also Murray, 114 and 134f.). 'The whole tenor of the Sandemanian presentation of the gospel became anti-emotional, to the point of coldness. The great enemy was pharisaism, or any form of trusting in oneself for salvation . . . Sandeman attacked, with great ingenuity, and repetitive vehemence, the idea that faith has any subjective element' (Murray, 133).

23. J. Fletcher, *Works* (1807/16) VII, 317.

24. Ibid., 341f.

25. Ibid., 343.

26. Rationality, as the essential characteristic of human creatureliness, and the insistence that God does not impose himself in any way upon human beings, are two central principles of the Dutch-English early Enlightenment. They are to be found both in Locke and Ostervald, where they are developed within the framework of the overarching conception of God as *law-giver*. Cf. J. F. Ostervald, *Compendium*, 66.

27. J. Fletcher, *Works* (1807/16) VII, 349f.

28. In this connection he was not following the criticism of his uncle, Crinsoz de Bionens, cf. P. Streiff, Dissertation, 247, n. 81.

29. J. Fletcher, *Works* (1807/16), VII, 360f.

30. See D. Shipley, 'Methodist Arminianism', ch. 4. Shipley misinterpreted Fletcher in this way because he was unaware of the concrete allusion in Fletcher's writing. At this point in his dissertation (which is otherwise generally valuable) he assumed an opposition between Scripture and experience, between outward and inner authority, which has no place in Fletcher's thought.

31. When he reverted to it, Fletcher extended the text: 'But if it be of *Works*, then it is no more *grace*; otherwise work is no more work' (Little notebook, Methodist Archives, Manchester, MAW Fl Box 20).

32. J. Fletcher, *Works* (1806) IV, 35–93 ('Salvation by the Covenant of Grace: A Discourse on Romans XI, 5.6' in 'An Equal Check to Pharisaism and Antinomianism').

33. MAW Fl Box 20, 12 (Foreword); the quotation shows, interestingly,

Notes to pages 108–112

how the word Methodism was understood to have been derived from 'method', not only by third parties with reference to the Holy Club in Oxford, but also by adherents of the Methodist movement themselves.

34. Fletcher spoke, like the Calvinist tradition, of covenant (covenant of works/covenant of grace), and not, like Locke, of law (law of works/law of grace). (In the quotations, the 1774 additions are omitted without acknowledgment.)

35. J. Fletcher, *Works* (1806) IV, 42f.

36. In a lengthy note of 1774, Fletcher called this grace 'gospel-grace', as opposed to 'original grace'. By so doing he wished to exclude the misconception that Adam before the Fall might have gained heaven through good works. All blessings conferred by the creator on his creation are pure grace, including the original covenant of works; cf. J. Fletcher, *Works* (1806) IV, 37f., note 3.

37. Ibid., 67–9.

38. Ibid., 78f.

39. In the original version of 1762, Fletcher mentioned six further grounds: the authority of God; reverence for God; the strengthening of the bonds of love with our heavenly Bridegroom(!); the commands of God; the power of our new nature, along with our sense of inadequacy; and the bliss of serving God.

40. J. Fletcher, *Works* (1806) IV, 91f.

41. Cf. letter to Ley, 3 July (1765): 'Works that spring from faith in the law may be good to men, but the very thought that they are good will (in my poor judgement) make them stink in the nostrils of God, as profitable as they might be to our neighbour; . . . the best way then is whether before or after Justification, to be faithful to ones light as to doing or omitting things. And to seek to lose even the rememberance of our works in the contemplation of Christs Love and *free* grace.'

42. Letter to John Wesley, 17 February 1766. Wesley's reply is recorded in his letter to Fletcher, 28 February 1766.

43. J. Fletcher, *Works* (1877) IX, 448–85; Benson, in whose possession the manuscript was found, no longer remembered how he had acquired it, nor when and for what purpose the manuscript had been composed.

44. J. Fletcher, *Works* (1877) IX, 450.

45. The Reformation, and with it Calvinism, interpreted the Fall in basic categories (rebellion, unbelief), whereas theologians conditioned by the Dutch-English early Enlightenment used moral categories (disobedience against the law of God). Both lines of thought are to be found in Fletcher, but in such a way that in his teaching on sin the more radical position of the Reformation dominates. Cf. also ch. 14 below.

46. The conflict between Traducianism and Creationism is to be found most notably in the third part of the document, which demonstrates the

reasonableness of the doctrine of original sin: J. Fletcher, *Works* (1877) IX, 475–77.

47. Ibid., 454; cf. also 474f. and 478f.

48. Ibid., 463.

49. Ibid., 467.

50. Ibid., 479.

51. Ibid., 481.

52. Ibid., 482. Fletcher often strung together very different arguments. He based his teaching on hell, e.g., on the following arguments: 1. Even in earthly things the human intellect is limited in its capacity for understanding. How much more so will it be in spiritual things. 2. Our daily experience of the fallen creation ought to be sufficient evidence for the existence of hell. 3. The opposition between God and the unconverted sinner makes it plain that the latter must stay in his wretchedness. 4. Every unbeliever is conscious, from time to time, of wretchedness in his heart. This is clear evidence of the existence of hell for the ungodly. 5. The fear of many and varied torments after death has been in all ages the stoutest bulwark against an overflowing of secret ungodliness.

53. Letter to Miss Hatton, 17 May 1766.

54. Letter to his societies, 30 October 1765.

55. Letter to the Countess of Huntingdon, 6 January 1761.

56. Letter to the Countess of Huntingdon, 19 December 1766.

57. Letter to the Countess of Huntingdon, 26 July 1762.

58. Letter to Miss Hatton, December 1764.

59. Fletcher combined the two in his letter to the Countess of Huntingdon, dated 3 January 1768. Cf. also the expectation of the power of the Spirit in his letters to the Countess of 3 April 1765, 19 December 1766 and 16 March 1767.

60. Letter to the Countess of Huntingdon, 10 February 1769; this letter was not known to me when I wrote my Dissertation.

61. Letter to the Rev. Mr Hull, 18 December 1770.

10. *Fletcher as a Clergyman of the Church of England*

1. Cf. ch. 7 above.

2. Letter to Rev. Mr Simpson, 4 August 1770.

3. Frank Baker, 'Sermon Notes', 30–33, and George Lawton, 'Pulpit Prayers', 2–6.

4. 'Il est certain que depuis quelques mois j'ai de tems en tems des scrupules – Je crois que je dis un mensonge en assurant que les Enfants que je *batise sont regenerés* – Et un autre quand je declare que je comets tous *mes morts a la terre* in sure & certain hope of resurection to Eternal life' [trans. 'Undoubtedly for some months I have had misgivings from time to

time – I believe I am telling a lie in giving the assurance that the *children I baptize* are regenerate – And another when I declare that I am committing all *my dead to the earth* in sure & certain hope . . .']. Letter to Charles Wesley, 22 August 1762; cf. also his dissatisfaction with Charles Wesley's reply in the letter to Wesley of 20 September 1762.

    5. Draft letter to Revd Mr Lewis, 3 February 1762.

    6. Cf. A. D. Gilbert, *Religion and Society*.

    7. But cf. the accounts in letters to Charles Wesley from that period.

    8. A. D. Gilbert, *Religion and Society*, 40, writes about 'old Dissent': 'It tended to remain exclusive and elitist while the new dissenting movements became, like Methodism, inclusive and conversionist . . . they [the old Dissenters] shared a common concern that religion should be "serious", that regularity should be preserved in matters of polity and liturgy, that high professional and intellectual standards should be maintained in the ministry, and that persons of rank and influence should not be driven from their congregations by any ill-advised popularisation of the dissenting tradition. They abhorred the "enthusiasm" of the New Dissent, its relative indifference towards denominational order and formal ministerial training, and its evangelical preoccupation with expansion which seemed too much like "trading in souls".'

    9. Abiah Darby, Diary in *JFHS* X, 79–92.

    10. Ibid., 90.

    11. 'An Answer to the Objections and Queries of Mrs. Darby in her Dispute with me John Fletcher Vicar of Madeley On Thursday the 22d Nov.br 1764. To which are added some Remarks upon what she calls a faithful Declaration of that Dispute, by Way of an Appendix', Methodist Archives, Manchester, MAW Fl Box 31 (original), and MAW Fl Box 20 (copy).

    12. 'An Answer to the Objections and Queries of Mrs. Darby', quoted from the copy in Methodist Archives, Manchester, MAW Fl Box 20.

    13. Letter to James Ireland, 30 December 1769.

    14. J. Fletcher, *Works* (1877) VIII, 490–2; cf. further 'An Answer to Popish Quibbles, I. Where was your Religion before Luther and Calvin?' in Methodist Archives, Manchester, MAW Fl Box 18.

    15. J. Fletcher, *Works* (1806) IV, 66, n. 20.

    16. John Wesley had asked Fletcher to establish such groups, which could be taken over by Wesley when Fletcher left Madeley: 'Votre frere [John Wesley] m[']a ecrit dernierem.ᵗ et me recommande de former incessament une société afin que ses predicateurs la prennent dans leur Circuit si je quitte Madeley' [trans. 'Your brother has written to me recently recommending me to form a society as soon as possible, so that his preachers may include it in their circuit if I leave Madeley']. Letter to Charles Wesley, undated (end of August 1762).

17. Letter to Charles Wesley, 8 June 1762; cf. the section 'Thomas Maxfield and the dispute over perfection' in the next chapter.

18. As he did later in a letter to Miss Hatton, 27 May 1766.

19. Salop, as the area around Madeley was also called, already had, according to Wesley's Conference statistics for 1766, 587 members! In the Minutes of Conference for later years, the area was included, in my judgment, under 'Cheshire', and not under 'Staffordshire' (against L. Tyerman, *Wesley's Designated Successor*, 100).

20. Letters from John Wesley to the Earl of Dartmouth, 19 April 1764, and to the Countess of Huntingdon, 20 April 1764, in J. Wesley, *Letters* (Standard Edition) IV, 236–9.

21. Ibid., 237.

22. Letter to Charles Wesley, 3 June 1764.

23. 'Votre frère ne me dit rien sur l[']article d'introduire ses predicateurs dans le voisinage, et je n'eus garde de remuer la cendre' [trans. 'Your brother said nothing to me on the subject of introducing his preachers into the neighbourhood, and I did not care to fan the flames']. Letter to Charles Wesley, 22 August 1764.

24. Cf. letter to Charles Wesley, 22 August 1764, and letter from John Wesley to Ebenezer Blackwell, 16 July 1761 in J. Wesley, *Letters* (Standard Edition) IV, 160.

25. Letter to Charles Wesley, 29 April 1765; see further Frank Baker, *John Wesley*, 183.

26. F. W. Macdonald, *Fletcher*, 89–91.

27. There are no letters to Charles Wesley from that period. If there had been, some comment might have been expected.

28. J. Wesley, *Letters* (Standard Edition) V, 143–4; cf. further ibid., 172.

29. Ibid., 84f.

11. *Fletcher and the Methodists (I: 1760–1770)*

1. Letter to Charles Wesley, 20 September 1762; Fletcher mentioned that he wrote to his mother with the same frequency.

2. Fletcher's reply to Charles showed that, despite his identification with the Wesleyan Methodists, he maintained an independent stance over against John Wesley: 'Je crois que vous ne *pouvez pas vous* empecher de communiquer à votre frere le dessein d'accepter une Eglise: S'il a quelque chose de materiel et de concluant à objecter il est bon que vous pesiez et suiviez ses raisons: Si elles ne sont pas de poids vous pouvez lui dire que vous ne les trouvez pas concluantes; vous etes toujours votre maitre, apres lui avoir montré la confiance d'un collegue et la cordialité d'un frere' [trans. 'I think you cannot avoid telling your brother of your plan to take on a parish. If he has solid and decisive reasons for objecting to it, it is good that

you should listen to and consider his arguments. If they are not weighty ones, you can tell him that you do not find them conclusive. You are always your own master, once you have shown him the trust of a colleague and the warm affection of a brother']. Letter to Charles Wesley, 12 October 1761. Charles Wesley did not take on a parish.

3. 'Votre frere m'a fait la grace de m'ecrire dernierement. l'extrait de sa lettre est: "Vous n'etes pas propre a etre seul, vous ferés et recevrez plus de bien parmi nous, venez et si vous ne voulez pas etre mon egal je serai au dessous de vous" etc' [trans. 'Your brother has recently been gracious enough to write to me. This is what he says in his letter: "You are not meant to be alone. You would do and receive more good if you were among us. Come, then, and if you do not wish to be an equal partner with me, I will be ready to serve under you", etc.']. Letter to Charles Wesley, 19 August 1761.

4. In most lists of names, the third place, after John and Charles Wesley, went to William Grimshaw, Rector of Haworth, who, however, was already over fifty years old (born in 1708), and who died in 1763.

5. John Wesley, *Letters* (Standard Edition) V, 4. Cf. also the letter from John Wesley to John Newton, 14 May 1765, with its reference to 'my brother, Mr. Fletcher, and I, and twenty thousand more', which underlines the high regard in which Wesley held Fletcher.

6. Cf. letter to John Wesley, 6 February 1773.

7. Fletcher did not name the writing in question. Probably it was neither 'Thoughts on Christian Perfection' (edited 1760) nor 'Farther Thoughts on Christian Perfection' (as I conjectured in P. Streiff, Dissertation, 266), but 'Cautions and Directions Given to the Greatest Professors in the Methodist Societies' of 1762.

8. And further: 'je vous ai dit que *je ne suis pas un homme a parti*, je ne suis *ni pour ni contre* les Temoins sans examen, je plains ceux qui se trompent j'honore ceux qui font honeur à leur profession, et je voudrois que nous trouvassions un moien de reconcilier la plus profonde humilité avec les plus . . . esperances de la grace, je crois que vous insistez sur l'un et *Maxfield sur l'autre*, et je vous crois tous deux sinceres dans votre voie . . . Ne croiez pas cependant que je suis pret à baiser la main des 350 sans examen – J'ai banni de ma Société deux faux temoins qui se disoient sans péché loin de participer à leur délusion' [trans. 'I have told you that *I do not want to take sides*. I am *neither for nor against* the witnesses without investigation. I pity those who delude themselves; I honour those who honour their profession; and I wish we could find a way of reconciling the deepest humility with the most . . . hopes of grace. I think that you lay the emphasis on one, and *Maxfield on the other*, and I believe that you are both sincere in the way you have chosen . . . Do not imagine, however, that I am ready to kiss the hand of the 350 without investigation. I have banished from my society two false witnesses who declared themselves to be without sin – far from

sharing in their delusion']. Letter to Charles Wesley, 20 September 1762 ('délusion' was probably a mistranslation into French of 'delusion' in English).

9. Letter to John Wesley, 22 November 1762.

10. Letter to Charles Wesley, 9 September 1763 (original in French).

11. 'Catholic' in the original sense of 'ecumenical, inclusive', as described in the previous chapter.

12. Letter to Charles Wesley, 8 August 1765 (original in French).

13. Cf. the retrospective comment of Fletcher from the year 1771 in L. Tyerman, *Wesley's Designated Successor*, 180f.

14. Letter to the Countess of Huntingdon, 27 April 1761.

15. For his part, John Wesley wanted to ask Fletcher to take on Samuel Furley as his curate, with a view to Furley's ordination as priest. (Letter from John Wesley to Samuel Furley, 9 December 1760.) It is unclear whether or when such a request reached Fletcher.

16. Letter to Charles Wesley, 31 January 1765. It was not stated explicitly in the letter that Harris's approach concerned a theological school, but later events make this interpretation likely. Cf. also Schlenther, *Queen of the Methodists*, 76.

17. The following journeys are known about: *c.* the early part of 1765, to Lewes; at the end of October 1765 to Bath and Bristol, as probably also in April/May 1766; in September and (or until?) November 1766 to Oathall and Brighthelmstone (Brighton) and London; in April 1767 with the Countess to Wales, and in the early summer to Huddersfield, Aberford, Haworth and Kippax, in Yorkshire. Information about journeys in the later 1760s is fragmentary.

18. At the end of October 1765 it was James Brown; at the end of 1766 Maxfield; in 1767 again Brown. In 1767 Fletcher also received a visit from Henry Venn, the Vicar of Huddersfield.

19. Letter to Lady Huntingdon, 5 November 1766.

20. Quotation from a note in the copy of the letter to Lady Huntingdon, 5 November 1766.

21. Letter to Lady Huntingdon, 24 November 1767; cf. further Fletcher's retrospective report of 1771 in L. Tyerman, *Wesley's Designated Successor*, 181.

22. Letter to Lady Huntingdon, 3 January 1768.

23. Letter from John Wesley to Charles Wesley, 14 May 1768, in J. Wesley, *Letters* (Standard Edition) V, 88.

24. Glazebrook's career is interesting: he worked in several of the Countess's chapels, and received episcopal ordination in 1771.

25. There was also a student called Williams. To distinguish between the two, Fletcher called the tutor '*Mr* Williams'.

26. It is not clear from Fletcher's letters whether this was the affair later

reported by Schlenther: 'a crisis surrounding the college housekeeper being made pregnant by the first college tutor' (*Queen of the Methodists*, 78).

27. Letter to Lady Huntingdon, 12 April 1769.

28. Letter to Lady Huntingdon, 10 November 1768.

29. In my opinion it is uncertain who proposed Benson as tutor. Contrary to suggestions in the secondary literature, John Wesley seems to have been hesitant about it: cf. the letters from John Wesley to Joseph Benson of 19 November 1769, 26 December 1769 and 27 January 1770.

30. Letter from John Wesley to Fletcher, 20 March 1768, in J. Wesley, *Letters* (Standard Edition) V, 83.

31. Letter to Walter Sellon, 7 October 1769.

12. Wesley's Conference of 1770, and the Calvinistic Methodists

1. R. E. Davies and G. Rupp (Gen. Eds), *A History of the Methodist Church in Great Britain* IV, 164.

2. Fletcher was able to support a statement conflicting with the rigid predestinarian thinking of his opponents by a quotation from Calvin's exegetical works, while acknowledging that there were contrary statements in Calvin's other writings. In connection with the self-styled Arminianism of the Wesleyans, Fletcher distanced himself from contemporary understanding of the term, but admitted that he had not himself read the works of Arminius.

3. *A History of the Methodist Church in Great Britain* IV, 164–5.

4. An interesting description of the events from the point of view of the Countess's circle is to be found in Schlenther, *Queen of the Methodists*, ch. 8: 'A papist unmasked, a heretic, an apostate'.

5. The biographer of Lady Huntingdon, Seymour, stated that, after the Conference, John Wesley had travelled to Bristol in order to await the Countess there, and then travel on with her to Trevecca for the celebration. The Countess had decided, however, to exclude John Wesley from all her pulpits, so long as he stood by the doctrines put forward at the Conference, and had written to him accordingly. Wesley had not answered her letter, but had gone off to Cornwall. The contents of this letter from the Countess are not known. It must, though, have included a formal refusal of permission to visit Trevecca. However, it is not possible for the Countess to have been aware of the wording of the conference minutes immediately after the end of the Conference (see below). She can only have been informed about it by word of mouth, either by Wesley himself or by a third party.

6. It is not clear from Fletcher's description whether we are dealing with a letter from the Countess to John Wesley in August, or an answering letter from Wesley to the Countess in October or November. Since Fletcher,

in his September letter, could say of the tensions: 'time will arrange these things', perhaps here it is Wesley's later answering letter that is meant.

7. 'Pour moi qui n'entre dans les partis et dans les disputes que pour tacher d'y mettre fin, Je suis le Serviteur des deux et m'estimerois heureux de pouvoir le demontrer par des actions' [trans. 'So far as I am concerned, I only enter into the debates and disputes in order to try to bring them to an end. I am the servant of both sides, and would be glad to show it by my actions']. Letter to Charles Wesley, September 1770.

8. Letter from Lady Huntingdon to J. Benson, 26 November 1770 in *PWHS* X (1916), 30.

9. Letter to Joseph Benson, 7 January 1771.

10. How very strongly the circle around Lady Huntingdon regarded Fletcher as belonging to them, is clear from the following comment: 'From what Lady Anne says, I fear very much for Mr. Fletcher that he will be carried off by Mr. Wesley's influence. What will be the end of this business I know not.' Letter from Lady Glenorchy to Lady Huntingdon, 10 January 1771, in (Seymour,) *The Life and Times of Selina Countess of Huntingdon* II, 111.

11. A compromise, perhaps like that put forward by John Wesley in letters to Benson (9 and 16 March 1771), whereby the witness of the Spirit is given to every believer, but an unbroken filling with the Spirit is only attained with Christian perfection, never materialized between Fletcher and Shirley.

12. Letter to John Wesley, 18 March 1771.

13. Letter from John Wesley to Fletcher, 22 March 1771, in J. Wesley, *Letters* (Standard Edition) V, 231.

14. 'To be short: such as I am, I love you well. You have one of the first places in my esteem and affection. And you once had some regard for me. But it cannot continue if it depends upon my seeing with your eyes or on my being in no mistake. What, if I was in as many as Mr. Law himself? If you were, I should love you still, provided your heart was still right with God. My dear friend, you seem not to have well learned yet the meaning of those words, which I desire to have continually written on my heart, "Whosoever doeth the will of My Father which is in heaven, the same is My brother and sister and mother." – I am, my dear Lady . . .' Letter from John Wesley to Lady Huntingdon, 19 June 1771 in J. Wesley, *Letters* (Standard Edition) V, 259f.

15. Quoted, with Fletcher's underlining (here in italics), from his letter to John Wesley, 24 June 1771.

16. Letter to John Wesley, 24 June 1771.

17. It is one of the unfortunate after-effects of the theological controversies within Methodism that even in the nineteenth century Methodist historical writing presented persons and events one-sidedly, favouring

either the Calvinistic or the Wesleyan point of view; cf. on one side (Calvinistic), *The Life and Times of Selina Countess of Huntingdon* II, 241f., and, on the other side (Wesleyan), L. Tyerman, *Wesley's Designated Successor*, 189f. and 204.

18. J. Wesley, *Works* 22, Journal and Diaries, V. 286f., footnote.

19. Cf. the arguments in P. Streiff, Dissertation, 294ff., and the valuable investigation by R. T. Kendall in *Calvin and English Calvinism to 1649*.

20. It is often not recognized that this was not already the case with Calvin. In the *Institutio*, Calvin asserted, in connection with the death of Christ and with his intercession as exalted mediator, that it was done 'for us', without specifying whether this applied only to the elect. However, in one place in the *Institutio* and in several places in his commentaries and sermons, he expressed the conviction that Christ died for all people, but that salvation becomes ours only through faith. Faith, again, is the work of the Spirit, and precedes repentance and sanctification. Thus the Holy Spirit is the bond by which Christ effectively binds us to himself. The doctrine of predestination was worked out by Calvin within the framework of pneumatology. It was meant to mediate assurance of faith. It was in this context that Calvin could quote John 17.9, and say that the intercession of the exalted Christ, through which we participate in the salvation wrought by him, applies only to the elect.

21. Rowland Hill completed his studies in Cambridge in 1769, and was known as a supporter of the Evangelical Revival. Altogether six bishops declined to ordain him, with the result that he finally became a minister among the Dissenters.

22. Richard Hill, *Five Letters*, 26f.

23. Ibid., 30f.

24. At this point Fletcher was not thinking of Luther, whose writings he did not know, but compared the view of his opponents to a 'Jesuitical' double will in God.

25. J. Fletcher, *Works* (1806) IV, 22.

26. Ibid., 19f.

27. Cf., e.g., J. Fletcher, *Works* (1806) III, 25f.; 206; 278–81.

28. Fletcher's second opponent, Toplady, was more consistent in his thinking than Hill, so that for him everything necessarily followed from the all-embracing activity of God: the elect person *has to* perform good works, the reprobate *has to* perform evil ones. In his critique of Toplady's teaching, while acknowledging that it was not open to the charge of theoretical anti-nomianism, Fletcher argued that Toplady's understanding of the providence of God, and of the necessary nature of everything that happened, would lead to fatalism, would make God the author of sin, and would deprive human beings of their responsibility before God and their fellows.

29. Hill objected to misquotation and the misuse of quotations on the part of Fletcher, but continued to complain, even when Fletcher got them right. Fletcher often answered his opponents point by point, but his arguments were not always heard or read. Cf. also Fletcher's description of Toplady's irrelevant and *ad hominem* methods of argument, in J. Fletcher, *Works* (1807) V, Preface, ivf.

30. Letter from Richard Hill to J. Fletcher, 20 August 1773. This letter was not known to me when I wrote my Dissertation.

31. Cf. the preface to the second part of the 'Scripture-Scales' in J. Fletcher, *Works* (1807) V, Preface, iii–ix.

13. The Controversies of the 1770s and their Precursors

1. Interestingly, similar conclusions to those of Arminius were drawn, in his teaching on faith, by Ames, one of the more important representatives of the English experimental predestinarian tradition (see ch. 12 above), though the two of them reasoned from different premises.

2. Limborch's *Theologia Christiana* is to be found in Fletcher's Library (Methodist Archives, Manchester, Fletcher's Library, MAW Fl 35). The first part is annotated by Fletcher.

3. I mention here only the most important: the exposition of salvation history, in which an economic understanding of the Trinity takes the place of an immanent one; the three persons of the Trinity have each their own time in the course of salvation history (by contrast with the orthodox statement that *opera trinitatis ad extra sunt indivisa*); there is a dialectic of universal–conditional and particular–absolute with reference to the will of God; there is a strongly pedagogically oriented concern; men and women are rational, morally responsible beings, who are not put under compulsion by God.

4. Again I mention only the most important: Fletcher usually speaks of 'covenant' in the orthodox, *two*-membered sense; the three-pronged exposition of the doctrine of the Trinity in salvation history only takes place in the context of the covenant of *grace*; the universal–conditional and particular–absolute will of God are not interpreted in the same way as by Amyraut.

5. Louis Tronchin (1629–1705) brought the ideas of Saumur to Geneva. J. F. Ostervald studied for three years in Saumur, and was decisively influenced by Amyraut's disciple, Claude Pajon, who had developed the theology of his teacher much farther. If the providence of God took centre stage for Pajon, and he taught that all things were strictly determined, the origins of this were already present with Amyraut, who was able to regard predestination as part of providence.

6. Election is not dependent on God's foreknowledge of faith and

perseverance, but rejection depends simply on his foreknowledge of human impenitence and lack of faith.

7. 'God hath not redeemed us by his son to be lawless. To be without law is to be without government.' R. Baxter, 'Right Method', *Works* (1830) IX, 57, quoted from I. Jeremias, 'Baxter', 247, n. 1. Cf. also the references in W. M. Lamont, *Richard Baxter and the Millennium*, especially 126ff.

8. I limit myself to writings and exchanges of letters which have a direct connection with Fletcher. The dissertation by Allan Coppedge, 'John Wesley and the Doctrine of Predestination', offers a comprehensive investigation into the writings of, and exchanges of letters between, the most varied adversaries. Cf. also W. Stephen Gunter, *The Limits of 'Love Divine'*.

9. Letter from John Wesley to Lady Maxwell, 8 February 1772, in J. Wesley, *Letters* (Standard Edition) V, 304.

10. Letter to J. Benson, 24 August 1771.

11. Letter to Lady Huntingdon, 5 September 1771. It is clear from the content of the letter that it must have been written in 1771, and not, as stated in the only preserved copy, 1773.

12. When Shirley informed Fletcher of the publication, Fletcher offered to buy copies from him for £10, to attach to it his own seal of approval, and to distribute it at no extra charge, provided that Shirley's account was correct. Fletcher received no response to his offer.

13. The case of Aldridge, a candidate for the ministry from Trevecca, illustrates this. Fletcher sought, with the agreement of the Countess, to help Aldridge obtain ordination. He secured his nomination in the neighbourhood, but by this time the Countess suspected that Fletcher was trying to entice Aldridge away from her, and dismissed Aldridge.

14. At first Wesley wanted to publish the sixth letter in London, along with the previous five, but Fletcher demurred, wrote two further letters related to the new circumstances, and expressed the desire to have these three published separately from the original five. Fletcher also specially asked Charles Wesley to shorten and amend the manuscript, and round off the corners. This second document appeared, like all the others, with the agreement and support of John Wesley. Fletcher once remarked that, without Wesley's support, he would not have sold even two dozen of his writings.

15. Cf. also the observations on Baxter above.

16. Fletcher regretted that Shirley had withdrawn his sermons after he, Fletcher, had quoted from them. By this over-hasty step, Shirley had also repudiated what was good in his sermons.

17. Cf. also, e.g., the admonition to the Methodists in Dublin not to love or honour Shirley any the less. The conflict of opinions ought not to detract from mutual love, but rather strengthen it. (Letter to the Methodist societies in Dublin, March 1772.)

18. J. Fletcher, *Works* (1806) II, 398.

19. Fletcher intended to deal with the disputed doctrine of Christian perfection in a third and final *Check*. In addition, he was asked, around the turn of the year 1771/72, to write a reply to a document by a Socinian Quaker, Elwall, who denied the Trinity.

20. John Wesley could thus offer his brother the following opinion of Fletcher's *Third Check*: 'In this he draws the sword and throws away the scabbard. Yet I doubt not they will forgive him all if he will but promise – to write no more.' Letter from John Wesley to Charles Wesley, 17 March 1772, in J. Wesley, *Letters* (Standard Edition) V, 311f.

21. The reference is to the writing against Elwall on the doctrine of the Trinity, mentioned in note 19 above.

22. This was an expression of Fletcher's self-understanding. He saw himself as mediator and reconciler between the two parties, although theologically he undoubtedly shared, and even further developed, Wesley's views.

23. Glazebrook was originally a miner from Madeley, who had come to faith through Fletcher, and had been one of the first students at Trevecca.

24. Cf. the letters from Richard Hill to Fletcher. The depreciatory judgment expressed in L. Tyerman, *Wesley's Designated Successor*, 286, does not do justice to the content or the tone of these letters.

25. The exchange of letters itself is unfortunately not preserved.

26. Letter to Charles Wesley, 20 February 1774.

27. J. Fletcher, *Works* (1806) IV, 153f.

28. Letter from John Wesley to Elizabeth Ritchie, 17 January 1775, in J. Wesley, *Letters* (Standard Edition) VI, 137. Similar judgments are to be found frequently.

29. Letter from John Wesley to Fletcher, 22 March 1775, in J. Wesley, *Letters* (Standard Edition) VI, 146. Wesley gave no further explanation of what he meant by the 'charms of Calvinism'.

30. Letter to Charles Wesley, 4 December 1775. On Fletcher's new-found understanding of God's gracious dealings, see ch. 14 below.

31. Letter to Charles Wesley, 24 November 1771.

32. John Wesley's appreciative judgment: 'I know not whether your last tract was not as convincing as anything you have written' (letter from John Wesley to Fletcher, 22 March 1775, in J. Wesley, *Letters* (Standard Edition) VI, 146) refers in my opinion to *The fictitious and the genuine creed* and not to the *Equal Check*. Hence it is in no way a devaluation of the former.

33. In this document, Fletcher dealt with the Calvinistic understanding of the covenant of grace, which John Wesley regarded as the cornerstone, and which had not previously been discussed in Fletcher's writings.

34. Letter to Miss Thornton, undated (*c.* July/August 1778).

35. On this question, we must go further than P. Fleisch, in his *Heiligungsbewegung* ['Holiness Movement']. Throughout the nineteenth century, Fletcher's life and theology found a place in Methodist literature. It is striking, however, that from the 1870s onwards numerous new biographies and editions of Fletcher's works were published. Were they intended as a Methodist contribution to the promotion of the Holiness Movement, or as a move to return to the Methodist understanding of Christian perfection? The history of the effects of Fletcher's theology is still largely unresearched. The links with Holiness and Pentecostal Movements are investigated by, among others, Daniel Brandt-Bessire, *Aux sources de la spiritualité pentecôtiste* ['On the sources of Pentecostal spirituality'], Donald W. Dayton, *Theological Roots*, and Laurence W. Wood, *Pentecostal Grace*.

36. In his dissertation, and in the article 'John Fletcher's Influence . . .', John A. Knight put forward the view that John Fletcher had contributed to the shift from the emphasis on grace to that on works in nineteenth-century American Methodism. W. Stephen Gunter, in *The Limits of 'Love Divine'*, largely followed him. In my view, their arguments are not convincing, since Fletcher's aim was to establish the foundations of both prevenient and sanctifying grace on God's saving act in Christ. If, in the early days of the controversy, Fletcher's statements were sometimes one-sided, he corrected the balance in subsequent writings. Both Knight and Gunter base their arguments especially on quotations from the *First Check*. It is possible that Methodists in the nineteenth century may have read the *First Check* (and the last one, on the doctrine of perfection) more closely and accepted them more readily, than the more theologically demanding parts of the *Equal Check*. Since Fletcher's writings arose out of actual situations, key sentences could be taken out of context and wrongly understood. In its more mature form, Fletcher's theology, in comparison with that of Wesley, was distinguished not by a stronger emphasis on the capability of the human will, but precisely by the greater pneumatological weight given to the doctrine of perfection.

37. How far overall Fletcher's writings were read by Calvinistic ministers and laypeople, or whether their distribution was limited, in the main, to a Wesleyan Methodist constituency, remains an unresolved question. How many copies of Fletcher's writings were printed is not known to me.

38. J. Wesley, *Fletcher*, 70. Grace is again understood here as effective power which justifies *and* sanctifies.

39. Letter to J. Benson, undated, around the beginning of 1776.

40. Fletcher explicitly criticized Rousseau in his writings.

41. Whereas Locke regarded the social contract as conducive to the common good, because such agreement would safeguard the property of

the individual, Fletcher argued in precisely the opposite direction, that the common good might necessitate restrictions on, or even the abolition of, personal property.

14. Fletcher's Dispensational Theology

1. Much of it was partially expressed in Fletcher's earlier *Checks*. In a few places, especially in connection with quotations from Bishop Hopkins and Baxter, we find observations which do not tally with other statements by Fletcher, but point rather to a mixture of faith and works.

2. In the corresponding chapter in P. Streiff, Dissertation, about 250 references are set out in detail.

3. The chief point of controversy in the Reformation, as Fletcher saw it, was, in terms of content, the doctrine of the Lord's Supper, and, formally, the scriptural principle – that Scripture rationally interpreted has supreme authority.

4. Thus, with regard to textual criticism, cf. J. Fletcher, *Works* (1806) II, 115.

5. In my opinion, Knickerbocker's Dissertation needs correcting at this point. He assigns a merely preparatory role to reason, and, by contrast, sees experience as the second most important authority alongside Scripture. Fletcher, however, with impressive frequency described Scripture and reason as the most important authorities. He referred to experience in the context of the appeal to reason – not the other way round. The significance of reason and experience in Fletcher's theology must be understood against the background of his origins in reasonable orthodoxy, and of the fundamental importance of Locke's epistemology in eighteenth-century England. The statement: 'Experience, thou best of judges, I appeal to thee', is thus to be understood as an emphatic turn of phrase. In this quotation, the category of experience is used only in the sense of universal, clearly evident, experience. Moreover, the quotation comes from the treatise on the doctrine of sin, which appealed strongly to reason (J. Fletcher, *Works* (1806) II, 62).

6. That does not mean that experience was not regarded as an implicit concomitant of faith. It was not, however, an independent criterion for theological argument. Fletcher expressed this in the short sentence: 'I build my faith not on my experience, though this increases it, but upon the revealed truth of God.' Letter to Mary Bosanquet, 7 March 1778.

7. Cf. the letter to Charles Wesley, 16 January 1773, in which Fletcher expressed his uncertainty as to whether one's own experience was the right category for deciding, in general, whether perfection was attained instantaneously or gradually. In his *Last Check* he left both possibilities open, and, following John Wesley, tried to link them together.

8. Zwingli is mentioned only by name. In two places Fletcher expresses an opinion on Luther (*Works* (1806) IV, 18f., and (1807) V, 289f.). Melanchthon is quoted once, in a positive sense, in connection with the question of the freedom of the will (*Works* (1806) II, 358). Only quotations from Calvin's writings appear more frequently (cf. also the judgment expressed in *Works* (1806) IV, 19f.). There are also isolated allusions to other Reformed theologians of the sixteenth and seventeenth centuries. For Fletcher's opinion of the Synod of Dordrecht, cf. *Works* (1806) IV, 20f. and 350n.

9. Among others, Bishop Burnet's *History of the Reformation* (*Works* (1807/16) VII, 46ff.), Vossius's *History of Pelagianism* (*Works* (1807) V, 116ff.) and a work by Whitby, with quotations from the church Fathers (*Works* (1807) V, 131ff.), are mentioned.

10. The *Checks* were, of course, originally undertaken as an explanation and defence of the teaching of John Wesley.

11. Quotation from the *First Check*, *Works* (1806) II, 235.

12. In the first five *Checks*, this balance was not always clear. Fletcher saw the purpose of the *Checks* initially as the defence of the second axiom. He defended the first axiom in his work on the doctrine of sin.

13. Fletcher could compare the bond between the two axioms with the mysterious bond between Christ and the church. The bond is an expression of unity in difference (*Works* (1807) V, 180ff.).

14. Cf. *Works* (1806) II, 213 and (1807) V, 225–50, where the teachings of the Reformers are presented and criticized.

15. Fletcher's strong emphasis on Adam's free will is not to be found in the same way in John Wesley, though it is, for example, in J. F. Ostervald, who stresses the following three faculties of the soul: understanding, will and freedom (J. F. Ostervald, *Compendium*, 114f.).

16. Cf. J. Calvin, *Institutio* II, 1.5–1.8. Over against this J. F. Ostervald in his *Compendium* defines sin as the deliberate transgression of a God-given law. God gave Adam a law, accompanied by promise and punishment, which Adam overstepped. Ostervald described the doctrine of original sin, with the related question as to how sin spread further, as obscure and insignificant (quae quaestio obscura est & nullius momenti – *Compendium*, 139). He held that the only important thing was that all people are prone to sin and mortal. Accordingly, he dealt in detail with wilful and freely committed actual sin (cf. on the whole question J. F. Ostervald, *Compendium*, De peccato, 137–50).

17. Much had been foreshadowed in John Wesley and, in part, in Richard Baxter, but not, as far as I know, in the clearly identifiable, systematically worked out form in which we find it in Fletcher.

18. *Works* (1806) II, 10. The understanding that all human beings were contained in Adam's seed is fundamental for Fletcher, cf. also his Traducianism in *Works* (1806) II, 129–33.

19. *Works* (1806) II, 125; it was only in this context that Fletcher spoke positively of a divine decree.

20. Rom. 5.18 is the standard text for these observations (already to be found in the *First Check*).

21. *Works* (1806) III, 349; cf. also *Works* (1806) IV, 306.

22. For Fletcher, in contrast with the Calvinistic view, there was no general grace which was not saving grace.

23. *Works* (1806) III, 23f.

24. Conversely it is true that only religious truths have a direct tendency to improve the will, *Works* (1806) IV, 175.

25. *Works* (1807) V, 390f. (in contrast with the absolute necessity propounded by Toplady).

26. 'To shew their mistake, I need only to produce the words of Mr. Locke . . . This excellent quotation encourages me . . .' *Works* (1807) V, 91f. The reference is to the only quotation from Locke in Fletcher's writings during the theological controversy.

27. J. Locke, 'Reasonableness', 252f.; J. Vernet, *Traité* vol. I, sect. II, 120f; J. F. Ostervald, *Compendium*, 404.

28. Fletcher did not always apply this notion consistently. Thus he could link together Jews and babes in Christ, and include them both under the economy of the Son.

29. So-called 'natural' religion was, for Fletcher, included in the first and lowest level of the revelation of God the Redeemer, in the dispensation of the Father.

30. Cf. *Works* (1806) II, 276–8 (*First Check*) and (1806) IV, 44f., n8. Earlier traces are to be found in *The Spiritual Manifestation of the Son of God*, *Works* (1807/16) VII, 343–5. Fletcher quotes, as examples of witnesses who agree with him, both a minister and helper of Whitefield and John Wesley. *Works* (1806) IV, 258–60.

31. There are indeed traces in John Wesley himself of the distinction between conditional and unconditional election by God (*Journal*, August 24 1743, in *Works* 19, 332–3 (later, however, modified in his letter of 8 August 1752 to his brother Charles (*Works* 26, 498–9)), as well as of a salvation-history way of thinking (e.g. *Works* 2, 110: Sermon 40 on Christian Perfection, where the Jewish and Christian dispensations are contrasted), though not in the trinitarian framework developed by Fletcher. In one of his later sermons, Wesley explicitly drew on Fletcher's contribution: cf. J. Wesley, *Works* 4, 492ff.: Sermon 106, On Faith.

32. Fletcher could, however, occasionally replace his trinitarian set of distinctions with a set related to biblical characters: Adam, Noah, Abraham, Moses, John the Baptist. See, e.g., *Works* (1806) IV, 5f.

33. A glance at Zinzendorf (whose theology was unknown to Fletcher) will reveal how widespread and varied were attempts to describe the

activity of God in terms of salvation history. Like Fletcher, Zinzendorf distinguished three epochs, or primary economies: a first one, in which God revealed himself as a father figure, and which lasted from the Fall until the bondage in Egypt; a second, in which God exercised his rule like a king, gave a law with promises and punishments, and identified Judaism; and a third, which began with Christ, and brought the Good News, the decisive turning point in human history. Zinzendorf thus distinguished more sharply between the old and the new covenant. Cf. E. Beyreuther, *Studien zur Theologie Zinzendorfs*, 264–8.

34. Over and over again, Fletcher maintained that a person could resist even the operation of the Spirit. The word of God is always effective. If it does not save, then it must judge.

35. In a more mature form, in *Works* (1806) IV, 426–42. For a demarcation from the Calvinistic understanding, cf. *Works* (1806) III, 424–8. In his response, Fletcher even goes back to Calvin's *Institutio*, quoting from this and other writings of Calvin.

36. Without free grace there can be no salvation; without free will, no righteous judgment.

37. Fletcher expounded his doctrine also by means of a comparison with the providence of God: as God in his providence distributes his natural blessing to people in varied ways, so that one person comes into the world a poor child, another the child of a king, one is born healthy, another blind or handicapped, so God is also perfectly free in the distribution of his spiritual gifts. *Works* (1807) V, 282f.

38. On the exposition of Rom. 9, see *Works* (1806) IV, 394–426; on Eph. 1, see *Works* (1806) IV, 442–55.

39. Thus Enoch, for example, is not under eternal condemnation, because he was excluded from participating in the blessing of the Jewish people, nor is David to be counted among the damned, because the special blessing of Christ's people was denied to him.

40. Alongside a partial election and rejection through the distinguishing grace of God, Fletcher recognized an impartial election and rejection through the retributive justice of God.

41. Fletcher deviated from his usual mode of expression in describing this (in *Works* (1807) V, 341f.) as the first of three covenants made by God. This first one was concluded with Adam after the Fall, and renewed with Noah. It embraces everyone. As a rule, however, Fletcher referred to it as the dispensation of the Father.

42. Already in Wesley's conference minutes, Acts 10.35 was the biblical text on the question of the salvation of the heathen who hear nothing of Christ.

43. Fletcher could also include Jews, as a special covenant people, under the dispensation of the Father. But the dispensation of the Son is given to

them as an explicit promise. As a rule Fletcher included them under the latter of these two dispensations.

44. Fletcher understood 'necessarily' not in terms of absolute, irresistible necessity, but as moral necessity.

45. This harmony was strongly emphasized by Fletcher. Cf., e.g., his pairing of living faith – loving obedience; believe as a sinner – work as a believer; free grace – free obedience; divine faithfulness – human fidelity.

46. Cf. T. L. Smith, 'How John Fletcher became the Theologian of Wesleyan Perfectionism'. Smith points out how, in the *Last Check*, Fletcher took into account John Wesley's correction, to the effect that 'babes in Christ' have received the Holy Spirit, though not in the same fullness as 'mature Christians'. Already in the *Equal Check*, in 'An Essay on Truth', Fletcher had replied to the misunderstanding that he was splitting up the operation of the triune God, and limiting the activity of the Holy Spirit to 'mature Christians'. Cf. *Works* (1806) IV, 238 and 261 n.

47. *Works* (1807) VI, 250.

48. According to Fletcher, if sin must remain in us, that contradicts the trinitarian activity of God. Indwelling sin is replaced by the indwelling Comforter.

49. If the law were done away for the Christian, it would no longer be possible to fall into sin.

50. A positive judgment on the mystics and on Thomas à Kempis can be found in *Works* (1806) II, 356f. On the positive judgment on the mystics, cf. also the letter to Charles Wesley, 4 December 1775: '. . . the truth lies between driving methodism and still mysticism.' Fletcher was critical of Molinos and the Quietists.

51. The accent in the above description of the dispensation of the Spirit and of Christian perfection thus lies on this second line of understanding which, in my opinion, represented Fletcher's more mature formulation of the doctrine of perfection.

52. As rational creatures, we are governed by God by means of laws. But where there is law, there must also be a day of judgment. Within the framework of the early Enlightenment this was a weighty argument.

53. Fletcher was attacked by his Calvinistic opponents because of this 'new' doctrine, and he defended it in detail and on the basis of tradition. What was mainly new was that Fletcher could use the term 'justification' in this context. Fletcher distinguished up to four kinds of justification: (a) the justification of all people (initial salvation); (b) justification through faith (sometimes called the first justification); (c) justification on the grounds of the fruits of faith, in accordance with the truth revealed; (d) the final justification according to the evidence of works of faith on the Day of Judgment (sometimes called the second justification).

54. Christ is the meritorious, faith the instrumental, and works the

evidential ground of salvation, and works are also the instrumental ground of continuance in faith.

55. Here are reflected Fletcher's axioms of God's free grace and human free will. How could God save the world without free grace, and how could he judge the world without human free will?

56. This reciprocity of gospel and law, which are related to each other as promise and demand, was also widely developed in John Wesley's doctrinal sermons.

57. Fletcher had already used the image of the different stars in his sermon on Romans 11. The parable of the Labourers in the Vineyard in Matt. 20.1–16, where all receive equal payment for unequal work, was nowhere taken up and expounded by Fletcher (the reference to Matt. 20.15 in *Works* (1807) V, 276, missed the point of the parable).

58. *Works* (1807) V, 226f. (without the underlining of the original). Cf. also *Works* (1806) IV, 306–11.

59. *Works* (1807) V, 54f. Cf. also V, 176–91.

60. Ibid., 376.

15. Fletcher and the Methodists (II: 1770–1777)

1. Letter to James Ireland, 21 September 1773.

2. In my opinion it is to this invitation that John Wesley's observation in a letter to Charles of 17 March 1772 refers: 'If Mr. F. does come, it will be for good. It does not follow, "You felt nothing, therefore neither did your hearers" ' (J. Wesley, *Letters* (Standard Edition) V, 312).

3. Letter from John to Charles Wesley, 26 April 1772, in J. Wesley, *Letters* (Standard Edition) V, 316. There is no indication that the papers were, in fact, deposited.

4. Letter from John Wesley to Fletcher, [15] January 1773, in J. Wesley, *Letters* (Standard Edition) VI, 11. The letter was not published until after the death of Fletcher and of John Wesley.

5. Letter from Charles Wesley to Davis, 1 January 1773, quoted from F. Baker, *John Wesley*, 208.

6. Letter to John Wesley, 6 February 1773.

7. The interpretation of Whitehead, that Fletcher declined the honourable task because it would have been too strenuous for him (cf. L. Tyerman, *Wesley's Designated Successor*, 264f.) tallies neither with the picture we have of Fletcher's character, nor with his own statements.

8. Letter from John Wesley to Fletcher, 21 July 1773, in J. Wesley, *Letters* (Standard Edition) VI, 34.

9. Cf. in ch. 16 below: 'The expectation of the outpouring of the Spirit'.

10. Letter from John Wesley to Fletcher, 1 October 1773, in Methodist Archives Manchester (copy) (see the list at the end of the book).

11. Letter to Charles Wesley, 2 July 1775.

12. Letter to J. Benson, 12 July 1775.

13. Letter to John Wesley, 1 August 1775. On the dating, cf. P. Streiff, Dissertation, 377.

14. Letter from John Wesley to Fletcher, 18 August 1775, in J. Wesley, *Letters* (Standard Edition) VI, 175.

15. Letter to John Wesley, 9 January 1776.

16. John Wesley's account of the journey in his biography of Fletcher differs from the account given above. He wrote that they had set out early in the year, and had covered between eleven and twelve hundred miles together. Wesley was describing the original itinerary, which had never been carried out. He could evidently no longer remember that their journey together had had to be shortened. Benson corrected Wesley's statements, but still spoke in his biography of a journey of Fletcher's with John Wesley in March 1776 through Gloucestershire, Worcestershire, Warwickshire, Staffordshire and Shropshire. This cannot be verified either from Wesley's *Journal* or from any remarks by Fletcher.

16. *Vicar of Madeley (II: 1770–1777)*

1. See the section on 'The Fall and its consequences' in ch. 9 above.

2. It is not clear from the description whether Fletcher had himself experienced these troubles. Probably he was referring to the riots of 1756. On this cf. B. Trinder, *Industrial Revolution*, 376–8.

3. J. Fletcher, *Works* (1806) II, 41.

4. Letter to the Madeley societies, 26 November 1777. The contents suggest, in my opinion, that it was written to members of the societies and not to the congregation as a whole.

5. The John Wilkes in question was not the one who had achieved notoriety about ten years earlier as a rebellious Member of Parliament, and to whom Fletcher had referred in his *Appeal*.

6. J. Fletcher, *Works* (1807/1816) VII, 239f.

7. Letter to Charles Wesley, 30 May 1773.

8. Letter to Charles Wesley, 11 May 1776.

9. Letter to Miss Perronet, 19 January 1777.

10. Letter to James Ireland, 21 September 1773.

11. Letter to Charles Wesley, January 1775.

12. L. Tyerman has confused this manuscript with the English translation of the sermon on the new birth from 1757 (*Wesley's Designated Successor*, 412). Many others have followed him in this, and therefore drawn false conclusions. The question as to whether this manuscript, or parts of it, are to be found in the Methodist Archives in Manchester can be answered only after all the Fletcher manuscripts held there have been

identified. It is possible that the manuscript remained in the hands of J. Benson.

13. Letter to T. Rankin, 25 June 1781. In my view Fletcher's difference of opinion from John Wesley, whose name might well have been mentioned, resurfaces in this letter. For Fletcher, the 'gift of the Spirit' signified the specific gift of the *fullness* of the Spirit, within the particular dispensation of the Spirit.

14. Letter to Charles Wesley, 4 July 1774.

15. Letter to Charles Wesley, 8 August 1775.

16. Letter to Joseph Benson, 8 May 1776.

17. Letter to Charles Perronet, 7 September 1772.

18. Letter to Lady Huntingdon, 28 May 1777.

19. Fully printed out in L. Tyerman, *Wesley's Designated Successor*, 362.

20. Cf. B. Williamson, 'The Spilsbury Portrait of John Fletcher', and also P. Forsaith, 'Portraits of John Fletcher of Madeley and Their Artists'.

21. Letter to parishioners in Madeley, 28 December 1776.

22. It is also clear from the letters that after payment of taxes, etc., Fletcher had only £50 left from his benefice. He passed this on to his deputy, Greaves.

23. Letter to James Ireland, 24 February 1777.

24. Letter to Lady Huntingdon, 28 May 1777.

17. Convalescence in Nyon

1. Even in the earliest biographies (J. Wesley, J. Gilpin, J. Benson, R. Cox) the two continental journeys were not always clearly distinguished from each other and sometimes they were actually intermingled. Cf. the more detailed analysis in P. Streiff, Dissertation 399ff. and notes.

2. An incident from Fletcher's journey to Rome, which was not explicitly mentioned in the analysis of the two continental journeys in my Dissertation, is referred to in a letter from John Pawson to Joseph Benson, dated 23 August 1804 (Bowmer and Vickers (eds), *The Letters of John Pawson* III, 105), and included by Benson in his biography.

3. 'It is said that Voltaire, when challenged to produce a character as perfect as that of Jesus Christ, at once mentioned Fletcher of Madeley' (Abbey and Overton, *The English Church*, 343). There cannot, however, have been a meeting between Fletcher and Voltaire, since Fletcher frequently expressed critical judgments on Voltaire and his thinking, without giving any indication whatever of having met him personally. The tradition reported by Overton is therefore, in my opinion, untenable. We should probably seek the answer to the question as to how this tradition arose in the various accounts of Fletcher's continental journeys. Ireland,

Fletcher's travelling companion, described a conversation with a wealthy, educated man who was vainly seeking for someone who lived his life selflessly in the measure that the Gospels and the epistles of Paul required. Ireland referred the man to Fletcher, and this resulted in long and comprehensive discussions between Fletcher and the stranger, going on for fourteen days. The stranger's respect for Fletcher grew, and on the latter's second visit to Marseilles years later he showed him great courtesy. By way of Gilpin's and Benson's biographies of Fletcher, this stranger became a follower of Voltaire. Then, possibly, as the tradition evolved, the account of a meeting with a follower of Voltaire led to the ascription to Voltaire himself of the opinion quoted above.

4. Letter from Magister Stroehlin to Eb. Gaupp, 3 November 1774, in Nachlass Johann Georg Müller, Fasc. 572/10, 14–16, Ministerial-Bibliothek, Schaffhausen, Stadtbibliothek Schaffhausen.

5. Cf. J. Chavannes, *J.-Ph. Dutoit*, 152f. and 315.

6. Cf. the biography by Cox, and the letters to Mary Bosanquet, 6 September 1781, and to John Ireland, undated, *c.* September 1781.

7. Letter to John and Charles Wesley, 17 May 1778.

8. Letter to James Ireland, 15 July 1778.

9. Letter to James Ireland, 2 February 1779.

10. Archives Cantonales Vaudoises, Lausanne: *Actes du colloque de Nyon*, 1735–1840, 79, in B db 42; *Registre des lettres de Classe envoyées à Leurs Excellences*, in B db 9, 31–4; *Registre de la Classe de Morges*, 1727–1780, 648 and 653, in B db 4; *Registre de la Classe de Morges dès l'an 1780*, 23, in B db 5.

11. Part of the long exchange of letters has been preserved and put together in booklet form.

12. Letter to the societies in and around Madeley, 1778.

13. Letter to the societies in and around Madeley, 11 February 1779.

14. On 28.2.1781, the sum of 44 gold louis, the equivalent of just under 700 francs. Cf. *Journal de henry Louys Delafléchère*, in Bibliothèque cantonale et universitaire, Lausanne, département des manuscrits (F 3639).

15. Letter to Greaves, 7 March 1780.

16. Letter to William Wase, 14 February 1781.

17. J. Wesley, *Fletcher*, 118.

18. *Later Writings in French (1779–1785)*

1. Letter to John and Charles Wesley, 17 May 1778.

2. Letter to James Ireland, 15 July 1778.

3. In the second part of the *Equal Check*, Fletcher had already introduced 'Candidus', an unprejudiced seeker after truth. This was doubtless a deliberate allusion to Voltaire's Candide.

4. The following is an extract from *La Louange:*

> *La nature* n'est rien, hors les *causes secondes*,
> et l'*ordre* que fixa le souverain des mondes:
> Apprends à distinguer *l'ouvrage* de *l'auteur*;
> Et ne prend plus les *loix* pour le *législateur*.
> . . .
> D'un abyme si grand ne cherche point le fond;
> Simonide s'y perd, Spinosa s'y confond.
> . . .
> Si résistant toujours aux mortels orgueilleux,
> Il comble de sa grace un coeur humble & pieux,
> Laisse au vain La Métrie exalter la matière,
> Et célebre, avec nous, cette cause première,
> Qui sauvant les pécheurs par son verbe incarné,
> Verse encore son courroux sur le Juif obstiné.
> Sans confondre la *grace* avec le *fanatisme*,
> Du sceptique insensé renverse le sophisme.
> Pour combattre l'erreur Dieu t'arma de Raison,
> Et non pour apprêter un funeste poison.
> . . .
> La plus saine Raison conduit à l'Evangile;
> A Christ, en la suivant, ton coeur sera docile;
> Veux-tu d'un Dieu Sauveur obtenir les bienfaits?
> Confesse ton orgueil, & pleure tes forfaits.
> Si, de tes passions brisant le joug funeste,
> Tu reçois dans ton coeur la sagesse céleste,
> Tel que l'humble *Pascal*, prenant Dieu pour soutien,
> Tu seras à la fois, *Philosophe* & *Chrétien*.
>
> (Canto III, 17–19)

[Translation:

> *Nature* has nothing to offer, apart from *secondary causes*
> and the order established by the sovereign ruler of the universe.
> Learn to distinguish the *work* from its *author*,
> and do not mistake the *laws* for the *lawgiver*.
> . . .
> Do not try to plumb the depths of so great an abyss,
> in which Simonides is swallowed up, and Spinoza is lost in
> confusion.
> . . .
> Leave la Mettrie to glory in his materialism,
> and celebrate with us this First Cause,
> who always resists arrogant mortals
> and showers with his grace a humble and devout heart.

He saves sinners by his incarnate Word,
while pouring out his wrath on the stubborn Jew.
Do not confuse *grace* with *fanaticism*,
but overturn the sophism of the demented sceptic.
God has armed you with Reason to fight against error –
not to prepare a dreadful poison.

. . .

Reason in its soundest form leads to the Gospel.
If you follow it, your heart will be submissive to Christ.
If you want to obtain blessings from God your Saviour,
confess your pride and weep for your crimes.
If you break the dire yoke of your passions,
and receive celestial wisdom into your heart,
then, like humble *Pascal*, taking God for your support,
you will be at one and the same time *Philosopher* and *Christian*.]

5. Letter to Mrs Thornton, 1777.

6. Therein, in my opinion, lies the difference from J. F. Ostervald, who similarly distinguished between the literal and the mystical sense, taking the literal sense to be the only true one, and seeing the mystical – i.e. allegorical, tropological or anagogical – as illustration and rhetorical embellishment, but not recognizing it as an argument in any rational process of argumentation. Cf. J. F. Ostervald, *Compendium*, 63f.

7. In my Dissertation, the addressees were not described with sufficient precision. For details on the origins and composition of the work, cf. P. Streiff, Dissertation, 421f. and notes.

8. It was thus fitting that Gilpin should have closely followed the detailed sections on Paul in his depiction of Fletcher's character.

9. J. Fletcher, *Works* (1807) VIII, 177.

10. In summaries and headings the English translator of *The Portrait of St. Paul* spoke of 'lively faith', whereas in the text he also used the words 'living faith'. The expression normally used by Fletcher himself was 'living faith', i.e. a faith which shows itself in discipleship. The stress is on the consequences of faith in the life of the believer. 'Lively faith', i.e. a faith that is alive, was a favourite term of the revival around the beginning of the nineteenth century, when the dimension of individual experience acquired a new significance. In the latter case the stress is on the experiential nature of faith, and on the feelings which it arouses.

11. J. Fletcher, *Works* (1807) VIII, 211.

12. Ibid., 248.

13. Ibid., 286f.

14. Ibid., 323.

15. Fletcher was far from calling for faith in the doctrines of the gospel on the grounds of their usefulness. For him, the truth of the gospel stood

firm in its own right. But the moral consequences had been called into question by his opponents, and it was for that reason that Fletcher here laid stress on the usefulness of Christian doctrine.

16. The sentence: 'The followers of Christ are required to tread in the steps of their Master, and not deeply to speculate upon the secret things of his invisible kingdom' also belongs in *this* context. J. Fletcher, *Works* (1807), VIII, 369.

19. Fletcher and the Methodists (III: 1781–1785)

1. Cf. T. Rankin's report, in J. Fletcher, *Works* (1806), I, 309f.

2. Letter to John Wesley, 6 June 1781.

3. The letter from John Wesley to Creighton, officially dated 29 September 1779, would fit perfectly the situation in Madeley in September 1781. Cf. J. Wesley, *Letters* (Standard Edition) VI, 356.

4. Draft of a letter to John Wesley at the end of August 1781, and letter from Charles Wesley to John and Mary Fletcher, 13 March 1782. (The letter is most often dated 1784. The last figure can be read as either 2 or 4. But the reference to the marriage, and the accompanying congratulations, clearly indicate that the letter was composed in 1782. In other words, it was the first letter from Charles Wesley after Fletcher's marriage.) The view that Fletcher first expressed his intention to marry in 1781 conflicts with a statement by John Wesley to a third party in 1774, which can scarcely bear any other interpretation than that Fletcher had once pressed Mary Bosanquet to marry him. Wesley quoted an extract from Mary Bosanquet's reply to him (Letter from J. Wesley to Ann Bolton, 20 January 1774, in J. Wesley, *Letters* (Standard Edition) VI, 70). In my opinion, however, preference must be given to Fletcher's own testimony. Possibly Mary Bosanquet's affection for Fletcher, of which the latter was himself unaware at the time, lies behind John Wesley's statement. The contradiction cannot be fully resolved on the basis of available sources.

5. T. M. Morrow, *Early Methodist Women*, 80.

6. Letters from Miss Bosanquet to John Wesley, 7 February 1776, and from Fletcher to Miss Bosanquet, 20 October 1777.

7. Letter to Thomas York, 15 September 1780.

8. T. M. Morrow, *Early Methodist Women*, 88f. (from Mary Bosanquet's diary).

9. Mary Tooth, who had been received by Mary Bosanquet into her extended family, came to Madeley with the Fletchers.

10. Cf. letters to Mary Bosanquet, 2 and 6 September 1781. Miss Adams (the housekeeper) later claimed that Fletcher had promised to marry her, and had outrageously broken his promise. Even John Wesley had heard the rumour, and he enquired of Fletcher whether any of it was true. Cf. notes

on the correspondence between Miss Adams and John and Mary Fletcher in
1782.

11. Letter to Mary Bosanquet, 2 September 1781.

12. In the draft of the letter to John Wesley at the end of August 1781, it
read: 'as persons who have a particular (and yet innocent [crossed out])
affection for each other', whereas Fletcher later said he had written: 'as
persons design'd for each other' (Letter to Mary Bosanquet, 11/12
September 1781).

13. A calculation of Fletcher's estate in Switzerland after his death can
be found in *Journal de henry Louys Delafléchère*, 32f., in Bibliothèque
Cantonale et Universitaire, Lausanne, Département des manuscrits (F
3639).

14. Thus Mary Bosanquet was also able to avoid selling the Leytonstone
property and had sufficient financial resources to provide support for the
members of the extended family there, as well as supplying her future
husband with a sizeable annual income.

15. A letter from Preston, in Morley near Leeds, 13 January 1783,
mentioned the name of Lord Dartmouth in connection with a deed of
conveyance, and a promissory note for £500. Both the place from which the
letter was sent and the matter with which it dealt suggest a connection with
the sale of Cross Hall.

16. Letter from John Wesley to Fletcher, 24 November 1781 in J.
Wesley, *Letters* (Standard Edition) VII, 93. Cf. also the letters from John
Wesley to Mrs Downes, 1 December, and to Hester A. Roe, 9 December
1781 in J. Wesley, *Letters* (Standard Edition) VII, 94ff.

17. Letter from Charles Wesley to John and Mary Fletcher, 13 March
1782.

18. *Minutes of the Methodist Conferences* I, 147. The order of the
names is significant!

19. Letter to T. Rankin, 25 June 1781. Who but John Wesley could be
meant here? It is unlikely that the note 'only' was meant to apply to Coke.
This part of the letter was omitted from the biographies by Benson and
Tyerman.

20. J. Wesley, *Works* 23, 218 (8 August 1781).

21. Letter to Mrs Thornton, 21 January 1783. The letter must, as the
reference in it to Greenwood shows, have been written in 1783.

22. The final step into Dissent was taken in 1782. On this, cf. B. S.
Schlenther, *Queen of the Methodists*, ch. 11.

23. Description by Charles Atmoor, quoted from L. Tyerman, *Wesley's
Designated Successor*, 545f. Cf. also the description in John Valton,
'Excerpts from John Valton's MS. Journal', 35. On the whole subject, cf. F.
Baker, *John Wesley*, chs 13–15.

24. Quoted from L. Tyerman, *Wesley's Designated Successor*, 546.

25. Letter from Charles Wesley to John and Mary Fletcher, 21 June 1784. Charles Wesley asked Fletcher to come to London after his death, and sort over the papers he would leave with his widow.

26. Letter to James Ireland, 13 September 1784.

27. Letter from John to Charles Wesley, 2 June 1785, in J. Wesley, *Letters* (Standard Edition) VII, 272.

28. Against this, cf. Wesley's statements in his memorial address on Fletcher's death, where, after again expressing the view that Fletcher would have improved his health if he had travelled for half the year, and would at the same time have been able to do more good than anyone else, he went on to say: 'However, though he did not accept of this honour, he did abundance of good in that narrow sphere of action which he chose, and was a pattern well worthy the imitation of all parochial ministers in the kingdom' (J. Wesley, *Works* 3, 619: Sermon 114).

20. Projected Theological Works

1. Letter from Charles Wesley to Fletcher, 11 October 1783.

2. Letter from John Wesley to Fletcher, 3 April 1785, in J. Wesley, *Letters* (Standard Edition) VII, 265.

3. The sections written by Fletcher are, in the first part, J. Fletcher, *Works* (1808) IX, 15–58; and in the second part, J. Fletcher, *Works* (1808) IX, 207–96.

4. The argument ran as follows: when the Socinians, in the seventeenth century, refused to believe in the union of the divine and the human in Jesus Christ, they were answered with the counter-argument that that was just as easy to accept as that human beings consisted of immortal souls and mortal bodies (an argument which had already appeared in J. Calvin, *Institutio* II, 14.1). Dr Sherlock had replied to the Socinians that they could not deny the former unless they also denied the latter. But this, according to Fletcher, was what some eighteenth-century philosophers, among them Priestley, had done: J. Fletcher, *Works* (1808) IX, 20f.

5. There were already signs of this deviation in the 1770s. In *The Spiritual Manifestation* Fletcher set aside miracles, as an ambiguous, dubious argument for the recognition of Jesus Christ: 'The bare outward sight of our Saviour's person and miracles rather confounded than converted the beholders' (J. Fletcher, *Works* (1807/1816) VII, 363. Fletcher's approach was rooted in his own independent study of Scripture, was pneumatologically based, and was implicitly related to the doctrine of the Trinity.

6. The explanation of the distinction between Father, Son and Spirit, belonged, according to Ostervald, to *docta ignorantia* ('learned ignorance') (J. F. Ostervald, *Compendium*, 100f.).

7. J. F. Ostervald built on this fourfold basis for the Messiahship of Jesus (*Compendium*, 204). On the other hand, he did not speak of manifestations of the Son of God in the Old Testament (ibid., 101f., 185f., 193f.). In an unpublished study, 'Die schweizerische Frühaufklärung', P. Barthel speaks, in this context, of the search for a Christology 'from below'.

8. In our context the significance of Christ in the Old Testament is particularly important (cf. Calvin, *Institutio* I, 13.9–11 (the divinity of Christ in the Old and New Testaments), and II, 6.2; 10.2, 4; 11.10 (the mediator in the Old Testament), though it is worth noting that Fletcher does not adopt Calvin's precise conception of the mediator, in whom the divine and human nature are combined (*Institutio* II, 14.2f., 5).

9. Like Calvin, Fletcher used the concept of *subsistentia*, or 'subsistence', to indicate the distinction between the Persons of the Trinity (cf. J. Calvin, *Institutio* I, 13.2, 6, 17). In his enumeration of the views of various theologians, Ostervald mentioned a similar distinction, which seemed to him more likely than other views, but which he still described as obscure and beset by many difficulties (J. F. Ostervald, *Compendium*, 100).

10. J. Fletcher, *Works* (1808) IX, 36.

11. Ibid., 36f.

12. Fletcher also disputed the validity of the comparison between the rejection by the Reformation of the veneration of the Host, and Priestley's proposed rejection of the veneration of the Son of God, since it was taken for granted that the former fell within the range of human comprehension. Fletcher rejected belief in the ubiquity of the exalted Lord, thereby remaining true to the Reformed tradition.

13. Fletcher, *Works* (1808) IX, 210.

14. In this, too, Fletcher differed from Ostervald and reasonable orthodoxy.

15. J. Fletcher, *Works* (1808) IX, 292–4.

16. On the doctrine of the Trinity, cf. Fletcher's personal covenant with God, made in 1754.

17. Letter to Lady Mary Fitzgerald, 11 February 1785.

18. The reference is to the two booklets *Spiritual Memoranda* and *Spiritual Extracts*, in Methodist Archives, Manchester, MAW Fl Box 20. The page numbering has been introduced by me.

19. *Spiritual Memoranda*, 1. Fletcher spoke of distinction, not of separation, but did not make clear that in the triunity of God there is no separation, and therefore no need for reunion. The need for reconciliation between God and the world is described in other sections.

20. Ibid., 4. The frequent allusions to the image of marriage in this notebook are, in my view, an indication of late composition, after Fletcher's marriage in the 1780s.

21. Ibid., 6.

22. Ibid., 11f.

23. In the 1760s, the contrast between the visible, which is transitory, and the invisible, which is eternal, was dominant.

24. The surprising thing is not the contrast as such, but the application of the notion of 'shadow' to creation, or the passing world. A comparison with Calvin makes the matter clearer: Calvin too could contrast Christ as the true, or the substance, with the shadowy. But he liked to apply the contrast between shadowy likeness and true substance (or between shadow and light), as in Col. 2.17 and Heb. 10.1, to the difference between the Old and New Testaments, setting Christ, as the true, the substance, over against the shadowy ceremonies and arrangements of the old covenant (J. Calvin, *Institutio* II, 7.1, 16; 8.34; 9.1, 3, 4; 15.6; 16.6; III, 20.18, and frequently). Calvin could also apply the contrast to the difference between the shadowy, intermittent faith of the condemned and the true, constant faith of the elect (J. Calvin, *Institutio* III, 2.11).

25. Fletcher stressed the separation especially in connection with the human capacity for knowledge: e.g., 'Finite can't take the infinite' (*Spiritual Memoranda*, 20). This was also a fundamental principle in Calvin's thinking.

26. *Spiritual Memoranda*, 15.

27. Ibid., 17.

28. *Spiritual Extracts*, 8.

29. Ibid., 10.

30. *Spiritual Memoranda*, 7; he also writes there of the sacrificial death and resurrection of Christ. Only in one place did Fletcher relate the God-likeness first to the angels, and divide the world into visible and angelic. Otherwise God-likeness is used with an exclusively christological reference.

31. *Spiritual Extracts*, 5. In a difficult section on 'creation' (*Spiritual Memoranda*, 12), in my opinion, Fletcher was seeking, within the framework of the contrast between the shadowy and the real, to underline the mediatorial work of Christ in creation and the christological connection of the image of God in humanity.

32. *Spiritual Memoranda*, 8.

33. Draft of sermon on Isa. 26.3, in J. Fletcher, *Works* (1807) VIII, 410f.

34. This understanding was not completely new. Already in 1771 Fletcher had written (in connection with his Arminianism): 'I must hold that sentiment, if I believe the bible is true, and God is Love.' (Letter to Joseph Benson, 7 January 1771, as transcript of a letter to Lady Huntingdon.) But at that time the statement that God is love had not yet become his starting point for all talk about God.

35. *Spiritual Memoranda*, 1f.

36. *Spiritual Extracts*, 7.

37. *Spiritual Extracts*, 2 and 6.

38. *Spiritual Extracts*, 8 and *Spiritual Memoranda*, 2.
39. *Spiritual Memoranda*, 2.
40. *Spiritual Extracts*, 5f.
41. *Spiritual Memoranda*, 5 and 16.
42. *Spiritual Extracts*, 12.
43. *Spiritual Memoranda*, 3.
44. *Spiritual Extracts*, 8.

21. *Sanctified Life and Service*

1. Report by Mrs Rogers, quoted by L. Tyerman, *Wesley's Designated Successor*, 467. From the start of the meeting, Mrs Rogers was greatly impressed by Fletcher: 'When I entered the room, where they were assembled, the heavenly man [Fletcher] was giving out the following verses, with such animation as I have seldom witnessed . . .' (ibid., 467).
2. Fletcher got on well with his brother Henri Louis, who was married. I suspect that it was Henri Louis who, in Nyon, advised John William to marry.
3. Cf. also Mary Bosanquet's statement: 'this I can say never had I any connection with a Creature that so drew me to the Lord as yours does.' (Letter from Miss Bosanquet to J. Fletcher, 1–4 September 1781.)
4. John Valton wrote in his Journal on 7 October 1781: 'We then had a comfortable lovefeast wherein several spoke, and among others Mr. Fletcher acknowledged to have received the gift of a new and clean heart.' (John Valton, 'Excerpts from John Valton's MS. Journal', 22.) Charles Wesley asked in a letter to John and Mary Fletcher, 13 March 1782: 'How much truth is there in that report that Mr. F– [Fletcher] declared before the Congregation – "I have attained[?]: I am [–?] perfect [–?]"' This extract was crossed out by a later hand in the original, and is barely decipherable in the copy to which I have had access.
5. '. . . at how much do you value the *best* Saviour, and the *best* friend in the world, and the *best* hopes – that of being filled with all the fulness of God? Such blessings are mine, thro' mercy divine.' (Letter to Mary Bosanquet, 2 September 1781. Cf. also the letter to John Wesley quoted below.)
6. '. . . and if God (blesses [crossed out]) smiles upon our [John Fletcher's and Mary Bosanquet's] intimacy by giving us spiritual blessings together, as he did particularly last wednesday when at a Meeting in Miss B. [Bosanquet's] house, I (was enabled to see [crossed out]) saw my christian privileges so clearly and felt so much of the power of faith and love as to be (enabled [crossed out]) constrain'd to profess (my being entered into the glorious liberty [crossed out]) a degree of the glorious liberty of God's children . . .' (Draft of a letter to John Wesley at the end of August 1781.)

7. Letter to Lady Mary Fitzgerald, January 1782.

8. In my opinion the main questions which arise in relation to responsible theological discussion of Christian perfection are the following: 1. whether a state of Christian perfection is attainable before death, in view of the extent to which human life, including that of Christians, is bound up with a world structurally conditioned by sin; 2. whether the concept of sin can be restricted to deliberate sins, and the extent to which such a view reflects the spirit of the age (early Enlightenment; absence of any knowledge of the unconscious); 3. whether it is possible to combine the notion of the attainment of Christian perfection (implying the highest stage in the Christian life) with that of further, ongoing growth; 4. whether a concept which all too often implies a *state* of perfection, rather than a relationship developing from the nature of love and making possible ever new growth and fulfilment, is tenable.

9. Letter to Lady Mary Fitzgerald, 28 August 1782.

10. Letter to Joseph Benson, 22 July 1783.

11. Statements such as those in the letter to Melville Horne, 10 May 1785, must be understood in the total context of Fletcher's life. For example, the statement that he seldom looked at any other book than the Bible is to be seen in the light of Horne's concern over the fate of a consignment of books. It should not be forgotten that only a year earlier Fletcher had read Ramsay's theological works with great interest!

12. Letter to Lady Mary Fitzgerald, 11 February 1785.

13. Letter to Henry Brooke, 28 February 1785.

14. J. Wesley, *Fletcher*, 94.

15. On the work amongst the sick, cf. J. P. Tuck, ' "Primitive Physic" – An Interesting Association Copy'.

16. We have no information from Fletcher himself on this visit, but John Wesley referred to it in his Journal (*Journal*, 20.12.1784), and later said of Simeon that he 'breathes the very spirit of Mr. Fletcher' (*Journal*, 30.10.1787).

17. Letter to Mrs Thornton, 21 January 1783. Contrary to the printed indication (1785), this letter must have been written before the death of Charles Greenwood on 21 February 1783. Most probably, therefore, it should be back-dated to January 1783.

18. Letter to Mrs Thornton, 20 June 1784.

19. Letter to Charles Wesley, 19 December 1782.

20. Cf. B. Trinder, *Industrial Revolution in Shropshire*, 376ff.

21. 'To the Magistrates & Gentlemen of Shropshire, who opend a Subscription at Wellington, Broseley, &c for the relief of the industrious Poor.'

22. *Three National Grievances; the Increase of Taxes: The Hardship of unequal Taxation; And the continual Rise of the Poor's Rates; with the*

Causes and Remedies of these Evils: humbly submitted to the Considera-
tion of the Legislature: in a Letter to the Right Honourable Lord John
Cavendish . . . Chancellor of the Exchequer, and one of the Lords of the
Treasury. London, November 1783.

23. Cf. the allusion to a 'motion' in a letter from Charles Wesley to
Fletcher, 11 October 1783.

24. It is clear from Fletcher's observation that a large number of children
could be employed in making nets if the fishing industry were not neglected,
that he regarded child labour as reasonable.

25. Cf. manuscripts in the Methodist Archives in Manchester: MAW
Fletcher, Box 17 and 18.

26. Mrs Fletcher said that her husband had become convinced that he
was called, not to London, but to the grave (M. Fletcher, *De la Fléchère*,
28f. and 34f.). That can, however, mean no more than that Fletcher – as
many times before – sensed the nearness of his own death. Even in his last
illness, he replied in the negative to the question whether he had any conviction that the Lord was calling him to himself, and added that he always
felt that death was very near (M. Fletcher, op. cit., 42).

27. Letter from W. Bosanquet to Mrs Fletcher, 16 May 1785, in L.
Tyerman, *Wesley's Designated Successor*, 556.

28. Letter to Lady Mary Fitzgerald, 19 July 1785.

29. M. Fletcher, op. cit., 44.

30. John Wesley, Sermon 114. Wesley included these final sentences
almost unchanged in his biography of Fletcher, but added, categorically,
'Nor do I expect to find another such on this side of eternity' (J. Wesley,
Fletcher, 226). Similarly, in the minutes of the Conference of 1786 it read:
'Q. 5. Who has DIED this year? A. John Fletcher, a pattern of all holiness,
scarce to be paralleled in a century' (*Minutes of the Methodist Conferences*
I, 183). The last half sentence exceeds what was normally written of
deceased preachers. The few and, up to that point defective, data which
Wesley was able to gather together for Fletcher's curriculum vitae make
clear the reticence with which Fletcher must have spoken of himself. In
March 1786 Wesley paid a further visit to Madeley, and preached a sermon
there.

31. Quoted from L. Tyerman, *Wesley's Designated Successor*, 567.

32. John Wesley would also have liked to write a biography of his
brother Charles, but he was unable to complete it.

Epilogue

1. 'He [Fletcher] is (I know, and he knows) a mule by nature: but is
become by grace, and by the wisdom from above, "easy to be entreated".'
Letter from Charles Wesley to John and Mary Fletcher, 13 March 1782.

2. Letter to Mary Bosanquet, 1 May 1781.

3. Letter from John Wesley to Sarah Wesley, 26 September 1788, in J. Wesley, *Letters* (Standard Edition) VIII, 93.

4. Letter to Charles Wesley, 4 December 1775.

Sources

A. LETTERS FROM AND TO FLETCHER

The first part of the following table includes all the letters from Fletcher to other people, while the second part lists letters from other people to Fletcher. In each case dated or datable letters are listed first, in chronological order, and letters which are undated or difficult to date are noted at the end. Also noted at the end are letters wrongly attributed to Fletcher. The details given in the right-hand column normally refer to the earliest or most complete publication of the archival material. Included in the table are some additional letters from and to Fletcher which were not mentioned in my Dissertation.

I would like again to express my gratitude to Peter Forsaith, of Wootton in Oxfordshire, for the valuable help he has given me in my search for archival material and in the compilation of this list.

The following abbreviations are used:

in capitals, for the form of the letter: O = original
     C = copy
     D = draft
     F = fragment
in lower case letters for the language: e = English
     f = French

in figures for the location:
1 = Cliff College, Calver, via Sheffield, UK
2 = Methodist Archives, Manchester – The John Rylands University Library of Manchester, Deansgate Building, Manchester, UK
3 = The Methodist Church Overseas Division, London, UK
4 = John Wesley's Chapel, New Room, Bristol, UK
5 = Shropshire County Archives, Shrewsbury, UK
6 = Wesley's Chapel, London, UK
7 = Westminster College (The Cheshunt Foundation) Cambridge, UK
8 = William R. Perkins Library, Manuscript Department, Duke University, Durham NC, USA
9 = The Robert W. Woodruff Library of Advanced Studies, Special Coll. Department, Emory University, Atlanta GA, USA

Other abbreviations (of book titles) will be found in the Bibliography.

			Oe2: Brown Folio Wesley Family II, 43+44		City Road Mag, 1872, 514ff. J.Wesley-Fl, 180-1
London	18.2.58	Charles Wesley	Oe2: Brown Folio Wesley Family II, 43+44	Fl-L 1791, 75–8 ?? IX, 152ff.	City Road Mag, 1872, 514ff. J.Wesley-Fl, 180–1
London	18.4.58	Mrs Glynne			
Tern	16.8.58	Charles Wesley	Of4	Fl-W 1806, I, 37–8	Tyerman-Fl, 33–4
	(Sept./Oct. 58)	Mr Richard Edwards			
Tern	12.10.58	Mrs Sarah Ryan	Ce2: Fl Vol., 74	Fl-L 1791, 78–80	
London	11.11.58	Mrs Gittoes			
London	12.12.58	Charles Wesley	Oe2: Fl Vol., 2		
London	26.12.58	Charles Wesley	Of2: Fl Vol., 81	(Fl-L 1791, 80–3)	
London	22.3.59	Charles Wesley '5'	OFf2: Fl Vol., 92+94	(Fl-L 1791, 83–5)	
	(April 59?)	Charles Wesley	OFf2: Fl Vol., 58	(Fl-L 1791, 84)	
	(April 59?)	Charles Wesley			
London	1.6.59	Charles Wesley '6'	Of2: Fl Vol., 82	(Fl-L 1791, 85–6)	
Tern	19.7.59	Charles Wesley	Of2: Fl Vol., 3	(Fl-L 1791, 86–8)	
Tern	4.9.59	Charles Wesley	Of2: Fl Vol., 4	(Fl-L 1791, 88–91)	
Tern	5.9.59	Mrs Sarah Ryan	Oe2: MAW Fl 36.1		
Tern	29.9.59	Charles Wesley '7'	OFf2: Fl Vol., 5	(Fl-L 1791, 93–5)	
Tern	1.10.59	Mrs Ryan and Miss Furley	Ce2: Fl Vol., 6	(Fl-L 1791, 95–7)	
De la Fonderie	24.10.59	Charles Wesley '10'	Of2: Fl Vol., 7	(Fl-L 1791, 91–3)	
	10.11.59	Charles Wesley	Of2: Fl Vol., 66		
London	15.11.59	Charles Wesley	Of2: Fl Vol., 61	(Fl-L 1791, 97–9)	

Place	Date	Recipient	Reference	Printed	Citation
	28.11.59	Charles Wesley	Of2: Fl Vol., 8		*City Road Mag*, 1872, 517
	'Mardi soir' 15 or 22.1.60	Charles Wesley	Of2: Fl Vol., 63		
Dunstable	30.1.60	Charles Wesley	OFf2: Fl Vol., 9	(Fl-L 1791, 83)	
	9.2.60	(Charles Wesley)	Ce2: MAW Fl 36.5		
	1.3.60	Charles Wesley '13'	Of2: Fl Vol., 83	(Fl-L 1791, 99–100)	
	'Mardi Matin' (April 60?)	Charles Wesley '15'	Of2: Fl Vol., 59		
	'Jeudi Matin' (7.5.60)	Charles Wesley '16'	Of4		
Tern	6.9.60	Lady Huntingdon	Ce2: Fl Vol., II, 39–47		(Seymour, I, 233–4)
Tern	14.9.60	Charles Wesley	Of2: Fl Vol., 11		*City Road Mag*, 1872, 516f.
Tern	26.9.60	Charles Wesley		Fl-L 1791, 103–6	(Seymour, I, 234–5)
	enclosed:	Lady Huntingdon		(Fl-L 1791, 104–5)	
Tern	3.10.60	Lady Huntingdon	Ce2: Fl Vol., II, 49–55		(Seymour, I, 236–7)

According to Professor Frank Baker, a letter to John Wesley dated 27 October 1760 (and perhaps other letters written by Fletcher) is held by the University of California in Santa Barbara, USA, but I did not have access to it before the present work went to press.

Place	Date	Recipient	Reference	Printed	Citation
Tern	28.10.60	Lady Huntingdon	Ce2: Fl Vol., II, 57–61		(Seymour, I, 237–8)
Tern	7.11.60	Charles Wesley	Of2: Fl Vol., 12	(Fl-L 1791, 108)	
Tern	19.11.60	Lady Huntingdon	Ce2: Fl Vol., II, 63–5		(Seymour, I, 238–9)
Madeley	6.1.61	Lady Huntingdon	Ce2: Fl Vol., II, 67–71		(Seymour, I, 239–40)

Madeley	10.2.61	Mrs Ryan	Oe2: MAW Fl 36.1		
Madeley	10.3.61	Charles Wesley	Of2: Fl Vol., 10	(Fl-L 1791, 106–7)	
Madeley	27.4.61	Charles Wesley '14'	Of2: Fl Vol., 13	(Fl-L 1791, 108–9)	
Madeley	27.4.61	Lady Huntingdon	Ce2: Fl Vol., II, 73–7		(Seymour, I, 240–1)
	(c. 61)	Lady Huntingdon			(Seymour, I, 318; fragment)
Madeley	19.8.61	Charles Wesley '17'	Of2: Fl Vol., 14	(Fl-L 1791, 110–11)	
Madeley	12.10.61	Charles Wesley '18'	Of2: Fl Vol., 84	(Fl-L 1791, 111–12)	
Madeley	5.1.62	Charles Wesley	Of2: Fl Vol., 15	(Fl-L 1791, 126–8)	
	3.2.62	Rev. Mr Lewis	Oe2: MAW Fl Box 18		
	3.2.62	Rev. Mr Prothero	Oe2: MAW Fl Box 31		Tyerman-Fl, 77–8 to: Mr Haughton
	May 62 (after 11.5.)	Haughton (?)/ Slaughter	2: MAW Fl Box 17: Indictment to: Mr Th. Slaughter jun.		
Madeley	16.5.62	Charles Wesley '19'	Of2: Fl Vol., 16	(Fl-L 1791, 113–14)	
Madeley	8.6.62	Charles Wesley '20'	Of2: Fl Vol., 17	(Fl-L 1791, 116–17)	
Madeley	19.7.62	Charles Wesley	Of2: MAW Fl Box 36.5	(Fl-L 1791, 114–16)	
Madeley	26.7.62	Lady Huntingdon	Ce2: Fl Vol., II, 79–83		(Seymour, I, 321)
Madeley	4.8.62	Rev. Mr Hatton			
Madeley	22.8.62 (end Aug. 62)	Charles Wesley '22'	Of2: Fl Vol., 85	(Fl-L 1791, 116f., 121)	WesMethMag 1829,175
Madeley		Charles Wesley	Of2: Fl Vol., 62		
Madeley	4.9.62	Mr Vaughan		Fl-L 1791, 118–20	
Madeley	4.9.62	Charles Wesley '23'	Of2: Fl Vol., 18	(Fl-L 1791, 120–1)	
Madeley	20.9.62	Charles Wesley '24'	Of2: Fl Vol., 1		

	Date	Recipient	Source	Fl-L reference	Other
Madeley	1.11.62	Miss Hatton		Fl-L 1791, 121–4	
Madeley	22.11.62	(John Wesley) '25'	Oe2: Fl Vol., 19	(Fl-L 1791, 124–6)	
Madeley	(30.11.62)	Charles Wesley '26'	Of2: Fl Vol., 21		
Madeley	28.1.63	Miss Hatton		Fl-L 1791, 128–9	
Madeley	14.3.63	Miss Hatton		Fl-L 1791, 129–30	
Madeley	22.4.63	Mr Samuel Hatton		Fl-L 1791, 131–2	
Madeley	9.5.63	Lady Huntingdon	Ce2: Fl Vol., II, 85–91		*City Road Mag* 1873, 331
Madeley	21.6.63	Charles Wesley '29'	Of2: Fl Vol., 28	(Fl-L 1791, 133)	
Madeley	26.7.63	Charles Wesley	Of2: Fl Vol., 22		
Madeley	3.8.63	Miss Hatton		Fl-L 1791, 134	
Madeley	19.8.63	Miss Hatton		Fl-L 1791, 135–6	
Madeley	9.9.63	Charles Wesley	Of2: Brown Folio Wesley Family II, 45	(Fl-L 1791, 142–4)	
Madeley	10.9.63	Lady Huntingdon	Ce2: Fl Vol. II, 93–9		(Seymour, I, 357)
Madeley	16.9.63	Charles Wesley '32'	Of2: Fl Vol., 23		*City Road Mag* 1872, 553f.
Madeley	26.12.63	Charles Wesley	Of2: MAW Fl Box 36.1	(Fl-L 1791, 146–9)	
Madeley	5.3.64	Miss Hatton	Oe2: Sidney Lawson Collection, 97		
Madeley	3.6.64	Charles Wesley '37'	Of2: Fl Vol., 102		*City Road Mag* 1873, 332f.
Madeley	4.7.64	Lady Huntingdon	Ce2: Fl Vol. II, 101–9		
Madeley	22.8.64	Charles Wesley	Of2: Fl Vol., 86		
Madeley	3.9.64	Miss Hatton		Fl-L 1791, 149–50	
Madeley	Dec. 64	Miss Hatton		Fl-L 1791, 151–4	
Madeley	3.11.65	Miss Hatton		Fl-L 1791, 154–5	

Madeley	31.1.65	Charles Wesley '33'	Of2: Fl Vol., 24		City Road Mag 1872, 554f.
Madeley	3.4.65	Lady Huntingdon	Ce2: Fl Vol. II, 111–16		
Madeley	12.4.65	Charles Wesley '34'	Of2: Fl Vol., 25		
Madeley	29.4.65	Charles Wesley '35'	Of2: Fl Vol., 26		
Madeley	9.5.(65)	Mr Ley	Oe2: Fl Vol., 76		
	10.5.65	Charles Wesley	Of2: Fl Vol., 27		
Madeley	2.6.65	Miss Hatton		Fl-L 1791, 156	
Madeley	3.7.(65)	Mr Ley	Oe2: Fl Vol., 77		
Madeley	8.8.65	Miss Hatton		Fl-L 1791, 157–62	
Madeley	8.8.65	Charles Wesley '38'	Of2: Fl Vol., 29		
Madeley	29.8.65	Lady Huntingdon	Ce2: Fl Vol. II, 117–25		
Madeley	23.9.65	Charles Wesley '39'	Of2: Fl Vol., 30		
Madeley	8.10.65	Charles Wesley '40'	Of2: Fl Vol., 31		
Madeley	20.10.65	Lady Huntingdon	Ce2: Fl Vol. II, 127–33		
Bath	30.10.65	(Societies in and around Madeley)	Ce2: (Fl Vol. II, 135–43)	Fl-L 1791, 1–5	
Madeley	6.11.65	Mr Henry Perronet			
Madeley	29.11.65 (65)	Lady Huntingdon Mr Alexander Mather	Ce2: Fl Vol. II, 135–45	Fl-L 1791, 162–3 (Fl-W 1806, I, 111: about 1764)	WesMethMag 1825, 744
Madeley	13.1.66	Miss Hatton		Fl-L 1791, 164–5	
Madeley	17.2.66	John Wesley	Oe2: MAW Fl Box 36.1 (not: Colman Coll. Box: Letters to John Wesley)		

Place	Date	Recipient	Archive	Fl reference	Notes
Bath	30.4.66	Mr D. Edmunds	Oe2: Fl Vol., 32	(Fl-L 1791, 1–5)	(Seymour, I, 487–8)
	1.5.66	(for societies)			
Madeley	May 66	Miss Hatton		Fl-L 1791, 166–7	
Madeley	27.5.66	Miss Hatton		Fl-L 1791, 167–9	
Madeley	21.6.66	Miss Hatton		Fl-L 1791, 169–71	
Madeley	July 66	Miss Ireland		Fl-L 1791, 171–5	
Madeley	July 66	J. Ireland, Esq.		Fl-L 1791, 175–8	
Madeley	17.7.66	Miss Hatton		Fl-L 1791, 179–81	
Madeley	28.7.66	Miss Hatton		Fl-L 1791, 181–2	
Madeley	30.7.66	Miss Hatton		Fl-L 1791, 182–3	
Madeley	Sept. 66	Miss Hatton		Fl-L 1791, 186	
Oakhall	23.9.66	(Societies in Madeley)		Fl-L 1791, 5–10	
London	15.10.(66)	Mr Wase	Oe5: 2280/16/1.2		
Oat (Oak?) Hall	5.11.66	Lady Huntingdon	Ce2: Fl Vol. II, 147–58		
Morley/	9./				
Madeley?	19.12.66	Lady Huntingdon	Ce2: Fl Vol. II, 159–69		(Seymour, I, 379)
Madeley	9.1.67	Miss Hatton		Fl-L 1791, 187–90	
Madeley	30.1.67	Mrs Hatton		Fl-L 1791, 190–1	
Madeley	Feb. 67	J. Ireland, Esq.		Fl-L 1791, 191–2	
Madeley	Feb. 67	Miss Brian/Bryan?		Fl-L 1791, 193	
Madeley	16.3.67	Lady Huntingdon	Ce2: Fl Vol. II, 171–5		
Madeley	30.3.67	J. Ireland, Esq.		Fl-L 1791, 194–5	
Madeley	27.4.67	J. Ireland, Esq.		Fl-L 1791, 195–6	
Madeley	18.5.67	G. Whitefield		Fl-W 1806, I, 112–14	
Madeley	3.7.67	G. Whitefield	Oe2: MAW Fl Box 36.1		

Sender / date	Recipient	Manuscript location	Printed edition	Secondary reference
Madeley 12.8.67	Lady Huntingdon	Ce2: Fl Vol. II, 177–81		(Seymour, I, 295f.)
Madeley 24.11.67	Lady Huntingdon	Ce2: Fl Vol. II, 183–9		(Seymour, II, 81f.)
Madeley 2.12.67	Lady Huntingdon	Ce2: Fl Vol. II, 191–5		
Madeley 3.1.68	Lady Huntingdon	Ce2: Fl Vol. II, 197–204	Fl-W 1883, IV, 373f.	MethMag. 1821, 435–7; (Seymour, II, 84–6)
Madeley 8.1.68	Lady Huntingdon	Ce2: Fl Vol. II, 205–12		(Seymour, II, 18–19)
Madeley 28.5.(68)	G. Whitefield	Oe2: MAW Fl Box 36.1	Fl-W 1877, IX, 254f.	(Tyerman-Fl, 135f.)
Madeley 30.7.68	J. Ireland, Esq.		Fl-L 1791, 196–8	
Madeley 14.10.68	J. Ireland, Esq.		Fl-L 1791, 198–9	
Lady Huntingdon's College and postscript 10.11.68 15.11.68	Lady Huntingdon	Oe7: Fl 1449		
Madeley 5.12.68	Miss Ireland		Fl-L 1791, 200–4	
1768/69	Miss Bryan/Brain	Ce2: MAW Fl Box 36.6 (correspondence collected in a booklet)		
Madeley 10.2.69	Lady Huntingdon	Oe7: Fl 1457	Fl-L 1791, 205–6	
Madeley 26.3.69	J. Ireland, Esq.			
Lady Huntingdon's College 12.4.69	Lady Huntingdon	Oe7: Fl 1464		

Place	Date	Recipient	Collection	Printed reference	Other
Madeley	20.5.(69)	Charles Wesley	Ofz: Fl Vol, 107 (C: Garrett Theological Seminary, Evanston, USA)		
Madeley	27.5.69	Lady Huntingdon	Oe7: Fl 1467	Fl-L 1791, 206–7	
Madeley	27.5.69	J. Ireland, Esq.			
Madeley	1.7.69	Lady Huntingdon			(Seymour, II, 97–8)
Madeley	7.10.69	Rev. Mr Sellon	Ce2: Fl Vol. II, 213–25	Fl-W 1807/16, VII, 430–1	
Madeley	30.12.69	J. Ireland, Esq.		Fl-L 1791, 207–8	
Trevecka	13.1.70	J. Ireland		Fl-L 1791, 208–10	
Madeley	23.7.70	Masters and Students of Lady Huntingdon's College	Oe8: J. Benson Collection	Fl-W 1806, I, 158–61	
Madeley	4.8.70	Rev. David Simpson		Fl-W 1877, IX, 256f.	
Madeley	10.8.70	Charles Wesley '41'	Ofz: Fl Vol., 33		
Wales	Sept. 70	Charles Wesley '42'	Ofz: Fl Vol., 34		
College	'Dimanche' (16.12.70)	Charles Wesley '43'	Ofz: Fl Vol., 35		
	18.12.70	Rev. Hull	Ce2: Fl Vol., 75		
	7.1.71	J. Benson enclosed: extract of a letter to Lady Huntingdon	Oe8: J. Benson Collection	(Fl-W 1806, I, 162–3)	(J.Wesley-Fl, 55f.)
	10.1.71	J. Benson	Oe8: J. Benson Collection	(Fl-W 1806, I, 163–4)	
Madeley	20.2.71	John Wesley	Oe2: Brown Folio Wesley Family II, 46		
College	7.3.71	Lady Huntingdon	Oe7: E4/7:1		

Place	Date	Correspondent	Source	Printed reference
'Saturday morning'	(9.3.71)	Lady Huntingdon	Oe7: E4 / 7:2	Tyerman-Fl, 177–9
Madeley	18.3.71	John Wesley	(Oe2: Letters to J. Wesley?)	
	22.3.71	J. Benson	OFe8: J. Benson Collection	(Fl-W 1806, I, 164–7)
Madeley	26.5.71	Charles Wesley '44'	Oe8: Wesley Family Collection	
Madeley	24.6.71	John Wesley	Oe2: Fl Vol., 36	Tyerman-Fl, 188–9
	24.8.71	J. Benson	Ce2: Fl Vol. II, 233–5 (date: 1773)	Tyerman-Fl, 209
	5.9.(71)	Lady Huntingdon	Oe2: Fl Vol., 37	(Fl-W 1806, I, 168–9)
Madeley	21.9.71	Charles Wesley '46' (postscript to Mr Benson)	Oe9: J. Wesley Coll., 1734–1864, AL	
Madeley	13.10.71	Charles Wesley	Oe2: Fl Vol., 39	
	(c. Oct./Nov.71)	J. and Ch. Wesley '49'	Ce2: Fl Vol. II, 227–31	(J.Wesley-Fl, 189)
Madeley	3.11.71	Lady Huntingdon	Oe8: J. Benson Collection	(Fl-W 1806, I, 169–70)
	23.11.71	J. Benson	Oe2: Fl Vol., 38	
Madeley	24.11.71	Charles Wesley	Oe8: J. Benson Collection	(Tyerman-Fl, 216–17)
	10.12.71	J. Benson	Oe2: Fl Vol., 40	(Fl-W 1806, I, 170: outline)
	(Dec.71)	John Wesley '50'	Oe2: Fl Vol., 71	
Madeley	7.1.72	Rev. Mr Sellon		
Madeley	21.1.72	Charles Wesley '52'	Oe2: Fl Vol., 41	(Tyerman-Fl, 219–20)

Place	Date	Correspondent	Archive	Printed references
Madeley	12.2.72	J. Benson	Oe8: J. Benson Collection	
Madeley	13.2.72	John Wesley	Oe2: MAW Fl Box 36.1 (not: Josey Bequest, Fletcher MSS / J. Wesley Folio No. 29)	Tyerman-Fl, 221–2
Madeley	March 72	Meth. Society, Dublin	Ce2: Fl Vol., 68	
Madeley	12.3.72	Charles Wesley '53'	Oe2: Fl Vol., 42	
Madeley	12.4.72	J. Benson	Oe2: Fl Vol., 43	
Madeley	'Last May' (31.5.)72	Charles Wesley '54'	Oe2: Fl Vol., 44	
Madeley	5.7.72	Charles Wesley	Oe2: MAW Fl Box 36.1	
Madeley	5.8.72	Charles Wesley '55'	Oe2: Fl Vol., 45	
Madeley	6.9.72	Henry Brooke	Ce2: MAW Fl Box 36.5	Fl-L1791, 212–14
Madeley	7.9.72	Charles Perronet (Charles Wesley) '56'	OFe2: Fl Vol., 46	Fl-W 1806, I, 173+174f.
Madeley	16.1.73	John Wesley	Oe8: Coll. Eugene Russell Hendrix	Fl-W 1806, I, 184–5; Fl-L 1791, 214–16; J.Wesley-Fl, 64–6
Madeley	6.2.73	Mr Vaughan	Oe2: Fl Vol., 47	
Whitchurch (?)	11.2.73	J. Benson		
Madeley	12.2.73	J. and Ch. Wesley '57' (with postscript to Charles Wesley)		
Madeley	28.2.73	John Wilkes	Oe2: Fl Vol., 87	
Madeley	23.3.73	Charles Wesley	Oe2: Brown Folio Wesley Family II, 48	
Madeley	20.4.73	(Charles Wesley)	Oe2: Fl Vol., 48	
Madeley	30.5.73	(Charles Wesley) '58'		
Madeley	24.8.73			Tyerman-Fl, 271

Place	Date	Recipient	Manuscript source	Printed source 1	Printed source 2
Madeley	21.9.73	J. Ireland, Esq.		Fl-L 1791, 216–18	
Madeley	17.10.73	'Dear Sir' (?)	Ce2: MAW Fl 36.5		
Madeley	17.10.73	(John Wesley)	Ce2: MAW Fl 36.1		
Madeley	6.2.74	J. Ireland, Esq.		Fl-L 1791, 219–21	
Madeley	20.2.74	Charles Wesley	Oe2: MAW Fl 36.1		
Madeley	20.3.74	Mr Benson	Oe8: J. Benson Collection	(Fl-W 1806, I, 179–80)	
Madeley	27.3.74	J. Ireland, Esq.		Fl-L 1791, 221–3	
	10.5.74	Vaughan			J. Wesley-Fl, 69f.
Madeley	4.7.74	Charles Wesley '60'	Oe2: Fl Vol., 49		
Madeley	14.8.74	Charles Wesley '61'	Oe2: Fl Vol., 50		
Madeley	Jan. 75	Charles Wesley		Fl-L, 1791, 223–4	
Madeley	30.3.75	Mr Valton	Oe2: Fl Vol., 70		
Madeley	2.5.75	Mr Benson	Oe8: J. Benson Collection	(Fl-W 1806, I, 181–3)	
Madeley	21.5.75	Charles Wesley '63'	Oe2: Fl Vol., 51		(PWHS IX, 1914, 133f.)
Madeley	2.7.75	Charles Wesley	Oe4		
Madeley	12.7.75	Mr Benson	Oe8: J. Benson Collection	(Fl-W 1806, I, 187+191)	Tyerman-Fl, 327–8 (W-J, VIII, 329f.)
	24.7.(75)	Mr Benson	Oe8: J. Benson Collection		(PWHS IX, 1914, 134)
Madeley	1./6.8.75	John Wesley	Oe2: Fl Vol., 88+89		
Madeley	8.8.75	Charles Wesley '64'	Oe2: Fl Vol., 52		W-J, VIII, 331–4
Madeley	4.12.75	Charles Wesley '67+68'	Oe2: Fl Vol., 90+91	(Fl-L 1791, 225-6-6+230)	
	75	Mrs Mary Cartwright		Fl-L 1791, 10–12	
Madeley	9.1.76	John Wesley	Oe2: Fl Vol., 103		

Place	Date	Recipient	Source	Reference
Madeley	(early 76)	Mr Benson	Oe8: J. Benson Collection	(Fl-W 1806, I, 189f., 193f.)
Madeley	3.2.76	J. Ireland, Esq.		Fl-L 1791, 226–7
Madeley	21.3.76	Mr Vaughan		Fl-L 1791, 227–9
Madeley	8.5.76	Mr Benson	Oe8: J. Benson Collection	(Fl-W 1806, I, 195f.)
Madeley	11.5.76	Charles Wesley '65'	Oe2: Fl Vol., 53	(Fl-L 1791, 229–31)
Bristol	11.7.76	Michael Onions (to a society?)		Fl-L 1791, 12–14
Bristol	12.7.76	Charles Perronet		(Fl-L 1791, 231) / Fl-W 1883, IV, 377
Madeley	18.8.76	J. Ireland, Esq.		Fl-L 1791, 232–3
Madeley	24.8.76	J. Ireland, Esq.		Fl-L 1791, 233–4
	(Aug. 76?)	Rev. V. Perronet		(Fl-W 1806, I, 175f.)
Madeley	7.9.76	J. Ireland, Esq.	Oe2: MAW Fl Box 36.1	Fl-L 1791, 235–6
Madeley	15.9.76	Charles Wesley		(Fl-L 1791, 236–7)
Bristol	(Sept. 76) –.10.76	Mr Benson Societies in and around Madeley		Fl-W 1806, I, 204f. Fl-L 1791, 14–16
London	12.11.76	Mr Hare, Terry, Fox, Good, Preston, Simpson and Ramsden	Oe2: MAW Fl Box 36.1	Fl-W 1807/16, VII, 440f.
Loestoff	21.11.76	Mr Benson		Fl-W 1806, I, 211–12
Newington	28.12.76	Church in Madeley		Fl-L 1791, 16–21 (published: London 1779 with date 1.1.77)

Place	Date	Recipient	Archive reference	Published reference	Notes
Newington	13.1.77	William Wase and Societies in and around Madeley	Oe2: MAW Fl Box 36.2	Fl-L 1791, 22–3 Fl-L 1791, 26–30	(Tyerman-Fl, 401; not to M. Bosanquet)
Newington	19.1.77	Rev. V. Perronet		Fl-L 1791, 238–9	
Newington	19.1.77	Miss Perronet		Fl-L 1791, 239–40	
Newington	29.1.77	J. Ireland, Esq.		Fl-L 1791, 240–2	
Newington	18.2.77	William Wase		Fl-L 1791, 23–4	
Newington	23.2.77	(Mrs Ford)	Ce9: J. Wesley Coll., 1734–1864, ALS		
Newington	24.2.77	J. Ireland, Esq.		Fl-L 1791, 243–4	
Stoke Newington	18.3.77	Lady Huntingdon	Oe7: Fl 1756		
Stoke Newington	22.3.77	Bishop of Hereford	Oe2: MAW Fl Box 36.2		Tyerman-Fl, 388–9
Newington	21.4.77	Miss Perronet		Fl-L 1791, 245–6	
Brislington	28.5.77	Mr and Mrs Greenwood		Fl-L 1791, 246–8	
Brislington	28.5.77	Lady Huntingdon	Oe7: A1 / 13:11	Fl-L 1791, 24–6	
Bath	8.7.77	Michael Onions		Fl-W 1806, I, 236–7	(J.Wesley, Fl, 96–8; with postscript)
Brislington	6.9.77	Rev. V. Perronet			
Brislington	10.10.77	Lady Huntingdon	Oe7: A1 / 13:12	Fl-L 1791, 254–5	Tyerman-Fl, 400–1
Bristol	20.10.77	Miss Bosanquet			
Madeley (Bristol?)	21.10.77	Lady Mary Fitzgerald			
Brislington	(Oct./77 Nov.?)	Mrs Thornton		Fl-L 1791, 249–51	

Place	Date	Person / Subject	Archive	Reference	
Brislington	(Oct./Nov.?) 77	Mrs Thornton		Fl-L 1791, 251–3	
Bristol	Nov. 77	Mr Th. York + D. Edmunds		Fl-L 1791, 31–4	
Bristol	Nov. 77	Mr Jehu		Fl-L 1791, 34	
Bristol	Nov. 77	William Wase		Fl-L 1791, 35–6	
Bristleton	19.11.77	Mr W. Perronet		(Fl-W 1806, I, 242) / Fl-W 1883, IV, 390f.	
Bristol	26.11.77	(Societies in Madeley)		Fl-L 1791, 36–40	
Reading	2.12.77	Rev. V. Perronet and Miss Perronet	Oe8: Frank Baker Coll. of Wesleyana and British Methodism, Perronet Family	(Fl-W 1806, I, 249–50)	(MethMag 1804, 520)
London	(end Nov.?) 77	Mr Greenwood		Fl-L 1791, 242–3	
London	(end Nov.?) 77	Mr and Mrs Greenwood		Fl-L 1791, 248–9	
Dover	2.12.77	Societies in Madeley	Oe2: MAW Fl Box 36.2	Fl-L 1791, 41	
	7.3.78	Miss Bosanquet			(Tyerman-Fl, 411–12)
	(early 78; March?)	Rev. Mr Greaves and church in Madeley		Fl-L 1806, 254–6	
Nyon	15.5.78	Mr (W.) Perronet	Oe2: Fl Vol., 54	(Fl-W 1806, I, 256f.) / Fl-W 1883, IV, 393f.	
Macon	17.5.78	J. and Ch. Wesley		Fl-L 1791, 256–9	
Macon	18.5.78	Rev. Dr Conyers		Fl-L 1791, 259–61	

Nyon	2.6.78	Mr (W.) Perronet	Oe8: Perronet Family Scrapbook, 39	(Fl-L 1791, 261-3) Fl-W 1883, IV, 391-93	Tyerman-Fl, 420-1 J.Wesley-Fl, 105f.
Nyon	20.6.78 (1778?)	Mr Power		Fl-W 1806, I, 262	
Nyon	15.7.78	Dr Turner		Fl-L 1791, 263-5	
Nyon	18.7.78	J. Ireland, Esq. (Rev. Mr Greaves and church in Madeley and societies in and around Madeley)		Fl-L 1791, 43-5	
Nyon	18.7.(78)	Mr Thomas York	Oe2: Brown Folio Wesley Family II, 49	Fl-L 1791, 52-3	
Nyon	(July/Aug. 78?)	Rev. V. Perronet and Mr W. Perronet		Fl-W 1883, IV, 394 and Fl-W 1883, IV, 392f.	
Nyon	(July/Aug. 78?)	Miss Thornton		Fl-W 1883, IV, 395	
Nyon	15.9.78	Mr Thomas York		Fl-L 1791, 45	
Nyon	15./	J. Ireland, Esq.		Fl-L 1791, 265-8: dated 25.9.78	
Nyon	25.9.78			(Fl-W 1806, I, 271-3: dated 15.9.78)	
Nyon	Dec. 78	J. and Ch. Wesley Society of Madeley	Oe2: Fl Vol., 57	Fl-L 1791, 41-3	
Nyon	78	Rev. V. Perronet		Fl-W 1883, IV, 395f.	
Nyon	2.1.79	Mr Greenwood		Fl-L 1791, 268-71	J.Wesley-Fl, 112 (in letter from W. Perronet to Greenwood)
Nyon	18.1.79			Fl-L 1791, 268-71	
Nyon	2.2.79	J. Ireland, Esq.		Fl-L 1791, 268-71	

Nyon	8.2.79	Rev. V. Perronet	Oe2: MAW Fl Box 36.1	Fl-W 1883, IV, 397	
Nyon	11.2.79	Societies in and around Madeley		Fl-L 1791, 48–9	
Nyon	11.2.79	William Wase	Oe2: MAW Fl Box 36.2	(Fl-L 1791, 46–7)	
Nyon	29.3.79	Rev. V. Perronet		Fl-W 1806, I, 282–3	
Nyon	18.5.79	Rev. Mr Greaves		Fl-L 1791, 49–50	
Nyon	18.5.79	Mr Michael Onions		Fl-L 1791, 50–2	
Nyon	22.5.79	Rev. V. Perronet		Fl-W 1806, I, 285	J.Wesley-Fl, 121f.
	22./	Mr Charles Greenwood		Fl-L 1791, 271–2: dated 22.5.79	
	24.5.79			(Fl-W 1806, I, 285f.: dated 24.5.79)	
Nyon	(May 79?)	–(a friend)		Fl-W 1806, I, 286–7	J.Wesley-Fl, 114
Nyon	30.7.79	Mons. Bridel	Ce2: MAW Fl Box 19; booklet with several letters: letter 2: 30.7.79; letters 3 to 6 and 9: without date; letters 7 and 8 missing		
Nyon	(5.11.79)	Rev. V. Perronet	Oe5: 2280/16/1.2	Fl-W 1883, IV, 397–8	
Nyon	'Thursday noon', 9.11.79	Mr W. Perronet	Oe6		WesMethMag 1826, 172
Nyon	18.11.(79)	Mr W. Perronet		(Fl-W 1883, IV, 398)	
Nyon	2.12.79	Mr W. Perronet	Oe2: Fl Vol., 55	(Fl-W 1806, I, 289)	WesMethMag 1825, 744

Nyon	15.12.79	'To a Nobleman'(?)		Fl-L 1791, 272–4	Tyerman-Fl, 437: to Lord North (?)
Nyon	25.12.79	Rev. Mr Greaves	Oe2: MAW Fl Box 36.2	Fl-L 1791, 53–6	
Nyon	31.12.79	Mr W. Perronet		Fl-W 1883, IV, 398	
Nyon	17.1.80	Mr W. Perronet		Fl-W 1883, IV, 399	
	'Friday', (25.2.80?)	Mr W. Perronet	Oe2: Fl Vol., 56	Fl-W 1883, IV, 399	
Nyon	7.3.80	Rev. Mr Greaves		Fl-L 1791, 56–7	
Nyon	7.3.80	William Wase		Fl-L 1791, 57–8	
	March 80	Mr W. Perronet		Fl-W 1883, IV, 399f.	
	'Good Friday' 80	Mr W. Perronet		Fl-W 1883, IV, 400	
Nyon	16.7.80	Mr W. Perronet		Fl-W 1883, IV, 400f.	
Nyon	15.9.80	Rev. Mr Greaves		Fl-L 1791, 58–60	
Nyon	15.9.80	William Wase		Fl-L 1791, 61	
Nyon	15.9.80	Mr Thomas York		Fl-L 1791, 62	
Nyon	15.9.80	Society of Madeley		Fl-L 1791, 62–3	
Nyon	20.9.80	Mr W. Perronet		Fl-L 1883, IV, 401f.	
Nyon	Tuesday 3.10.80	Mr W. Perronet		(Fl-W 1806, I, 299–300) Fl-W 1883, IV, 401	
Nyon	5.12.80	Rev. V. Perronet		(Fl-W 1806, I, 300) Fl-W 1883, IV, 402f.	
Nyon	Thursday 31.12.80	Mr W. Perronet	Oe8: Perronet Family Scrapbook, 37	Fl-W 1883, IV, 403	WesMethMag 1830, 831
Nyon	14.1.81	Mr W. Perronet	Oe2: MAW Fl Box 36.2	Fl-W 1883, IV, 403	

Place	Date	Recipient	Source	Reference	Additional reference
Nyon	1.2.81	Mr W. Perronet	Oe2: Brown Folio	Fl-W 1883, IV, 404	
Nyon	10.2.81	Mr W. Perronet	Wesley Family II, 50–1	(Fl-W 1806, I, 302)/ Fl-W 1883, IV, 404	
Nyon	14.2.81	Mr John Owen with a letter to the society in Madeley		Fl-L 1791, 64–5	
Nyon	14.2.81	William Wase	Oe2: MAW Fl Box 36.2	Fl-L 1791, 66–7	
Nyon	'Mardi'	Mr W. Perronet		Fl-W 1883, IV, 405	
Nyon	20.2.81				
Nyon	March 81	Mr Michael Onions		Fl-L 1791, 67–8	
Lyons	6.4.81	Mr W. Perronet		(Fl-W 1806, I, 305f.) Fl-W 1883, IV, 405f. Fl-W 1883, IV, 406f.	J.Wesley-Fl, 122f.
Newington	28.4.81	Rev. V. Perronet	Oe2: MAW Fl Box 36.2		
Brislington	1.5.81	Miss Bosanquet		Fl-W 1883, IV, 384	Tyerman-Fl, 448–50
Madeley	24.5.81	Miss Loxdale	Oe2: MAW Fl Box 18		
Madeley	31.5.81	Rev. Mr Greaves		Fl-W 1883, IV, 384	
Madeley	6.6.81	John Wesley			ArmMag 1782, 47–8 Tyerman-Fl, 460–2 J.Wesley-Fl, 124f.
Madeley	12.6.81	Ch. Greenwood	Oe2: MAW Fl Box 36.3	Fl-W 1806, I, 312f.	
Madeley	22.6.81	Miss Loxdale		Fl-W 1883, IV, 385	
Madeley	24.6.81	John Wesley		Fl-W 1883, IV, 386	ArmMag 1782, 49
Madeley	25.6.81	Mr T. Rankin	Oe8: J. Benson Collection	(Fl-W 1806, I, 310–11)	ArmMag 1797, 352–3
Madeley	20.7.81	Mr Benson		(Fl-W 1806, I, 313–14)	

Place	Date	Recipient	Archive ref.	Printed ref.	Other ref.
Cross-hall	27.8.81 (end Aug. 81)	Mr Merryweather (John Wesley)	Oe2: Fl Vol., 106		
(Madeley	c. Sep. 81	J. Ireland, Esq.	Oe2: MAW Fl Box 36.4		MethMag 1817, 863f.
Madeley	2.9.81	Miss Bosanquet	OFe2: MAW Fl Box 36.3		
Madeley	3.9.81	Lady Mary Fitzgerald	Oe2: MAW Fl Box 36.3	Fl-L 1791, 274–5	
Madeley	4.9.81	Miss Perronet and Rev. V. Perronet	Oe2: MAW Fl Box 36.3	Fl-L 1791, 276–7/ Fl-W 1883, IV, 386f.	
Madeley	6.9.81	Miss Bosanquet	Oe2: MAW Fl Box 36.3		
Madeley	10.9.81	Miss Bosanquet	Oe2: MAW Fl Box 36.3		
Madeley	11./12.9.81	Miss Bosanquet	Oe2: MAW Fl Box 36.3		
Madeley	22.9.81	Miss Bosanquet	Oe2: MAW Fl Box 36.3		(Tyerman-Fl, 487f.)
Madeley	22.9.81	Cl. Bosanquet, Esq.	Oe2: MAW Fl Box 36.4		Tyerman-Fl, 488–90
Madeley	22.9.81	S. Bosanquet, Esq.	Oe2: MAW Fl Box 36.4		Tyerman-Fl, 490–91
Madeley	29.9.81 (after 2.12.81)	Lady Mary Fitzgerald Rev. V. Perronet		Fl-L 1791, 277–80 Fl-W 1806, I, 308f./ Fl-W 1883, IV, 408	
Cross Hall	26.12.81+ 1.1.82	'The Hon. Mrs C.'	Oe2: MAW Fl Box 36.3	Fl-L 1791, 280–3	
Madeley	Jan. 82	Lady Mary Fitzgerald		Fl-L 1791, 283–4	
Madeley	17.3.82	Miss Loxdale	Ce2: MAW Fl Box 36.5		
Madeley	20.4.82	Mr Henry Brooke and Society of Dublin			PWHS 1914, IX, 139 Tyerman-Fl, 508
*Madeley	28.8.82 (before 19.12.82)	Lady Mary Fitzgerald (M. de Luc)	Oef2: MAW Fl Box 19	Fl-L 1791, 284–7	

Place	Date	Recipient	Archive	Reference	Source
Madeley	19.12.82	Charles Wesley	Ce2: Fl Vol., 73	(Fl-L 1791, 287–8)	(Tyerman-Fl, 531–2)
*Madeley	21.1.(83)	Mrs Thornton		Fl-L 1791, 302–3	
*Madeley	3.3.83 (June or July 83)	Mrs Thornton		Fl-L 1791, 288–90	
		Rev. Bouverot (Geneva)	Ce2: MAW Fl Box 36.5		
Madeley	22.7.83	J. Benson	Oe8: J. Benson Collection		
*Dublin, Bristol	23.8.83	Lady Mary Fitzgerald		Fl-L 1791, 290–1	
	Sunday Morning (19.10.83)	Mary Fletcher-Bosanquet	Oe2: MAW Fl Box 36.4		
Bristol	21.10.83	Mary Fletcher-Bosanquet	Oe2: MAW Fl Box 36.3		
Madeley	20.11.83	Mr Hindmarsh	Oe4		
*Madeley	Nov. 83	William Smith, Esq	Ce2: MAW Fl Box 36.4	Fl-L 1791, 292–4	
*Madeley	Nov. 83	Society of Dublin		Fl-L 1791, 294–5	
Madeley	27.4.84	Mr Henry Brooke		Fl-L 1791, 297–9	
Madeley	20.6.84	Mrs Greenwood		Fl-L 1791, 300	
Madeley	13.9.84	J. Ireland, Esq		Fl-L 1791, 300–2	
Madeley	28.11.84	Mr John Fennel		Fl-W 1807/16, VII, 468–9	MethMag 1801, 93
Madeley	11.2.85	Lady Mary Fitzgerald		Fl-L 1791, 303–4	
*Madeley	28.2.85	Mr Henry Brooke		Fl-L 1791, 304–7	WesMethMag 1825, 745
Madeley	29.3.85	Rev P. Dickenson	Oe6		
Madeley	10.5.85	Mr Melvill Horne		Fl-L 1791, 307–9	

	Date	Recipient	Archive	Printed source
**Madeley	3.6.85	Mr George Gibbons	Oe8: J. W. Fletcher papers	
*Madeley	19.7.85	J. Ireland, Esq		Fl-L 1791, 309–10
Madeley	19.7.85	Lady Mary Fitzgerald	Oe2: MAW Fl Box 18	Fl-W 1807/16, VII, 472–3

* = signed by John and Mary Fletcher

** = first part: Mary Fletcher; second part: John Fletcher

Undated letters from Fletcher (with conjectured dates in brackets)

	Date	Recipient	Archive	Printed source
Madeley	(62–64)	Miss Hatton		Fl-L 1791, 136–140
	'Good Friday', (62–64)	Miss M. Hatton	Oe2: MAW Fl Box 36.4	
	(63/64?)	Mr Vaughan		Fl-L 1791, 145–6
	(66?)	Miss		Fl-L 1791, 183–5
Madeley	2.9.– (68–70)	Mrs Glynne		Fl-L 1791, 140–2
Madeley	(before 70)	Lady Huntingdon	Oe7: A3/3:25	
	(71?)	Mr –/'To C. B.'		Fl-L 1791, 210–11
	(75?)	(Charles Wesley) '51'	Ofe2: Fl Vol., 60	
	(78–80?)	Mr and Mrs Greenwood		Fl-W 1883, IV, 395
Madeley	(after 81)	(Mrs Goodwin)	Oe5: 2280/16/1.2	
	'Thursday evening'	Mr Henry Burder	Oe2: MAW Fl Box 36.4	
	12.7.–			MNCMag 1815, 124 ('To C. B.')

—	'The Hon. Mrs–'		Fl-L 1791, 100–3	Tyerman-Fl, 540–1: Lady Mary Fitzgerald
—	'Sir' (Lord Gower)	ODFe2: MAW Fl Box 36.4	
—	Mrs King	Ce6	
Madeley 7.3.–	Mr York and Miss Simpson			WesMethMag 1829,

Letters not written by Fletcher

Gainsborough	6.7.73	Lady Huntingdon	Oe7
Gainsborough	13.1.74	Lady Huntingdon	Oe7

In my opinion these two letters were written by a different Fletcher. Cf. also W-L VI 23 (1.4.73) and W-L VI, 34–5 (30.7.73).

28.2.77	'Much esteemed, tho' unknown Friend'	C(?)e2: MAW Fl Box 36.2

In my opinion this does not refer to a letter by Fletcher.

Nov 83	Mrs Dolier	Ce2: Fl Vol., 67	Fl-L 1791, 296–7

Though signed by John and Mary Fletcher, this and the following two letters were written, in my opinion, by Mary Fletcher.

July 83	Mr Valton	MethMag 1798, 597–8
27.4.84	Mrs Smyth	Tyerman-Fl, 539–40

Dated or datable letters to Fletcher

Madeley Wood	21.9.62	Mr Slaughter, sen.	Oe2: MAM Fl 6.10
	24.9.62	J. Henshaw	Oe2: MAM Fl 3.8

Place	Date	Recipient	Source	Reference
Lewisham	28.2.66	John Wesley	Oe2: S. L. V, 3; W. L. File	W-L V, 3–4 (from London)
Vauxhall	16.8.66	C. Tilbury	Oe2: MAM Fl 7.1	
Walcot, near Bath	10.12.67	Lord Erskine, Earl of Buchan	Oe2: MAM Fl 2.13	(Seymour, II, 21)
	(Jan. 68?)	Lady Huntingdon		ArmMag 1797, 244–6
Birmingham	20.3.68	John Wesley	Oe2: MAM Fl 7.1	W-L V, 82–5
Vauxhall	18.6.68	C. Tilbury	Oe2: MAM Fl 7.1	
	3.11.68	C. Tilbury	Oe2: MAM Fl 1.12	
Bristol	3.10.69	Brain	Oe2: MAM Fl 1.12	
Bristol	6.1.70	Brain	OFe2/ MAM Fl 1.12	
Bristol	20.2.70	Brain	Oe2: MAM Fl 1.12	
Bristol	29.7.70	Brain	Oe2: MAM Fl 1.12	
Bristol	14.10.70	Brain	Oe2: MAM Fl 1.12	
Hay	14.1.71	Walter Churchey	Oe2: S. L. V, 217; T. S. C.	(The letter reached Fletcher by way of John Wesley)
London	16.1.71	John Wesley		W-L V, 217
London	27.2.71	John Wesley	Cfe8: J. Benson Collection	(in letters to J. Benson 2.3.71)
Parkgate	22.3.71	John Wesley		W-L V, 231
London	6.10.71	John Wesley		W-L VI, 179 (not 1775)
London	12.10.71	John Wesley		W-L V, 281–2
	(1772/73?)	Joseph Benson	Oe2: PLP 7.7.2	
Shoreham	15.1.73	John Wesley		W-L VI, 10–12
Lewisham	21.7.73	John Wesley	Oe2: S. L. VI, 33; W. L. File	W-L VI, 33–4

Place	Date	Recipient			
Hawkstone	31.7.73	Richard Hill	Oe2: Letters relating to Wesley Family II, 97		Tyerman-Fl, 285–6
Hawkstone	20.8.73	Richard Hill	Oe2: Letters chiefly to Charles Wesley VI, 93		Tyerman-Fl, 286–7
Bath	9.9.73	M. Tucker	Oe2: MAM Fl 7.1		
Bristol	1.10.73	John Wesley	Ce2: W. L. File; Lamplough Coll. and Research Centre		
Hawkstone	23.12.73	Richard Hill	Oe2: MAM Fl 7.18		Tyerman-Fl, 287–8
High-Town	24.2.74	Th. Wright		W-L VI, 75	
London	26.2.74	John Wesley	Oe2: MAM Fl 2.1		
Bristol Wells	7.9.74	A. Cranage	Oe2: MAM Fl 2.14		
Shrewsbury	28.12.74	J. Eddowes		W-L VI, 146	
Northwich	22.3.75	John Wesley		W-L VI, 174–5	
Brecon	18.8.75	John Wesley			
South Petherton	26./28.8.75	Thomas Coke	Oe3/Ce2: PLP, No 1		Tyerman-Fl, 331
Newcastle u.T.	(75/76?)	Lady Huntingdon		W-L VI, 221	(Seymour, II, 246–7)
	1.6.76	John Wesley			
London	11.7.76	K. E. Keysall	Oe2: MAM Fl 4.8		
Clapham	30.7.76	J. Thornton	Oe2: MAM Fl 7.4		
London	12.9.76	Charles Wesley	Oe2: Lamplough T. S. C.		
	(1776?)	T. Olivers	Oe2: PLP 80.23.2		
	17.6.77	T—(?)	Oe2: MAM Fl 7.1		
Nyon	18.6.79	Mons. Bridel, pasteur	Ce2: MAW Fl Box 19 (letter 1 in a booklet with several letters)		

Place	Date	Recipient	Source	Reference
Kidderminster	25.5.81	J. Ireland, Esq.	Ce2: MAW Fl Box 18 (in a letter to Greaves, dated 31.5.81	(Macdonald, 156)
Leeds	12.6.81	J. Benson	Oe2: PLP No 9	
Alexton	15.6.81	Rev. Th. Davenport	Oe2: MAM Fl 2.7	
Cross Hall	1.–4.9.81	Mary Bosanquet	Oe2: MAM Fl 37.6	(Tyerman-Fl, 491)
Forest House	2.10.81	S. Bosanquet, Esq.	Oe2: MAM Fl 1.8	
London	24.11.81	John Wesley		W-L VII, 93
	8.3.82	Miss Adams	Ce2: MAW Fl Box 37.1	(W.R.Davies Diss., 118)
London	13.2.82	Charles Wesley	Oe9: J. Wesley Coll., 1734–1864, ALS	(*WesMethMag* 1828, 531)
Morley	13.1.83	H. Preston	Oe2: MAM Fl 5.11	
(Dublin)	Oct. 83	Society of Dublin	Oe2: MAM Fl 2.7	
Chesterfield-street	11.10.83	Charles Wesley	Oe2: Lamplough T. S. C.	Tyerman-Fl, 521–2
London	25.11.(83)	Hindmarsh	Oe2: MAM Fl 3.8	
	Nov. (83)	H. and A. Brooke	Oe2: MAM Fl 1.15	
	6.1.84	Thomas Coke	Ce2: PLP No 16	
London	21.6.84	Charles Wesley	Oe2: Lamplough T. S. C.	Tyerman-Fl, 531
	22.6.84	Abiah Darby	(Oe2: untraceable)	(Macdonald, 185–8)
	(84)	H. Brooke	Oe2: MAM Fl 1.15	(Trinder, 370)
London	1.9.84	Hindmarsh	Oe2: MAM Fl 3.8	
Nyon	Oct. 84	Henri-Louis de la Fléchère	Of2: MAW Fl Box 42.1	
Dublin	19.11.84	K. Rudd and D. Johnson	Oe2: MAM Fl 4.5	
Bradford	24.11.84	J. Valton	Oe2: MAM Fl 7.6	
Cleobury, North	27.11.84	Th. Warter	Oe2: MAM Fl 7.12	

Sheffield	14.12.84	Th. Holy	Oe2: MAM Fl 3.8
Hawkstone	16.12.84	Sir Richard Hill	Oe2: MAM Fl 3.8
Cleobury, North	15.1.85	Th. Warter	Oe2: MAM Fl 7.12
Manchester	2./3.4.85	John Wesley	Oe2: S. L. VII; 214; W. L. File W-L VII, 264–5
Marylebone	24.5.85	Charles Wesley	Tyerman-Fl, 556f.

Undated letters to Fletcher

	22.2. (68–70?)	Brain	Oe2: MAM Fl 1.12
	21.1. (68–70?)	Brain	Oe2: MAM Fl 1.12

Letters which may or may not have been written to Fletcher

Foundery	16.7.65	T. Olivers	Oe1: Fletcher MSS, No. 20
Bristol	12.5.68	Brain	Ofe2: MAM Fl 1.12
	—	C. Carthy	Oe2: MAM Fl 2.1 (The letter was not accessible to me)

Letters addressed to Mary Fletcher

Scott Hall	10.4.84	W. Burrowes	Oe2: MAM Fl 1.2

Letters not addressed to Fletcher

London	15.11.59	—	Oe2: MAM Fl 4.8
Stockton	9.1.80	Woodcock	Oe2: MAM Fl 7.8

This list contains all the works by Fletcher known to me. Many of these were in letter form, but because of their character as theological writings they are here listed separately from the letters. Personal letters which appeared as forewords to theological writings have been regarded as forming part of those writings. Unpublished sermons, booklets dealing with specific problems within the parish, and personal notebooks are not included in this list. Reference has been made to them in the notes to the relevant chapters.

Since I have not been able to check and identify the manuscripts in the Methodist Archives in Manchester and compare them with published versions, normally only the place of publication indicated in the first edition of Fletcher's Works is given in these pages. The list is divided up as follows:

(a)   works published during Fletcher's lifetime;
(b)   posthumously published works, and unpublished works which can be dated;
(c)   works which have not yet been recovered.

In the left-hand column an approximate date of origin is sometimes given. In some such cases the date given indicates when the work was begun, in others, when it was finished. The middle column contains the full title and description of the original publication. In the case of translations into German, French or English, the place and date given are also those of the first publication. The right-hand column shows where each particular work appears in editions of Fletcher's Works.

(a) Works published during Fletcher's lifetime

1759   *Discours sur la Régénération.* Londre 1759, 48pp.; f: Genéve 1823;
     e: ed. H. Moore 1794; German 1841   e: Fl-W 1807/16 VII, 275–312 with changes and abridgements

1771   *A Vindication of the Rev Mr Wesley's Last minutes: In five letters to the Hon and Rev Author of the circular letter. By a Lover of quietness and liberty of conscience.* Bristol 1771, 98pp. (later: *First Check to Antinomianism*)

1771   *A Second Check to Antinomianism; occasioned by a late narrative in three letters to the Hon and Rev Author. By the Vindicator of the Rev Mr Wesley's Minutes.* Bristol 1772, xi + 109pp.   Fl-W 1806 II, 317–428

1772   *A Third Check to Antinomianism. In a Letter to the Author of Pietas Oxoniensis. By the Vindicator of the Rev Mr Wesley's Minutes.* Bristol 1772, 114pp.   Fl-W 1806 III, 1–112

1772   *An Appeal to Matter of Fact and Common Sense or A rational demonstration of man's corrupt and lost estate.*   Fl-W 1806 II, 165–212
     To which is added an Address to such as enquire what must we do to be saved? Bristol 1772, 210 + 72 + 8pp. abridged: f: 1832; German: Pennsylvania 1839, Cincinnati 1841, Bremen & Zürich 1866   Fl-W 1806 II, 213–18

1772   *Logica Genevensis; or, a Fourth Check to Antinomianism.* Bristol 1772, 237pp.   Fl-W 1806 III, 113–329

1773   *The Penitent Thief; or, a narrative of two women . . . who visited in prison a highwayman (J. Wilkes) . . . With a letter to a condemned malefactor; and a penitential office . . .* London 1773, 36pp.   Fl-W 1877 VIII, 205–39

1773	*A dreadful phenomenon, described and improved . . . And the substance of a sermon preached the next day.* Shrewsbury 1773, 104pp.	Fl-W 1806 II, 209–74
1773	*Logica Genevensis Continued; or, the first part of the Fifth Check to Antinomianism.* London 1773, iv + 48pp.	Fl-W 1806 III, 331–78
1774	*Logica Genevensis Continued; or, the second part of the Fifth Check to Antinomianism.* London 1774, 44pp.	Fl-W 1806 III, 379–418
1774	*The first part of an Equal Check to Pharisaism and Antinomianism.* Shrewsbury 1774, x + 264pp.	Fl-W 1806 IV, 1–269
1774	*Zelotes and Honestus reconciled; or, An equal check to Pharisaism and Antinomianism – continued. Being the first part of the Scripture Scales . . . By a lover of the whole truth as it is in Jesus.* Shrewsbury 1774, xx + 175pp.	Fl-W 1806 IV, 271–455
1775	*The fictitious and the genuine creed; being 'A creed for Arminians', composed by Richard Hill, Esq; to which is opposed A creed for those who believe that Christ tasted Death for every man.* London 1775, 52pp.	Fl-W 1806 III, 419–64
1775	*Zelotes and Honestus reconciled; or, An equal Check to Pharisaism and Antinomianism – continued. Being the second part of the Scripture Scales.* Shrewsbury 1775, xii + 223pp. (pages 177–412 of the equal Check)	Fl-W 1807 V, 1–210
1775	*The Last Check to Antinomianism. A polemical essay on the twin doctrines of Christian Imperfection and a Death Purgatory.* London 1775, 327pp. abridged: f: *Le grand privilège des croyants,* Paris & Lausanne 1842	Fl-W 1807 VI, 115–420
1776	*A Vindication of the Rev Mr Wesley's 'Calm Address to our American Colonies'; in some letters to Mr Caleb Evans. By John Fletcher, Vicar of Madeley, Salop.* London 1776, 70pp.	Fl-W 1807/16 VII, 1–71

1776	American Patriotism. Farther confronted with Reason, Scripture and the Constitution. Being observations on the dangerous politicks taught by the Rev Mr Evans, MA and the Rev Dr Price. With a scriptural Plea for the revolted colonies. By John Fletcher, Vicar of Madeley, Salop. Shrewsbury 1776, viii + 130pp.	Fl-W 1807/16 VII, 73–196
1776	The Bible and the Sword; or, the Appointment of the general Fast vindicated; in an Address to the Common People, concerning the propriety of repressing obstinate licentiousness with the sword, and of fasting when the sword is drawn for that purpose. London 1776, 22pp.	Fl-W 1807/16 VII, 197–208 (without introduction)
1776	An Answer to the Rev Mr Toplady's Vindication of the decrees, &c. By the Author of the checks. London 1776, V + 128pp.	Fl-W 1807 VI, 1–113
1777	A Reply to the principal arguments by which the Calvinists and the Fatalists support the Doctrine of Absolute Necessity; being remarks on the Rev Mr Toplady's 'Scheme of Christian and Philosophical Necessity'. London 1777, 80pp.	Fl-W 1807 V, 385–459
1777	The Doctrines of Grace and Justice. Equally essential to the pure Gospel. London 1777, 39pp.	Fl-W 1807 V, 211–50
1777	The Reconciliation; or, An easy method to unite the professing people of God . . . (containing: Bible Arminianism and Bible Calvinism, a twofold essay. 1777, 84pp.) London 1777, 187pp.	Fl-W 1807 V, 251–384
1781	La Louange, Poème Moral et Sacré, tiré du Psaume CXLVII. Nyon 1781, viii + 196pp.	—
1783	Three National Grievances: the Increase of Taxes: The Hardship of unequal Taxation: And the continual Rise of the Poor's Rates: with the Causes and Remedies of these Evils: humbly submitted to the Consideration of the Legislature: in a Letter to The Right Honourable Lord John Cavendish . . . Chancellor of the Exchequer, and one of the Lords of the Treasury. London, November 1783 (manuscript in Oe2: MAW Fl Box 18)	—

Date	Work	Reference
1784	*Essai sur la Paix de 1783, Dédié à l'Archevêque de Paris, par un Pasteur Anglican.* Londre 1784, 70pp.	e: ed. J. Gilpin, 1785
1785	*La Grace et la Nature, Poème,* Seconde edition, plus complète. Londre 1785, 442pp.	e: ed. M. Martindale, 1810

As editor Fletcher published in 1777:

Bunyan, A Race for eternal life: being an Extract from the Heavenly Footman. By the Rev Mr Fletcher. 16pp.

(b) Posthumously published works, and unpublished works with their date of origin

Date	Work	Reference
1755	*Prophecies of the remarkable events now taking place in Europe.* In a letter to the late Rev Mr John Wesley dated London, November 29, 1755. Bath 1793, xii + 20pp.	Fl-W 1808 IX, 429–40
1758	*Test of a new creature; or, Heads of examinations for adult Christians.* New York 18—, 8pp.	Fl-W 1807 VIII, 426–32
1761	'A letter to the Rev Mr Prothero, in Defense of Experimental Religion' (July 25, 1761).	Fl-W 1877 IX, 404–32
176?	*The Nature and Rules of a Religious Society; submitted to the consideration of the serious inhabitants of the Parish of Madeley.* (With a prefatory epistle, by M. Horne) Madeley 1788.	—
1766	'A Dialogue between a minister and one of his parishioners, on man's depravity and danger in his natural state.'	Fl-W 1877 IX, 448–5 (with preface by J. Benson, 446–7)
1767	*Six Letters on the Spiritual Manifestation of the Son of God.* (ed. M. Horne) Leeds 1791; f: nouv. éd. Toulouse 1863	Fl-W 1807/16 VII, 313–73
1779–	*The Portrait of St. Paul; or, The true model for Christians and pastors.*	Fl-W 1807 VIII, 1–394

81 (?)	(translated from f to e by J. Gilpin) edn enlarged with 'The Character of Mr Fletcher' by J. Gilpin. Shrewsbury 1790, 2 vols.	(without addition)
1784/ 85 (?)	*A Rational Vindication of the Catholic Faith; being the first part of a vindication of Christ's Divinity; inscribed to the Rev Dr Priestley.* edn enlarged by J. Benson, London 1788, 223pp.	Fl-W 1808 IX, 1–196 (by Fletcher: 15–58)
1784/ 85 (?)	*Socinianism Unscriptural; or, The Prophets and Apostles vindicated from the charge of holding the doctrine of Christ's mere humanity; being the second part of a vindication of His Divinity.* edn enlarged by J. Benson, Birmingham 1791, 239pp.	Fl-W 1808 IX, 197–396 (by Fletcher: 207–96)
??	*The Furious Bucher bumbled. A true and remarkable story.* London (1795?), 8pp.	—

The following sermons and drafts of sermons were published:

f: Sermons, Bruxelles 1836 (7 sermons)		—
e: Sermons		Fl-W 1877 VIII, 339–456
e: Drafts of sermons		Fl-W 1807 VIII, 410–26 and Fl-W 1877 VIII, 457–506

(c) *Works which have not yet been recovered*

1776/ 77 (?)	Manuscript with the probable title 'An Essay on the Birth of the Spirit'

John Wesley mentions as Fletcher's first publication 'A Christmas Box for Journeymen and Apprentices', but nothing is known of such a work apart from this reference (J. Wesley, *Fletcher*, 36–7).

Bibliography

1. PRIMARY LITERATURE

This bibliography contains only printed works. For handwritten material by Fletcher the reader is referred to the section on Sources above. Other archival material is not listed here, but is indicated, together with its location, in the appropriate notes. Abbreviated titles, as used in the Sources section above, are shown in bold type.

1.1 Fletcher and Wesleyan Methodism

Arminian Magazine, Consisting chiefly of Extracts and Original Treatises on Universal Redemption, London, 1778–1797 (ed. John Wesley until 1791) (**ArmMag**).

Bowmer, John C. and Vickers, John A. (eds), *The Letters of John Pawson (Methodist Itinerant, 1762–1806)*, Vol. 1: To the Conference of 1794, WMHS Publications, Peterborough 1994; Vol. 2: From the Conference of 1794 to the Conference of 1799, Peterborough 1995; Vol. 3: Closing Years (1799–1806), Peterborough 1995.

Fletcher, John William, or de la Fléchère, Jean Guillaume, *Discours sur la Régéneration*, réimprimé sur l'édition de Londre, de 1759, et suivi de trois autres discours, Genève 1823.

——, *La Grace et la Nature*, poème (seconde édition plus complète), London 1785.

——, *La Louange*, poème moral et sacré, tiré du psaume CXLVIII, Nyon 1781.

——, *A Poem entitled Grace and Nature*, with copious notes, moral and theological, translated by Miles Martindale, Leeds 1810.

——, *Posthumous Pieces of the late Rev. John William de la Fléchère*: pastoral and familiar letters, six letters on the spiritual manifestation of the Son of God, fragments, ed. M. Horne, London 1791 (**Fl-L 1791**).

——, *The Works of the Rev. John Fletcher, in eight volumes*, and *A Supplement to the eight volumes*, ed. J. Benson, London 1806–1808 (vol. VII bears the publication date 1816) (**Fl-W 1806–08**).

——, *The Works of the Rev. John Fletcher*, 9 vols, London 1877 (**Fl-W 1877**).

——, *The Works of the Rev. John Fletcher*, 4 vols, New York/Cincinnati 1883 (**Fl-W 1883**).

Hodson, James H., 'John Fletcher's Covenant with God', *Experience*, October 1914, 58–60.

Methodist Magazine, Being a continuation of The Arminian Magazine . . ., London 1798–1803 (**MethMag**).

——, New Series, London 1804–1807 and 1817–1821 (**MethMag**).

Methodist Magazine, or Evangelical Repository, for the year . . ., containing original and select pieces, designed to promote experimental religion amongst all denominations of Christians, printed for the New Connection, Leeds 1815 (**MNCMag**).

Minutes of the Methodist Conferences, Vol. 1: 1744 to 1798, ed. Wesleyan Conference Office, London 1862.

Proceedings of the Wesley Historical Society, Leicester etc. 1896/97– (**PWHS**).

Tyson, John R. (ed.), *Charles Wesley, A Reader*, Oxford 1989.

Valton, John, 'Excerpts from John Valton's MS. Journal', *PWHS* VIII (1912/13), 21–3, 33–5.

Wesleyan Methodist Magazine, Being a continuation of The Arminian or Methodist Magazine, Third Series, London 1822–44; Fourth Series, London 1845–54; Fifth Series, London 1855–76 (**WesMethMag**).

Wesley, Charles, *The Journal of the Rev. Charles Wesley, to which are appended Selections from his Correspondence and Poetry*, ed. Thomas Jackson, 2 vols, London 1849.

Wesley, John, *The Journal of the Rev. John Wesley*, Standard Edition, ed. Neh. Curnock, 8 vols, London 1938 (**W-J**).

——, *The Letters of the Rev. John Wesley*, Standard Edition, ed. John Telford, 8 vols, London 1931 (**W-L**).

——, *The Standard Sermons of the Rev. John Wesley*, ed. Edward H. Sugden, 2 vols, Seventh edition, London 1968.

——, *The Works of the Rev. John Wesley, reproduced from the authorized edition published by the Wesleyan Conference Office in London, England, in 1872*, Michigan (no date).

——, *The Works of John Wesley* (Bicentennial Edition), Oxford 1975–/ Nashville 1984–.

1.2 *Other Primary Literature*

'Berner Synodus, mit den Schlussreden der Berner Disputation und dem Reformationsmandat' in *Dokumente der Berner Reformation*, Bern 1978.

Budé de, E. (ed.), *Lettres inédites adressées de 1686–1737 à J.A. Turrettini, théologien genevois*, I–III, Paris 1887.

Calvin, Johannes, *Institutio Religionis Christianae*, nach der letzten Ausgabe übersetzt und bearbeitet von Otto Weber, 3 vols, Neukirchen 1936–38.

Crinsoz de Bionens, Théodore, *Apologie de Mr. de Bionens, contre un écrit intitulé 'Défense de la Dissertation de Mr. Turrettin sur les Articles Fondamentaux de la Religion, etc.'*, Yverdon 1727.

——, *De Divina Scripturae sacrae origine (Exercitatio theologica nona)*, Bern 1714.

——, (published anonymously) *Essai sur l'Apocalypse, avec des éclaircissemens sur les prophéties de Daniel qui regardent les derniers tems*, 1729.

——, *Lettre de Mr. T.C. à un Ami, Où Examen de quelques endroits de la dissertation de Monsieur Jean Alphonse Turrettin sur les Articles fondamentaux de la Religion*, undated (1727?).

Darby, Abiah, 'Extracts from the Diary of Abiah Darby', *JFHS* X, 79–92.

Evans, Caleb, *A Letter to the Rev. Mr. John Wesley, occasioned by his Calm Address to the American Colonies. – A new edition. To which are prefixed, some interesting observations on the Rev. Mr. Wesley's late Reply to Americanus*, Bristol 1775.

——, *A Reply to the Rev. Mr. Fletcher's Vindication of Mr. Wesley's Calm Address to our American Colonies*, Bristol (1776?).

Fabricius, C. (ed.), *Corpus Confessionum*, Abtlg. 17, Band 1: *Die Kirche von England, Ihr Gebetbuch, Bekenntnis und kanonisches Recht*, Berlin and Leipzig 1937.

Hill, Richard, *The Finishing Stroke: Containing some strictures on the Rev. Mr. Fletcher's pamphlet, entitled, Logica Genevensis, or a fourth check to Antinomianism*, London 1773.

——, *Five Letters to the Reverend Mr. Fletcher, relative to his Vindication of the minutes of the Reverend Mr. John Wesley. Intended chiefly for the comfort of mourning backsliders, and such as may have been distressed and perplexed by reading Mr. Wesley's Minutes, or the Vindication of them. By a Friend*, London 1771.

——, *A Review of all the Doctrines taught by the Rev. Mr. John Wesley; containing a full and particular answer to a book entitled, 'A Second Check to Antinomianism'. In six letters to the Rev. Mr. F—r. Wherein the Doctrines of a twofold Justification, free will, men's merit, sinless perfection, finished salvation, and real antinomianism, are particularly discussed; and the Puritan Divines and Protestant Churches vindicated from the charges brought against them of holding Mr Wesley's doctrines. To which are added, a Farrago; and some remarks on the 'Third Check to Antinomianism'. By the author of Pietas Oxoniensis*, London 1772.

——, *Three Letters, written by Richard Hill, Esq. to the Rev. J. Fletcher,*

Vicar of Madeley. In the Year 1773. Setting forth Mr. Hill's reasons for declining any further controversy relative to Mr. Wesley's principles, Shrewsbury 1774.

Hill, Rowland, *Friendly Remarks occasioned by the Spirit and Doctrines contained in the Rev. Mr. Fletcher's Vindications, and more particularly in his Second Check to Antinomianism, to which is added a postscript, occasioned by his Third Check. In a letter to the Author, by ******* *****, London 1772.

Locke, John, 'The Reasonableness of Christianity (as delivered in the Scriptures), übersetzt von Prof. Dr. T. Winckler, mit einer Einleitung herausgegeben von Prof. Lic. L. Zscharnack', *Studien zur Geschichte des neueren Protestantismus 4*. Quellenheft, Giessen 1914.

——, *Versuch über den menschlichen Verstand*, 2 vols, 1981.

——, *Zwei Abhandlungen über die Regierung*, ed. und eingeleitet von Walter Euchner, Frankfurt a.M. 1977.

Ostervald, Jean Frédéric, *Catéchisme ou Instruction dans la religion chrétienne*, Neuchâtel 1708.

——, *Compendium Theologiae Christianae*, Basel 1739.

Shirley, Walter, *A Narrative of the principal circumstances relative to the Rev. Mr. Wesley's Conference, held in Bristol, August the 6th, 1771, at which the Rev. Mr. Shirley, and others, were present. With the Declaration then agreed to by Mr. Wesley, and fifty-three of the Preachers in Connexion with him. In a letter to a Friend*, Bath 1771.

Thomas à Kempis, *L'imitation de Jésus-Christ*, Collection Gallica, London and Paris (undated).

Toplady, Augustus Montague, *Free-will and Merit fairly examined; or, men not their own saviours. The substance of a discourse preached in the Parish Church of St. Anne, Black-Friars, London: on Wednesday, May 25, 1774*, Manchester, 5th edn (undated).

Turrettin, Jean-Alphonse, *Défense de la Dissertation de Mons. Turrettin sur les articles fondamentaux de la Religion; Contre une brochure intitulée, Lettre de Mr T.C., c'est à dire, de Mons. Théodore Crinsoz, qu'on appelle ordinairement Mon. De Bionens, etc.*, Genève 1727.

Vernet, Jacob, *Traité de la vérité de la religion chrétienne, tiré du Latin de M. J. Alphonse Turrettin*, Tome I, Section I + II, Genève 1730; Section III, Genève 1731.

2. SECONDARY LITERATURE

2.1 *Fletcher*

Baker, Frank, 'John Fletcher's Sermon Notes', *PWHS* XXVIII, 1951/52, 30–3.

Benson, Joseph, *The Life of the Rev. John Fletcher, compiled from the Narratives of the Rev. Mr. Wesley, the biographical notes of the Rev. Mr. Gilpin, from his own letters, and other authentic documents*, London 1806.

Coulton, Barbara, 'Tutor to the Hills: the Early Career of John Fletcher', *PWHS* XLVII, 1989, 94–103.

Cox, Robert, *The Life of the Rev. John William Fletcher*, London 1822 (**Cox-Fl**).

Cubie, David L., 'Perfection in Wesley and Fletcher, Inaugural or Teleological?', *WTJ* XI, 1976, 22–37.

Davies, William R., 'John William Fletcher of Madeley as Theologian', unpublished dissertation, Manchester 1965 (**W.R.Davies-Diss.**).

——, 'John Fletcher's Georgian Ordinations and Madeley Curacy', *PWHS* XXXVI, 1967/68, 139–42.

(Fletcher, Mrs Mary), *A Letter to Mons. H.L. De la Fléchère on the Death of his Brother, the Reverend John William De la Fléchère . . .* , London 1786.

Forsaith, Peter S., 'The Eagle and the Dove, John Fletcher of Madeley – towards a new assessment', unpublished thesis, Wesley College, Bristol 1979.

——, *John Fletcher, Vicar of Madeley*, in series People called Methodists, Foundery Press, Peterborough 1994.

——, 'Portraits of John Fletcher of Madeley and Their Artists', *PWHS* XLVII, 1990, 187–201.

——, 'Wesley's Designated Successor', *PWHS* XLII, 1979, 69–74.

Gilpin, Joshua, 'The Character of the Rev. Mr. Fletcher', reprinted in *ArmMag* 1792, 643–51, and 1793, 3–7, 57–62, 113–19, 169–75, 225–30, 281–4, 337–41, 393–5, 449–55, 505–11, 551–6, 617–21.

Kinghorn, Kenneth Cain, 'Faith and Works: A Study in the Theology of John Fletcher', unpublished dissertation, Emory University 1965.

——, 'Fletcher, John William', *Encyclopedia of World Methodism*, Gen. Ed. N. B. Harmon, 1974, I, 852.

Knickerbocker, Waldo Emerson, Jnr, 'Doctrinal Sources and Guidelines in Early Methodism: Fletcher of Madeley as a Case Study', *MethH*, April 1976, 186–202.

——, 'The Doctrine of Authority in the Theology of John Fletcher', unpublished dissertation, Emory University 1972.

Knight, John A., 'Aspects of Wesley's Theology after 1770', *MethH* VI/3, April 1968, 33–42.

——, 'John William Fletcher and the Early Methodist Tradition', unpublished dissertation, Vanderbilt University 1966.

——, 'John Fletcher's Influence on the Development of Wesleyan Theology in America', *WTJ* XIII, 1978, 13–23.

Lawton, George, 'John Fletcher's Pulpit Prayers', *PWHS* XXX, 1955/56, 2–6.

——, 'The Incumbency at Madeley', *London Quarterly and Holborn Review*, 1956, 281ff.

——, *Shropshire Saint; A Study in the Ministry and Spirituality of Fletcher of Madeley*, London 1960.

Lelièvre, Matthieu, 'Fletcher (John William)', *Encyclopédie des sciences religieuses* (ed. F. Lichtenberger), Paris 1878, IV, 773–5.

Macdonald, Frederic W., *Fletcher of Madeley*, London 1885 (**Macdonald**).

Marrat, Jabez, *John Fletcher: Saint and Scholar*, London 1902.

Mattke, Robert A., 'John Fletcher's Methodology in the Antinomian Controversy of 1770–76', *WTJ* III, 1968, 38–47.

Maycock, J., 'The Fletcher–Toplady Controversy', *London Quarterly and Holborn Review*, July 1966, 227–35.

Nuelsen, John L., *John William Fletcher; Der erste schweizerische Methodist*, Zürich 1929.

Rowe, Kenneth E. (ed.), *Methodist Union Catalog: Pre-1976 Imprints*, Vol. IV: Do-Fy, Mituchen NY/London 1979.

Shipley, David Clark, 'Methodist Arminianism in the Theology of John Fletcher', unpublished dissertation, Yale University 1942.

Smith, Timothy L., 'How John Fletcher became the Theologian of Wesleyan Perfectionism 1770–1776', *WTJ* XV, 1980, 68–87.

Sommer, C. Ernst, *Der designierte Nachfolger John Wesleys*, Beiträge zur Geschichte der Ev.-meth. Kirche, Beiheft 6 (ed. Studiengemeinschaft für Geschichte der Ev.-meth. Kirche), Stuttgart 1977.

——, 'John William Fletcher (1729–85) Mann der Mitte; Prolegomena zu seinem Verständnis', in Festschrift *Basileia*, *Walter Freytag zum 60. Geburtstag*, ed. J. Hermelink und H. J. Margull, Stuttgart 1959, 437–53.

Streiff, Patrick Ph., *Jean Guillaume de la Fléchère, John William Fletcher 1729–1785: ein Beitrag zur Geschichte des Methodismus*, Bern 1984.

——, 'Der ökumenische Geist im frühen Methodismus. Mit besonderer Berücksichtigung der Kontroverse zwischen calvinistischen und wesleyanischen Methodisten im 18. Jahrhundert', *Pietismus und Neuzeit Bd. 11: Ökumenische, soziale und politische Wirkungen des Pietismus*, Festschrift für A. Lindt, Göttingen 1985, 59–77.

Turner, George Allen, 'The Baptism of the Holy Spirit in the Wesleyan Tradition', *WTJ* XIV, 1979, 60–76.

Tyerman, L., *Wesley's Designated Successor*, London 1882 (**Tyerman-Fl**).

Vie de M. de la Fléchère de Nyon: Pasteur de Madeley, dans le Shropshire en Angleterre, traduit de l'Anglais (anonymous, based on Benson's *Life*), Lausanne 1826 (**Vie de-Fl**).

Wesley, John, *A short account of the Life and Death of the Rev. John Fletcher*, London 1786 (**J.Wesley-Fl**).

Wiggins, James Bryan, 'The Pattern of John Fletcher's Theology: As developed in his poetic, pastoral, and polemical writings', unpublished dissertation, Drew University 1963.

Williamson, Barry, 'The Spilsbury Portrait of John Fletcher', *PWHS* XLVII, 1989, 44–9.

2.2 *Other Secondary Literature*

Abbey, Charles J. and Overton, John H., *The English Church in the Eighteenth Century, A new Edition, revised and abridged*, London 1887.

Amiel, Henri-Frédéric et Bouvier, Auguste, *L'enseignement supérieur à Genève depuis la fondation de l'académie, le 5 juin 1559 jusqu'à l'inauguration de l'université, le 26 octobre 1876; facultés et chaires – professeurs et recteurs – étudiants*, Genève 1878.

Armstrong, Anthony, *The Church of England, the Methodists and Society 1700–1850*, London 1973.

Armstrong, Brian G., *Calvinism and the Amyraut Heresy*, Madison, Milwaukee and London 1969.

Baker, Frank, *Charles Wesley as Revealed in His Letters*, Madison 1995 (revised edition).

——, *John Wesley and the Church of England*, London 1970.

——, 'The Shaping of Wesley's "Calm Address"', *MethH* XIV/1, October 1975, 3–12.

Barnaud, Barthélemy, *Mémoires pour servir à l'Histoire des troubles arrivés en Suisse, à l'occasion du Consensus*, Amsterdam 1726.

Barthel, Pierre, 'Die Schweizerische Frühaufklärung am Beispiel des Katechismus von J. F. Ostervald (1663–1747)' (unpublished research).

Bassett, Paul M., 'A Study in the Theology of the Early Holiness Movement', *MethH* XIII/3, April 1975, 61–84.

Bertrand, Claude-Jean, *Le méthodisme*, Paris 1971.

Beyreuther, Erich, *Studien zur Theologie Zinzendorfs*, Neukirchen 1962.

Borgeaud, Charles, *Histoire de l'Université de Genève, I: L'Académie de Calvin 1559–1798*, Genève 1900.

Brandt-Bessire, Daniel, *Aux sources de la spiritualité pentecôtiste*, Labor et Fides, Genève 1986.

Brown-Lawson, Albert, *John Wesley and the Anglican Evangelicals of the Eighteenth Century; A Study in Co-operation and Separation – with special reference to the Calvinistic Controversies*, Edinburgh 1994.

Budé de, E., *Vie de Jacob Vernet, théologien Genevois 1698–1789*, Lausanne 1893.

Chamberlain, Jeffrey S., 'Moralism, Justification and the Controversy over Methodism', *JEH* 44, 1993, 652–78.

Chavannes, Jules, *Jean-Philippe Dutoit*, Lausanne 1865.

Christie, Jan R., *Wars and Revolutions, Britain 1760–1815* (vol. 7 of *The New History of England*), London 1982.

Coppedge, Allan, 'John Wesley and the Doctrine of Predestination', PhD thesis, University of Cambridge 1976.

Core, Arthur C., 'Die Evangelische Vereinigte Brüderkirche in den Vereinigten Staaten von Amerika (Evangelical United Brethren Church; in Deutschland: Evangelische Gemeinschaft)', *Geschichte der Evangelisch-methodistischen Kirche*, ed. K. Steckel und C. E. Sommer, Stuttgart 1982, 59–84.

Coulton, Barbara, *A Shropshire Squire, Noel Hill, First Lord Berwick, 1745–1789*, Shrewsbury 1989.

——, 'Tern Hall and the Hill Family: 1700–75', *Transactions of the Shropshire Archaeological Society* LXVI, 1989, 97–105.

Crow, Earl P., Jr, 'John Wesley's Conflict with Antinomianism in Relation to the Moravians and Calvinists', PhD thesis, University of Manchester 1964.

Dallimore, Arnold, *George Whitefield; The Life and Times of the Great Evangelist of the 18th Century Revival*: I, London 1970; II, Edinburgh 1980.

Darby, Henry Clifford (ed.), *A New Historical Geography of England after 1600*, Cambridge 1976.

Davies, Rupert E., *Methodism*, London 1963.

Davies, Rupert E., and Rupp, Gordon (Gen. Eds), *A History of the Methodist Church in Great Britain* I, London 1965.

Dayton, Donald W., *Theological Roots of Pentecostalism*, Scarecrow Press, Metuchen 1987.

Feller, Richard, *Geschichte Berns: III Glaubenskämpfe und Aufklärung, 1653–1790; IV Der Untergang des alten Bern, 1789–1798*, Bern/Frankfurt a.M. 1974.

Fleisch, Paul, *Zur Geschichte der Heiligungsbewegung: I Die Heiligungsbewegung von Wesley bis Boardman*, Leipzig 1910.

Foras, le Cte E.-Amédée de, *Armorial et Nobiliaire de l'ancien Duché de Savoie: II*, Grenoble 1878.

Garlick, Kenneth B., *Mr. Wesley's Preachers, An alphabetical arrangement of Wesleyan Methodist Preachers and Missionaries, and the stations to which they were appointed, 1739–1818* (published for the World Methodist Historical Society, British Section), London 1977.

Geiger, Max, *Die Basler Kirche und Theologie im Zeitalter der Hochorthodoxie*, Zürich 1952.

Gilbert, Alan D., *Religion and Society in Industrial England; Church, Chapel and Social Change, 1740–1914*, London/New York 1976.

Gindroz, André, *Histoire de l'instruction publique dans le pays de Vaud*, Lausanne 1853.

Gunter, W. Stephen, *The Limits of 'Love Divine'*, Abingdon Press, Nashville 1989.

Hadorn, W., *Geschichte des Pietismus in den schweizerischen reformierten Kirche*, Konstanz/Emmishofen 1901.

Harrison, A.W., 'The Perronets of Shoreham', *PWHS* XVI, 1928, 40–7.

Heitzenrater, Richard P., *Wesley and the People Called Methodists*, Abingdon Press, Nashville 1995.

Heyer, H., *Catalogue des Thèses de théologie*, Genève 1898.

Hurst, John Fletcher, *The History of Methodism, I–III: British Methodism*, New York 1902.

Jackson, Thomas, *The Life of the Rev. Charles Wesley, I–II*, London 1841.

Jeremias, Isolde, 'Richard Baxter's Catholic Theology, ihre Voraussetzungen und Ausformungen', unpublished dissertation, Göttingen 1956.

Jones, William, *Memoirs of the Life, Ministry, and Writings of the Rev. Rowland Hill, M.A.*, London 1834.

Keller-Hüschemenger, Max, *Die Lehre der Kirche im frühreformatorischen Anglikanismus; Struktur und Funktion*, Gütersloh 1972.

Kendall, R. T., *Calvin and English Calvinism to 1649*, Oxford 1979.

Kirkham, Donald H., 'John Wesley's Calm Address: The Response of the Critics', *MethH* XIV/1, October 1975, 13–23.

Lamont, William M., *Richard Baxter and the Millennium, Protestant Imperialism and the English Revolution*, London 1979.

Lang, August, *Puritanismus und Pietismus, Studien zu ihrer Entwicklung von M. Butzer bis zum Methodismus*, Darmstadt 1972 (reprint of the edition Neukirchen 1941).

Lechler, Gotthard Victor, *Geschichte des englischen Deismus*, Stuttgart/Tübingen 1841.

Léonard, Emile G., *Histoire générale de Protestantisme, III: Déclin et renouveau (XVIIIe–XXe siècle)*, Paris 1964.

Leu, Hans Jacob, *et al.*, *Allgemeines Helvetisches/ Eydgenössisches/oder Schweizerisches Lexicon* in 26 Bänden, 1750–1850.

Lindström, Harald, *Wesley und die Heiligung*, Frankfurt a.M. 1961.

Lyles, Albert M., *Methodism Mocked, The Satiric Reaction to Methodism in the Eighteenth Century*, London 1960.

Macfadyen, Dugald, 'Glasites (Sandemanians)', *Encyclopedia of Religion and Ethics*, ed. James Hastings, VI, fourth edition, Edinburgh/New York 1959.

Mann, Golo und Nitschke, August (eds), *Propyläen Weltgeschichte*, VII, Berlin/Frankfurt/Wien 1964.

Milburn, G. E., 'Early Methodism and the Huguenots', *PWHS* XLV, 1985, 69–79.

Moltmann, Jürgen, 'Prädestination und Heilsgeschichte bei Moyse Amyraut', *ZKG* LXV, 1953/54, 270–303.

Montet, Albert de, *Dictionnaire biographique des Genevois et des Vaudois*, II, I–Z, Lausanne 1878.

Morrow, Thomas M., *Early Methodist Women: Sarah Crosby, Hannah Ball, Frances Pawson, Mary Fletcher, Sarah Bentley*, London 1967.

Murray, Derek Boyd, 'The Social and Religious Origins of Scottish Non-Presbyterian Protestant Dissent from 1730–1800', D.Phil. thesis, University of St Andrews, 1976.

Mützenberg, Gabriel, *Genève 1830, Restauration de l'école*, Lausanne 1974.

Neuser, Wilhelm, 'Dogma und Bekenntnis in der Reformation', *Handbuch der Dogmen- und Theologiegeschichte*, ed. C. Andresen, Göttingen 1980, II, 165–352.

Nuttall, Geoffrey F., *Richard Baxter*, London/Edinburgh 1965.

——, *The Significance of Trevecca College 1768–91*, Epworth Press, London 1969.

Orcibal, J., 'Les spirituels français et espagnols chez John Wesley et ses contemporains', *Revue de l'Histoire des Religions* CXXXIX, 1951, 50–109.

Podmore, C. J., 'The Fetter Lane Society', *PWHS* XLVII, 1990, 156–86.

Rack, Henry D., 'Early Methodist Visions of the Trinity', *PWHS* XLVI, 1987, 38–44, 57–69.

——, *Reasonable Enthusiast, John Wesley and the Rise of Methodism*, London 1989.

Recueil de généalogies vaudoises, publié par la Société vaudoise de généalogie, I, Lausanne 1923.

Rowe, Kenneth E., *The Place of Wesley in the Christian Tradition*, Essays delivered at Drew University in celebration of the commencement of the publication of the Oxford Edition of the Works of John Wesley, with a selected Bibliography by Lawrence D. McIntosh, Metuchen 1976.

Ryle, John Charles, *The Christian Leaders of England in the Eighteenth Century*, fourth edn, London 1868.

Saladin, J. L., *Mémoire historique sur la vie et les ouvrages de Mr. J. Vernet*, Paris & Genève 1790.

Sangster, W. E., *The Path to Perfection*, New York 1943.

Schieder, Theodor (ed.), *Handbuch der europäischen Geschichte*, IV: *Europa im Zeitalter des Absolutismus and der Aufklärung*, Stuttgart 1968.

Schlenther, Boyd Stanley, *Queen of the Methodists: The Countess of Huntingdon and the Eighteenth-Century Crisis of Faith and Society*, Durham 1997.

Schmidt, Martin, 'Englischer Deismus', *RGG*[3] II, 59–69.

——, *John Wesley* I, Zürich/Frankfurt a.M. 1953; II, Zürich/Frankfurt a.M. 1966.

——, 'Priestley, Joseph', *RGG*[3] V, 582f.

Schweizer, Alexander, *Die protestantischen Zentraldogmen in ihrer Entwicklung innerhalb der reformierten Kirche* II: *Das 17. und 18. Jahrhundert*, Zürich 1856.

Semmel, Bernard, *The Methodist Revolution*, London 1974.

(Seymour, A. C. H.) (published anonymously) *The Life and Times of Selina Countess of Huntingdon* I and II, London 1840 (**Seymour**).

Smith, George, *History of Wesleyan Methodism* I: *Wesley and his times*, London 1857.

Speck, William Arthur, *Stability and Strife, England 1714–1760* (*The New History of England*, Vol. 6), London 1977.

Stelling-Michaud, Sven and Suzanne, *Le livre du Recteur de l'Académie de Genève (1559–1878)*: I, Genève 1959; IV, *Notices biographiques des étudiants H-M*, Genève 1975.

Stevens, Abel, *The History of the Religious Movement of the 18th Century called METHODISM, considered in its different denominational forms, and its relations to British and American Protestantism*. I: Nineteenth Thousand, New York (undated); II: Thirteenth Thousand, New York 1860; III Seventeenth Thousand, New York (undated).

Streiff, Patrick, 'Die Breitenwirkung des Methodismus im 18. Jahrhundert als Grundlage seines Einflusses auf die Erweckungsbewegung' in U. Gabler (ed.), *Erweckung am Beginn des 19. Jahrhunderts*, Amsterdam 1986, 59–72.

——, 'Wie 'methodistich' war die Erweckung in der französischsprachigen Schweiz?', *Mitteilungen der Studiengemeinschaft für Geschichte der Evang.-meth. Kirche*, 16/2, Stuttgart 1995, 30–56.

Sykes, Norman, *Church and State in England in the XVIII*[th] *Century*, Cambridge 1934.

Telford, John, *Two West-End Chapels: Sketches of London Methodism from Wesley's Day*, London 1886.

Toon, Peter, 'Der englische Puritanismus', *HZ* 214, 1972, 30–41.

Trinder, Barrie, *The Industrial Revolution in Shropshire*, London/ Chichester 1973 (**Trinder**).

Tuck, John P., '"Primitive Physic" – An Interesting Association Copy', *PWHS* XLV, 1985, 1–7.

——, 'Some Pocket Books in the Methodist Archives', *PWHS* XLVI, 1987, 32–7.

Tyerman, Luke, *The Life and Times of the Rev. John Wesley* I–III, New York 1872.

Tyson, John R., *Charles Wesley on Sanctification, A Biographical and Theological Study*, Francis Asbury Press, Grand Rapids 1986.

Vuilleumier, Henri, *Histoire de l'Eglise réformée du Pays de Vaud sous le régime bernois*: II: *L'orthodoxie confessionnelle*, Lausanne 1929; III: *Le refuge, le piétisme, l'orthodoxie libérale*, Lausanne 1930; IV: *Le déclin du régime bernois*, Lausanne 1933.

——, 'Quand et comment la Formula consensus a-t-elle été définitivement abrogée?', *RThPh* XII, 1879, 471–8.

——, 'Théodore Crinsoz de Bionens et son interprétation prophétique de l'Ecriture', *RThPh* XX, 1887, 113–35, 294–319, 481–504.

Walsh, J. D., 'Elie Havély and the Birth of Methodism', *THS* (fifth series) XXV, 1975, 1–20.

Watson, J. Steven, *The Reign of George III, 1760–1815* (*The Oxford History of England*, Vol. XII), Oxford 1960.

Welch, Edwin (ed.), *Cheshunt College, The Early Years, A Selection of Records*, Hertfordshire Record Society 1990.

Wernle, Paul, *Der schweizerische Protestantismus im XVIII. Jahrhundert* I–III, Tübingen 1923–25.

Winkoop, Mildred Bangs, *A Theology of Love, the Dynamic of Wesleyanism*, Kansas City 1972.

Wood, Laurence W., *Pentecostal Grace*, Wilmore 1980.

Index

(2) following a page number indicates two separate references on that page. 'n.' following a page number indicates additional information located in the notes on pp. 311–54.